for the beauty of the
earth

a christian vision for creation care

second edition

steven bouma-prediger

D0082657

BakerAcademic

a division of Baker Publishing Group
Grand Rapids, Michigan

© 2001, 2010 by Steven Bouma-Prediger

Published by Baker Academic
a division of Baker Publishing Group
P.O. Box 6287, Grand Rapids, MI 49516-6287
www.bakeracademic.com

Printed in the United States of America

All rights reserved. No part of this publication may be reproduced, stored in a retrieval system, or transmitted in any form or by any means—for example, electronic, photocopy, recording—without the prior written permission of the publisher. The only exception is brief quotations in printed reviews.

Library of Congress Cataloging-in-Publication Data
Bouma-Prediger, Steven.
    For the beauty of the earth : a Christian vision for creation care / Steven Bouma-Prediger.—
2nd ed.
      p.   cm.   (Engaging culture)
    Includes bibliographical references (p.   ) and indexes.
    ISBN 978-0-8010-3695-8 (pbk.)
    1. Human ecology—Religious aspects—Christianity. I. Title.
BT695.5.B69 2010
261.8'8—dc22
                                    2009050032

Unless otherwise indicated, all Scripture quotations are from the New Revised Standard Version of the Bible, copyright © 1989, by the Division of Christian Education of the National Council of the Churches of Christ in the United States of America. Used by permission. All rights reserved.

Scripture quotations labeled GNT are from the Good News Translation—Second Edition. Copyright © 1992 by American Bible Society. Used by permission.

Scripture quotations labeled KJV are from the King James Version of the Bible.

Scripture quotations labeled NIV are from the HOLY BIBLE, NEW INTERNATIONAL VERSION®. NIV®. Copyright © 1973, 1978, 1984 by International Bible Society. Used by permission of Zondervan. All rights reserved.

Scripture quotations labeled Phillips are from The New Testament in Modern English, revised edition—J. B. Phillips, translator. © J. B. Phillips 1958, 1960, 1972. Used by permission of Macmillan Publishing Co., Inc.

Scripture quotations labeled RSV are from the Revised Standard Version of the Bible, copyright 1952 [2nd edition, 1971] by the Division of Christian Education of the National Council of the Churches of Christ in the United States of America. Used by permission. All rights reserved.

Chapter 3 is adapted from Steven Bouma-Prediger, "Is Christianity Responsible for the Ecological Crisis?" *Christian Scholar's Review* 25, no. 2 (1995). Copyright © 1995 by *Christian Scholar's Review*. Reprinted by permission.

Chapter 6 is adapted from Steven Bouma-Prediger, "Creation Care and Character: The Nature and Necessity of the Ecological Virtues," *Perspectives on Science and Christian Faith* 50, no. 1 (March 1998): 6–21. Used by permission.

Chapter 7 is adapted from Steven Bouma-Prediger, "Why Care for Creation: From Prudence to Piety," *Christian Scholar's Review* 27, no. 3 (1998). Copyright © 1998 by *Christian Scholar's Review*. Reprinted by permission.

The lines of poetry on page 154 are from "Whatever Is Foreseen in Joy," from *Sabbaths* by Wendell Berry. Reprinted by permission of North Point Press, a division of Farrar, Straus and Giroux, LLC.

In keeping with biblical principles of creation stewardship, Baker Publishing Group advocates the responsible use of our natural resources. As a member of the Green Press Initiative, our company uses recycled paper when possible. The text paper of this book is comprised of 30% postconsumer waste.

10 11 12 13 14 15 16   7 6 5 4 3 2 1

To my students—
in Belize, Chicago, Holland, Los Angeles, New Zealand, and Toronto—
for you have been my teachers

For the Beauty of the Earth

For the beauty of the earth,
For the beauty of the skies,
For the love which from our birth,
Over and around us lies,
Lord of all, to thee we raise,
This, our hymn of grateful praise.

For the wonder of each hour,
Of the day and of the night,
Hill and vale and tree and flower,
Sun and moon and stars of light,
Lord of all, to thee we raise,
This, our hymn of grateful praise.

For the joy of ear and eye,
For the heart's and mind's delight,
For the mystic harmony,
Linking sense to sound and sight,
Lord of all, to thee we raise,
This, our hymn of grateful praise.

For the joy of human love,
Brother, sister, parent, child,
Friends on earth and friends above,
For all gentle thoughts and mild,
Lord of all, to thee we raise,
This, our hymn of grateful praise.

For thy Church that evermore,
Lifteth holy hands above,
Off'ring up on ev'ry shore,
Her pure sacrifice of love,
Lord of all, to thee we raise,
This, our hymn of grateful praise.

Folliott S. Pierpoint

contents

illustrations

acknowledgments

I would like to gratefully acknowledge a number of people who assisted me with this book. Their comments, questions, and suggestions improved both the substance and the style of the text. First, my colleagues in the religion department at Hope College read and discussed various chapters of this new edition and the previous edition. So a heartfelt thanks to Barry Bandstra, Wayne Brouwer, Jenny Everts, Steve Hoogerwerf, Mark Husbands, Lynn Japinga, Phil Muñoa, Lyra Pitstick, Jeff Tyler, and Boyd Wilson. It is a privilege to work with such a talented group.

Many thanks also to Dean Bill Reynolds, Provost James Boelkins, and President James Bultman. Through their steady encouragement and timely financial support over the years, they have cultivated an ethos at Hope College in which excellence in teaching and in scholarship has flourished. I am one grateful beneficiary of their tireless efforts.

A number of friends and colleagues elsewhere read and commented on either this edition or the earlier one. Thanks to Ryan Atwell, Peter Bakken, Tom Boogaart, Kent Busman, and Brian Walsh. Some former Hope students have done research that contributed to this new edition, so a word of thanks to Justine Post, David Rye, and Allison Schneider. I also wish to thank Bill Dyrness and Rob Johnston, who as coeditors of the Engaging Culture series originally invited me to write this volume. It is a pleasure to be a part of this set of books.

At Baker Academic, Bob Hosack has been, as always, encouraging of this project, and Brian Bolger and his crew helped to polish my prose and make the text more readable. Thanks for your careful attention to detail.

As with previous writing projects, I owe an enormous debt of gratitude to my wife and children—Celaine, Anna, Chara, and Sophia. A simple thank you is a woefully inadequate expression of appreciation for your patience and forbearance, care and concern.

As the dedication indicates, the book could not have been written (or re-written) without my students, for this text has been forged and tested in the classroom. To all whom I have had the privilege of teaching, a hearty thank you. I have learned much from you. May we together continue to learn how best to care for each other and our home planet—to God's glory and for the beauty of the earth.

introduction

ecology and theology in dialogue

Any error about creation also leads to an error about God.

Thomas Aquinas[1]

"What does ecology have to do with theology?" Andrew asked, as I finished going over the course syllabus. Along with the standard fare of subjects usually found in a philosophical theology class—arguments for God's existence, the nature of religious experience, evidence for and against miracles, the problem of evil and human suffering—I had included ecology as one of the topics to be covered in a summer school course I was teaching at a seminary in California. This student (and many others, I was soon to discover) wondered what such a topic had to do with this class. What do sandhill cranes and chinook salmon have to do with God? What possible relevance does ecology have for Christian theology?

Susan's hand shot up in the air like fireworks on the Fourth of July in response to my question to the undergraduates in my Earth and Ethics course, "Who among you agrees with Wendell Berry's assertion that 'Our destruction of nature is not just bad stewardship, or stupid economics, or a betrayal of family responsibility; it is the most horrid blasphemy'?"[2] While Susan was persuaded that Berry was correct in his first three claims, she was certain he was wrong in his last. Our despoilation of creation was not, she strenuously argued, "the most horrid blasphemy." After Susan stated her case, others entered the fray to express their disagreement with Berry's seemingly outrageous claim. How can Berry assert that polluting a stream is worse than killing another human being or cursing God? Theologically speaking, what is so wrong with ecological degradation?

"How many of you have in the last year heard a sermon on stewardship?" This was my question to a group of thirty adults in a Sunday school class I was guest teaching at a local church. While I suspected I already knew the answer, I was genuinely curious about what my informal poll would reveal. Many people raised their hands to indicate they had heard such a sermon, but when I inquired about the specific content, it became clear that the message had been on tithing and had nothing to do with caring for the natural world. I already knew from previous discussions that most of the people in the class were avid gardeners, walked wherever they could, and bought produce at the local farmers' market. But they engaged in these activities, it seemed, not because of any explicit theological rationale but for other reasons. What connection, their responses implied, is there between caring for the earth and Christian faith? What has stewardship to do with earthkeeping?

These three anecdotes prompt a number of questions. Why did the seminary students so readily assume that attention to the earth is not a proper concern of Christian theology? The students were steeped in theology, but their theological convictions had no apparent connection to the earth. Why did the college students—persuaded that degradation of the natural world is a serious economic, ecological, and ethical issue—not attribute any theological relevance to their views of nature? These students had ecological awareness aplenty but saw no relationship between their ecological commitments and theological categories. Finally, why did the folks in the Sunday school class, who in fact engaged in various earth stewardship practices, not explain their actions in terms of their faith? These earthkeepers perceived little relationship between their behavior and their basic religious beliefs. In sum, why do many people see little, if any, connection between ecology and theology?

In this book I intend to explore these questions by putting contemporary ecology (broadly construed) and Christian theology into dialogue. But this endeavor is more than a dialogue. It sets forth a thesis. It is, to be honest, a piece of rhetoric in the classical sense of the term. I mean in these pages not only to inform but to persuade. My central claim is simple: authentic Christian faith includes care for the earth. Earthkeeping is integral to Christian discipleship.

As the epigraph at the beginning of this chapter implies, much is at stake. Other luminaries in the Christian tradition could be cited, but St. Thomas Aquinas puts it succinctly: "Any error about creation also leads to an error about God." If we do not properly understand our home planet, we will not properly understand the nature and character of the God we worship and claim to serve. Nothing less than our understanding of God is at stake. There is, in other words, an inner theological rationale for attending to the blue-green planet we inhabit with its plethora of other earth-creatures.

But more is at stake. The earth is groaning, to use St. Paul's metaphor from Romans 8. As chapter 2 lays out in agonizing detail, the world in which we live is not doing well. Its vital signs are not healthy. This includes a great many humans—humans who are hungry, sick, homeless. So human health and flourishing, as well as that of our many nonhuman neighbors, is at stake. The health of all earth-dwellers is at stake if we humans don't properly understand our place and calling in God's scheme of things. This leads to one more thing that is at stake: how we comprehend who we are and what we are supposed to do. Our own individual and collective self-understanding is at stake—in summary, how we understand God, the world, and ourselves.

The conversation and argument that follow are divided into eight chapters. Since I am convinced that much of our current malaise stems from not knowing our place, chapter 1 answers the question: where are we? In this stage of the dialogue, ecology has its say as we strive to increase what David Orr calls our "ecological literacy."[3] Do we really know our place? And what can we learn from our home planet? A survey of the current state of the planet follows in chapter 2: How goes it with earth, air, water, and fire? And what about claims by those who say that things aren't so bad? Amid the welter of data, where lies the truth?

The conclusion of many responsible earth-watchers is that the earth is not doing very well. A wealth of evidence supports the claim that creation is indeed groaning. Chapter 3 explores why this is so. More exactly, I address the claim that Christianity is the culprit—that the Christian tradition is the reason we are in this ecological mess. In dealing with what James Nash calls "the ecological complaint against Christianity,"[4] I sort out what is right and what is wrong. And I offer (ever so briefly) an alternative explanation for what ails us. As a number of perceptive historians conclude, while we Christians have much to confess, the real answers to the question of the origin of our ecological sins lie elsewhere.

For Christians, especially evangelical Christians, the Bible plays a central role in theological reflection—indeed, in all of life. We are people of the book. Is the Bible the problem, as some assert? Or are there ecological riches and resources in Scripture, if only we have the eyes to see? For example, with whom does God make a covenant (Gen. 6–9)? Who is at the center of things (Job 38–41)? What does God's good future look like (Rev. 21–22)? Chapter 4 addresses these questions and more. My central claim is that, properly understood, the Bible is not the problem but rather contains great wisdom and a winsome vision of the earth as our home and of humans as earthkeeping homemakers.[5]

How then should we think of the earth and its creating-redeeming God? What are the main tenets of an ecological theology informed by science and guided by Scripture? In chapter 5, I set forth an evangelical theology of care for the earth. More than merely a theology of creation, an ecological theology addresses the whole range of traditional topics in theology. I also lay out in this chapter a spectrum of different perspectives in ecological ethics, since many theories exist and sorting them out is not easy, and I indicate which overarching ethical position from among these views is, in my estimation, most adequate and why.

Chapter 6 gives much fuller attention to ethics. Indeed, in it I develop my own ecological ethic. In contrast to much contemporary environmental ethics, my conviction is that a more fundamental question than, what ought we do? is, who must we be? More precisely, what kind of people ought we be in order to be faithful earthkeepers? What virtues ought we embody and need we enflesh to properly bear witness to the hope that lies within us? Phrasing the question this way directs attention to what I and others call "ecological virtues." This chapter zeros in on this important issue.

When all is said and done, why care for the earth? Why worry about spotted owls and the Pacific yew tree? Why care about Kirtland's warblers and jack pine forests? Why be concerned for marmots and mountains and meadows? Chapter 7 presents an apologia for earth-care. More exactly, I offer ten arguments—moving from prudence to piety—for why people, especially Christians, ought to care for our home planet, this blue-green orb called earth.

As Aldo Leopold perceptively noted, "one of the penalties of an ecological education is that one lives alone in a world of wounds."[6] While many would challenge the claim that we ever really live alone, few these days would question the truth about living in a wounded world. To become ecologically literate is to open yourself to seeing and feeling the woundedness of the world. To lament the loss of that aged oak. To ache over a stream despoiled. To grieve over what is now gone—the Santa Barbara song sparrow and the solace of open spaces. In such a world, where is there hope? If one is a Christian, for what and in whom does one hope? I reflect on these questions in the concluding chapter.

I stated above that this book sets forth a thesis and contains an argument. But arguments, while important, have their limits. The best apologetic, as the venerable St. Augustine stated centuries ago, is a life well lived.[7] Or as one more recent theologian put it: "A believer is an evangelist primarily by who he is and how he lives—not by what he says. What he says is important; but unless his speaking tallies with what he is and does, he had better keep quiet."[8] Each of these theologians rightfully reminds us that the goal of theology is eminently practical—wisdom in living well. I intend for such a goal to infuse this entire work. Whether I realize this intention, only you the reader can judge.

A word about terminology: This is not a book about "the environment." While the term "environment" is for many the term of choice, it is not without its problems. For starters, it is abstract, lacking the concreteness of marmot or mountain or meadow. Few people describe where they live by speaking of their "environment." Furthermore, it suggests something that we live in but that is apart from us, rather than the home we inhabit and of which we are an integral part. In other words, it connotes a disjunction between human and nonhuman that is simply not true to the way things are. We do not exist over against something called "the environment." Finally, the term "environment" is sterile. It fails to capture the plethora of creatures in dynamic interaction that is the natural world. The term "environment" is, in short, too tame.

Nor is this a book about "nature." As a number of scholars have argued, and as I have argued elsewhere,[9] the term "nature" all too often denotes something over against culture or history, as if humans are not a part of the natural world and as if nonhuman creatures have no history. We often assume, in other words, that "nature" excludes us—an often fatal presumption. In addition, for many the term "nature" implies a God-less universe, a cosmos for which there is no maker, whereas the term "creation" implies a Creator, a claim at the very heart of Christian faith and one very few Christians would be willing to give up. The term "nature," in sum, is too secular.

Nor, finally, is this a book about "creation." Though a much better term than "environment" or "nature," "creation" is, nevertheless, also problematic. As Christopher Kaiser insightfully points out, biblically the term "creation" includes everything except God: angels, humans, other creatures both celestial and terrestrial.[10] To speak of caring for creation, as many do, thus literally implies concern for angels, and for our moon, and for the constellation Draco, whatever that might mean. Does God really expect us to care about things distant in the cosmos? Does God expect us to care for all the heavenly host? Thus "creation" takes in too much. Unless it is delimited (as it often de facto is) to mean something like the terrestrial world—the seas, the land, the lower atmosphere, and all their inhabitants—it is too expansive and all-encompassing. The term "creation" is, then, too broad.

This book is about "the earth." The term "earth" is not abstract; it is concrete, denoting both the planet on which we live and the very stuff of which we are made. "Earth" does not imply that we humans are somehow separate from or above what is not human (nor does it necessarily imply that we humans are only so much oxygen and nitrogen and calcium); it includes us with all the other inhabitants of our spinning globe. "Earth" does not promote an unhealthy dualism of culture over against nature; creatures human and nonhuman together inhabit this one home planet. "Earth" does not carry a presumption of atheism; it can easily be seen as the work of God's hands. "Earth" does not refer to angels or stars or pulsars; it includes only that part of creation sometimes called the biosphere. "Earth" is anything but a sterile term. This book is about the earth—the earth God created and continues to lovingly sustain and redeem and will one day make whole—and it is about our responsibility and privilege as humans to care for the earth.

"What does ecology have to do with theology?" my student asked. Many today pose, in one form or another, this very same question. Pioneering ecological theologian Joseph Sittler, whose eloquence and insight on these matters remain unsurpassed, years ago offered his answer to this important and timely question. His hard but honest words fittingly conclude this introduction and launch us on our journey into chapter 1.

When we turn the attention of the church to a definition of the Christian relationship with the natural world, we are not stepping away from grave and proper theological ideas; we are stepping right into the middle of them. There is a deeply rooted, genuinely Christian motivation for attention to God's creation, despite the fact that many church people consider ecology to be a secular concern. "What does environmental preservation have to do with Jesus Christ and his church?" they ask. They could not be more shallow or more wrong.[11]

where are we?

an ecological perception of place

An individual is not distinct from his place; he is that place.

Gabriel Marcel[1]

What do you remember from your childhood about the earth? What from your growing-up years comes most to mind when you think about the natural world? Perhaps you remember your family flower garden—daffodils, geraniums, impatiens, petunias. Or maybe it is the vegetable garden—sweet corn, string beans, radishes, lettuce, rhubarb. Or maybe it is playing in the local creek—looking for tadpoles, stalking salamanders, catching crayfish. Or maybe you remember walks in the local park or swinging under the shade trees in the school playground down the street.

What animals come to mind? Pet dog Fido or cat Florence? Horses or chickens or pigs? A turtle or a parakeet or a snake? Deer (or its scat), skunk (or its smell), raccoon (or its print)? Or do you remember a particular tree: sap-rich white pine, scaly sycamore, white-bark birch, bent-topped hemlock, towering maple or oak or beech?

Or maybe what you remember are the seasons. The sweet scent of spring—that freshness of early April when the breathing earth sucks in carbon dioxide and exhales oxygen for us, the days that grow slowly longer, the night rains that wash our fields and sidewalks and souls. The lushness and fullness of summer—freshly cut grass, swimming in the local lake or pond or pool, family camping

1

trips at Ludington or Yellowstone or Grandma's backyard. The waning light of autumn—a crisp chill in the October air, dead leaves, cold rain, and the first flakes of snow. The wonder of winter—short days, frosted windows, snowdrifts covered with footprints and snow angels and animal tracks.

But, alas, these are, by and large, memories from the American upper Midwest.

If you grew up in another part of North America, maybe in your mind's eye you see southern magnolia, or feel a Pacific silver fir, or smell the delicious vanilla-cinnamon aroma of ponderosa pine. Or perhaps your memories include sighting California condors, or catching Mississippi catfish, or swatting the Minnesota state bird—the mosquito. Or maybe you hear the crash of the North Sea surf, or the trickle of a meadow stream high up in the Alps, or the cry of howler monkeys in the muggy Belizean night. In your mind's eye right now, what do you remember? What do you see and hear, smell and taste and feel?

But these are memories of places rural and wild. Most of us these days grow up and live in cities and towns. So perhaps what you hear is the cooing of mourning doves or the caw-caw-caw of crows in the treetops. Maybe what you see are blue jays at the feeder or an opossum dead by the side of the road. Even in large cities you may smell a skunk or spy a falcon roosting atop a skyscraper. Such urban memories, like their country cousins, attest to at least some knowledge of and feeling for particular places. And these remembrances point to the power of place in shaping who we are and how we see the world. As Spanish philosopher Jose Ortega y Gasset famously put it, "Tell me the landscape in which you live and I will tell you who you are."[2]

Such musings, furthermore, prompt the following questions: Do we know our place? Do we know where we are? What exactly does that mean? And what might greater knowledge of place mean for how and why we care for the earth? Or put differently, could it be that contemporary ecological degradation is a result, in part, of us not knowing our places, our own local habitats on this our home planet? All too often, I fear, we do not know our places, and such ignorance contributes to the ecological despoilation we see today. Precisely what the nature and extent of that degradation is will be discussed in the next chapter. Here our focus is on places and what we can learn about ourselves and the earth if we attend with care to what is around us.

Ecological Perception of Place

Do you know where you are? Certainly you can state that you are on 12th Street or 10th Avenue, in Lansing or Lincoln or Los Angeles, in Oregon or Ontario, in the United States or the United Kingdom or the United Arab Emirates. But ecologically speaking, do you know where you are? In a more than geopolitical sense, do you know where you are? What is your ecological perception of place? Some questions might help us gauge our awareness of where we are.

What is the soil like around your home? Silty loam? Loamy sand? Sandy clay? Rocks and pebbles? Wet or dry? A few precious inches of soil atop ancient Canadian shield, or eighteen inches of rich, fertile gardener's gold? What are five agricultural plants in your region? Corn, wheat, alfalfa, beans, sorgum? Or maybe grapes or cherries or oranges? And how long is the growing season? A precious few weeks? Or all year long? What geological events or processes have influenced the land where you live? Glaciers, volcanoes, earthquakes? Uplifting mountains or rivers carving canyons to the sea? What confluence of water and wind?

What trees live where you do? Sitka spruce or Douglas fir, bald cypress or incense cedar, Norway maple or American chestnut? Northern white cedar or western hemlock, Ohio buckeye or California live oak, beech or basswood or birch? Desert mesquite or water-loving cottonwood? Young upstart poplar or ancient bristlecone pine? What about birds, resident and migratory? The common loon or the uncommon meadowlark? Mallard or merganser? House finch or goldfinch? A goose with a gaggle or a murder of crows? Yellow-bellied sapsucker or white-crested warbler? Bluebird or blackbird or redheaded woodpecker? Kingfisher or cormorant or sandhill crane? What raptors roam the skies above your house? Osprey, northern harrier, red-tailed hawk? What owls dine at night? Barred owl, barn owl, burrowing owl?

What flowers bloom where you live? Poppies or peonies? Tiger lilies or tulips? Daisies or daffodils? Crocus or columbine? Bird-of-paradise or star-of-Bethlehem? What animals share your place? Long-tailed weasel or white-tailed deer? Grey wolf or red fox? Alligator or armadillo? Manatee or marmot or moose? Which animals are extinct in your neck of the woods? Wolverine, grizzly bear, passenger pigeon, prairie dog?

How many days until the moon is full? And what kind of moon is it: waxing or waning, crescent or gibbous? Were the stars out last night? If so, what constellations did you see? When did it last rain or snow or sleet or hail? From where you are reading this, which way is north? From what direction do the prevailing winds blow? From where does your water come? To where does your garbage go?

These questions test our knowledge of our place. And they all too often, truth be told, expose our ecological ignorance. To face such a battery of questions forcibly reminds us of how little we know about the world and how it works. Do we know our place? Do we know the natural history of the land? Do we know its flora and fauna? And perhaps most importantly, do we know how what we do affects the world around us?

If the answer to these questions is "no," then we really do not know where we are. Despite our education we remain ecologically illiterate. Or perhaps because of our education we remain ignorant of how the world works. As Aldo Leopold perceptively puts it: "One of the requisites for an ecological comprehension of land is an understanding of ecology, and this is by no means co-extensive with 'education'; in fact, much higher education seems deliberately to avoid ecological concepts."[3] Contemporary environmental activist and culture critic David Orr agrees. In no uncertain terms he presents the challenge ahead.

> The crisis of sustainability, the fit between humanity and its habitat, is manifest in varying ways and degrees everywhere on earth. It is not only a permanent feature on the public agenda; for all practical purposes it is *the* agenda. No other issue of politics, economics, and public policy will remain unaffected by the crisis of resources, population, climate change, species extinction, acid rain, deforestation, ozone depletion, and soil loss. Sustainability is about the terms and conditions of human survival, and yet we still educate at all levels as if no such crisis existed.[4]

Hence, we desperately need, according to Orr, increased ecological literacy. Just as we educate for numeracy, or the ability to calculate, and literacy, or the ability to read, so also we must educate for the ability to understand how the world works—"ecolacy," as famous biologist Garrett Hardin calls it. Like Orr, Hardin argues that such a mental filter or way of viewing the world is absolutely essential if we are to live responsibly and wisely.[5]

But what exactly is ecolacy? What does it mean to be ecologically literate? In a clear and compelling account, Orr argues that the essence of ecological literacy is "that quality of mind that seeks out connections."[6] In contrast to the narrow specialization that characterizes so much education today—across virtually all the academic disciplines—an ecological frame of mind seeks to integrate, to bring together, to see things whole. In Orr's words, "The ecologically literate person has the knowledge necessary to comprehend interrelatedness, and an attitude of care or stewardship," and this must be accompanied by "the practical competence required to act on the basis of knowledge and feeling." Hence "knowing, caring, and practical competence constitute the basis of ecological literacy."[7] Not only must we know; we must care. And not only must we care, but we must have the wherewithal to act responsibly, informed by such knowledge and passion.

But concretely what does this mean? If we are truly to know our place, what do we need to learn? Orr offers a list of five necessary components of seeing things whole. First, we need "a broad understanding of how people and societies relate to each other and to natural systems, and how they might do so sustainably."[8] This presumes knowledge of how the world as a biophysical system works—knowledge of keystone species and succession, entropy and energy flow, niches and food chains. Ecological literacy, in short, implies a modicum of knowledge about the inextricable interconnectedness of all creatures great and small.[9]

Second, we need to know "something of the speed of the crisis that is upon us."[10] While some would argue that "crisis" is too strong a term, the preponderance of evidence suggests otherwise.[11] Hence, we need to know the vital signs of our home planet—the trends concerning population growth and climate change, soil loss and species extinction, deforestation and desertification, energy use and air pollution.[12] A prescription is only as good as the diagnosis on which it is based. Our attempts to achieve wellness must, therefore, be based on a sober and honest assessment of the health of the earth.

Third, ecological literacy, according to Orr, "requires a comprehension of the dynamics of the modern world."[13] In other words, we need some understanding of the historical, political, economic, and religious forces that have molded the modern world. What social pressures have brought us to where we are today? What economic and political systems mold our everyday life? And that all too often neglected question: how has religion played a part in shaping the world in which we live? To be more specific, how did "the Columbian exchange" of 1492 and subsequent years influence both old and new worlds?[14] What was (and still is) nature's role in American history?[15] And how exactly do societies choose to fail or succeed, and what are the major contributing factors to societal collapse or flourishing?[16] In short, what ideas and forces have shaped the world in which we live?

Fourth, ecological literacy requires "broad familiarity with the development of ecological consciousness."[17] Of special importance here is explicit attention to ethics and the nature of nature. Environmental issues are laden with questions of value. Are we humans, for example, "conqueror of the land-community" or "plain member and citizen of it?"[18] Do animals or plants or endangered species or ecosystems have value, and if so, why? And how do we portray the natural world: as "red in tooth and claw," as an Edenic paradise, or neither? Whether and how we "follow nature," to use Holmes Rolston's phrase,[19] depends in large part on our idea of what it is. Is it nature or Nature or the environment or the biosphere or Creation? Are humans included in it? Is God? Ecological literacy does not require an elaborate answer to each of these questions, but it does presuppose some wrestling with issues such as these.

Fifth and finally, Orr maintains that we need "alternative measures of well-being" and "a different approach to technology."[20] For example, in contrast to the typical indicators of societal well-being, such as the Gross Domestic Product (GDP), we need more inclusive and more accurate metrics to honestly assess how our society is doing.[21] For example, the Index of Sustainable Economic Welfare (ISEW) includes the depletion of nonrenewable natural resources and the costs of water and air pollution in its calculation of overall welfare, as does the Genuine Progress Indicator (GPI), while the Weighted Index of Social Progress (WISP) includes both social and environmental conditions.[22] What all these indicators show is that while GDP has grown in the United States over the last decades, genuine well-being has not. And along with these alternative measures of well-being we need to rethink our use of technology. The work of E. F. Schumacher, to mention only one well-known example, illustrates how technology can and must be appropriate to the scale and needs of a people and its culture.[23] Many other examples exist, almost all of which emphasize sustainability and a proper sense of place.[24]

Ecological literacy, Orr states in summary, echoing one of the central tenets of the Christian tradition, is "built on a view of ourselves as finite and fallible creatures living in a world limited by natural laws."[25] Ecological literacy, in other words, is founded upon the theological insight that we are creatures—limited and liable to error—living in a world not of our own making. Being ecologically literate, hence, ought to engender humility and a thoughtful keeping of God's earth.

Such a detailed description of ecological literacy may seem quite daunting. How is it possible to learn so much? Gain knowledge of entropy, economic history, ethics? Read Thoreau, Ehrlich, Schumacher? Build bat houses and compost bins? Surely, some may argue, such a program of "knowing, caring, and practical competence" is utterly unrealistic—a pipe dream unattainable for those paddling upstream in the powerful currents of popular culture. While it may be difficult, increasing one's ecological literacy is not as daunting, nor as dour, as it may seem. Learning more about how the world works is interesting and exciting. And it can be a joy-filled learning process in countless ways as we go about our everyday lives.[26] Regardless of difficulty, David Orr is right: "the fit between humanity and its habitat" is *the* agenda of the twenty-first century, a matter of human survival. We simply must become more ecologically literate. We have no choice.

Learning from Our Home Planet

If ecological literacy of the sort described by Orr is a desideratum of knowing where we are, how best do we gain the kinds of knowledge described above? How do we develop the ability to see things whole? How do we attain the "knowing, caring, and practical competence" required to live properly in our place? The hardest piece of this puzzle has to do with cultivating an attitude of care. Knowledge of the second law of thermodynamics and the ability to build a compost bin mean nothing without an affection for place (and the placed people) that puts that knowledge and skill to work. So one fruitful beginning point for cultivating care is reflection on specific places.

My modest strategy here is simply to focus on three places and see what can be learned about the natural world and our role in it. These places have not been randomly selected. They are, rather, places that have taught me something about how the world works and fostered in me a care-full attitude toward the earth.[27] We all have such places. As Gabriel Marcel states in the epigraph for this chapter, in a real sense we are the places that have formed us. And more than that, we have an inbuilt love of place. To use the neologism of cultural geographer Yi-Fu Tuan, we humans exhibit topophilia.[28] Not only are we formed by places, but we have an abiding affection for places. Here are three of my favorites.

Forest

A riot of green visually greets you as you first encounter the rain forest in Belize. Shades and hues of green abound in all directions. One hundred thirty feet and more into the sky, an emergent layer of scattered trees towers above the canopy, itself sixty to ninety feet from the floor. With sunlight aplenty and a seemingly impenetrable ceiling of chlorophyll green, the canopy produces 80 percent of the forest's food. Tropical rain forests are impressive solar collectors, capturing more sunlight per unit area than any other natural ecosystem.[29] Though you can see little of it, the sunlight-bathed canopy is abuzz with a plethora of living things: flowering trees, lianas, orchids, bromeliads, not to mention bees, bats, and a profusion of birds. And of course there are larger (and more well-known) animals, such as howler monkeys and three-toed sloths.

Of the trees perhaps the most conspicuous to your eye is the cecropia or trumpet tree, with its thin, gray, circular-ringed trunk and large deeply lobed leaves spread umbrella-like above you. Growing up to eight feet a year, this pioneering tree flourishes in forest gaps where there is abundant sunlight. Living inside the stem of the cecropia are biting ants (genus *Azteca*), feeding on the nectar produced at the leaf axil, where the leaf attaches to the stem. In exchange for room and board, the ants trim the tree of vines and air plants, which would otherwise shade the cecropia and thus inhibit its growth, and also attack any intruder, whether human or nonhuman, that tries to cut or damage the tree. This is but one example of rain forest symbiosis—in this case, mutualism, a relationship between two different organisms that is mutually beneficial.

The sacred tree of the Mayans, the ceiba or kapok, also grows exceedingly fast—up to ten feet a year. What strikes you immediately about this light-loving tree is its buttressed roots—large above-ground roots flaring out in all directions from the base. With most nutrients located not in the soil but in the forest floor and litter,[30] the roots of the ceiba break through the earth and grow along the ground. Common along forest edges and river banks, the ceiba is deciduous, dropping its leaves in the dry season. A single ceiba flowers only every five to ten years, though it is capable of producing five hundred to four thousand fruit, each with two hundred or more seeds. Hence, a single ceiba tree can produce as many as eight hundred thousand seeds in one year of flowering.[31] Surrounded by silky fibers called kapok (thus the name), the seeds are easily dispersed by the wind, especially since the flowering occurs after the leaves drop. A better example of floral reproductive effectiveness would be difficult to find.

All around you see vines of various sorts. Lianas entwine the trees and hang from the crowns. Other vines, the climbers, go straight up the trunks. And still others, the stranglers, wrap themselves around the trees, often killing them. The strangler fig, for example, begins from a seed dropped by a bird or monkey into the tree crown that grows down and around the tree, eventually putting its own roots into the ground. After penetrating the forest floor, the fig sucks up much more water and grows more quickly than the tree it surrounds. Because of either constriction or shading, or both, the host tree often dies and decomposes, leaving the fig standing alone.

Perhaps most amazing among the flora of the rain forest are the epiphytes, or air plants. These plants live on trees, with no roots connecting them to the earth. They draw their nutrients from the decayed remains of algae, moss, and leaves and absorb needed moisture through their tissue from rainfall and/or via their roots from the damp air. For example, bromeliads trap water with their overlapping leaf pattern. This tiny pool of water provides not only sustenance for the plant but also habitat for mosquitoes, tree frogs, salamanders, and snails. Some species of crabs "complete their lifecycles in the tiny aquatic habitats provided by the cuplike interiors of bromeliads."[32] With roughly thirty thousand species of epiphytes in the tropics, you see them virtually everywhere, for in this Central American rain forest they constitute approximately one-quarter of the flora.[33] Neither harming nor benefiting their host, these nonparasitic plants display yet another form of symbiosis, namely, commensalism.

The canopy is dense, so dense that little sunlight filters through to the floor beneath. Even with a blazing sun in a clear sky, inside the rain forest it is dark, so dark that it is not easy to see the vibrant bird life in the understory or the various inhabitants on the forest floor. Though unable to see much, you very readily hear all manner of sounds. Indeed, the cacophony of sound is at times deafening, especially early in the morning. The cicadas provide the background music with their sawing sounds. A trogon softly calls "cow, cow, cow," while tree frogs squeak their "peep, peep, peep" and a woodpecker sounds its staccato "rap-tap-tap." On a lucky day (or more likely at the zoo) you might see the brightly colored scarlet macaw—red chest, blue and yellow tail feathers, white beak and face—or perhaps a keel-billed toucan, with its yellow throat and long banana-shaped green, orange, and red beak.

As your eyes adjust to the darkness, you notice on the ground a hairy brown lump meandering slowly away from you. As you bend down to get a better look, you recognize what it is—a tarantula. As big around from leg to opposite leg as your fist, this much-feared spider with long glistening hairs moves gracefully, even elegantly, along the litter of the forest floor. Not an aggressive or easily provoked creature, this spider is a reminder of how we often misunderstand and unfairly characterize our nonhuman neighbors.

Hunched down close to the ground, you also notice a moving line of green. Upon closer inspection you see small leaf clippings moving single file in a long line on a well-worn highway cleared of leaves, twigs, and other debris. Carrying these clippings are leaf-cutter ants. These industrious ants are engaged in a massive gardening project, for contrary to expectation, they do not eat the leaves. Rather, they cut and carry the clippings to their underground nests, where they chew the leaves and defecate on the organic mulch before placing it on an already growing fungal bed. Once planted, the ants weed their garden of other fungi and use body secretions to suppress bacterial growth. Hence the leaf-cutter ant's other name: fungus garden ant.

This symbiotic relationship is fascinating. The ants disperse and plant the fungus, they cultivate and protect it from competing species, they supply the fungus with necessary amino acids, and they furnish the plant medium with enzymes to produce additional nitrogen. When a new queen, after twenty years or so, migrates to found a new colony, she stuffs a small bit of the precious fungus into her mouth in order to start a new garden. In short, "the ants are the expert gardeners of the insect world." The fungus, for its part, digests cellulose, an energy source that is indigestible to the ants, and so "by eating the fungus, ants can tap into the immense abundance of energy in rain forest leaves." This fungus (*Basidiomycetes*) is the ants' only food, and these ants (genus *Atta*) are the only cultivator of this fungus. Thus both ants and fungi "are totally dependent on each other."[34] A more perfect example of obligate mutualism—a relationship in which each organism is completely reliant on the other to survive—would be difficult to find.[35]

Examples of mutualism and commensalism should not mislead. Not all is sweetness and light in the rain forest. There is ample evidence of the three *p*'s: predation, parasites, and pathogens. Aggressive and poisonous pit vipers such as the fer-de-lance. Hunting wasps that lay eggs on wolf spiders, leaving the eggs to hatch into larvae, which eat the spiders alive. The inch-long bullet ant, which packs a mighty sting. Debilitating diseases such as yellow fever, malaria, and hepatitis. Internal parasites such as blood flukes and hookworms. Ingenious insects such as the botfly.[36] The forest is a complicated mix of different kinds and patterns of interrelationship.

If you are fortunate on your rain forest hike, you might glimpse some of the larger animals that live there. Perhaps a band of agoutis by day or pacas by night—both members of the rodent order. Maybe a herd of collared peccaries—fifty- to sixty-pound wild pigs with bristly black and gray hair and a musky smell. Or perhaps an anteater or armadillo. If you are very fortunate, you may see the relative of the rhino—the tapir or mountain cow. The national animal of Belize, this stout-bodied, short-legged, herbivorous creature is, despite its appearance, shy and unaggressive. If you are very, very fortunate, a wild cat may briefly show its face—perhaps a big-eared ocelot, or the weasel-like jaguarundi, or, least likely but best of all, the secretive jaguar. At six feet and three hundred pounds, the solitary and noctural *Felis onca* reigns at the top of the food chain. The black-on-tan spotted jaguar—meaning "he who kills with one leap" in the language of the peoples native to this place—is, though rarely seen, a constant reminder that life in the rain forest is precarious. It also reminds us that some things to this day remain, as they should, forever wild.

After some time spent exploring the rain forest, the overwhelming impression you get is of the sumptuous luxuriance of living things. This place—a lowland rain forest in Blue Hole National Park in central Belize—teems with life. Indeed, scientific studies confirm your casual observations: species richness, the number of different species in a given area, is staggering. Approximately 3,300 different species of birds—367 species of tyrant flycatchers alone—live in the neotropics. There are over 100 species of bats, compared to 40 in the entire United States. In Costa Rica alone, one researcher identified 550 butterfly species. In a Peruvian rain forest, Harvard biologist E. O. Wilson once counted 43 species of ant on a single tree, an amount equal to all ant species found in the British Isles.[37] A typical four-square-mile patch of rain forest contains 125 mammal species, 400 bird species, 100 reptile species, 60 amphibian species, and 150 different kinds of butterflies.[38] In all three ways—within a given habitat, between different habitats, and over the entire region—tropical forests are incredibly diverse.[39] The biological exuberance of the neotropical rain forest is simply astounding, as are the incredibly complex patterns of adaptation and interdependence.

Mountain

In many ways, the contrast between the mountains of California and the rain forest of Belize could not be more striking. The air around you is cool and dry. Compared to the hot and humid climate of the rain forest, this alpine air is bracing. You see what some would call a stark, austere landscape. Mountain pinnacles and peaks, like spires on a medieval cathedral, shoot high into the azure sky. Everywhere you look there are granite slabs, polished to a high gloss by ancient glaciers and water of more recent times. Large boulders, called glacial erratics, are strewn haphazardly hither and yon. Snow in the cracks and crevices, even in August, is melting and cascading its way into an interlaced chain of deep blue-turquoise lakes, whose surfaces mirror the crags above. All in all, a stunningly beautiful scene.

The air is bracing for yet another reason. At 11,407 feet above sea level, the oxygen is scarce. Just walking from campsite to stream to fetch water can leave you winded. And you have carried a forty-pound pack up steep mountain trails—the only way to get to this piece of God's good earth. To the north, as the sun nears its diurnal circuit, you can barely make out Forester Pass—a small notch in the Kings-Kern Divide, sandwiched between Cal Tech Peak on the left and Diamond Mesa on the right. At 13,200 feet, this pass is higher than most mountains in the continental United States. To the west, into the red-orange glow of the setting sun, you see the magnificent Great Western Divide—a long series of 13,000-foot peaks forming the north-south boundary between the Kern River and Kaweah River watersheds. To the south is a precipitous drop-off. In the valley over 3,000 feet below where you stand is the Kern River, flowing icy cold and clear from its snowy origins above. And to the east, on fire with the burning light of alpenglow, is the magnificent Sierra crest—Tyndall, Versteeg, Barnard, Russell, Whitney, Muir. As you gaze, transfixed, at the rugged peaks now pierced by this ethereal light, you recall something written by the most famous of the persons immortalized on that list of mountains. John Muir, writing some twenty-five years after his first experience hiking and living in the Sierra Nevada of central California, penned these now famous words:

> Then it seemed to me the Sierra should be called not the Nevada, or Snowy Range, but the Range of Light. And after ten years spent in the heart of it, rejoicing and wondering, bathing in its glorious floods of light, seeing the sunbursts of morning among the icy peaks, the noonday radiance on the trees and rocks and snow, the flush of alpenglow, and a thousand dashing waterfalls with their marvelous abundance of irised spray, it still seems to me above all others the Range of Light, the most divinely beautiful of all the mountain-chains I have ever seen.[40]

From your vantage point on Bighorn Plateau, smack dab in the middle of north-central Sequoia National Park, the contrast with life-teeming Belize could not be more clear. In this the Hudsonian or subalpine zone, little life is immediately visible. But first impressions to the contrary, you are on no moonscape. On a closer look you notice life virtually everywhere. Most immediately evident are the trees, for at this elevation—at timberline—the trees are eye-catching to say the least. Near you is a copse of rugged survivors—foxtail pines. With bleached yellow-brown trunks three to four feet in diameter and gnarled beyond description, upper branches helter-skelter to the sky, these thirty- to forty-foot-tall drought-resistant trees possess spreading root systems that penetrate deeply into the well-drained rocky soil. Their name comes from needles that clothe branchlets in a manner resembling a fox's tail—needles that may persist seventeen years, much longer than on any other pine. Native only to California, foxtails often live, despite the harsh climate, for one thousand years. Sentinels evoking an almost mystical allure, the foxtail would be right at home in any C. S. Lewis novel or Harry Potter adventure.

Nearby is a clump of battered white-bark pines—the foxtail's comrade in high altitude living. A smaller, more shrublike tree, the sprawling white-bark also lives on the very frontier of arboreal existence. Found only between ten thousand and twelve thousand feet in the southern Sierra, it can grow as a tiny wind-pruned shrub huddled in the lee of rocks extending up into the alpine zone. Unlike most pines, its purple thick-scaled cones disintegrate on the tree when the seeds are ripe. White-barks provide essential food and shelter for native inhabitants of the high country, such as chickarees, chipmunks, and blue grouse.

In a nearby white-bark you see a Clark's nutcracker—pale gray-white body with black wings and big as a crow. Taking a break from its work to check out your unexpected arrival, he soon resumes his appointed task of dismantling a pinecone, extracting and eating the seeds. You hear, not too far away, the telltale call of the mountain chickadee: "chick-a-dee-dee-dee." With its familiar call this hardy avian—with black throat, black crown, and white over the eyes and on cheeks and breast—welcomes you to this high country perch. Though lacking the species richness of the rain forest, the Sierra high country nevertheless exhibits its own intricate web of life.

On some rocks near your campsite you spy a pika, or coney, scurrying from rock to rock. A pale-gray animal the size of a small rabbit, the pika has rabbitlike nose and teeth (four upper teeth rather than two) and a rabbitlike hop—hence its other name, the rock rabbit. Heard more often than seen, with its sharp whistle call of alarm, the pika feeds on green vegetation, putting away enough to last through the entire winter, for unlike many of its high-altitude neighbors, he does not hibernate. As might be expected in this land of short summers and long, brutal winters, "the pika's link to snow and cold is an ancient one, for they are among the creatures known as glacial relicts. Widely distributed during the Ice Age, they now occur only where the climate is still similar to Ice Age type, hence are scattered disjunctively in the far North and on mountains in North America and Eurasia."[41] Evolutionary adaptation and habitat fit are as evident in this climatic zone as in the tropical rain forest.

The rock-loving pika is not to be confused with that other common high-altitude mammal, the marmot. As you look for a place to pitch your tent, you spot a fat yellow-bellied marmot basking in the sun on a nearby rock. The relative of the woodchuck or groundhog, this charming creature forages in the alpine meadows, eating to put on sufficient fat for his long winter hibernation. With a sharp whistle to warn its comrades, the marmot goes into hiding, only to emerge when the coast is clear. Your quiet patience in waiting out the marmot is rewarded when he peeks his blackish-brown whiskered face out at you from only a few feet away.

Despite the harsh climate, there is no dearth of things for these vegetarian, rock-hugging mammals to eat, for interspersed among all the rock gardens are gardens of a different sort—lush meadows sporting a variety of grasses and wildflowers. Even above timberline in the alpine zone at the very edge of subsistence, plants with fitting names such as rockfringe and prickly phlox and yellow alpine columbine manage to survive. Against the onslaught of wind and heat and cold, these highest of all Sierra flora hug the ground, put down deep and wide roots, and preserve moisture by hook and by crook. In so doing, they provide a powerful testimony to the tenacity of life.

Perhaps the prime example of the tenacity of life lies not high up in the alpine zone but farther down, in the transition zone between 5,000 and 7,500 feet. In your hike up to Bighorn Plateau you passed through many forests of large trees—sugar pine, Douglas fir, Ponderosa pine, mountain hemlock—but no tree was as breathtaking as the giant sequoia. This famous sequoia—*Sequoiadendron giganteum*, not to be confused with the taller though slimmer coastal redwood, *Sequoia sempervirens*—grows to an enormous size. For example, the famous General Sherman tree stands at a height of 275 feet and has a basal diameter of 36 feet. The biggest living thing on earth, its trunk totals over 50,000 cubic feet in volume.[42] One of its branches, 130 feet off the ground, measures almost 7 feet across and is 140 feet long—bigger than most entire trees in the forests of the eastern United States.[43] And at 2,700 years old, the General is still growing at the same pace as when he was a mere adolescent.[44] Only the bristlecone pine, one estimated at 4,500 years of age, is older than this giant.

The giant sequoia is a particularly fine example of ecological adaptation. Limited to about 75 small groves within a 250-mile stretch of the Sierra Nevada, the tree has very specific needs. Above 7,500 feet the temperature is too cold and the growing season too short. Below 5,000 feet there is too little moisture. The sun-loving sequoia flourishes in the relatively mild, sheltered basins on the western slopes of the Sierra. In the thin soil, the sequoia sends its roots far and wide in search of water, with a root base that can extend for hundreds of feet.

Due to lightning storms, fire is common in this forest zone, and prior to human arrival and the ubiquity of Smokey Bear, any given area would experience a fire at least once every five to ten years. The giant sequoia defends itself in a variety of ways. Its cinnamon-colored bark is two feet thick and very resistant to fire. The soft and spongy bark also offers insulation against the heat. And even when the bark burns and forms a scar, new bark creeps over the wound until the breach is covered and the tree is again protected. But the giant sequoia has not only adapted to survive fires; it has also learned to take advantage of them. Each tiny sequoia cone—only one to one and a half inches long—contains one hundred to three hundred seeds, each seed so small that it takes ninety-one thousand of them to weigh one pound. Unlike other trees in the conifer forest, the giant sequoia retains its cones, rather than dropping them when they reach maturity. As a ground fire sweeps through the forest, the updrafts cause the old cones to dry and open, and within a week or two they release a cascade of seeds onto the forest floor. In addition to providing the heat necessary for the cones to release their seeds, fire clears away underbrush and purifies the soil, thus preparing the floor for the coming rain of seeds. In short, fire is crucial to the life cycle of the giant sequoia.

The ecological web is even more intricate, however. Also helping the giant sequoia prosper are squirrels and beetles, which munch on mature cones and thus spread seeds during the times between fires. And while the moist and mild climate of the transition zone forest provides an excellent habitat for fungi, the giant sequoia has developed certain internal chemical compounds that render it unpalatable to fungi and to many insects. Thus "large sequoias are highly resistant to the ravages of insects even though more than a hundred species are known to inhabit them."[45] An impressive witness not only to the interrelatedness of the natural world but to the vast physical and temporal scale of living things, the giant sequoia evokes in us a proper humility. Verna Johnston states it well: "Throughout the fires and storms of centuries, through the rise and fall of Rome, the Mayan empire, Spain, through Magna Carta, the Renaissance, 1776, the birth of the United Nations, this statesman has heralded each sunrise anew for nearly three millennia."[46]

As with the description of the Belizean rain forest, this sketch of the mountains of central California is merely the tip of the proverbial iceberg. Much, much more could and should be said. But the spirit of the Sierra Nevada is perhaps best captured in the ringing words of John Muir:

> The snow on the high mountains is melting fast, and the streams are singing bank-full, swaying softly through the level meadows and bogs, quivering with sun-spangles, swirling in pot-holes, resting in deep pools, leaping, shouting in wild, exulting energy over rough boulder dams, joyful, beautiful in all their forms. No Sierra landscape that I have ever seen holds anything truly dead or dull, or any trace of what in manufactories is called rubbish or waste; everything is perfectly clean and pure and full of divine lessons. This quick, inevitable interest attaching to everything seems marvelous until the hand of God becomes visible; then it seems reasonable that what interests Him may well interest us. When we try to pick out anything by itself, we find it hitched to everything else in the universe.[47]

Lake

Water and trees. Blue and green as far as the eye can see. A land of forest, lake, and stream. Such is the third and last place I will briefly describe. A labyrinth of water on this the water planet is the Quetico-Superior wilderness of northeastern Minnesota and western Ontario. A canoe paddler's paradise, this two-million-acre expanse of enchanted lakes, meandering rivers, and dense forest contains some of the oldest exposed rock on earth. With outcrops dated to three billion years ago, this ancient Precambrian bedrock, called the Canadian Shield, stretches in a vast arc from the Atlantic to the Arctic Sea across the upper part of North America. Walking on rock so old prompts you to marvel at the temporal scale of the natural world. We humans are such latecomers to this aged earth.

You notice that the forest floor where you stand has very little topsoil. Scoured by glaciers two miles thick at least four times in the last two million years, most recently a mere ten thousand years ago, the soil around you is seldom more than ten inches deep, and often it is much less.[48] No thick taproots probe this earth. The lay of the land before you, you quickly deduce, is in large measure the legacy of the glacier. On an exposed rock to your right you notice splotches of orange and brown. A closer look reveals, clinging to the rock, that most marvelous of plants—the lichen. A combination of two primitive plants, fungi and algae, lichens often grow in places too harsh for other plants. After the glacier receded, these strong and hardy creatures were the first to colonize the barren landscape. Over aeons, by slowly breaking down the rock, the lichens helped produce the humus necessary for other plants to grow. The fungi provide moisture for the algae while the algae furnish sugars, produced from the light of the sun, for the fungi. Thus, the fungi and algae live symbiotically, each benefiting the other and playing an integral part in the development of the forest ecosystem.

Nearby is a large pond. On one end you see a dam, built by a colony of beavers. A marvel of engineering prowess, with sticks and logs and mud every which way, the dam is able to bear your weight and then some, as well as hold back the water.[49] Not far from the dam you notice a large dome-shaped lodge. Twelve feet across and six feet high above the water, with two underwater entrances and walls four feet thick—to keep the inner chamber free from predators such as the lynx and bobcat, as well as above freezing even in the coldest winter—the lodge is a snug and safe haven. As you quietly approach the lodge, you spot a beaver—black and brown fur glistening, long whiskers on dark nose, wide and flat tail—just before it dives underwater. Weighing in at up to sixty pounds, the beaver is the second largest rodent in the world, after the South American capybara, and ranks second only to humans in its ability to deliberately alter its environment.[50] With large front teeth that are, due to timber cutting, constantly resharpened, the beaver is able to down a two- to three-inch-diameter aspen in thirty seconds and has been known to fell trees one hundred feet long and twelve inches thick.[51]

Such prodigious tree-cutting ability is a necessity when not only your shelter but your food is at stake, for the beaver is entirely vegetarian, preferring the bark of aspen and birch, as well as twigs and leaves. Though able to move (albeit slowly) on land, the beaver vastly prefers the water, and so its industrious dam building serves to make available trees and vegetation otherwise inaccessible. By flooding large areas, the average colony can more easily forage a large expanse for food—six to ten acres of water and up to four hundred yards from the water's edge.[52]

The effects of the beaver's dam building are profound, for over time the forest itself will change. From a stand of aspen and birch comes "a rushy, sedge-grown, semi-aquatic world, part swamp, part lake. The shallow slow-moving waters attract a host of living things—from algae and plankton to fish and crustaceans. These creatures in turn have their own parasites and predators—from mosquitoes to hawks."[53] Eventually, these beavers will consume all the food within their reach and have to abandon this pond for a more promising home elsewhere. In so doing they set the stage for the death of the pond, for the dam will slowly disintegrate and release its impounded water, the aquatic creatures will no longer be able to live there, and the pond will eventually dry out—only to be succeeded by a meadow. After a few decades the meadow will be inhabited by colonizing trees such as aspen and birch, and if the stream does not dry up altogether, another group of hungry beavers will begin the story all over again. Such is one of the many cycles of the northwoods forest.

While wading in the pond your eye catches the zigzag pattern of water striders skittering over the surface of the water. Buzzing just above the water is a dragonfly, its long body powered by two pairs of veined wings. Exiting the pond you shake your feet in the water to rinse off the mud—except one piece of mud does not rinse off your left big toe. You reach down—and, behold, it's a leech. Four inches long and a half inch wide, with a gray-brown body, this wormlike bloodsucker evokes a near universal disdain. But leeches are an important part of the food web, providing nourishment for fish such as northern pike and walleye and also breaking down dead organic matter, thereby making crucial nutrients available to plants and all manner of aquatic organisms. Even the lowly leech has its role—its niche[54]—in the functioning of the pond ecosystem.

As expected this time of year, a small cloud of blackflies hovers around your blue bandana. Seemingly omnipresent in the Quetico-Superior area during May and June, the pinhead-sized female blackfly, like the mosquito, needs blood to provide protein for her developing eggs. However, despite their sometimes annoying presence and welt-producing bite, the blackfly's penchant for blue serves an important ecological function, since they are an important pollinator of the tiny white flowers that later become wild blueberries. The presence of blackflies "also indicates excellent water quality, since nearly any pollution will kill off the larva."[55] Like the leech, the dreaded blackfly has its utility.

On your leisurely walk from pond back to lakeshore campsite, you travel through a forest of balsam fir and white spruce, with some northern white cedar near the water's edge. No birches or aspens stand among these conifers, for the forest through which you walk is a fine example of a boreal forest.[56] Sometimes nicknamed "the spruce-moose forest," the boreal forest circumnavigates the earth, for it is found not only in the northern climes of North America but also in Finland, the Ukraine, and northern China. As one naturalist astutely states, "the globe wears the boreal forest around its head like a spruce-studded crown."[57] As you walk you see many balsam fir, with their famously fragrant needles, as well as pyramidal, Christmas-tree-like spruce here and there. Near the shore is the ubiquitous white cedar, with its scaly needles and peeling bark. You wonder why all the cedar branches are the same height and then remember that deer browse on the cedar in the winter. The lowest level of these branches represents the highest reach of the hungry deer.

So-called natural disasters are an integral part of this forest community. Windfall, insect attack, and fire all contribute to the continuation of this spruce-fir forest. This forest, in other words, "depends on continuing disturbance to maintain itself."[58] Put differently, succession—"the natural change in the plant life of an area that involves the gradual, continuous replacement of one group of species by another"[59]—in this case involves maintenance through disturbance. This beautiful conifer forest would not be what it is without periodic disruption.

As with the giant sequoia forests, fire is especially important to the boreal forest. Among other things, fire releases nutrients into the soil, burns off the acidic mat of accumulated humus, and opens the canopy, allowing more light to fall on the plants on the forest floor. After a fire in the north woods, aspen and birch and jack pine colonize, and often white or red pine if conditions are right. These pioneers endure for a generation, which may be quite a while in the case of the majestic white pine, some of which in this locale grow to be four hundred years old. But below the canopy of pines are somewhat younger white spruces and, a bit lower down, the shade-tolerant balsam fir, biding their time until the relatively short-lived aspens and birches fall.

At dusk, back at your campsite on a large island-studded lake, you hear the rhythmic "peep" of the spring peepers and the guitar-pluck "guunng" of the green frog along the water's edge. Each male sings out to demarcate and defend his territory. You also observe the erratic flight of numerous little brown bats, flying low as they scoop in up to three hundred mosquitoes and other insects in a single hour. Without the maligned mosquito, these bats would be malnourished. Though not blind, contrary to what many believe, at night the bat must rely on its acute hearing to locate its prey. Using an amazing process called echolocation, bats send out ten to twenty high-pitched calls every second.[60] Like underwater sonar, these sounds bounce off objects and return to the bat as echoes. Able to distinguish a flying beetle from a moth, the bat's sense of hearing is incredibly acute and discriminating, as it must be if it is to survive.

Your reverie in observing bats is broken by a quavering sound, one of the haunting calls of that prototypical northwoods bird, the common loon (*Gavia immer*). This vibrato laugh you hear is the tremelo, a distress call indicating danger. Another loon, this one more distant down the lake, joins in, and you are serenaded with a tremelo duet. Just then you hear another of the loon's four distinctive calls—the wail. This plaintive three-note call, long and mournful like the cry of the wolf, is a way of saying, "Where are you?" or, "Here I am." On this night you hear a third distinctive loon cry—the yodel of the male. A complex chain of three to four three-part squeals, this call is used to attract a mate and defend territory. You now know where the expression "crazy as a loon" comes from. Only the quiet "hoot" eludes your listening ears on this night.

Of all the creatures of the north woods, by common consent the most alluring is not the moose, the black bear, or the timber wolf, but rather the common loon. Large birds with a wingspan of about five feet, weighing up to fifteen pounds, and marked by a jet black head, red eyes, white plumage, and a long sharp bill, the loon is easy to recognize. Loons are fishing machines, built for diving. Their bodies are streamlined, with legs far to the rear for effective padding, and their red eyes allow them to see more clearly underwater. Their bones are not hollow, like other birds, but solid, thus giving them a low-in-the-water look and the ability to dive to great depths. Believe it or not, loons have been taken in fishing nets 240 feet deep.[61] Able to stay underwater for up to fifteen minutes, loons swim fast enough to catch game fish such as trout and perch, spearing their prey with their beak and then, after surfacing, swallowing it whole.[62] Being built for diving makes flying more difficult, but loons are, in fact, powerful fliers. Requiring as much as one hundred yards before they can get airborne, once in wing the loon cruises at 75 miles per hour and has been clocked as fast as 108 miles per hour.[63] Loons leave the north woods every fall to winter along the south Atlantic coast from North Carolina to Florida and beyond, only to return in the spring when the ice melts off the lakes. An amazingly well-adapted creature in this land of water, the loon is an unforgettable inhabitant native to this place—a vivid reminder in this wilderness that we humans are only visitors.

Darkness settles in, like a gentle friend blanketing the land. With a new moon the stars blaze back at you brighter than you have ever seen them— Big Dipper and Little Dipper, Draco and Boötes, Cassiopeia and Cepheus, the summer triangle of Cygnus, Lyra, and Aquila, these constellations and many more in all their stellar glory. And then, out of the corner of one eye, you see a strange dancing light just over the horizon. After a few seconds you realize you are witnessing the famed aurora borealis, or northern lights. Sigurd Olson describes the indescribable as well as anyone:

> The lights of the aurora moved and shifted over the horizon. Sometimes there were shafts of yellow tinged with green, then masses of evanescence that moved from east to west and back again. Great streamers of bluish white zigzagged like a tremendous trembling curtain from one end of the sky to the other. Streaks of yellow and orange and red shimmered along the flowing borders. Never for a moment were they still, fading until they were almost completely gone, only to dance forth again in renewed splendor with infinite combinations and startling patterns of design.[64]

Caused by great solar flares that traverse the ninety-three million miles from our star to our home planet and enter the earth's magnetic field, the northern lights are perhaps the most beautiful reminder that, in the words of a poem whose author I have long forgotten, "though things near and distant are, they are connected from afar."

How the World Works

From these three different places, what can we learn from and about our home planet? What can and what should we learn about how the world works? Here are ten learnings—call them *principles of ecology*—gleaned from attending to the world around us.

First, everything is hitched to everything else, as John Muir put it. Or in the words of G. Tyler Miller, every one of us is downwind or downstream of everyone else.[65] This is the first of the "laws of ecology" for Ernest Callenbach: "All things are interconnected."[66] For Garrett Hardin, too, this is "the first law of ecology."[67] We live in an intricate web of a world in which all creatures are in some way interrelated. The cecropia tree and the biting ants. The giant sequoia and the squirrels. The beaver and the birch. Carbon, hydrogen, nitrogen, oxygen, phosphorus, and sulfur recycling among all living organisms. We are all in this together. Call it *the principle of interrelatedness*.

The second follows from the first: we can never do only one thing.[68] Our actions always have many consequences, some of which we do not know and cannot predict. I flip a light switch in Holland, Michigan, and contribute to acid rain falling in the Adirondacks of upstate New York. You eat a salad whose ingredients came from your backyard organic garden and local farmers' market and end up not only boosting the local economy but also, with the scraps, providing the worms in your compost bin with supper. As when a pebble falls into a still pond, our actions ripple out far beyond their immediate spatial or temporal context. This is *the principle of multiple effects*.

Third, there is no throwing things "away." Callenbach's version is, "Everything goes somewhere."[69] We may think our garbage has gone away, but in reality we have merely moved it from one place to another. In the natural world there is no waste. The waste, including dead bodies, of one form of life is invariably the food for other forms of life. A fundamental principle of physics, this insight is called the law of the conservation of matter. We cannot create or destroy matter; matter merely changes form (which could be energy). Matter is conserved. Let's call it *the principle of matter conservation*.

Fourth, we cannot get something for nothing. It takes energy to get energy. In his third law of ecology, Callenbach puts it this way: "There's no such thing as a free lunch."[70] In physics this is the law of the conservation of energy. Often known as the first law of thermodynamics, it states that within any isolated system, we cannot create or destroy energy. Energy simply changes form (which could be matter). A further implication is that in terms of energy quality, when energy changes from one form to another, some of the useful energy is degraded or becomes less useful. This is the second law of thermodynamics: in energy conversion, entropy or disorder increases. We could call this *the principle of energy conversion*.

Fifth, everything fills a niche. Every organism has a function within its habitat. Every species has a role to play or adaptively fits a role in its ecosystem. The leaf-cutter ants cultivate a particular fungus. The ragged white-bark pines provide a home to chipmunks. The omnipresent blackfly pollinates wild blueberries. The tropical rain forest provides an especially clear example of a diverse array of species occupying specialized niches. At every layer of the forest, from soil to canopy, many different organisms function in the trophic system. This is *the principle of fittingness*.

Sixth, things change. We live in an incredibly dynamic universe. The earth's living organisms and natural cycles are constantly changing. Gone is the view that all things reach a form of permanent homeostasis—that the world is basically static. As Daniel Botkin states, we must recognize "the dynamic rather than the static properties of the Earth and its life-support system," for "nature is a moving picture show."[71] A blowdown in the Belizean rain forest means more light reaches the forest floor and thus new plants colonize the forest. A ground fire in the Sierra Nevada causes the sequoia cones to drop their seeds. A beaver dam in the Quetico-Superior changes water flows and levels and thereby alters the landscape. On a larger scale, tectonic plates sliding and colliding rearrange the very skin of the earth. In a variety of spatial and temporal scales, the world is constantly changing. Call this *the principle of dynamic systems*.

Seventh, you adapt or die. Given the ineluctable reality of change, individual organisms, populations, and species either adapt to their surroundings or cease to exist. Bromeliads trap water or die. The pika finds sufficient vegetation to outlast the winter or it dies. Bats get good at echolocation or they die. For some organisms the tolerances of survival are thin, while for others there is much more leeway. With conditions always changing, organisms (e.g., via natural selection) and communities (e.g., via ecological succession) either adapt or go out of existence. Let's call it *the principle of adaptation*.

Eighth, the earth swims in diversity. Biodiversity has at least three forms: the genetic variety within a given species (genetic diversity), the many different individual species of organisms (species diversity), and the diversity of different kinds of natural systems (ecosystem diversity). In the three places described above, the second form of biodiversity is perhaps the most evident, and never more so than in the species-packed tropical rain forest; but diversity in all its forms is visible all over our planet. For example, there are four thousand to five thousand species of bacteria in a single gram of beech forest soil, not to mention all the beetles, centipedes, earthworms, and the like.[72] This is *the principle of diversity*.

Ninth, there is not always more. Except for our energy income from the sun, the world is finite. Numbers of individual organisms (e.g., buffalo and passenger pigeons) may seem limitless, but they are not. Species may appear to be beyond counting (e.g., beetles and flycatchers), but they are finite in number. Our life-support systems (soil, water, and air) may seem beyond abuse, but there are limits to what they can bear. Like it or not, we are finite creatures living in a finite world. Hence, *the principle of limits*.

Tenth and last, the natural world is more complex than we think. Indeed, as G. Tyler Miller Jr. reminds us, the world is more complex than we can ever possibly imagine.[73] The burgeoning field of complexity theory is but one example that demonstrates the truth of this claim.[74] The world is not fundamentally like a machine—understandable by a dissection and cataloguing of its parts. It is, rather, an incredibly complex system whose properties cannot be fully explained by knowing its constituent components. In other words, the whole is more than the sum of its parts. In the natural world there are nonlinear systems, such as the weather, whose behavior can never be easily predicted. Hence, the butterfly effect: a butterfly flapping its wings in Tokyo affects the rainfall in Chicago. Also, in complex systems there are properties that unexpectedly emerge, such as social life among certain insects. The more we learn about the world, the stranger and more mysterious it gets. Call this *the principle of complexity*.

There are, of course, many other important things we could learn, but this short list will suffice. What would it mean to acknowledge and live by these principles? How would our world be different if we took these learnings to heart? Would this knowledge of how the world works increase our love of and care for our place?

Places of the Heart

We care for only what we love. We love only what we know. We truly know only what we experience. If we do not know our place—know it in more than a passing, cursory way, know it intimately and personally—then we are destined to use and abuse it. So we need to experience our home place firsthand. In my case, only if I see the great blue heron arch its prehistoric wings in flight, only if I hear the song sparrows and the chickadees, only if I smell the scent of skunk or wild onion, only if I feel the warm sun of spring or the brisk breeze of autumn, only, in short, if I take the opportunity to know my place will I feel motivated to care for it.

Important as it is to have a solid sense of our connectedness to the larger whole, we all live in particular places, discrete locales, specific homes. I live in southwestern Michigan, in a temperate transition zone of conifers, such as spruce and hemlock, and of hardwood deciduous trees, such as maples and beeches and oaks, above layers of sand deposited thousands of years ago by glaciers a mile high, along the shore of that great inland sea we call the Great Lakes—holder of one-fifth of all the fresh water on the surface of the earth.

More exactly, my home is the Macatawa watershed. I live in an area drained by countless creeks and streams, all flowing inexorably into the Macatawa River, which itself flows west into Lake Michigan. Sometimes called the Black River, the river comes by its alternate name honestly. The water is black, very black. With phosphorus levels four times what they should be, the lake is eutrophic: there is not enough oxygen to support the normal food chain. In addition, the turbidity is quite high. That is, the blackness of the river and its feeder streams is due in large measure to large quantities of suspended silt and organic matter in the water. Put in layperson's language, soil is being eroded into the streams and thus contributing to the problems in the river. In short, the watershed is not in very good shape. That's the bad news.

The good news is that things are changing for the better. For example, the Macatawa Area Coordinating Council has launched a campaign to clean up the watershed. Aimed at farmers, industry, private homeowners, and local municipalities, this watershed conservation program is raising awareness of how we can and must do a better job of caring for our place by using less fertilizer, installing erosion strips on stream banks, protecting remaining wetlands, and the like. In addition, the Macatawa Greenway Partnership, a nonprofit organization whose mission is to protect and connect green spaces, streams, and natural lands, has been working to preserve remaining area along the Macatawa River and build trails for walking, running, and bicycling. Convinced that one sure way to cultivate care for the watershed is by getting people out into it, the people of the Greenway Partnership envision a series of public waterfront pathways for the enjoyment of all. These groups are merely two examples in my local community of people who know their place and are working to make it better—for humans and nonhumans alike.

So where are we? Do we know our place? If we wish to properly care for our homes—not only for ourselves but for our children and our children's children—then we, and all our fellow dwellers in our place, must love our homes. And we must love them for more than merely our own gain. And to love them we must know them—up close and personal. When asked by a questioner what he could do to stem the tide of ecological degradation and work to improve the state of our home planet, contemporary poet Gary Snyder gave this sound advice: "Settle down, get to know your place, and dig in."

what's wrong
with the world?

the groaning of creation

For the creation waits with eager longing for the revealing of the children of God; for the creation was subjected to futility, not of its own will but by the will of the one who subjected it, in hope that the creation itself will be set free from its bondage to decay and will obtain the freedom of the glory of the children of God. We know that the whole creation has been groaning in labor pains until now; and not only the creation, but we ourselves, who have the first fruits of the Spirit, groan inwardly while we wait for adoption, the redemption of our bodies.

Romans 8:19–23

"One in Four Bird Species Declining"
"Silicon Valley Fears Toxin Is Far Worse Than First Believed"
"EPA Report Finds Coastal Waters Still Awash in Problems"
"Polluted Asia Air Makes Easy Trip to US across Pacific"
"Comprehensive Study Bolsters Link between Warming and Changes in Nature"

This small sampling of recent newspaper headlines pointedly illustrates that all is not well. Indeed, it is a rare week that passes without learning about some ecological degradation. With each newspaper and television report, or because of our own firsthand observations, we are regularly shaken from our comfortable ignorance about the state of our earthly home. Global warming, toxic wastes, oil spills, acid rain, drinking water contamination, destruction of rain forests, overflowing landfills, topsoil erosion, species extinction, smog— this is the bald-faced reality of our life in the world today.

If anecdotal observations or media reports need any confirmation, there are plenty of highly trained earth-watchers speaking out about the current state of the planet. For example, biologist Calvin DeWitt states that we humans "have exceeded our capacity to be responsible stewards, and in our over-reach, we have brought destruction and degradation as never before, on a grand scale." DeWitt identifies four areas of major concern—planetary energy exchange, land and soils, forest and habitats, and biotic species and biodiversity—and documents how we have "significantly restructured the biosphere."[1] Biologist Stuart Pimm reaches a similar conclusion in his environmental audit of the earth. In his overall summary he states that the earth "is suffering from huge and unmistakable human impacts," some of which (e.g., loss of species) "are about to become irreversible" unless we act very quickly.[2] As Aldo Leopold succinctly puts it: to those with the eyes to see, we live in a world of wounds.[3] Or, to paraphrase the words of St. Paul from the Romans 8 epigraph above: creation is groaning.

Creation is groaning. The state of the world is not good. But what exactly is wrong? In what precise ways is the earth groaning? In this chapter I survey and explain a number of ways in which our home planet is being degraded. If in the previous chapter we examined how the world works and what we can and must learn to be responsible earthkeepers, here we take an honest and often painful look at how things are not, ecologically speaking, the way they are supposed to be. The problems are many, and they are profound. But we dare not, ostrich-like, stick our heads in the sand and ignore them. If, in short, we truly are to know our place, then such knowing must include an accurate and sober assessment of how God's blue-green earth is out of kilter.

Population

When were there half as many people in the world as there are today? In 1883? 1924? 1965? A guess of 1924 seems reasonable, but in fact, in 1924 there were approximately two billion people—less than a third of the 2008 population of 6.7 billion. The correct answer is 1965. The global population doubled in only forty-three years, and it continues to increase by 77 million each year.[4] As figure 1 indicates, human population growth in the last century has been exponential, not linear. In other words, the time it takes for the population to double has dramatically decreased. At these growth rates global population is expected to reach 9 billion by 2050.

Figure 1. World Population Development

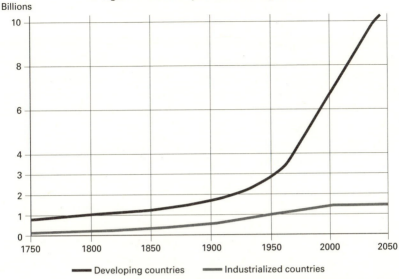

Billions

——— Developing countries   ——— Industrialized countries

UNEP/GRID-Arendal, *UNEP/GRID-Arendal Maps and Graphics Library*, Philippe Rekacewicz
cartographer, available at http://maps.grida.no/go/graphic/world_population_development.

As many demographers assert, this increase in population will take place almost exclusively in the so-called developing world. Indeed, 95 percent of the current population growth is in developing countries, with the highest growth rate in Africa, which is expected to double its population to 2.3 billion by 2050. Not to be forgotten are China and India, which today account for 37 percent of the total world population. China, whose age pyramid shows that 35 percent of its population is in the prime child-bearing ages of fifteen to thirty-four,[5] is expected to reach 1.4 billion by 2050, and projections indicate that India will overtake China as the most populous country, with 1.6 billion people, by the year 2050.[6] In short, even though the rate of world population growth is slowing, in many countries the population is expected to increase dramatically in the next three or four decades.

One need not be a mathematician to grasp the significance of this trend and to ask a number of important questions. For example, what are the social and environmental effects of such population growth, and how long can such an increase in human population be sustained? In answer to the first question, Lester Brown expresses the view of many when he puts population growth at the top of his list of seven key "environmental trends shaping the new century." He states, "The projected growth in population over the next half-century may more directly affect economic progress than any other single trend, exacerbating nearly all other environmental and social problems." In a concise summary he explains the challenge facing us: "Our numbers continue to expand, but the Earth's natural systems do not."[7] Likewise, James Speth begins his list of "ten drivers of environmental deterioration" with population, since it "has been a huge driver of environmental decline," placing additional pressures on already over-strapped resources for many impoverished people and places.[8] Christopher Flavin also points to human population growth as "a driving force behind many environmental and social problems." Indeed, in his view it is one of the three global problems that "still stand in the way of achieving a sustainable world," along with human-induced climate change and the loss of biodiversity.[9]

In response to the question concerning sustainability, Brown echoes the views of many when he concludes that "population growth has already surpassed sustainable limits on a number of environmental fronts. From cropland and water availability to climate change and unemployment, population growth exacerbates existing problems, making them more difficult to manage."[10] In other words, population growth is already a serious threat to ecological sustainability. But Flavin rightly adds that "population growth cannot be adequately considered without reference to the resource consumption levels of individual nations."[11]

> Roughly 1.5 billion people in the world's consumer class—who drive automobiles, own refrigerators and televisions, and shop in malls—consume the bulk of the world's fossil fuels, metals, wood products, and grain. A newborn in the United States requires more than twice as much grain and 10 times as much oil as a child born in Brazil or Indonesia—and produces far more pollution. In fact, a simple calculation shows that the annual increase in the U.S. population of 2.6 million people puts more pressure on the world's resources than do the 17 million people added in India each year.[12]

Brown himself acknowledges the pivotal role of resource consumption. When asked, "How many people can the Earth support?" he perceptively responds, "At what level of consumption?"[13]

These comments point to the importance of acknowledging that more than population is at work in determining environmental impact. Indeed, there are at least three majors factors that influence impact, namely, population, affluence, and technology. This is captured in the much-used formula I=PAT. Environmental Impact (I) equals Population (P) times Affluence (A) times Technology (T), where A is essentially consumption per capita and T is a measure of overall technological efficiency. The formula is an oversimplification, but it reminds us that population is only one factor in determining environmental impact. Consumption rates per person and technological efficiency are also important. So the environmental impact of an increasing population could actually go down if consumption per capita decreased and/or various technologies became more efficient. With characteristic force and self-critical honesty Wendell Berry questions whether population per se is the problem:

> I would argue that, at least for us in the United States, the conclusion that "there are too many people" is premature, not because I know that there are *not* too many people, but because I do not think we are prepared to come to such a conclusion. I grant that questions about population size need to be asked, but they are not the *first* questions that need to be asked. The "population problem," initially, should be examined as a problem, not of quantity, but of pattern. Before we conclude that we have too many people, we must ask if we have people who are misused, people who are misplaced, or people who are abusing the places they have. . . . I would argue that it is not human fecundity that is overcrowding the world so much as technological multipliers of the power of individual humans. The worst disease of the world now is probably the ideology of technological heroism, according to which more and more people willingly cause large-scale effects that they do not foresee and that they cannot control.[14]

Human population growth is a critical factor in assessing the groaning of the earth. Creatures human and nonhuman are imperiled, in some instances, simply because there are so many of us humans. But as Berry reminds us, both affluence and technology play crucial roles in determining environmental impact. The question is not simply how many humans can the earth sustain, but at what level of consumption and using what kind of technology?

Hunger

If the hungry people in the world today were lined up shoulder to shoulder, how long would the line stretch? From New York to Los Angeles? Around the world once at the equator? Would you believe around the world at the equator thirteen times?[15] Incredibly, the line of those who have too little to eat to meet their daily energy needs would extend around the world thirteen times, for roughly 850 million people are undernourished.[16] Further, these undernourished are often also malnourished, so not just food quantity but food quality is lacking.[17]

Hunger is a grim reality for approximately one in eight people, and unfortunately the prospects of increasing food production are not promising. While the inference drawn from figure 2 might seem heartening, given the dramatic increase in world grain production in the last fifty years due in large measure to the use of fertilizers and pesticides developed as part of the so-called Green Revolution, figure 3 is more sobering.[18] When grain production per person is charted, rather than total grain production, the gains in the last five decades are much more modest. Indeed, the grain output per person peaked in 1984 and has been decreasing ever since. In short, grain production is not keeping up with population growth.

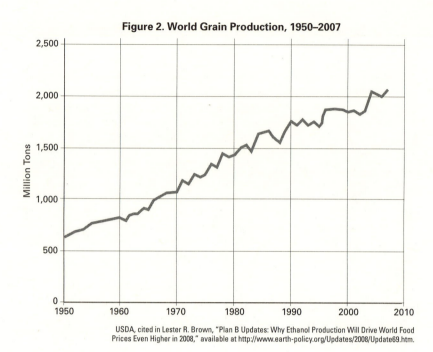

Figure 2. World Grain Production, 1950–2007

USDA, cited in Lester R. Brown, "Plan B Updates: Why Ethanol Production Will Drive World Food Prices Even Higher in 2008," available at http://www.earth-policy.org/Updates/2008/Update69.htm.

Of particular concern are two other trends. First, in the last fifty years there has been a 50 percent decrease in world grain harvested area per person—from .23 hectares to .12 hectares.[19] In other words, while more land is being used for agriculture now than fifty years ago, due to the increase in population there is less land per person. Assuming that in the next decades the total harvested area remains constant (a questionable assumption given urbanization and land degradation), the harvested area per person will shrink even further. In addition, water tables around the world are falling, and the oceanic fish catch is leveling off and in some places severely declining. In sum, measured per person, the resource base on which we depend to feed ourselves is growing ever smaller.

Second, since the year 2000 world grain consumption has outpaced world grain production, with the shortfall covered by world grain stocks, that is, the amount left over from the last harvest when the next harvest begins. But in 2007 the world grain stocks, measured as days of consumption, were less than half of what they were in 2000. As of January 2008 we had fifty-four days of grain in reserve to feed the world—the lowest on record.[20] Carryover stocks of grain are, for many experts on global food policy, the most basic measure of world food security. When our cushion of food to feed a hungry world becomes perilously low, it is clear we have a serious problem on our hands. And in light of these trends, the specter of hunger will not go away any time soon. Alas, the line of the hungry grows ever longer.

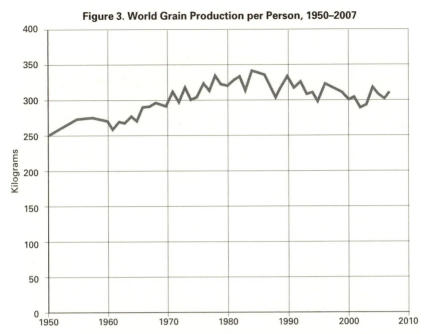

Figure 3. World Grain Production per Person, 1950–2007

USDA/United Nations, cited in Lester R. Brown, "Plan B Updates: Why Ethanol Production Will Drive World Food Prices Even Higher in 2008," available at http://www.earth-policy.org/Updates/2008/Update69.htm.

Biodiversity

Does another species of plant or animal life become extinct every year? Every week? Every eight hours? While estimates vary, a scientifically reasonable figure is three species per day, or one every eight hours. John Tuxill summarizes the data:

> Scientists who study the fossil and archeological record of the recent geologic past—called the Quaternary Period—have accumulated substantial evidence to suggest that extinction rates have increased over the past several millennia. Most estimates of the current situation are that at least 1000 species are lost per year, an extinction rate 100 to 1000 times above the background rate even when calculated with conservative assumptions. Like the dinosaurs 65 million years ago, human society now finds itself in the midst of a mass extinction: a global evolutionary convulsion with few parallels in the entire history of life. [21]

This astonishing conclusion is portrayed in figure 4, from the Millennium Eco-system Assessment. In the words of the authors of this exhaustive scientific study: "Over the past few hundred years, humans have increased species extinction rates by as much as 1000 times the background rates that were typical over Earth's history."[22] Three species every day. Every eight hours another species

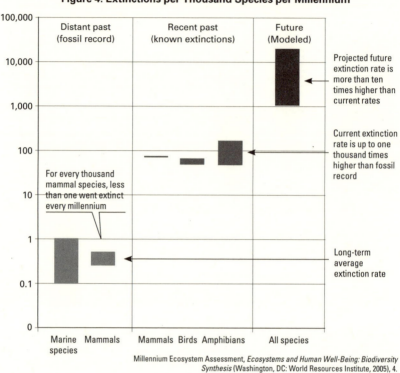

Figure 4. Extinctions per Thousand Species per Millennium

Distant past (fossil record) | Recent past (known extinctions) | Future (Modeled)

Projected future extinction rate is more than ten times higher than current rates

Current extinction rate is up to one thousand times higher than fossil record

For every thousand mammal species, less than one went extinct every millennium

Long-term average extinction rate

Marine species | Mammals | Mammals | Birds | Amphibians | All species

Millennium Ecosystem Assessment, *Ecosystems and Human Well-Being: Biodiversity Synthesis* (Washington, DC: World Resources Institute, 2005), 4.

gone forever. The conclusion of biologist Norman Myers is inescapable: we are experiencing a "human-caused biotic holocaust."[23]

More specific data can be seen in figure 5, from the World Conservation Union (also known as the International Union for the Conservation of Nature, or IUCN).[24] According to the IUCN's "Red List" terminology, there are three categories of threat (in escalating order of peril): vulnerable, endangered, and critically endangered, all of which are included within the technical term "threatened." As of 2006, among the vertebrates approximately 12 percent of the world's bird species, 23 percent of mammals, 31 percent of amphibians, 40 percent of fish, and 51 percent of reptiles were threatened. The invertebrates were even worse, with 53 percent threatened, while the plants faced even greater danger of extinction, with 70 percent of those evaluated listed as threatened. In sum for 2006, of the 40,168 species evaluated, 16,118 (or 40 percent) were threatened. As Elroy Bos puts it in his understated summary, these numbers "demonstrate the ongoing decline of global biodiversity and the impact that humankind is having on life on Earth."[25] The message is clear: the web of life is unraveling.

Figure 5. Threatened Species, by Major Groups of Organism, 2006

Organism	Described Species (number)	Species Evaluated (number)	Threatened Species (number)	Threatened Species as Share of Known Species (percent)	Threatened Species as Share of Species Evaluated (percent)
Vertebrates					
Mammals	5,416	4,856	1,093	20	23
Birds	9,934	9,934	1,206	12	12
Reptiles	8,240	664	341	4	51
Amphibians	5,918	5,918	1,811	31	31
Fishes	29,300	2,914	1,173	4	40
Subtotal	58,808	24,284	5,624	10	23
Invertebrates					
Insects	950,000	1,192	623	0.07	52
Mollusks	70,000	2,163	975	1.39	45
Crustaceans	40,000	537	459	1.15	85
Others	130,200	86	44	0.03	51
Subtotal	1,190,200	3,978	2,101	0.18	53
Plants					
Mosses	15,000	93	80	0.53	86
Ferns and allies	13,025	212	139	1	66
Gymnosperms	980	908	306	31	34
Dicotyledons	199,350	9,538	7,086	4	74
Monocotyledons	59,300	1,150	779	1	68
Subtotal	287,655	11,901	8,390	3	70
Others					
Lichens	10,000	2	2	0.02	100
Mushrooms	16,000	1	1	0.01	100
Subtotal	26,000	3	3	0.01	100
Total	1,562,663	40,168	16,118	1	40

IUCN, cited in Elroy Bos, "Threats to Species Accelerate," *Vital Signs 2007–2008* (Washington, DC: Worldwatch Institute, 2008), 97. Used by permission of W. W. Norton & Company, Inc.

Some of the species recently included on the Red List are the polar bear, the dama gazelle of the Sahara, the angel shark, and the common hippopotamus. Not included on this short list of charismatic megafauna are many less well-known but equally (if not more) important species.[26] The causes of species extinction are not difficult to identify. Loss of habitat, overhunting, invasions of exotic species, and pollution are the leading causes. Tuxill captures the essence of the matter:

Human activities fueling vertebrate declines and attendant biodiversity losses include conversion, fragmentation, and disruption of native habitats (by far the most important factor); overexploitation of species for their meat, hides, horns, or medicinal or entertainment value; and aiding (intentionally and unintentionally) the spread of invasive species—highly adaptable animals and plants that "hitch-hike" with humankind around the globe. Environmental contamination by synthetic chemicals and toxic pollution is a lesser problem, but has the potential to grow much larger in the near future.[27]

And it is becoming increasingly clear that climate change is significantly affecting the world's biodiversity, with many negative impacts.[28] In various and sundry ways, often unknowingly, we have diminished our native flora and fauna and, in all too many cases, extinguished them altogether.

The effects of this "biotic holocaust" are profoundly disturbing, for biodiversity constitutes a fundamentally necessary condition for human life. We are inextricably and essentially dependent on the goods and services provided by the natural world.[29] The foreword to the *Global Biodiversity Assessment*, commissioned by the United Nations Environment Programme and to which over fifteen hundred scientists worldwide contributed, summarizes the serious consequences facing us in the future:

> Biodiversity represents the very foundation of human existence. Yet by our heedless actions we are eroding this biological capital at an alarming rate. Even today, despite the destruction that we have inflicted on the environment and its natural bounty, its resilience is taken for granted. But the more we learn of the workings of the natural world, the clearer it becomes that there is a limit to the disruption that the environment can endure.
>
> Besides the profound ethical and aesthetic implications, it is clear that the loss of biodiversity has serious economic and social costs. The genes, species, ecosystems, and human knowledge which are being lost represent a living library of options available for adapting to local and global change. Biodiversity is part of our daily lives and livelihood and constitutes the resources upon which families, communities, nations, and future generations depend.[30]

Without the original worldwide web, we simply cannot exist.

Deforestation

Tropical forests are currently destroyed at what annual rate? An area the size of metropolitan Chicago? Or Massachusetts? Or Indiana? The answer: Indiana, roughly twenty-five million acres each year.[31] Trees figure prominently in our language. Consider these terms and expressions: family tree, decision tree, branching out, finding roots, becoming uprooted.[32] Yet the prominence of trees in our language is no guarantee they will be cared for in real life. Indeed, we have, especially in the last 150 years, destroyed many of our forests. In the last 50 years, the pace of forest destruction has quickened. Can it be true that an area of tropical forest the size of Indiana vanishes each year?

As with the previous three topics, the facts here are simply staggering. Half of the forests that covered the earth eight thousand years ago are now gone.[33] Between 1980 and 1995 at least two hundred million hectares of forests vanished—an area larger than Mexico. From 1990 to 2005 in Brazil alone the area of forests cut was the size of California.[34] The amount of deforestation from 1990 to 2005, not just in Brazil but elsewhere in the world, is clearly evident in figure 6. In South America, Central America, sub-Saharan Africa, Southeast Asia, and Indonesia, the trees continue to fall at an alarming rate. Figure 7 reveals the extent of tropical rain forest destruction more lucidly than any raft

Figure 6. Global Deforestation

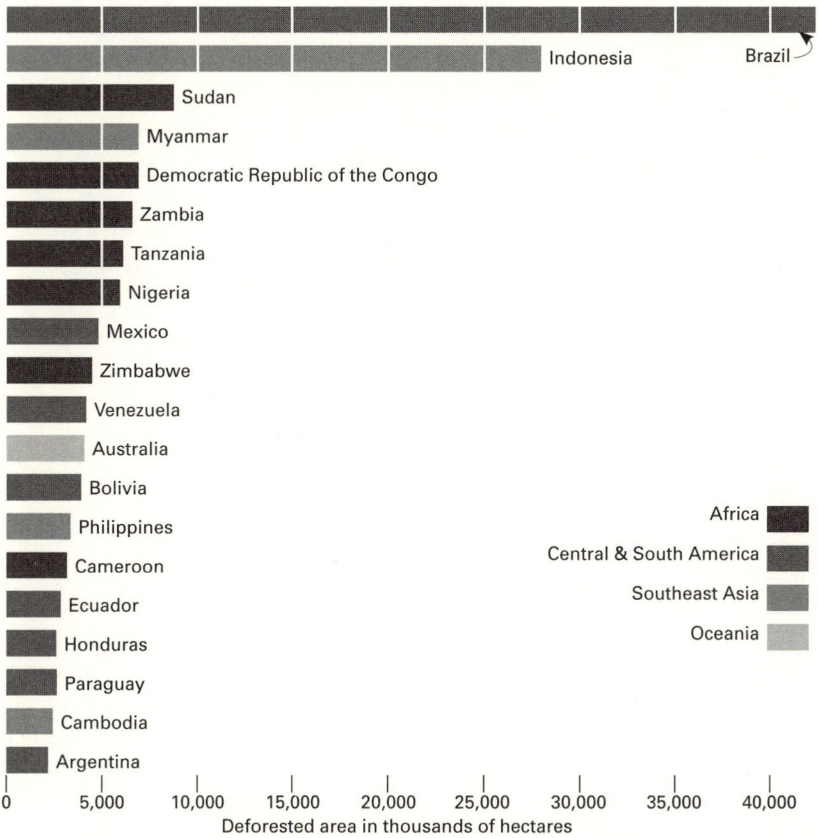

Deforested area in thousands of hectares

Original graphic by Robert Simmon, based on data provided by individual countries to the U.N. Food and Agriculture Organization for the Global Resources Assessment Report 2005, cited in "Causes of Deforestation: Direct Causes," NASA Earth Observatory, available at http://earthobservatory.nasa.gov/Features/Deforestation/deforestation_update3.php.

of statistics. The area covered by dense forest in Borneo, represented by dark shading in the figure, has sharply receded in the last sixty years to a mere fraction of its previous size. Such a pattern of forest degradation is, unfortunately, not unique to Indonesia.

Figure 7. Deforestation in Borneo

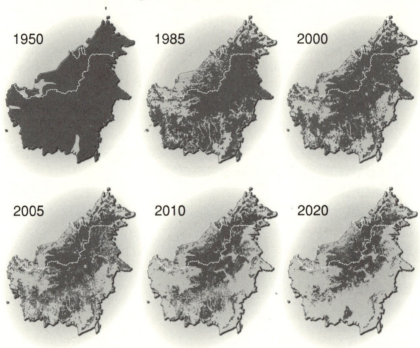

UNEP/GRID-Arendal, "Extent of Deforestation in Borneo 1950–2005, and Projection towards 2020," *UNEP/ GRID-Arendal Maps and Graphics Library,* Hugo Ahlenius cartographer, available at http://maps.grida .no/go/graphic/extent-of-deforestation-in-borneo-1950-2005-and-projection-towards-2020.

The major causes of deforestation are logging, ranching, plantation farming, small-holder agriculture, cutting for fuelwood, and road construction, though the causes vary according to place. In Southeast Asia logging is the primary cause, while in East Africa fuelwood is the primary driver, and in South America cattle ranching and road building are the major contributors. As one example of the interrelationship between different degradations, roughly one-quarter of all the atmospheric carbon produced by human activities comes from cutting and burning forests (with the other three-quarters coming from burning fossil fuel). Since the 1980s there has been a net release of carbon into the atmosphere from the world's forests.[35] In short, the world's forests are no longer carbon sinks but instead are carbon sources and thus major contributors to global climate change.

Our patterns of forest use also merit scrutiny. In 2000 the world used more than 3.5 times as much paper as it did in 1961, and consumption continues to grow.[36] In the United States, paper products make up roughly 40 percent of the municipal solid waste stream, and more than half of the wood brought to a sawmill leaves as chips and sawdust. Less than 20 percent of the world's population (the United States, Europe, and Japan) consumes over 50 percent of the world's industrial timber and 67 percent of its paper.[37] Such is our use and abuse of the forests.

Forests need not be cut to be degraded, however. Existing uncut forests may appear healthy when in fact they are not. Charles Little, in his book *The Dying of the Trees*, gives more than ample evidence that many of the forests in North America are dying. Little documents case after tragic case of forest decline, from the dogwood to the giant sequoia, from the sugar maple to the balsam fir: "For the trees are dying everywhere, including everywhere in the United States of America. They are dying on the ridges of the Appalachian chain and in the sugar bush of Vermont. They are dying in the mixed mesophytic of the mid-South border states, in the thick forests of central Michigan, on the mountainsides of Colorado and California, on the gulf of Mexico, and in the deserts of the southwest. And they are dying in the Northwest, too—even before they are cut."[38] Little persuasively argues that our forests are in deep trouble because of what we humans have done (and not done) over the last few centuries.

> Thus do the causes—direct or indirect—proliferate, a growing list of human actions that so modify the natural environment that tree death and forest decline eventuate: too much ground-level ozone and not enough stratospheric ozone; acidified soils over vast forest regions; a pattern of nutrient loss and an excess of other nutrients, such as nitrogen, that prove toxic; the deposition of heavy metals—cadmium, lead, copper, zinc, mercury—and the mobility of poisonous aluminum normally locked in the soil; the loss of beneficial mycorrhizal fungus; the destructive edge effects of clearcutting; the genetic weakness of replacement trees in impacted ecosystems; a host of plagues and diseases anxious to take advantage of the debilitated trees and forests; the unwonted effects of too-rapid climate change.[39]

Needless to say, we imperil ourselves when we wreak havoc on the forests, for the goods and services that forests provide are many. In addition to timber, the forests provide goods such as food, fodder, fish, oils, resins, spices, and medicines. The services forests provide include purification and regulation of water; decomposition of waste; cycling of nutrients; creation and maintenance of soil; provision of pollination, pest control, and habitat; moderation of disturbances such as floods and storms; regulation of local and global climates; and the sustenance of millions of people, including educational, recreational, and cultural benefits.[40] In short, forests are invaluable. We simply cannot live without them.

Water

Roughly how many people in the world do not have an adequate supply of water? If you guessed over 50 percent you would be right. In 2008 about 1.1 billion people did not have safe drinking water, and 2.6 billion people lacked water for proper sanitation.[41] This constitutes 56 percent of the global population. Worldwide, about six thousand children under the age of five die each day from diarrhea-related diseases.[42] The issue here is twofold: having enough water (water supply) and having uncontaminated water (water purity). Both are important aspects of water degradation.

Water scarcity is perhaps the most unacknowledged ecological problem in the world today. Most of us in the United States simply turn on a tap and out flows a seemingly endless supply. Water, however, is increasingly being diverted from rivers, lakes, and aquifers for a variety of human uses, including agricultural irrigation, domestic consumption, and industrial use. So much is this the case, as is evident in figure 8, that "the amount of fresh water withdrawn [from these sources] has risen 35-fold in the past three hundred years," and "over half of that increase has occurred since 1950."[43] According to one projection, the amount

Figure 8. Global Trends in Water Withdrawals, 1900–2000

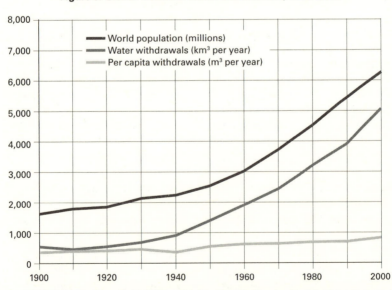

UNESCO/Gleick, "At a Glance: The World's Water Crisis," *Our Planet: The Magazine of the United Nations Environment Programme* 14, no. 1 (2003): 18, available at http://www.unep.org/OurPlanet/imgversn/141/images/glance/glance1.jpg.

of water available per person will fall 73 percent between 1950 and 2050, and given that many of these shortages will likely occur in countries already facing scarcity, the effects will be traumatic.[44]

Examples of water overconsumption are easy to find. So much water is taken from the mighty Colorado River that it no longer reaches the Gulf of California. The once voluminous Nile now trickles to the Mediterranean. Due to excessive water diversion and mismanagement, the Aral Sea in the former Soviet Union, once the world's fourth-largest lake, contains less than one-fourth of its previous volume, and the fish catch, which once totaled 44,000 tons per year, has dropped to zero.[45] Water tables are falling in China, India, Pakistan, Lebanon, Mexico, and the United States; indeed, significant groundwater depletion is taking place in virtually every part of the globe.[46] For example, the Ogallala aquifer, which underlies much of the south-central United States, is being drawn down much faster than it is being replenished. In some parts of Texas, Oklahoma, and Kansas, the water table has dropped 150 feet.[47] In short, we are using water faster than it can be replenished. If this continues, according to one estimate, "a billion people will be living in countries facing absolute water scarcity by 2025."[48] Sandra Postel puts it bluntly: "The upshot of this survey of groundwater use is that many food-producing regions are sustained by the hydrologic equivalent of deficit financing."[49]

Water purity is also a troublesome problem. For example, the largest freshwater ecosystem in the world, the Great Lakes, is home to 20 percent of the earth's surface fresh water. It is also home to a toxic brew of chemicals, including mercury, PCBs, DDT, and dioxins. Hence the ubiquitous fish consumption advisories against eating too much Great Lakes fish, for many of the chemicals become more concentrated as they move up the food chain. While some of these chemical pollutants are released directly into the water, many enter indirectly, for example, as runoff. Indeed, research has pointed to the deposition of airborne pollutants as a major source of water pollution.[50]

Water purity is a serious problem not just in North America, but the world over, with a demonstrable link between lack of potable water and infant mortality. More exactly, lack of clean water causes various diseases that in turn increase infant mortality. For example, 1.8 million people (of whom 90 percent are children under the age of five) die each year from diarrheal diseases, with 88 percent of diarrheal disease attributed to an unsafe water supply and/or inadequate sanitation.[51] The lesson is clear: where access to clean water is limited, more children die; where access to clean water is readily available, more children live. Hence it is not just water but safe water that is badly needed in many parts of the world. The human impacts on freshwater ecosystems are many and varied, with negative consequences on both water supply and water purity.[52] The irony is inescapable and profound: on this the water planet, a great many people do not have enough good water to drink.

Land

In the United States the amount of topsoil lost each year is 3,000 tons? 300,000 tons? 3 billion tons? The answer, believe it or not, is 3 billion tons—topsoil lost annually due to wind and water erosion.[53] While this seems like a most disturbing fact, it is not in itself troubling, for soil is naturally created. The problem is that the rate of natural soil formation in the United States is between one-half and one ton of topsoil per hectare per year, while the erosion rate is 10 tons per hectare per year. In other words, we are losing topsoil 10 to 20 times faster than it is being replaced. According to soil expert David Pimentel, "90% of US cropland now is losing soil faster than its sustainable, replacement rate."[54] Furthermore, soil erosion is most severe in some of the most agriculturally productive areas. For example, because of erosion 50 percent of the fertile topsoil of Iowa has been lost in the last 150 years, and 40 percent of the rich topsoil in the Palouse region of the Pacific Northwest has been lost in the last century. The economic costs of soil erosion in the United States are a staggering $37.6 billion a year in lost productivity.[55]

Worldwide, the statistics on soil erosion are equally stunning. Scientifically informed estimates put the total soil loss from agricultural systems alone (that is, not including range land or forests) at 75 billion tons a year.[56] In addition, according to Pimentel, "about 80% of the world's agricultural land suffers moderate to severe erosion, while 10% experiences slight erosion." As a result, "during the last 40 years about 30% of the world's arable land has become unproductive and much of that has been abandoned for agricultural use."[57] Indeed, each year approximately 10 million hectares of cropland, an area the size of South Korea, are abandoned because of lack of productivity due to erosion. The message is clear: we are losing soil—another feature of our earthly inheritance essential to our existence—at an alarming rate.

Another form of land degradation is desertification. Figure 9 (see pp. 40–41) illustrates the scope of this lesser-known yet ecologically serious phenomenon. In a variety of places around the world deserts are growing. While some desertification occurs naturally—as a result of prolonged drought, hotter than normal temperatures, and high winds—in recent years much has clearly been a result of human action. Practices such as overgrazing, cultivation of marginal land, and deforestation, among others, have contributed to the growth of desert areas on the earth. In the last half of the twentieth century the amount of desert increased 3.1 million square miles, an area the size of Brazil, with another 23,000 square miles, or an area the size of West Virginia, of new desert formed each year.[58]

But decreasing the quality of the land, via topsoil erosion and desertification, is only one kind of land degradation. Another form involves decreasing the quantity of land available. In the United States the most dominant example of this is sprawl—low-density, automobile-dependent development beyond the edge of service and employment areas. In addition to increasing traffic congestion, worsening air pollution, and exacerbating flooding, sprawl is gobbling up farmland (and forests and wetlands) at a frightening rate. For example, between 1970 and 1990 in the United States more than nineteen million acres of rural land were "developed"—that is, built on, bulldozed under, or paved over.[59] While population accounts for some urban growth (urban here includes cities and their suburbs) in the last decades, in many cases sprawl is the decisive factor. For example, from 1950 to 1970, while the population of Phoenix grew 300 percent, its urban area grew 630 percent. From 1970 to 1990 the population of Charlotte, North Carolina, grew by 63 percent while its urban area grew 129 percent. Even more telling: from 1970 to 1990 Chicago's population grew only 1 percent while its urban area grew by 24 percent, and Detroit's population dropped 7 percent while its urban area increased by 28 percent.[60] Urban areas are currently expanding at about twice the rate that urban population is growing, in many cases gobbling up land once used for food production.[61] In short, a myriad of statistics points to the reality and harmful effects of this haphazard and car-crazy growth pattern called sprawl. Land degradation, unfortunately, takes many forms.

Waste

Each year we in the United States generate enough municipal solid waste to fill a bumper-to-bumper convoy of garbage trucks that would stretch from Los Angeles to New York? From Los Angeles to Calcutta? Around the world at the equator almost 4 times? Though literally incredible, the convoy of trucks containing municipal solid waste (MSW) from the United States would extend around the planet 3.8 times. Just one year's worth of garbage, from only one country. In 2006 the United States produced 251 million tons of MSW.[62] This amounts to 1,645 pounds per person per year, which means that at this rate the typical U.S. citizen throws away 62 tons of garbage over a 75-year lifetime. As is evident in figure 10 (see p. 42), from 1960 to 1990 the amount of MSW generated annually increased dramatically, from 88 to 205 million tons. Some of this was due to increasing population, but most was due to increasing waste per person, since the per capita generation rate during that same period went from 2.68 to 4.5 pounds per person per day. Since 1990 the total amount of MSW has increased, but at a much slower rate, while the per capita waste generation rate has leveled off and actually started to go down.

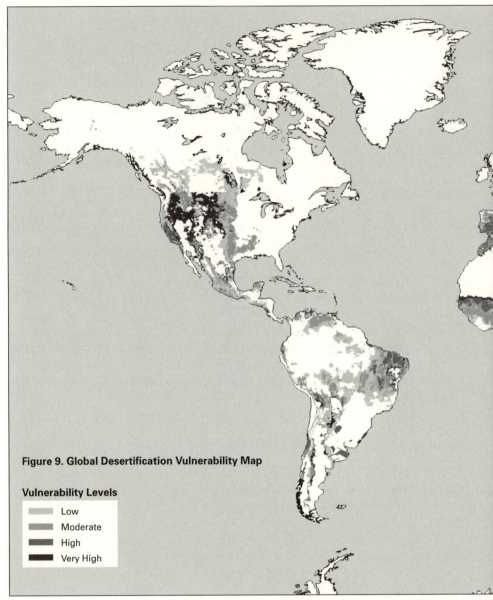

Figure 9. Global Desertification Vulnerability Map

Vulnerability Levels

- Low
- Moderate
- High
- Very High

U.S. Department of Agriculture, National Resources Conservation Service (NCRS),
available at http://soils.usda.gov/use/worldsoils/mapindex/desert.html.

The reason for these latest trends is an increase in solid waste recycling. Since 1985 there has been a significant increase in both total MSW recycled and percent MSW recycled. From 1985 to 2006 total MSW recycled per year has risen from 16.7 to 81.8 million tons, while the percent recycled each year has jumped from 10.1 to 32.5.[63] That's the good news. The bad news is that only 32.5 percent of our MSW is currently being recycled. The rest is

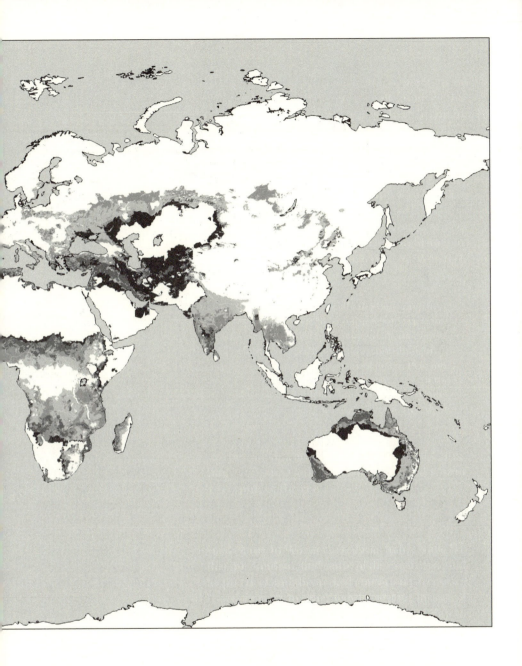

dumped into landfills (55 percent) or burned in incinerators and waste-to-
energy plants (12.5 percent). Though much of what we throw away could
easily be reduced (food waste), reused (yard waste), or recycled (paper), a very
large amount is still "thrown away." In fact, paper and paperboard products
account for 34 percent of our solid waste, with yard waste and food scraps
making up 25 percent.[64] In other words, we could dramatically (and relatively

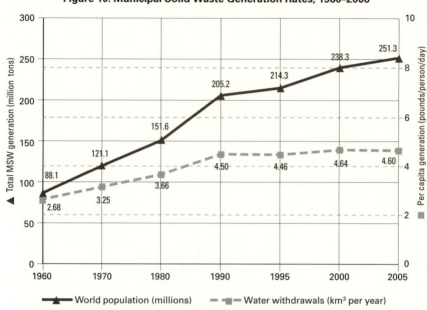

Figure 10. Municipal Solid Waste Generation Rates, 1960–2006

"Municipal Solid Waste Generation, Recycling, and Disposal in the United States: Facts and Figures for 2006," U.S. Environmental Protection Agency, 2007, available at http://www.epa.gov/waste/nonhaz/municipal/pubs/msw06.pdf.

easily) reduce our waste by more seriously embracing the three r's: reduce, reuse, and recycle.

What it means to live in a throwaway society can perhaps best be understood through the following examples: In one year we in the United States throw away enough aluminum to rebuild the country's entire commercial airline fleet every three months. Enough disposable diapers are disposed of each year to reach, if linked end-to-end, to the moon and back seven times. And if laid flat, the tires thrown away each year in the United States would encircle the earth almost three times.[65] And this, note well, is only municipal solid waste; it does not include industrial waste or agricultural waste. Indeed, though mind-boggling, the above-mentioned convoy of garbage trucks encircling the globe almost four times accounts for only a meager 1.5 percent of the total waste generated each year in the United States. Only 1.5 percent! The other 98.5 percent comes from mining, oil and natural gas production, agriculture, industry, and sewage.[66] Almost all of this enormous amount of waste is unseen by us, since it is not included in the trash we haul to the street.

Of the many questions prompted by these statistics—for example, what happens when we run out of certain stuff? and where will we dispose of our waste?—perhaps the most important is this: does our soaring consumption really make us happy? Despite the widespread belief that more is always better, numerous culture-watchers have deduced that having more stuff has not made us any happier. For example, Alan Durning describes "the dubious rewards of consumption"—the fraying social fabric of consumer society, the decline of attachments to people and places, the commercialization of the household economy, the erosion of civic identity, the acceleration of the pace of life—all of which lead him to declare that "the consumer society fails to deliver on its promise of fulfillment through material comforts."[67] After an exhaustive review of the literature, David Myers confirms Durning's analysis: *"Our becoming much better-off over the last thirty years has not been accompanied by one iota of increased happiness and life satisfaction."*[68] And in a discussion of "real growth," in which a variety of indicators of well-being are put forward as alternatives to GDP, James Speth asks: "Has America's pursuit of growth and ever-greater material abundance brought true happiness and satisfaction in life?" His answer is a clear and resounding "no."[69] Our culture's materialistic assumption that "whoever dies with the most toys wins" (to quote an infamous bumper sticker) is patently false.

In short, solid waste, while a serious problem in itself, is also symbolic of a larger cultural trend well captured in the neologism "affluenza."[70] We in the wealthy West are addicted to the consumption (and disposal) of material goods. And the dubious rewards of this disease, combined with the considerable environmental costs, render the ailment most debilitating. Given this diagnosis, what is the proper prescription? What antidote is there to affluenza?

Energy

With about 5 percent of the world's population, the United States uses approximately what percentage of the world's commercial energy? 5 percent, 15 percent, or 25 percent? If you chose the last option, you are correct. The United States is the world's biggest user of energy, devouring roughly one-quarter of what is available.[71] This consumption rate for total energy mirrors the consumption rate for oil, with the United States consuming 24 percent of the global total—about 21 million barrels of oil a day.[72] Figure 11 dramatically portrays the differences between regions of the world in total energy use and per capita energy consumption. An average North American consumes 2.5 times the energy of the average European and 28 times as much energy as an average African. Needless to say, this disproportionate usage of energy by the United States and Canada is not lost on other countries. Many naturally ask questions about energy equity. Of special note is the fact that Japan has a higher GDP per capita than the United States but at half the energy expenditure; likewise, England, France, and Germany have only a slightly lower GDP per capita than the United States at roughly half the energy consumption.[73] In other words, one does not need to expend nearly as much energy as we do in the United States in order to have a high standard of living.

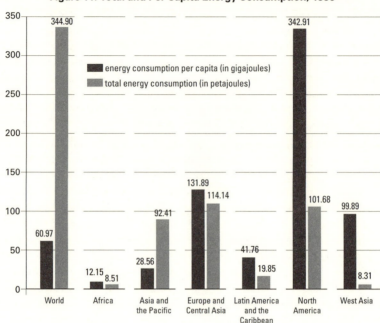

Figure 11. Total and Per Capita Energy Consumption, 1995

Legend:
- ■ energy consumption per capita (in gigajoules)
- ▨ total energy consumption (in petajoules)

Values shown:
- World: 60.97 / 344.90
- Africa: 12.15 / 8.51
- Asia and the Pacific: 28.56 / 92.41
- Europe and Central Asia: 131.89 / 114.14
- Latin America and the Caribbean: 41.76 / 19.85
- North America: 342.91 / 101.68
- West Asia: 99.89 / 8.31

Data compiled by UNEP GRID Geneva from UNSTAT 1997, available at Global Environmental Outlook 2000 (UNEP), http://www.unep.org/geo2000/english/i5a.htm.

Overall, in the past fifty years the world's demand for energy has increased fivefold, over twice as fast as its population growth. And according to projections from the U.S. Department of Energy and the Intergovernmental Panel on Climate Change, if present trends continue, 86 percent of the global energy increase in the first four decades of the twenty-first century will be a result of rising consumption per person, while only 14 percent will result from sheer growth in numbers.[74] Figure 12 vividly illustrates patterns of world energy consumption in the last third of the past century and the first years of this century. The rise in energy use has come almost entirely from the increased consumption of fossil fuels. Oil consumption doubled from 1965 to 1980. Coal consumption doubled and natural gas consumption more than tripled from 1965 to 2005. At present, the use of all three fossil fuels continues to increase.

However, world oil production per person reached a peak in 1979 and has been declining ever since, and it is estimated that global oil production will peak around 2008–2010.[75] Reserves of coal and natural gas are more plentiful than oil, but those too are finite and have significant ecological costs—for example, air and water pollution. In short, the days of heavy fossil fuel use are limited. Whether because of resource scarcity or environmental quality, other forms of energy must be utilized. Lester Brown speaks for many when he concludes, "A shift to renewable energy sources, such as solar energy and wind power, holds great promise for meeting future energy demands without adverse ecological consequences."[76]

That shift is now underway. The world has (finally) become aware of its over-reliance on oil and the pressing need to find alternatives. World wind energy production has been on a steep upward curve since the year 2000 and is currently one of the fastest growing energy sources. In 2006 the United States led the world in new wind energy installations, with Texas passing California to become the country's top wind power generator. As of 2008 Germany and Spain led the world in overall wind power capacity, with the United States third and China sixth (but catching up rapidly). Over fifty nations now use wind to produce power, with Asia experiencing the strongest growth.[77]

Solar power is growing even faster than wind, with a sixfold increase since the year 2000. In 2006 global production of photovoltaic cells rose 41 percent over the previous year, and grid-based installations (i.e., not including off-the-grid sources) increased 47 percent. Germany, Japan, and the United States lead the way in solar energy installations, with a 60 percent increase in the United States since 2005. And this increase came despite a shortage in polysilicon, one of the main ingredients in photovoltaic cells.[78]

So there are some strong signs that sustainable energy is catching on. There is, however, precious little evidence that our addiction to fossil fuel will abate any time soon. While some experts argue "that energy efficiency improvements

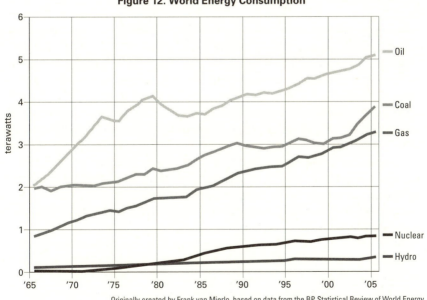

Figure 12. World Energy Consumption

Originally created by Frank van Mierlo, based on data from the BP Statistical Review of World Energy, June 2006, available at http://en.wikipedia.org/wiki/File:World_Energy_consumption.png.

and renewable energy could displace a significant share of fossil fuel use and reduce global emissions," the International Energy Agency "projects that, if unchecked, global energy use will rise more than 50 percent by 2030, with fossil fuel remaining the dominant energy source."[79] Will energy supply keep up with energy demand, and if so, at what cost and to whom? And which scenario will carry the day? Will we make the transition to an alternative fuel economy, or will fossil fuels continue to be our dominant energy source? Finally, can our seemingly insatiable desire for more energy be sustained?

Air

Mention of fossil fuel consumption leads to a discussion of air pollution and, in particular, acid rain. In Sweden the number of lakes seriously affected by acid rain is 100? 1000? 14,000? Believe it or not, in Sweden there are 14,000 bodies of fresh water where acid rain has caused widespread damage to plant and animal life.[80] Indeed, damage to flora and fauna is widespread not only in Sweden but in much of Scandinavia, central Europe, and the United Kingdom. For example, in West Germany and the United Kingdom acid rain has damaged more than half the forests. In Greece acid rain is eroding the Parthenon and other ancient buildings. In Poland acid rain has even weakened railroad tracks.[81] New evidence indicates that acid rain is becoming a major problem in Asia, with acid deposition levels "particularly high in areas such as southeast China, northeast India, Thailand, and the Republic of Korea."[82] This is no surprise given the increasing use of coal and oil in those areas. Acid rain in Asia is linked to a reduction in wheat production and a significant decline in the growth of pine and oak forests.

In Canada acid rain has been a serious problem for some time. According to Environment Canada, "although the acidity of acid rain has declined since 1980, rain is still acidic in eastern Canada" with "the average pH of rain in Ontario's Muskoka-Haliburton area about 4.5."[83] Acidity is measured by the pH scale—a logarithmic scale that measures hydrogen ions in solution and ranges from 0 (most acidic) to 14 (most basic), with 7 being neutral. So a pH of 6 is ten times more acidic than 7, and a pH of 5 is 100 times more acidic than 7. Natural precipitation has a pH of 5.6 or 5.7. Hence the rain falling in this area north of Toronto is over ten times more acidic than normal. The negative effects include the disappearance of crayfish and clams, then fish (e.g., bass, walleye, trout), and then the birds that feed on the fish (e.g., loons).

As can be seen from figure 13, acid rain is a serious problem for much of the United States, especially in the east. The average pH of rainfall in the state of New York ranges from 4.5 to 4.0, or ten to thirty times more acidic than normal.[84] In the Adirondacks of upstate New York approximately one-quarter of the 2,759 lakes and ponds are fishless because of acid deposition, or they

Figure 13. Hydrogen Ion Concentrations as pH, from Measurements Made at the Central Analytical Laboratory, 2006

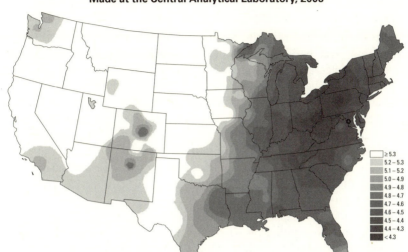

National Atmospheric Deposition Program (NRSP-3) 2009. NADP Program Office, Illinois State Water Survey, Champaign, Illinois, available at http://nadp.isws.illinois.edu/isopleths/maps2006/phlab.pdf.

have been damaged to the point that fish populations have been substantially reduced.[85] More than simply a process that decreases pH and makes lakes inhospitable to fish, acidification also changes soils and disrupts nutrient cycles. In short, the damage is more extensive than first believed. Thus, while the emissions that produce acid rain have dramatically decreased in the past three decades, surface water recovery in the Adirondacks is small and slow, given the accumulated acids in the watershed.[86]

As indicated in the previous paragraph, the effects of acid deposition are many, and they are harmful: fish and aquatic plant mortality due to inability to reproduce; contamination of fish with toxic methylmercury that is released in more acidic waters; tree mortality as a result of the leaching of calcium, potassium, and other nutrients from the soil; damage to tree roots and weakening of trees because of the release of naturally occurring aluminum; leaching of toxic metals such as copper and lead from home water pipes; aggravation of many human respiratory diseases.[87] These effects, furthermore, often go unnoticed. As Chris Bright notes, after chronicling the damaging and often cascading chemical effects of acid rain on tree and forest health, "Acid-induced decline may unfold for decades as a hidden process that escapes casual notice."[88] The hiddenness of the various problems, combined with the synergistic effects of multiple stresses on the ecosystem, often means that by the time the damage is noticed, it is too late. An invisible threshold is crossed, and the damage is done—dying trees, disappearing fish, degraded soil.

While the effects of acid rain, or more accurately acid precipitation, are often hidden, the causes are well known. Most of the acidity comes from sulfur dioxide and nitrogen oxides. These compounds combine with moisture and heat in the atmosphere to form sulfuric acid and nitric acid, which then fall to the earth as rain, sleet, hail, fog, snow, and other forms of precipitation. The sulfur dioxide originates largely from coal-burning power plants. The nitrogen oxides are produced by the burning of fossil fuels, especially from motor vehicles.[89] Acid rain is no respecter of national or international borders either. It floats and falls where it wills. And with the building of ever-taller smokestacks, acid rain is no longer merely a local issue. As E. G. Nisbet observes, "Polluted air masses have been tracked across the Atlantic and over the North Pole from Eurasia to North America. About 50% of the sulfates falling in eastern Canada probably come from the United States."[90] The wind has yet to learn to read our maps or take note of our geopolitical barriers.

As the plethora of data suggests, acid rain is a serious problem. But acid rain is only one form of air pollution. There are, unfortunately, many others, such as smog, one component of which is ozone. Ozone, among other things, irritates the lungs and impairs breathing. We have too little ozone in the stratosphere (the well-known "ozone holes" in the Arctic and Antarctic) and too much ozone in the troposphere. Another air pollutant is carbon monoxide, an odorless, invisible gas that reduces blood flow. And then there is particulate matter, especially PM10 (particulates smaller than ten microns), which not only reduces visibility but penetrates deeply into the lungs, causing respiratory ailments.

The good news is that we have made significant progress with respect to both acid rain and high-level ozone. As a result of the Clean Air Act of 1963, its extension in 1970, and its amendments in 1990, emissions of both sulfur dioxide and nitrogen oxides have decreased substantially.[91] And the United Nations–brokered Montreal Protocol of 1987 has reduced the amount of ozone-destroying gases such that the ozone holes are no longer growing. Even the infamous air in Los Angeles is cleaner today than it was thirty years ago, because of a variety of public policy changes and laws. That being said, we must remember that air is one of the absolute essentials of life, and yet in our day the air we breathe is often not what it should be.

Climate

Which decade contains the eight warmest years on record? Is it 1918–28, 1978–88, or 1998–2008? The eight hottest years have been since 1998, and the fourteen warmest years (as of 2007) have occurred in the last seventeen years.[92] As figure 14 shows, according to James Hansen and colleagues at the NASA Goddard Institute for Space Studies, since at least 1880 the mean surface temperature of the earth has been rising. There has been an especially strong

Figure 14. Global Land-Ocean Temperature Anomaly

Global Temperature Change (°C)

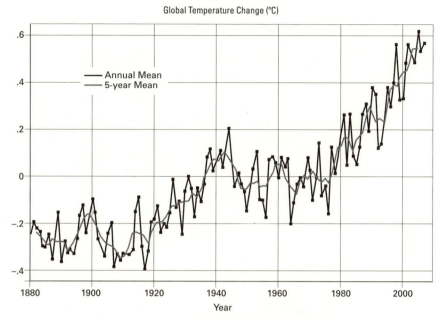

"GISS Surface Temperature Analysis," NASA Goddard Institute for Space Studies, December 26, 2008 (updated January 13, 2009), available at http://data.giss.nasa.gov/gistemp/2008/.

warming trend during the past thirty years. Figure 15 shows the variations in the earth's surface temperature over the last thousand years, with the warming trend strikingly clear.

These conclusions are fully supported by the Intergovernmental Panel on Climate Change (IPCC). Established in 1988 by the World Meteorological Organization and the United Nations Environment Programme, the IPCC is widely recognized as the leading source of reliable scientific information on global climate change. The IPCC's fourth assessment report (2007) contains the most up-to-date data and definitive judgments.[93] Concerning the scientific basis for climate change, the report came to this succinct conclusion: "Warming of the climate system is unequivocal."[94] The evidence is incontrovertible: the earth is warming up.

It is also very clear that the concentration of carbon dioxide (CO_2) in the atmosphere is increasing. Figure 16 is the famous "Keeling Curve," named after David Keeling, who as a young post-doc at Cal Tech in 1957 started measuring carbon dioxide (CO_2) from the Mauna Loa Observatory in Hawaii. From a level of 315 parts per million (ppm) in 1958, CO_2 has risen to 387 ppm in 2008 and is currently increasing at a rate of 1.9 ppm per year. We also know, from air trapped in ice cores taken in Greenland and Antarctica, that in 1750 the CO_2

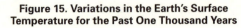

Figure 15. Variations in the Earth's Surface Temperature for the Past One Thousand Years

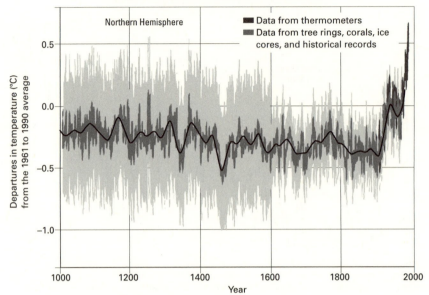

Intergovernmental Panel on Climate Change, Third Assessment Report, "Climate Change 2001," Working Group 1, "The Scientific Basis," fig. 1, available at http://stephenschneider.stanford.edu/Climate/Climate_Science/VariationsSurfaceTemp.html.

concentration was roughly 280 ppm and has been rising at an increasing rate ever since.[95] In fact, analyses of the history of the earth's atmosphere indicate that the carbon dioxide level in the troposphere, or lowest layer of the atmosphere, is now the highest it has been in at least 800,000 years.[96]

Carbon dioxide is a greenhouse gas. Greenhouse gases—including ozone (O_3), methane (CH_4), nitrous oxide (N_2O), chlorofluorocarbons (CFCs), and water vapor, in addition to carbon dioxide—are those gases in the troposphere that trap heat by preventing infrared radiation from escaping into space. As with the glass of a greenhouse or a car windshield, which allows light to enter but prevents heat from radiating out, these important gases capture heat and thus help maintain the earth's surface temperature at a level conducive to life as we know it. There is nothing wrong, therefore, with greenhouse gases; on the contrary, they are absolutely essential to life on earth. What is at issue is the proper concentration of these gases. Too high a concentration, and the planet warms up. There is no doubt that the greenhouse effect exists. Certain gases trap heat.

So if greenhouse gases increase, other things being equal, the earth will warm up. Increase the thickness of your car windshield and it will be even hotter on that sunny spring day. This warming, it is important to note, is an average increase for the whole planet over a given time scale. It may actually be colder

**Figure 16. Monthly Average Carbon Dioxide Concentration,
May 2009 (Mauna Loa Observatory, Hawaii)**

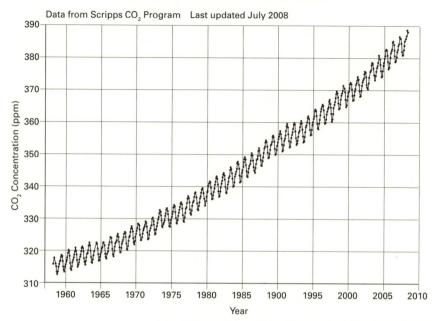

Data from Scripps CO_2 Program   Last updated July 2008

Scripps CO_2 Program, Scripps Institution of Oceanography, available at http://scrippsco2
.ucsd.edu/graphics_gallery/mauna_loa_record/mauna_loa_record.html.

in some places while, on the whole, the average temperature is rising. For example, New York City in January 2004 was 4°F colder than the average January in New York (with 1951 to 1980 as the baseline period), and yet the average global temperature in January 2004 was above normal. In other words, global warming does not mean that it is always getting warmer everywhere.

Unfortunately, carbon dioxide is not the only greenhouse gas on the rise. Methane and nitrous oxide are also increasing. Methane has a relatively brief life span of 7 to 10 years, but it has by weight nearly one hundred times the effect as that of CO_2. Nitrous oxide lasts about 120 years in the troposphere and is about two hundred times more potent at warming the earth than a molecule of CO_2.[97] According to the latest IPCC data, since 1750 methane has increased from 715 parts per billion (ppb) to 1,774 ppb, a value that far exceeds the natural range of the last 650,000 years, and nitrous oxide has risen from 270 ppb to 319 ppb in the last 250 years.[98] In sum, while carbon dioxide increases have received most of the press, the lesser-known greenhouse gases are also on the rise.

The earth is warming up and greenhouse gas concentrations are increasing. Is this merely a coincidence? Or is there not only a positive correlation but a causal connection between the two? There has been much discussion of this question, but the debate is now settled. The 2007 IPCC report clearly states: "Most of the observed increase in globally averaged temperatures since the mid-20th century is *very likely* due to the observed increase in anthropogenic greenhouse gas concentrations."[99] In other words, there is better than a nine in ten chance (the technical meaning of "very likely") that we humans are causing most of the warming. Primarily from burning fossil fuels we have changed the chemistry of the atmosphere and caused the world to warm up. Furthermore, if our greenhouse gas emissions continue at or above current rates, the best predictions indicate that by the end of this century the average global temperature will increase 3 to 7°F, a substantially higher increase than we had in the twentieth century. In short, we humans are warming the earth, and if we continue with business as usual, we ain't seen nothin' yet.

In summary thus far, the argument is impeccable: If greenhouse gases increase, then (other things being equal) the world will warm up. Greenhouse gases are in fact increasing—because of humans. Therefore, the world is getting warmer—because of humans. The real scientific debate is not over whether global warming is real, but rather is over how much and how fast average global temperature might rise, whether other factors in the climate system will counter or amplify a temperature rise, and what the specific effects will be. However we answer those questions, this much is clear: "We have changed the atmosphere—changed it enough so that the climate will change dramatically."[100]

Where do greenhouse gases come from? As indicated above, we are pumping large amounts of carbon dioxide into the air primarily from our burning of fossil fuels. But deforestation also contributes to this problem, for in cutting our forests we are destroying one of our major carbon sinks. Methane is produced naturally from a variety of sources (e.g., bacteria that decompose organic matter), but much of it comes from human activities: landfills; leaks from natural gas pipelines and storage tanks, furnaces, dryers, and stoves; the guts of domesticated animals, such as cattle, sheep, pigs, goats, and horses. Even termites—growing in number as deforestation proceeds apace—produce methane as they digest dead wood. Finally, nitrous oxide is released from the breakdown of nitrogen in fertilizers, animal wastes, and the burning of biomass.

Why worry about global warming, you may ask? In a word, global warming comes with very serious consequences. Already observed ecological changes include shrinkage of glaciers, thawing of permafrost, later freezing and earlier break-up of ice on rivers and lakes, lengthening of mid-latitude growing seasons, poleward and altitudinal shifts of plant and animal ranges, declines of some plant and animal populations, and earlier flowering of trees, emergence of insects, and egg-laying in birds.[101]

In the future there will very likely be more outbreaks of insects, but declining numbers of fish and reptiles. Migratory patterns may be disrupted so that the timing between the arrival of birds and the availability of fruit and seeds will be thrown out of kilter. Rising sea levels will rise even higher, threatening coastal wetlands, just as melting glaciers will continue to disappear. Every ecosystem on earth will be affected: coral reefs and rain forests, savannas and alpine tundras, deserts and rivers and oceans.[102] Because of global climate change, in these and countless other ways the ecological systems of our planet will be altered and its various inhabitants affected, often for the worse.

In addition to the ecological effects, as if these were not serious enough, global warming will also directly affect humans. Potential problems include a reduction in crop yield, decreased water availability, an increase in the number of people exposed to vector-borne diseases (e.g., malaria) and water-borne diseases (e.g., cholera), and a widespread risk of flooding of many cities and towns, affecting tens of millions of inhabitants. The most vulnerable people and countries will most likely suffer the worst, with the present disparity between rich and poor even more greatly exacerbated. While some of these are matters of speculation, most are not. Indeed, we are already seeing ample evidence consistent with earlier predictions from climate change models: more intense heat waves and longer cold spells; severe droughts and intensive flooding; more destructive storms and less controllable wild fires.[103] As only one example from the recent past, figure 17 lists extreme weather events from the summer of 2004. Weather that year was unusual, and destructive, literally all over the world. Weather-related disasters in 2004 caused nearly $105 billion in losses, almost twice the total from 2003, and thousands died in weather-related events such as floods and hurricanes. From 1980 to 2004 the number of weather-related disasters has doubled.[104] In sum, the potential effects of global climate change are many, and they are profound—indeed, potentially catastrophic.

Figure 17. Extreme Weather Events, Summer 2004

- In late July, much of northern Europe, which had sweltered in the brutally hot summer of 2003, was plagued by near-winter-like temperatures and even periodic snowfalls.
- In late July, wildfires were spreading throughout the western U.S. at a record pace, with conflagrations from Alaska to southern California spreading at double the average rate of the previous decade.
- After seeing crops destroyed by floods and drought earlier in the year, residents of Peru near the Bolivian border needed airlifts of food after the worst frost and snowstorms in 30 years devastated food supplies.
- In mid-August, the most powerful typhoon to hit China in at least seven years killed 115 people and injured 1,800.
- In mid-August, an unprecedented flash flood deluged Cornwall, England, pouring two inches of rain in two hours and washing cars and buildings away.

- In mid-August, a flash flood in Death Valley National Park in southern California closed roads, knocked out power, severed sewer lines and killed two people.
- Lake Mead, in Nevada, is at its lowest level in 39 years and officials have been trucking in water from as far away as Canada. The governor has urged authorities to declare the drought-stricken state as a disaster area.
- In Alaska, unusually hot weather along with a lack of rain triggered forest fires which consumed a record 5 million acres by mid-August.
- A powerful typhoon displaced more than 3,000 people and left 12 dead in Japan and Korea, ripping up railroad tracks and washing away homes.
- In New Zealand, a storm, described as the most severe in 40 years, ripped off roofs, downed power lines and brought transportation to a stand-still.
- Typhoon Aere triggered mudslides and flash floods in Taiwan then turned toward China, forcing the evacuation of half a million people.
- In July, downpours that meteorologists called a "1,000-year storm," deluged parts of New Jersey, Pennsylvania, and Maryland: bursting dams, snarling traffic, and delaying scores of trains.
- In Bangladesh, a month of heavy rains and flooding created hundreds of islands in delta regions, killing hundreds and marooning more than two million people.
- In the western U.S., infestations of beetles are devastating drought-parched pine forests from Alaska to Arizona to South Dakota, in an outbreak experts are calling "unprecedented."

The State of the Planet

Exploding population growth, increasing hunger, loss of biodiversity, deforestation, water scarcity and impurity, land degradation, accumulating waste, expanding energy consumption, acid rain, global climate change—such is the long litany of ecological woe. The state of our home planet is not good. The earth is groaning.

On the other hand, as suggested earlier, not all the news is bad. The California condor, sandhill crane, and gray wolf have all made astonishing comebacks in their respective habitats. The air in Los Angeles is better now than it was thirty years ago. The Cuyahoga River in Ohio no longer catches fire, and Lake Erie is recovering as a viable fishery. All these (and the list could go on) are causes for real celebration and hope.[105] So the state of the planet, truth be told, is mixed. It is not all doom and gloom, and neither is it all sweetness and light. However, in contrast to those who think all is well concerning our earthly home, in my judgment the overarching conclusion is not pretty.[106] To again use the language of St. Paul, creation is groaning.

After his own survey of the state of the planet, earth scientist E. G. Nisbet offers this summary of global environmental change, its causes and its consequences: "The evidence detailed in the previous chapters is that the Earth has been damaged and that the damage will become worse. The accusation is that the past and present behavior of humanity is responsible for the damage, which is increasing to the point where the well-being of all people, animals, and plants is threatened."[107] He then asks, with respect to the question of human culpability, "What would a jury of reasonable people decide?" After presenting evidence pro and con, he comes to the conclusion that "a reasonable jury finds for the prosecution. The evidence is strong enough. There may be some mistakes, but the case is overwhelming."[108] In other words, the case is overwhelming that we humans are responsible for the damage to our home planet. "Mea culpa" we must reply—a powerful and sad irony for a species called *Homo sapiens*, wise human. Obvious questions prompted by such a conclusion include: Why is the earth groaning? How did we get into this ecological mess? What explanations can be found as to why we have despoiled our home planet? To these queries we now turn.

is christianity
to blame?

the ecological complaint
against christianity

Nature, the world, has no value, no interest for Christians. The Christian thinks only of himself and the salvation of his soul.

Ludwig Feuerbach[1]

Why is the earth groaning? How did we get into this ecological mess? These are the questions with which the last chapter concludes. The epigraph above, from a prominent mid-nineteenth-century writer, indicates one common answer: Christianity is to blame for the ecological crisis. If nature has no value for Christians, who think only about the salvation of their souls, then it is no surprise that the earth is in such sorry shape, given the influence Christianity has had and continues to have around the world. Updated versions of this argument go something like this:

> To the extent that man fulfills the command to be fruitful and multiply, his assault on this planet will continue. Religions assume that whatever sacrifices may be necessary to accommodate more of humanity should be made by species other than us.
>
> Having created God in man's own image, Western religion has adopted an anthropocentric mythology that separates God from Creation, soul from body, and

man from Earth. It is this dualism that prevents us from relating not only to the natural world, but to ourselves.

These statements were made in an issue of *Sierra*, the official publication of the Sierra Club, in answer to the question of whether organized religion has benefited or harmed the planet.[2] Some people blame Christianity (or religion in general) for the present ecological crisis. Directly or indirectly, they argue, the Christian faith is responsible for ecological degradation since in various ways it encourages the exploitation of the earth. Christianity legitimates ecological degradation. Such, in sum, is the "ecological complaint against Christianity."[3]

In this chapter we examine this claim. More exactly, we seek to answer two questions. First, what is the ecological complaint against Christianity? And second, are these various criticisms concerning the contribution of Christianity to ecological degradation well founded? My contention is that the ecological complaint against Christianity, correctly understood, is not cogent. If I am right, a further question presents itself: what are more credible explanations for our current ecological predicament?

It is important, before we examine the complaint itself, to acknowledge the need for confession. Despite the fact that, as I will argue, the ecological complaint against Christianity is seriously flawed, a satisfactory response to the complaint must include, as James Nash insists, "a forthright confession that at least much of the complaint is essentially true."[4] Nash's comments on this matter deserve a full hearing:

> It will not do to draw a neat distinction between Christianity and Christendom, between the faith itself and perversions of it by its practitioners. That distinction may be formally or logically true, as I agree, but it is facile and unconvincing when applied to history. We cannot so easily distinguish between the faith and the faithful. The fact is that Christianity—*as interpreted and affirmed* by billions of its adherents over the centuries and in official doctrines and theological exegeses—has been ecologically tainted. . . . The bottom line is that Christianity itself cannot escape an indictment for ecological negligence and abuse.[5]

Nash's point must be taken very seriously. As he quite properly acknowledges, "Christianity has done too little to discourage and too much to encourage the exploitation of nature"; thus "ongoing repentance is warranted."[6] This bears repeating: ongoing repentance is warranted. The Christian faith as affirmed by many over the centuries has been, to use Nash's words, ecologically tainted. We Christians have been complicit in much ecological woe and thus have much to confess. We cannot escape culpability for our ecological sins of omission and commission, neglect and abuse. A clear call to confession, therefore, is much needed.

Like Wendell Berry, however, I remain persuaded that there is merit in a distinction between authentic Christian faith and misunderstandings or perversions of it by Christians themselves. Berry minces no words when he claims that "the indictment of Christianity by the anti-Christian conservationists is, in many respects, just." He continues: "Christian organizations, to this day, remain largely indifferent to the rape and plunder of the world and its traditional cultures. It is hardly too much to say that most Christian organizations are as happily indifferent to the ecological, cultural, and religious implications of industrial economies as are most industrial organizations."[7] So, like Nash, Berry rightly calls Christians to confession.

But that is not the end of the matter. Berry argues that "however just it [the indictment of Christianity] may be, it does not come from an adequate understanding of the Bible and the cultural traditions that descend from the Bible." This implies, he continues, "the making of very precise distinctions between biblical instruction and the behavior of those peoples supposed to have been biblically instructed." Given that there are "virtually catastrophic discrepancies between biblical instruction and Christian behavior"—and not disreputable behavior but "allegedly respectable Christian behavior"—a distinction between biblical instruction and the behavior of Christians is legitimate and important. Indeed, it is precisely because of this distinction that Berry concludes, "Our predicament now, I believe, requires us to learn to read and understand the Bible in the light of the present fact of Creation."[8] We must learn to read the Bible anew precisely because our behavior is out of line with the ecological vision of Scripture.

Thus, it is not only non-Christians who must be convinced that Christianity is not necessarily ecologically bankrupt, but many Christians as well. They must be persuaded, put more positively, that their faith calls them to care for the earth. Indeed, the rhetorical task applies as much (or more) to Christians as to non-Christians. We Christians must learn to read the Bible with new eyes, eyes that are open to its ecological wisdom, and we must come to know and appropriate our own traditions, including their ecological insights. What, then, of the charge that Christianity is the problem?

The Ecological Complaint

The ecological complaint against Christianity claims, in general, that the Christian faith is at fault for the current ecological crisis. As Nash states, "The ecological complaint is the charge that the Christian faith is the culprit in the crisis. Christianity is the primary or at least a significant cause of ecological degradation."[9] Christianity, especially Christian theology, is ecologically bankrupt, and given its influence in Western culture, it is morally blameworthy with respect to the plight of the earth. The implication usually drawn from this claim is that people today must discard the Christian tradition and look elsewhere for a perspective that provides an adequate response to the ecological challenges before us.

There are a variety of specific arguments given to support this complaint. Here are four of the most common.

The first is that *monotheism in general, and Christianity in particular, is the primary if not sole cause of the despoilation of the earth.* For example, influential British historian Arnold Toynbee asserts that "some of the major maladies of the present-day world—for instance the recklessly extravagant consumption of nature's irreplaceable treasures, and the pollution of those of them that man has not already devoured—can be traced back in the last analysis to a religious cause, and . . . this cause is the rise of monotheism."[10] Specifically, Toynbee argues that the Genesis 1:28 command to have dominion over the earth has not only permitted but directed humans to dominate and exploit creation.[11] Given this diagnosis, Toynbee claims that the remedy for what ails us "lies in reverting from the *Weltanschauung* of monotheism to the *Weltanschauung* of pantheism."[12] Only by repudiating the worldview of monotheism and adopting a worldview in which God and world are seen as one and the same will we be able to extricate ourselves from our ecological abyss.

American historian Roderick Nash also points to the use of Genesis 1:28 as a decisive sanction for ecological destruction. He argues that given the harsh imagery of "absolute domination" signified by the verbs in that verse, "it followed that the Christian tradition could understand Genesis 1:28 as a divine commandment to conquer every part of nature and make it humankind's slave." Such an interpretation served as "intellectual lubrication for the exploitation of nature."[13] Genesis 1 in particular, and Christianity more generally, is anti-ecological.

American novelist and essayist Wallace Stegner more than hints at a similar view: "Our sanction to be a weed species living at the expense of every other species and of the Earth itself can be found in the injunction God gave to newly created Adam and Eve in Genesis 1:28: 'Be fruitful and multiply, and replenish the earth, and subdue it.'"[14] Stegner contrasts this biblical view with that of Native Americans, who "stressed the web of life, the interconnectedness of land and man and creature."[15] In sum, this argument asserts that the Bible, especially Genesis 1, sets humanity over against nature and thus encourages humans to conquer and exploit the natural world.

The second argument is that *the emphasis within the Christian tradition on dualisms of soul and body and of spirit and matter denigrates the earth and sanctions its misuse and exploitation.* More exactly, the claim is that since there is a dualism between spirit and matter, and/or soul and body, such that the former is of greater value than the latter, and since lack of value implies lack of ethical obligation, Christianity fosters a care-less attitude toward matter and the body, and thus is at fault for the plundering of the earth. Wendell Berry gives voice to this argument for why Christianity is to blame for the current ecological crisis. "I have been talking, of course, about a dualism that manifests itself in several ways: as a cleavage, a radical discontinuity, between Creator and creature, spirit and matter, religion and nature, religion and economy, worship and work, and so on. This dualism, I think, is the most destructive disease that afflicts us. In its best known, its most dangerous, and perhaps its fundamental version, it is the dualism of body and soul."[16] Philosopher John Passmore likewise points to the presence of various dualisms within the Christian tradition, especially the "dualism between God and nature," as a major cause of ecological degradation. By means of such a hierarchical view of reality, Passmore claims, "Christianity has encouraged man to think of himself as nature's absolute master, for whom everything that exists was designed."[17] A dualism between Creator and creation, in this view, necessarily implies an anthropocentric attitude of domination toward the natural world.

Contemporary feminist theologian Rosemary Radford Ruether lodges a similar criticism when she speaks of "the male ideology of transcendent dualism."[18] This involves a chain of dualisms—male/female, soul/body, spirit/matter, culture/nature—in which the second half of each pair is seen as subject to the first. The latter is an object for conquest, whether in the case of the domination of women by men, the control of the body by the soul, or the exploitation of the nonhuman world by humans. In short, Christianity harbors a number of world-negating dualisms that have provided intellectual justification for the neglect and abuse of the earth and thus contributed to the current ecological crisis.

The third argument in the ecological complaint against Christianity is that *Christianity is to blame for much ecological degradation because of its role in the rise of modern Western science and technology*. For example, medieval historian Lynn White Jr., in his famous and often reprinted 1967 essay, "The Historical Roots of Our Ecologic Crisis," argues that by emphasizing both divine and human transcendence over nature, and thus by desacralizing nature, "Christianity made it possible to exploit nature in a mood of indifference to the feelings of natural objects."[19] In addition, White argues that the Christian doctrine of creation implies that "since God had made nature, nature also (in addition to the Bible) must reveal the divine mentality," thus encouraging empirical investigations of the natural world so that humans could "understand the mind of God by discovering how his creation operates."[20] In short, White claims that "modern Western science was cast in a matrix of Christian theology." More precisely, it was the "Judeo-Christian dogma of creation" that gave the impetus to modern Western science.[21]

White, therefore, concludes that since Christianity made possible the growth of modern science and technology, and since science and technology have given us unprecedented and uncontrolled power over nature—power the misuse of which Christianity has sanctioned—Christianity is responsible for the current plight of the earth. White's own summary of his argument is worth quoting in full:

We would seem to be heading toward conclusions unpalatable to many Christians. Since both *science* and *technology* are blessed words in our contemporary vocabulary, some may be happy at the notions, first, that, viewed historically, modern science is an extrapolation of (Christian) natural theology and, second, that modern technology is at least partly to be explained as an Occidental, voluntarist realization of the Christian dogma of man's transcendence of, and rightful mastery over, nature. But, as we now recognize, somewhat over a century ago science and technology—hitherto quite separate activities—joined to give mankind powers which, to judge by many of the ecologic effects, are out of control. If so, Christianity bears a huge burden of guilt.[22]

Christianity is responsible for the current ecological crisis.

The ubiquity of White's essay—found in almost every environmental philosophy, theology, and/or ethics anthology and referred to in virtually every textbook—is matched only by the unquestioned faith in its thesis. For many, in circles both religious and secular, it is (or until recently has been) an unexamined contention. As environmental philosopher Max Oelschlaeger confesses, "The roots of my prejudice against religion . . . grew out of my reading of Lynn White's famous essay blaming Judeo-Christianity for the environmental crisis."[23] In sum, Christianity is at fault because of its intellectual support for Western science and technology.

A fourth argument often cited by critics asserts that *Christian eschatology underwrites the exploitation of the earth.* The Christian view of the future negates any rationale for preserving the earth, some argue, since Christians believe the return of Jesus will usher in a completely new earth and an utterly different form of existence. The doctrine of the second coming of Jesus thus militates against caring for the earth because it posits that this world is ephemeral and ultimately unimportant. Humans need not care for this present world.

The popularity of books by Hal Lindsey and Tim LaHaye attests to the allure of this eschatology.[24] Lindsey's *The Late Great Planet Earth* sold millions in the 1970s, but its popularity is dwarfed by the Left Behind series, coauthored by Tim LaHaye and Jerry Jenkins.[25] While this series is technically fictional, the authors are very clear that the fiction is merely a cover for an otherworldly dispensationalist eschatology in which Christians will be raptured from the earth and the world will be destroyed. As Jenkins admitted to an interviewer: "I believe the kind of stuff I'm writing about [that all saved Christians dead and alive get snatched into heaven and a seven-year tribulation of plagues ravages the earth] is going to happen some day."[26]

With books such as those mentioned above, purporting to espouse orthodox Christian theology, it is easy to see why some argue that Christianity is otherworldly and thus anti-ecological. For example, one of Roderick Nash's reasons for criticizing Christianity is its "pervasive otherworldliness."

Christians' aspirations were fixed on heaven, the supposed place of their origins and, they hoped, their final resting. The earth was no mother but a kind of halfway house of trial and testing from which one was released at death. . . . Indeed Christians expected that the earth would not be around for long. A vengeful God would destroy it, and all unredeemed nature, with floods or drought or fire. Obviously this eschatology was a poor basis from which to argue for environmental ethics in any guise. Why take care of what you expected to be obliterated?[27]

Or as Bill Moyers asks, quoting a column from the online journal *Grist*: "Why care about the earth when the droughts, floods, famine, and pestilence brought by ecological collapse are signs of the apocalypse foretold in the Bible? Why care about global climate change when you and yours will be rescued in the rapture?"[28] In sum, this argument contends that because Christians believe the world will ultimately be destroyed, they feel no need to care for it. All four of the above arguments require further examination. To that task we now turn.

The Cogency of the Complaint

Problems abound with these arguments. Beginning with the first, then, in Genesis 1:28, does *dominion* mean *domination*? Do the first two chapters of Genesis actually license the exploitation of creation? Is a monotheism that is informed by the first few chapters of Genesis the problem?

First, chapters 1 and 2 of Genesis each speak about who humans are and what humans are to do. With respect to who we are as humans, Genesis 1:26 clearly distinguishes between human creatures and nonhuman creatures by speaking only of the former as created *imago Dei*—in the image (*ṣelem*) and likeness (*dĕmūt*) of God. Humans are distinct in some important sense—unique among all the creatures to come from God's hand.

The story of the naming of the animals in Genesis 2:19–20, among other things, also points to human uniqueness. The human creature is handed the responsibility of giving names to the other creatures—no small task given the importance of names in the Bible, for names signify identity. Abram becomes Abraham—ancestor of a multitude. Jacob becomes Israel—one who wrestles with God. Saul the persecutor becomes Paul the apostle. To name something well implies knowledge of its essence. To get the name right one must intimately know the creature named. But naming also indicates a kind of authority over. To know a name is to have power, as any substitute teacher quickly learns when attempting to control a class of students. Clearly, according to Genesis 1–2, humans are unique in important ways. We usually state this by saying that only humans are persons.[29] We are response-able and responsible creatures. That is an inescapable part of who we are.

But what is often ignored or intentionally overlooked is that humans are not only distinct in some sense but are also similar to other creatures. We are embedded in creation. For example, the creation of humans does not occur on a day different from the creation of other animals. There is no separate day for humans. On the sixth day, as Genesis 1:24–31 tells it, all kinds of living creatures came forth: domestic animals and wild animals and creeping things. Humans and the animals of the earth, the text implies, have something in common. And as Genesis 2:7 indicates, the human earth-creature (*'ādām*) is made from the earth (*'ădāmâ*). Humans are made of dust. To carry the Hebrew wordplay into Latin, we are humans because we are from the humus. We, too, are earthly and earthy creatures. Other creatures, to take seriously the language of Joseph Sittler, are our sisters and brothers.[30] In sum, these texts indicate that we humans are not only different from but significantly similar to our nonhuman neighbors. We are both responsible persons and earthly creatures. That is who we are.

With respect to what we are supposed to do, the Hebrew verbs in Genesis 1:26–28 indicate that one dimension of the human calling is mastery. The earth-creature is called to subdue (*kābāš*) and have dominion over (*rādâ*) other creatures. We are called to dominion. But what does this mean? Does dominion, as is often assumed, necessarily mean domination? A larger canonical perspective sheds light on this important question. For example, Psalm 72 speaks most clearly of the ideal king—of one who rules and exercises dominion properly. The psalm unequivocally states that such a ruler executes justice for the oppressed, delivers the needy, helps the poor, and embodies righteousness in all he does. In short, the proper exercise of dominion yields shalom—the flourishing of all creation. This is a far cry from dominion as domination. And Jesus, in the Gospel accounts, defines dominion in terms clearly contrary to the way it is usually understood. For Jesus, to rule is to serve. To exercise dominion is to suffer, if necessary, for the good of the other. There is no question of domination, exploitation, misuse. Humans, therefore, are called to rule, but ruling must be understood rightly.

But this is only part of the picture. Yes, we are called to exercise dominion, but we are also called to service. For example, Genesis 2:5 speaks of humans serving the earth (*'ādām* is to *'ābād* the *'ădāmâ*). And Genesis 2:15, the last part of which is painted on the door of every Chicago police car, defines the human calling in terms of service: we are to serve (*'ābād*) and protect (*šāmār*). We are to serve and protect the garden that is creation—literally, to be slaves to the earth for its own good, as well as for our own benefit. Taking these texts seriously implies that dominion must be defined in terms of service. We are called to dominion as service. In short, to focus only on the dominion texts and then to interpret them as necessarily entailing domination, as Toynbee does, is faulty exegesis. It is a selective and tendentious reading of Genesis 1–2.

With respect to the argument that Genesis 1:28 gives unconditional permission to humans to use and abuse the world, Wendell Berry states:

> Such a reading of Genesis 1:28 is contradicted by virtually all the rest of the Bible, as many people by now have pointed out. The ecological teaching of the Bible is

simply inescapable: God made the world because He wanted it made. He thinks the world is good, and He loves it. It is His world; He has never relinquished title to it. And He has never revoked the conditions, bearing on His gift to us of the use of it, that oblige us to take excellent care of it. If God loves the world, then how might any person of faith be excused for not loving it or justified in destroying it?[31]

Berry's final question presses the issue pointedly: If God loves the world, then how can any Christian be justified in destroying it? In short, there is scant evidence to support the claim that Genesis 1–2 licenses the exploitation of the earth.

In addition, even if Toynbee's reading of Genesis were correct, is it true that the ecological crisis can be traced back, as he argues, to a single cause? James Nash, among others, rightly cautions against any such historical explanation:

The single cause theory for the emergence of our ecological crisis is pathetically simplistic. Lynn White generally recognized this fact, but he too succumbed finally to oversimplification. And most other complainants have been undeterred by fears of reductionism. They have often structured their complaint on a single, flimsy biblical text (Gen. 1:28) dealing with "dominion," and have ignored the fact that the Christian faith and its cultural influences have been far more complicated and ambiguous than that. Theirs is proof-texting of the worst sort. They have accused Christianity of being the parent of ecologically debilitating forms of industrialization, commercialism, and technology. However, in historical reality, many complex and interwoven causes were involved—and Christian thought was probably not the most prominent one.[32]

The historical work of both Carolyn Merchant and Clarence Glacken, among others, also repudiates any theory of single causation with respect to ecological degradation.[33] Ecological decline, past and present, has many causes. As Nash succinctly states, "The ecological complaint against Christianity appears to be a serious historical oversimplification."[34] In sum, there are a number of significant problems with this first argument.

The second argument, likewise, invites a number of questions. For example, are these dualisms (spirit and matter, soul and body) biblical? And even if they are, do they represent the only perspective within the Christian tradition? While this is not the place to engage in an extensive discussion of this issue, a few comments are apposite. First, it is not at all clear that either the Old Testament or the New Testament supports the kind of body/soul dualism assumed by advocates of this argument.[35] Widely accepted readings of biblical anthropology affirm either a functional holism or a holistic dualism.[36] In neither case is the body devalued. While the body is separate from and inferior to the soul for Plato,[37] this is not the case for Scripture. Wendell Berry summarizes well the correct biblical view:

The formula given in Genesis 2:7 is not man = body + soul; the formula there is soul = dust + breath. According to this verse, God did not make a body and put a soul into it, like a letter into an envelope. He formed man of dust; then, by breathing his breath into it, He made the dust live. The dust, formed as man and made to live, did not *embody* a soul: it *became* a soul. "Soul" here refers to the whole creature. Humanity is thus presented to us, in Adam, not as a creature of two discrete parts temporarily glued together but as a single mystery.[38]

The same is true with respect to the supposed dualism between matter and spirit, in which matter is devalued. A variety of biblical texts—from Genesis to Revelation—and many basic Christian doctrines derived from the Bible—creation, incarnation, eschatology—affirm that for God, matter matters. God is, to put it sharply, an undeviating materialist. Thus, since the initial premise is unacceptable—the claim that the Bible promotes a dualism between soul and body or between spirit and matter—this argument is not sound.

But what about the Christian tradition? While a *contemptus mundi* tradition based on dualisms of this sort does exist within the Christian faith, such a tradition is but one among many. As Nash reminds his readers, "Christianity is no monolith: it has had multiple strains with radically different emphases."[39] More precisely, Nash rightly states that this form of the ecological complaint "overlooks the complex, ambiguous, and diversified character of Christian history" and thus misses "the varied voices—albeit minorities—for ecological sensitivity in Christian history."[40] As Paul Santmire has clearly shown, Christianity has within it creation-affirming as well as creation-negating traditions. In contrast to the "spiritual motif," which adopts certain of these dualisms, the "ecological motif" stands as one of the dominant theological themes in Christian history.[41] This vision of human existence eschews the dualism of spirit and matter by acknowledging human rootedness in the world of nature, and it desires to celebrate God's presence in and with the entire natural order. Therefore, the claim that the Bible and Christian tradition necessarily perpetuate creation-denying dualisms, and thus are at fault for the ecological crisis, is simply false.

A great deal of ink has been spilt responding to the third argument—the so-called Lynn White thesis. Wesley Granberg-Michaelson concisely summarizes a number of the conclusions reached since White's article was first published: "First, White's description of biblical teaching regarding the environment is selective and highly distorted. Second, his argument that Christianity paved the way for the scientific and technological revolutions is very questionable. And third, his assumption that environmental destruction has flowed solely from the mindset of Western culture, and not from others, is historically dubious."[42]

From what has been argued heretofore, it should be obvious that White's description of biblical teaching is, as Granberg-Michaelson claims, distorted. Like Toynbee, White focuses exclusively on certain texts while ignoring others. Thus his premise that historical Christianity understands dominion only as domination is mistaken. Also, White's claim that Christian thought was a necessary condition for the rise of modern science in the West is disputed. While this thesis has its able defenders,[43] it also has its compelling critics.[44] The precise role of Christian theology in the rise of modern science is a complex question admitting of no simple answer. And so another of White's premises is, at the very least, questionable.

Finally, as Granberg-Michaelson points out, White's historical claim that ecological degradation is somehow linked uniquely with the modern Western worldview is dubious indeed. As James Nash, among many others, rightly states, "ecological crises are not peculiar to Christian-influenced cultures. Non-Christian cultures have also caused severe or irreparable harm to their ecosystems."[45] Plato describes deforestation in ancient Greece. Augustine laments desertification in fourth-century North Africa. The great Mayan cultures of Meso-America collapsed around the year AD 800 due to deforestation and soil erosion.[46] Ecological degradation is no respecter of religions. It predates Christianity and can be found in places where Christianity has asserted little or no influence. In a number of significant respects, therefore, White's argument is problematic.

But let us grant, for the sake of argument, that White is correct about all his claims. Let us assume that his premises are acceptable: Christianity was an essential contributor to the development of modern science and technology. Science and technology have given us great power over nature. The Christian tradition encourages mastery over nature, thereby promoting the "if we can, we must" logic of our technological society. Even if we accept his premises, his argument is still problematic, for his conclusion that "Christianity bears a huge burden of guilt" for the ecological crisis does not follow. This is so because the conclusion relies on the questionable historical claim that science and technology are the principal causes of the crisis. While science and technology certainly have played a role in contributing to the current situation, many argue that other factors, especially economic factors, are equally if not more important.[47] There is, in other words, reason to doubt White's assumption about the dominant causal role of science and technology. In short, while extremely influential, the Lynn White thesis is not as plausible as many believe. In fact, there are compelling reasons to reject it.

It is interesting to note, in concluding this discussion of White's argument, that most references to White's thesis stop with his declaration that Christianity is at fault. However, in an often ignored section of his influential article, entitled "An Alternative Christian View," White goes on to argue that "since the roots of our trouble are so largely religious, the remedy must also be essentially religious, whether we call it that or not." And thus given his diagnosis, White proceeds to offer a prescription: "I propose Francis [of Assisi] as a patron saint for ecologists."[48] In other words, contrary to many accounts, White's own response to what ails us is not to abandon Christianity but to draw upon earth-affirming aspects of that very tradition. In this way White himself is an admirable model for reappropriating the Christian tradition—a tradition assumed by many to be barren of ecological insight and hence unredeemable.

The fourth argument in the ecological complaint focuses on Christian eschatology. If the earth will be burned up, why care about it? Why care for something that will (sooner or later) be destroyed? Why care for the earth if the Rapture is imminent? But is this eschatology biblical? Will the earth be destroyed in the eschaton? Does Christian eschatology necessarily entail an ecologically bankrupt ethic?

In responding to these questions, at least two key biblical texts deserve attention here (while others will be discussed in the next chapter). A text often cited or alluded to in support of an anti-ecological eschatology is 2 Peter 3. The question at issue has to do with what will happen when Jesus comes again, especially what will happen to the earth. After responding to those who ridicule the hope of Christ's coming by arguing that God is not slow but rather patiently forbearing, not wanting any to perish (v. 9), the author states that "the day of the Lord" will most certainly come, but its coming will be unexpected, like a thief in the night (v. 10). Furthermore, when Jesus comes again the heavens, with a loud rushing sound, will pass away, and the elements (heavenly bodies? the basic matter of the cosmos?), burning, will be loosened, and "the earth and the works that are upon it will be burned up" (v. 10 RSV). Almost all English versions translate this last clause in a similar creation-negating manner. For example, "the earth also and the works that are therein shall be burned up" (KJV); "the earth with everything in it will vanish" (GNT); "the earth and everything in it will be laid bare" (NIV); "the earth and all that is in it will be burned up to nothing" (Phillips).

A survey of translations into languages other than English reveals a similar pattern. The French and Spanish equivalents of the Good News Translation render the last verb "will cease to exist [*cessera d'exister*]" and "will be burned up [*sera quemada*]," respectively. The Afrikaans translation reads, "the earth and all the works on it will burn down [*sal verbrand*]." Swedish, Russian, and Chinese versions read, "the earth and the works upon it will be burned up." The German Bible (*Deutsche Bibelgesellschaft Stuttgart*) comes closer to the correct reading when it translates the last clause as "the earth and the works upon it will find their judgment [*werden ihr Urteil finden*]."

The New Revised Standard Version (NRSV) renders this text more accurately: "and the earth and everything that is done on it will be disclosed." But the 1975 Dutch translation (*Niewe Vertaling, Het Nederlandsch Bijbelgenootschap Amsterdam*) even more faithfully captures the meaning of the best Greek text: "and the earth and the works upon it will be found [*en de aarde en de werken daarop zullen gevonden worden*]."

To put it bluntly, this verse represents perhaps the most egregious mistranslation in the entire New Testament. The last clause of verse 10 in Greek is: *kai gē kai ta en autē erga heurethēsetai*. The Greek verb in question here is *heurethēsetai*, from *heurēskein*, "to find," from which we get the English expression "eureka."[49] In other words, the text states that after a refiner's fire of purification (v. 7), the new earth will be *found*, not burned up. The earth will be *discovered*, not destroyed.[50] John Calvin's take on this text is instructive. Summarizing his interpretation, Susan Schreiner states: "Therefore, in Calvin's view, the fires of judgment will not destroy creation but will purify its original and enduring substance. With this argument, Calvin portrayed God as faithful to his original creation. Just as God brought the cosmos into being, closely governs and restrains its natural forces, so too he will renew and transform its original substance."[51] This text does not refer to the Rapture. It is not about the destruction of creation. It refers, rather, to the purification and renewal of creation. As Thomas Finger insists in his careful study of this text, "The main emphasis of the text is that everything will be scrutinized or assessed by God, and not necessarily destroyed."[52] Thus, 2 Peter 3 rightly rendered speaks of a basic continuity rather than discontinuity of this world with the next. Creation is not ephemeral and unimportant—some second-rate way station until the eschaton—but rather, it is our proper home. Biblical eschatology affirms the redemption and restoration of creation.

The other biblical text that deserves some attention here is 1 Thessalonians 4. Often cited as the proof text for "the Rapture," this chapter from the apostle Paul's earliest letter actually teaches the exact opposite of what the Left Behind authors say it does. In the latter part of this chapter Paul is answering questions about what will happen when Jesus returns. Paul states that those who have died in Christ will go first to meet the risen Jesus, followed by those who are alive (v. 15). When Jesus the coming king descends from heaven, the dead in Christ will rise first (v. 16). Then, Paul writes, "we who are alive, who are left, will be caught up in the clouds together with them [the dead] to meet the Lord in the air; and so we will be with the Lord forever" (v. 17). The English expression "will be caught up" is from the Greek word *harpagēsometha*, which is the future middle/passive indicative first person plural form of *harpazō*, which means "to seize, take away, or catch up." So "we will be caught up" is a good translation. Where did the word *rapture* come from? In the Vulgate, the early fifth-century Latin translation of the Bible, the Greek verb was translated using the Latin verb *rapere*, "to rapture"; hence the English noun *rapture* is from the Latin *raptus*.

What is most crucial, however, is not the translation of the first verb in verse 17 but the translation of the second verb. The Greek expression is *eis apantēsin tou kuriou*—rendered "to meet the Lord" in the NRSV. The verb used is *apantaō*, which means to go out to meet a visiting dignitary in the final stage of his journey in order to escort him back to your city. For example, Cicero writes of people who went out "to meet" Julius Caesar and Octavian.[53] In a parable Jesus speaks of five wise bridesmaids who went out "to meet" the bridegroom so they could escort him back to the wedding banquet (Matt. 25:6). Luke tells how believers from Rome went as far as the Forum of Appius (forty-three miles from Rome) and Three Taverns (thirty-three miles from Rome) in order "to meet" the apostle Paul so they could be part of his entourage as he entered the capital city (Acts 28:15). So when Paul writes in 1 Thessalonians 4 that we—the living and the dead—will meet the Lord in the air, this does *not* refer to some rapture. It refers, rather, to those in Christ joining the royal procession of Jesus the king coming to reign on a renewed and renovated earth. We are not whisked off the earth; rather, we join Christ as he comes to the earth. N. T. Wright clearly captures Paul's meaning: "When Paul speaks of 'meeting' the Lord 'in the air,' the point is precisely not—as in the popular rapture theology—that the saved believers would then stay up in the air somewhere, away from earth. The point is that, having gone out to meet their returning Lord, they will escort him royally into his domain, that is, back to the place they have come from."[54] In no uncertain terms Barbara Rossing draws the proper conclusion from these (and other) texts: "This [Rapture] theology is not biblical. We are not Raptured off the earth, nor is God. No, God has come to live in the world through Jesus. God created the world, God loves the world, and God will never leave the world behind!"[55]

Christian eschatology, properly understood, is not creation-negating. As Thomas Finger concludes after surveying all four major eschatological schemes—postmillenialism, dispensationalism, historic premillennialism, and amillennialism: "*All evangelical eschatologies anticipate significant degrees of continuity between our present earth and the future world.* To be sure, this contrasts greatly with what seems to be believed in some evangelical churches: that our ultimate destiny is an immaterial, spaceless heaven, and that our present earth will be wholly destroyed. Wherever these views may come from, they have no sound foundation in either evangelical theology or Scripture."[56] He goes on to argue that "the general environmental implications of this affirmation would be that since God will transform the earth we now have, this earth must be precious to God, and that proper stewardship of nonhuman nature is a task with eternal consequences."[57] The claim that Christian eschatology is essentially anti-ecological is badly mistaken.

Finally, with respect to this fourth argument, even if LaHaye and Jenkins are correct about the eventual destruction of the earth at the eschaton, why does it necessarily follow that we should not care for creation now? It is a non sequitur to argue that because the earth will be destroyed in the future, humans should exploit it in the present. To use an analogy, is it permissible for me to plunder your house just because some time in the future it will be torn down? The fact that something will eventually be destroyed gives no license to abuse or neglect it. So this last argument, too, has significant problems. At least one of the central premises is unacceptable, and even if one grants this premise, the logic is fallacious, for the conclusion does not follow. The argument that we should not care for creation because it will one day be destroyed should be rejected.

In my judgment the ecological complaint against Christianity is seriously flawed. James Nash provides a succinct summary of the problems with this complaint, stating that it tends "to reduce the explanation of the complex ecological crisis to a single cause, to exaggerate the authority of Christianity in cultures, to minimize the fact that non-Christian cultures also have been environmental despoilers, to overlook the number of dissenting opinions in Christian history, and to underestimate the potential for ecological reform in Christianity."[58] The ecological complaint thus fails to substantiate the assertion that Christianity is the cause of the ecological crisis. As a result, the implication that Christianity itself must be rejected is likewise unjustified. But having said all this, we Christians need to be (again) reminded that we have not always been good keepers of the earth. We need to begin (and end) with confession and repentance, for while the Christian faith is not necessarily anti-ecological, we have all too often acted as if it were. Many of our beliefs, habits, and practices have in fact not served the earth but rather despoiled it.

Some Better Explanations

If the ecological complaint against Christianity is not cogent, then what might be a more plausible explanation of why we are in this environmental mess? We cannot escape this question. We must find an adequate explanation if there is any hope of moving beyond our current situation, for knowing how to extricate ourselves from our current predicament is possible only if we have some idea of how we got ourselves into it.

Materialism

In a direct refutation of Lynn White's thesis, environmental historian Donald Worster argues that "we don't have to look so far back as the book of Genesis nor do we have to indict the entire Christian heritage for our situation" since "we have a much shorter and distinctly *modern* cultural history to understand and fix." In Worster's opinion, "The most important roots [of the environmental crisis] lie not in any particular technology of production or health care . . . but rather in modern culture itself, in its world-view that has swept aside much of the older religious outlook."[59] He calls this modern worldview "materialism" and argues that it has two intertwined parts, economic and scientific.

By economic materialism Worster means, put bluntly, "worshipping the god of GNP." According to this worldview, "improving one's physical condition— i.e., achieving more comfort, more bodily pleasure, and especially higher levels of affluence—is the greatest good in life, greater than securing the salvation of one's soul, greater than learning reverence for nature or God." Success, therefore, is defined in terms of material possessions and economic productivity. Worster claims, correctly in my view, that while there are examples in history of particular individuals who embraced such a vision of life, not until the modern age do we find a whole culture "unabashedly materialist in its ultimate goals and daily strategies."[60]

Economic materialism—with its corollary commitments to secularism, the idea of progress, and the ability of human reason to discover the laws of nature—is wedded to scientific materialism, or the view that "nature is nothing but physical matter organized under and obeying physical laws, matter rationally ordered but devoid of any spirit, soul, or in-dwelling, directing purpose."[61] Worster scrutinizes the usual cast of suspects—René Descartes, Francis Bacon—but nominates Adam Smith as the person who best exemplifies this materialist spirit. The famous economist is "the representative modern man, the most complete embodiment of that cultural shift" called materialism, and the person "whom we must understand if we are to get down to the really important roots of the modern environmental crisis."[62]

The reasons for Worster's choice are many. Though born and raised in the seaside town of Kirkcaldy, Scotland, Smith "seems to have lived his entire life utterly oblivious of the nature around him. He set out to revolutionize the study of human economics in total disregard of the economy of nature." Smith believed that a system of "natural liberty" in which every person is free to pursue his own interest in his own way is in harmony with our acquisitive human nature. Smith, like Locke before him, argued that the natural world has no intrinsic value or value apart from its usefulness to humans; rather, "a thing has value only when and if it serves some direct human use ('value in use') or can be exchanged for something else that has value ('value in exchange')."[63] The wealth of which he spoke in his famous tome, *The Wealth of Nations*, has nothing to do in his mind with what we today call "nature's services"—that is, the goods and services rendered by the flora and fauna and biotic systems of the natural world. In all these ways and more, Smith exemplifies the prototypical modern person.

It is this ethos—this set of basic beliefs, convictions, and attitudes—that lies at the root of our modern ecological malaise. The natural world is scenery, not habitat. Individual freedom is paramount. Self-interest is natural. Wealth is the greatest good. Nature has no value in itself. God is dead, or on holiday.

However, insofar as every human economy derives its resources from the larger economy of nature, Worster insightfully argues, "Every economy that humans have devised must appear as only a dependent economy, deriving from that greater one." This implies, Worster insistently reminds us, that "the human economy requires for its longterm success that its architects acknowledge their dependence on the greater economy of nature, preserving its health and respecting its benefits. By this standard every modern economy, whether built on the principles of Adam Smith or Karl Marx, is an unmitigated disaster."[64] Given some such acknowledgment that the economy of nature is real and vital, Worster concludes that our "entire modern way of thinking appears in a withering light as overweening pride in inadequate intelligence and skill."[65] Our individual and collective hubris is leading us, whether we realize it or not, to an ecological and cultural collapse not unlike that of the great civilizations of the past. Therefore, Worster concludes that "the ecological crisis we have begun to experience in recent years is fast becoming *the* crisis of modern culture, calling into question not only the ethos of the marketplace or industrialism but also the central story that we have been telling ourselves over the past two or three centuries: the story of man's triumph by reason over the rest of nature."[66] In short, we are in the midst of a worldview crisis—a shaking of the very foundations of Western culture.

So why is creation groaning? Materialism. If the preceding analysis is correct, religion in general and Christianity in particular are not primarily to blame. In fact, religion has often acted to resist the pressures of materialism. Worster's own summary bears quoting at length:

> If my argument is right and the environmental crisis is really the long-preparing consequence of this modern world-view of materialism, economic and scientific, then it makes no sense to blame any of the traditional religions of the world. Religion, on the whole, acted to check that materialism, to question human arrogance, and to hold in fearful suspicion the dangerous powers of greed. Religion, including Christianity, stood firmly against a reductive, mechanistic view of the world. It pointed to a subordinate and restrained role for humans in the cosmos. And, most importantly for the sake of the biosphere, it taught people that there are higher purposes in life than consumption.[67]

Worster thus validates the distinction made earlier between a form of Christianity that embraces earthkeeping—serving God, not mammon—and a form that capitulates to the materialistic spirit of the age.

The Denial of Creation

Norman Wirzba adds additional clarity to Worster's analysis. In his book *The Paradise of God*, Wirzba argues that one fundamental cause of the environmental crisis is "the steady erosion of the practical and theoretical conditions necessary for the experience of the world *as creation*."[68] In other words, various historical developments in the last four hundred years have undermined our ability to know the world as a gift made and sustained by God. More precisely, Wirzba says, "If it was central to Scripture that the whole of reality (ourselves included) exists as the expression of God's good pleasure and that reality is therefore a reflection of a divine intention and goal, it is clear today, especially given naturalist, materialist, and consumer assumptions, that the world has little purpose other than the instrumental purposes humans ascribe to it." Our way of seeing the world reflects modern scientific, technological, and economic views "that place humanity and its interests over and against the natural world."[69] Nature has been reduced to a site for the expression of human desire.

Wirzba proceeds to outline five aspects of "culture as the denial of creation." First, modern science and industrial technologies have "promoted a radical transformation in social structures and meanings."[70] For example, the rise of modern science with Galileo and Bacon removed God from the sphere of meaning such that the creating-sustaining-redeeming God of the Bible was replaced by the god of deism. This God of deism, according to Wirzba, "has no intimate, abiding relationship with the world, and so the world can no longer be considered as a created realm daily sustained and directed by the divine creative spirit. The rational laws that govern the material realm bear no intrinsic relation to the reason within the divine mind, because the nominalist philosophy that sits behind much of modern thought dictated that God is entirely inscrutable. God's domain is the supernatural, a domain that stands apart from the natural world we inhabit."[71] One consequence of this "eclipse of divine transcendence" was that humanity filled the hole left by a banished God. Meaning and purpose now found their source in the rational will of the autonomous human.[72] Another consequence was that the natural world was reduced to the status of objects, since things no longer were believed to have integrity of their own and were not seen as directed by God to some end or purpose.

The social and economic consequences of these intellectual developments, Wirzba argues, were immense, for "when value has its source and goal in the autonomy of the individual, then the conditions for a new economic order emerge"—for example, work is no longer understood as vocation, the economy is no longer limited by a vision of divine justice, and so forth.[73] The upshot was "a crisis of meaning." As Wirzba puts it,

> whereas premodern cultures understood value to be embedded within the world, the modern mind separated fact and value, housing the former in an objective world and the latter in a form-giving subject. The sense of the world as creation, as ordered in terms of a divine plan, is largely gone. The sense of humans as microcosms of creation, as containing within themselves the responsibility to bring creation to its perfection in God, is eclipsed by the autonomous self who, with the aid of scientific technique, transforms the world according to a human plan. That this should all end in crisis is, perhaps, not surprising, for if the world is without value, are we too, as members of this world, also without value? Can the value of the world, and thus its integrity and safety, be maintained without an appreciation for its sanctity?[74]

In sum, the eclipse of divine transcendence meant that creation was no longer seen as the all-encompassing reality that united God, humanity, and the earth.

Second, "the transformation of agrarian into industrial and urban societies" has undercut "the intimate knowledge of and sympathy for the earth that are indispensable in the care of creation."[75] Most urban people today, Wirzba observes, have lost any sense of their vital connection with the earth and hence view the earth merely as a commodity or resource. Any sense that "our lives are maintained and supported by the gifts of the earth" is consequently lost.[76] Our non-agrarian lives, moreover, have insulated us from the effects of our everyday decisions and increased our ignorance about the responsibilities of life on earth. As indicated in chapter 1, we think we throw things "away," but we fail to realize there is no away. Contrary to agrarian life, in which the connections between behavior and consequences are usually immediate and direct, we today all too often assume we do not have to live with the effects of what we do.

Furthermore, Wirzba argues that our mobility has rendered us placeless and thus ignorant of how (or why) to care for our home place. In contrast to an agrarian life rooted in a particular place, we (post)modern nomads never seem to stay in one place long enough to care for it.[77] Tutored by Wendell Berry, Wirzba asks, "How will we care for what we do not know or appreciate? This is the central dilemma of urban life. Since we are now raising generations of children who are ignorant of where food and energy come from and under what conditions it is produced, we cannot seriously expect them to care for the soil and water, to tend and serve the garden of life."[78] The eclipse of agrarian life is yet another recent historical development that makes it increasingly difficult to experience the world as creation, and thus to have the motivation and practical competence to care for our home planet.

Third, modern technology has "changed the nature of our experience in profound ways."[79] Both particular technologies and a technological mind-set have transformed our attitudes and practices in such a way that we now experience the world through a technological grid or filter. Echoing the analyses of Neil Postman, Albert Borgmann, and others, Wirzba writes:

> One change in sensibility can be seen in the enframing character of technological media that further contribute to the modern disenchantment with the world. We do not engage reality on its own terms, but rather as packaged or framed by someone else and in terms set by the limits of the medium. Not only do we feel cut off from a direct experience with reality, we now wonder, given the power of media to manipulate image and information, if what we see is really real. We have become spectators of a world of someone else's invention and control, particularly when we realize how many hours are spent weekly in front of a television or computer screen.[80]

What's the problem? Unlike participants, spectators have no direct encounter with reality, and hence have little knowledge unmediated by the media. And knowledge is reduced to data or bits (bytes?) of information, leaving behind the larger ecological and social contexts necessary to achieve genuine understanding. The complexity of real life is lost. The deleterious environmental effects are not hard to imagine.

Behind the rise of modern technology, Wirzba argues, is an urge to control and master nature. In keeping with Francis Bacon's metaphor that nature must be made a slave, the technological impulse seeks to tame and manipulate nature. As Wirzba says, "Unlike the artisan who works from an affinity with nature learned through years of attentive practice, the masters of technology, at once proud, fearless, and determined, manipulate the world according to their own ends."[81] The technological mind-set empties the world of its integrity. The end result of pledging allegiance to technology is the devastation of the earth, for in this view the natural world is merely a collection of resources to be used.

Fourth in Wirzba's list is his observation that contemporary culture has "forgotten, denied, or scorned" the interdependencies that are necessary for the flourishing of life. To flourish, Wirzba rightly insists, we must acknowledge and learn from two forms of interdependence: the physical/biological and the historical/traditional. In other words, we must "acknowledge and respect the life-giving sources of food, energy, and water without which we could not live," and we must "remember and cultivate the ties of community and tradition that infuse biological life with spiritual and moral significance and that guide cultural development with the memory of past success and failure."[82]

Our current culture, however, has largely failed to do either of these things. As a consequence we mistakenly assume that we can and do live alone, without acknowledging our embeddedness in the biophysical world or our dependence on human community and culture. Some examples: Instead of viewing "waste" as food or fuel in a larger ecological order in which there is no waste, we throw things "away" and live in a "throwaway society." Rather than living in city neighborhoods where the houses and people look different and you can walk almost anywhere, we live in suburbs where the houses and people all look the same and you have to drive everywhere. According to Wirzba, an "abstract culture" leads to "neglect and disregard, a general inconsiderateness toward the needs of others" since "the very character of our lives, the practical shape of our living arrangements and the advertised goals of our striving, limits our capacity to appreciate and address the need around us."[83] In other words, certain cultural conditions make it difficult to care for people or the earth.

The fifth and final obstacle "to a recovery of the full meaning of creation," according to Wirzba, "is the growing irrelevance of God." There can be no creation, properly understood, without a Creator. And yet while we may voice our belief in God the Creator, it has become increasingly difficult to truly mean it. As Wirzba observes, "the conditions that would enable us to recognize or feel with honesty and depth the presence of God are mostly gone. Though we may claim that God exists, it does not matter, since the patterns of our day-to-day lives, as well as the goals of our culture, proceed on terms set by economic demands and without reference to God."[84] While we may profess belief in God, our lives reveal that, practically speaking, God is irrelevant. "As we have become controllers of our own fate," Wirzba states, "God has simply become an unnecessary hypothesis. We, rather than God, run the world. Talk of God as a creator who is intimately and concernfully involved in the daily affairs of existence is simply quaint, a reflection of the refusal to deal with the naturalistic assumptions of modern science. How, then, can we think of ourselves and the world as creation, when the idea of a creator has been so severely compromised?"[85] If we find it difficult to think of the world as creation, what does that mean for any attempt to care for creation? How will we encounter God, or feel God's presence, in a world increasingly of our own making?

The Church

While the previous two explanations of our contemporary environmental crisis point to factors other than Christianity, the church is not off the hook. In the spirit of James Nash's admonition that Christians ought to confess their own complicity, Wesley Granberg-Michaelson offers both a perceptive explanation of our current crisis and an honest assessment of the church. His account finds the roots of our environmental malaise in five interrelated claims.

First, the church is captive to modern Western culture. According to Granberg-Michaelson, "Christian faith in the West has been captive to the assumptions of modern culture which sever God from the creation and subject the creation to humanity's arrogant and unrestrained power."[86] Our de facto theology has all too often been deistic—affirming that God exists and that God creates but denying that God is related in any meaningful way to the created order. According to this view "nature" is autonomous, operating like a self-sustaining machine, not needing divine assistance. The natural world is, furthermore, viewed merely as a repository of raw material or resources for human exploitation.[87] It is not difficult to see how such a materialistic worldview underwrites the pillage and plunder of the natural world.

The fact that the church has been captive to the modern Western worldview is well documented, and the fact that this captivity warrants critique is no less clear.[88] While scientific and/or technological examples are usually given as evidence of "humanity's arrogant and unrestrained power," many argue that the most obvious and pernicious examples of such abusive power are economic. That is, the captivity of the church to modernity is most fundamentally its subservience to the gods of consumption and wealth. This critique is no more trenchant than in the words of Wendell Berry: "Despite its protests to the contrary, modern Christianity has become willy-nilly the religion of the state and the economic status quo. Because it has so exclusively dedicated itself to incanting anemic souls into Heaven, it has been made the tool of much earthly villainy. It has, for the most part, stood silently by while a predatory economy has ravaged the world, destroyed its natural beauty and health, divided and plundered its human communities and households."[89] Given even a modicum of truth to such criticism, it is understandable why many today call the church to confession and renewal.

Second, the church has accepted the anthropocentrism of modernity. In the words of Granberg-Michaelson: "Modern cultural and theological assumptions have placed humanity at the center of purpose and meaning in the universe."[90] Having banished God or rendered God harmless, we have enthroned ourselves at the center of things. We believe we humans are the measure of all things—*homo mensura*. This human-centeredness is evident in countless ways. We assume rights apply only to humans. Bioethics (the ethics of life) assumes that the only important life is a human life. The earth is viewed as a stage on which humans perform. Land is of value only if human labor is mixed with it. The weather is considered bad if it rains or snows, regardless of whether the land and its creatures need the precipitation. Once again, it is not difficult to see how such a perspective on the world and one's place in it legitimates and sanctions the despoilation of creation.

However, as James Gustafson states, while humankind is no doubt the "*measurer*" of all things, "there are some good reasons for asking in our time and in light of the Western religious tradition whether the apparent assumption that man is the moral measure of all things can be sustained."[91] Or as Holmes Rolston III maintains, "Man may be (in some advanced senses) the only *measurer* of things, but it does not follow that man is the only *measure* of things."[92] Happily, the case for a theocentric perspective in theology and ethics is being made with increasing frequency, eloquence, and power.[93]

Third, we in Western culture have made technology into a god. Bhopal, Chernobyl, Exxon Valdez—the list of technological disasters in recent memory is long. And those are only the large-scale examples of our technological hubris. "Our culture adheres to a blind faith in technological progress," Granberg-Michaelson observes, "as the means to resolve environmental problems and the maldistribution of world resources."[94] If you doubt the veracity of this claim, simply eavesdrop on any conversation about environmental degradation or world hunger. Without fail someone will opine that while we have serious problems, technology will save us. As one Chicago corporation unabashedly put it, "Science and technology must answer our problems. If they don't, nothing else will."[95]

Granberg-Michaelson is not trashing technology per se, nor am I. The power to shape and form culture is a God-given dimension of human existence. Technology is an inescapable feature of human life, often producing much good. The question is not whether we use technology, but what kind of technology, how much, for whom, and at what cost? Neil Postman summarizes this well:

> Most people believe technology is a staunch friend. There are two reasons for this. First, technology is a friend. It makes life easier, cleaner, and longer. Can anyone ask more of a friend? Second, because of its lengthy, intimate, and inevitable relationship with culture, technology does not invite a close examination of its own consequences. It is the kind of friend who asks for trust and obedience, which most people are inclined to give because its gifts are truly bountiful. But,

of course, there is a dark side to this friend. Its gifts are not without a heavy cost. Stated in the most dramatic terms, the accusation can be made that the uncontrolled growth of technology destroys the vital sources of our humanity. It creates a culture without a moral foundation. It undermines certain mental processes and social relations that make human life worth living. Technology, in sum, is both friend and enemy.[96]

As Langdon Gilkey insightfully observed some years ago, technology is ambiguous.[97] It is and can be both blessing and bane. Insofar as we give our ultimate allegiance to technology and its products, we have misplaced our faith and engaged in idolatry.

Fourth, the church has forgotten creation. "The Western Church's modern theology has fought between being personalized or politicized, and largely has forgotten the theology of creation as its starting point."[98] We have forgotten that the Apostles' Creed begins with an affirmation of God as Maker of heaven and earth. We have forgotten that Genesis begins with creation, not redemption, and that Revelation ends with a redeemed, renewed creation. We have forgotten that, in the words of St. Paul, all things were created and hang together in Christ (Col. 1:16–17). While reading the book of Scripture, we have forgotten to read the book of nature.[99] Because of such forgetfulness we operate with a faith so focused on redemption that we have lost sight of the cosmic scope of God's work. Conversion is limited to people. Spirituality concerns only certain kinds or spheres of action. The kingdom of God is reduced to church activities. By so confining faith to individual "spiritual" well-being, we deny the full power of God's grace. And by implication, "in such a mindset, environmental problems are at best nothing more than another issue over which Christians may have different opinions, all largely unrelated to the gospel."[100]

Many have commented on the eclipse of the doctrine of creation, none more astutely or eloquently than Joseph Sittler. Because of "this virtual demise of a vigorous doctrine of the Creation," argues Sittler,

> it is difficult but possible to get men to understand that pollution is biologically disastrous, aesthetically offensive, equally obviously economically self-destructive and socially reductive of the quality of human life. But it is a very difficult job to get even Christians to see that so to deal with the Creation is *Christianly* blasphemous. A proper doctrine of creation and redemption would make it perfectly clear that from a Christian point of view the ecological crisis presents us not simply with moral tasks but requires of us a freshly renovated and fundamental theology of the first article whereby the Christian faith defines whence the Creation was formed, and why, and by whom, and to what end.[101]

As Clarence Glacken states in his magisterial study of nature and culture in Western thought, in contrast to other religions of the ancient world, Christianity is "a religion and a philosophy of creation."[102] While not the central message of Scripture, creation is "the underlying foundation" without an understanding of which "our understanding of both sin and redemption will inevitably be distorted."[103] Creation, fall, and redemption well summarize the biblical drama. To the extent that we have a truncated story line, we have forgotten where and whose we are and thereby contributed to our current condition.

The fifth and final reason for our ecological predicament, according to Granberg-Michaelson, is the hubris of the Western church, which "has been theologically arrogant and inattentive as well as condescending toward non-Western Christian perspectives."[104] Colonialism has wreaked an enormous toll, affecting not just the economies and politics of the so-called developing nations but also the very mind-set of the church. Examples abound. We in the West (or, more accurately, the North) assume that our creeds and confessions are binding on Christians elsewhere. We in the United States send missionaries to other countries but then chafe at the idea that others might send missionaries to us. Though our numbers continue to plunge while the church elsewhere is flourishing, we in North America and Europe still often assume we are at the theological center of things.

In contrast to the prevailing attitude of pride and condescension, we in the Northern church have much to learn from our sisters and brothers living in other parts of the world. The Eastern Orthodox tradition, for example, has theological and liturgical riches that could help reshape our own thought and life in more earth-friendly ways.[105] Asian, African, and South American churches have wisdom to share that we neglect at our own peril.[106] And we Christians have much to learn from religious traditions other than our own.[107] In short, we must acknowledge our pride and open our eyes to what the Holy Spirit has done and is doing among all the peoples of the world.

If Worster, Wirzba, and Granberg-Michaelson are on the mark, then the way forward is clear. We must renounce the idols to which we have pledged our allegiance—the false gods of scientism, technicism, and materialism, among others—and return to a faith refined of hubris and marked instead by humility. We must cultivate a (sub)culture of creation, in which we gratefully acknowledge a loving God who creates and sustains and redeems all things, and whose vision of shalom includes a flourishing natural world of meaning and value. We must call the church out of its captivity to Western culture and into a faithful obedience to Jesus. For insight into that vision, we need to look to Scripture. To that important task we now turn.

what is the connection between scripture and ecology?

biblical wisdom and ecological vision

And the angel showed me the river of the water of life, bright as crystal, flowing from the throne of God and of the Lamb through the middle of the street of the city. On either side of the river is the tree of life with its twelve kinds of fruit, producing its fruit each month; and the leaves of the tree are for the healing of the nations.

Revelation 22:1–2

As indicated in the preceding chapter, according to many people the Bible contributes to the ecological crisis. Scripture, they argue, sanctions the exploitation and degradation of the earth. It is anti-ecological, and so we should discard it. Thomas Berry, for example, advocates putting the Bible on the shelf for a decade or two.[1] Many seem to believe Scripture is of no good use, so why not scrap it and find insight and inspiration in other places?

I have attempted to rebut a number of specific charges, for example, by explicating Genesis 1–2 and 2 Peter 3:10. But having done that, there remains much more to say with respect to Scripture. Indeed, any responsible Christian perspective must attend to the Bible, since within the Christian tradition in its many varieties—Orthodox, Catholic, Protestant—sacred Scripture functions as both source and norm for thinking properly and living rightly. The canonical Scriptures, as the term implies, are the standard according to which all claims are judged. Christianity is, like it or not, a religion of the Book.

For evangelical Protestants this affirmation of the centrality of Scripture is especially important. With respect to virtually any issue, evangelicals instinctively turn to the Bible for insight and direction. Indeed, for evangelicals the Bible is not simply one of the places to go—along with tradition, reason, and experience—when seeking knowledge of God or guidance on how to live; the Bible is *the* source and norm that takes precedence over all others. To use the classical terminology, the Bible is the *norma normans*—the ultimate norm, that which trumps all other authorities.

But the matter does not end there, with discussion of the Bible as source and norm, for views regarding Scripture are not the same as uses of Scripture. That is, one's actual reading of the Bible may be only loosely connected to the view one has of the nature and authority of the Bible. A person with a "high" view of Scripture—for example, where the Bible is taken as inerrant or infallible divine revelation—may read it carelessly or with his or her own agenda (unconsciously) in mind; someone with a "low" view of the Bible—for example, where the Bible is taken as only a collection of human fables—may in fact read the text with great care and insight.[2] In short, Scripture must be interpreted. All of which is to say that the problem of interpretation, or hermeneutics, is an inescapable and important issue that (if only briefly here) must be addressed.[3]

The Use and Abuse of Scripture

We all read from somewhere. As many contemporary philosophers have acknowledged, there is no view from nowhere.[4] This is not a lamentable fact of our existence but simply an honest recognition of our inescapable finitude. What we see depends, in part, on where we stand. In addition, what we see is shaped by our self-seeking and pride. We are not only finite but faulted. Our hearts are, to use Luther's famous image, curved in on themselves. Such admissions, however, need not imply epistemic relativism. The fact that what we see (or read) is contingent on where we stand and influenced by inordinate pride does not necessarily entail that truth is, in the famous phrase of Richard Rorty, "what our peers will let us get away with saying."[5] Truth is not a wax nose, endlessly malleable and conformable to one's own dreams, desires, or quest for power. So while Paul Ricoeur's three "masters of suspicion"—Karl Marx, Friedrich Nietzsche, and Sigmund Freud—have much to teach us,[6] the conclusion some draw from their writings—that "truth" is merely a fiction used by those in power to dominate the powerless—is unwarranted. We Christians can, in other words, appropriate the important insights of modern philosophers such as Marx, Nietzsche, and Freud, as well as those of postmodern philosophers such as Michel Foucault, Emmanuel Levinas, and Jacques Derrida, without necessarily accepting all the conclusions they or some of their followers draw.[7]

To borrow a phrase from philosopher Richard Bernstein, the proper view of human knowing lies somewhere between an objectivism that purports to offer "the only truth" (and is absolutely certain of possessing it) and a relativism that says "anything goes" (often with, ironically, equal certitude).[8] In other words, with respect to reading texts, including the Bible, often there is more than one good reading, and almost always some readings are absolutely implausible. In each case arguments can be given, though they may not be persuasive to all.

By analogy, consider a symphony playing a musical score. Different conductors offer different interpretations, and some performances are better than others—more faithful to the score, more technically proficient, more creative. So judgments of quality are possible; to a trained ear some performances are clearly better than others. But while reasons can be given as to why some performances are superior to others, there may not be universal agreement over which one is "the best." The same can be said in regard to the reading of the Bible. Some readings are better than others, and one can argue why that is the case. But sometimes there is legitimate disagreement over which is better and which is worse. And often it is only through the clarifying lens of history that the truth can be most clearly seen.

Willard Swartley, among others, offers detailed evidence of our finite and fallen readings of the Bible. In his illuminating volume *Slavery, Sabbath, War, and Women*, he documents how Christians through the ages have used (and abused) Scripture when dealing with the four issues listed in the title of his book.[9] In the United States in the mid-nineteenth century, Christians, all of whom were using the Bible as their source of authority on the matter, reached diametrically opposed conclusions on the issue of slavery, sometimes by appealing to the very same texts. For centuries Christians with similar views of the Bible have differed on the proper role, if any, of Christians in war. And in more recent years Christians with a "high" view of the nature and authority of Scripture have come to divergent conclusions on the issue of women in ministry. Swartley's study makes this important point exceedingly clear: while Scripture is infallible, our readings of it most certainly are not.

In the context of an exegetical discussion of the first chapters of Genesis, Old Testament scholar Bernhard Anderson summarizes the matter well:

> Clearly, we read the Bible "where we are": as people who are conditioned by the times in which we live and by the history that we share, including our philosophical heritage (capitalism and its Marxist counterpart) and our scientific outlook. This sober realization does not, in my estimation, mire us in interpretive relativism. . . . To be sure, we come to the Scriptures in a particular time and place.

But the words of Scripture, spoken or written in their own context, may criticize where we stand, limit our use of them, and challenge us with their strange social setting and theological horizon.[10]

If we ignore or refuse to acknowledge our "placedness" in reading Scripture, we blind ourselves to what the Bible has to teach us. Awareness of our own preunderstandings and openness to the otherness of the text, as Hans-Georg Gadamer reminds us, are two prerequisites to normative interpretation. Humility and courage, in short, are necessary virtues.

This very brief excursus into contemporary hermeneutics requires, first, that I readily acknowledge that I read the Bible from somewhere. Like everyone else, I can do no other. Pretenses to objectivity, defined in Enlightenment fashion as the ability to escape our own skin and see things as God does, must be abandoned. And, second, I honestly state that my readings are informed by what we know of how the world works and of what is currently wrong. My reading, in other words, is informed by the challenges we face as we attempt to be faithful followers of Jesus in an ecologically imperiled age. Therefore, while my interpretations of the biblical texts in the pages that follow may seem implausible to some, they are, I believe, good interpretations—rooted in the text, warranted by what we know of the time and place and culture of that now-ancient world of meaning, and put into explicit conversation with the questions and challenges of our own time. My reading, in short, is a faithful attempt to hear the message of Scripture, while attentive to a groaning earth.[11]

Claims about the appropriateness of certain interpretive assumptions or ways of approaching the biblical text cannot, of course, be justified in advance. As Paul Santmire honestly and rightly admits, one's interpretive framework "can only be justified in terms of its legitimate exegetical fruits."[12] The hermeneutical proof is in the exegetical pudding. And so it is to the reading of specific texts that we now turn.

Indwelling the Biblical Story

In order to understand more fully the biblical story, and thus grasp the rich biblical theology and ethic of care for the earth, I here examine a few texts in some detail. In chapter 3, I dealt with 2 Peter 3, and thus will not consider it here. So also, in chapters 6 and 7 I will address a great number of other biblical passages, including Psalm 104, Leviticus 25, and Luke 4; therefore, they will not be the focus of this chapter. Though I dealt with Genesis 1–2 in chapter 3, the focus was on the question, who is the human? In this chapter I pose a different question with respect to that key passage. In what follows, therefore, I attend to five texts and, in regard to each one, ask and attempt to answer one central question.

"In the beginning God created the heavens and the earth." So reads (in the NRSV) the first verse of the book of beginnings. As many have commented, regardless of the tradition-historical roots of Genesis 1–11, its final form as a skillfully written piece of literature and its placement at the beginning of the canon are of great significance.[13] Terence Fretheim captures this significance well:

> Genesis stands at the beginning because creation is such a fundamental theological category for the rest of the canon. God's continuing blessing and ordering work at every level is creational. Moreover, only in relationship to the creation can God's subsequent actions in and through Israel be properly understood. The placement of creation demonstrates that God's purposes with Israel are universal in scope. God's work in redemption serves creation, the *entire* creation, since it reclaims a creation that labors under the deep and pervasive effects of sin.[14]

Thus if one wants to answer the question, where are we? there is no better place to begin than the first chapter of the first book of the Bible. Let's look again (perhaps for the first time) at this evocative and powerful text.[15]

> In the beginning was God.
> And over a deep, dark, watery abyss—
> a formless void of nothingness—
> God's creative Spirit swept,
> hovering like an eagle over her brood.
> Like a rushing wind God's Spirit moved
> when it was time to create the heavens and the earth.
>
> And in the midst of this chaotic darkness, God spoke,
> and light, like the pulse of a quasar, came to be.
> And God saw that this brilliant light was good,
> and so pushed back the darkness to make room for the light.
> God named the light Day and the darkness Night.
> Evening and morning, the first day.
> God spoke, and it was so.
> Out of chaos, order.
> From what was empty and dark came a fullness of light.
>
> And God spoke again,
> and in the midst of the chaotic waters God fashioned a dome—
> a celestial roof carving out space between the waters above
> and the waters below.
> So the waters were put in their place,

and God named this protective space Sky.
Evening and morning, the second day.
God spoke, and it was so.
Out of chaos, order.
From what was fluid and flowing came a bounded firmament.

And God spoke again,
and the disordered waters under the sky were gathered together
so that dry land appeared.
And God named the dry land Earth and the gathered waters Seas.
God saw that this, too, was good.
And God spoke yet again,
and the earth gave birth to plants and trees of every kind.
And this too—this greening, living earth—God saw was good.
Evening and morning, the third day.
God spoke, and it was so.
Out of chaos, order.
From the sea came land, and on this dry land fruit trees flourished.

And God spoke again,
and the earth's greater and lesser lights and the stars were created.
To separate day from night
and to serve as celestial signs of the seasons,
God set the sun and the moon in the dome.
To rule over day and night
God made the two great lights.
And God saw that all this, too, was good.
Evening and morning, the fourth day.
God spoke, and it was so.
From emptiness to fullness.
Heavenly space was filled with brilliant lights.

And God spoke again,
and with this speaking
the waters below brought forth swarms of living things of every kind,
and the sky above was filled with winged birds of every kind.
Shrimp and suckers and sea monsters.
Warblers and waxwings and woodpeckers.
And God saw that these creatures were good,
and God blessed them.
God spread his blanket of blessing upon them,
that they might be fruitful and multiply
and fill the space created for them.

Evening and morning, the fifth day.
God spoke, and it was so.
From emptiness to fullness.
Water and sky were filled with creatures great and small.

And God spoke again,
and by this word the fecund earth brought forth
living land creatures of every kind:
cattle and kangaroo and cobra.
And God saw that all these creatures—
domestic and wild and creeping upon the ground—
were good.
And then God spoke another word.
In consort with the heavenly court,
God willed to make an earth-creature in God's own image—
after God's own likeness—
to rule the fish and the fowl, the creatures domestic and wild.
So male and female God created these his own image-bearers,
and God blessed them.
In their filling and ruling of the earth,
they were to mirror God.
And God gave to these earth-creatures and to every living creature
green plants and fruit to eat.
And God beheld all that God had made,
and it was very, very good.
Evening and morning, the sixth day.
God spoke, and it was so.
From emptiness to fullness.
The earth was filled with living creatures of every kind,
including the divine image-bearing human.

And so the heavens and the earth
and all their multitude of creatures
were made,
and on the seventh day God rested from his work.
And God blessed this day and made it holy,
for on it God ceased from his labor of love.

What does this primal story of origins—this Word of God in human words—
tell us about the world in which we live? In both its substance (what it says)
and its style (how it says it), how does this founding story answer the question,
where are we?

First, God is the Creator of all things. The merism "the heavens and the earth" (*haššāmayim wĕ'ēt hā'ereṣ*) indicates that the heavens and the earth and everything in between come to be as a result of God's creative Word and energizing Spirit. Also, verses 1 and 2 of chapter 1, meant to apply to all that follows, like bookends form an inclusio with verses 1 through 3 of chapter 2, again emphasizing that everything is formed by God. In addition, both the regions of the cosmos (days 1–3) and their various inhabitants (days 4–6) are created by God. None of the celestial beings—sun or moon or stars—has the power to create. And though living beings procreate, none has the power God has to create ex nihilo. In contrast to the competing creation myths of the day, this text clearly affirms that the sovereign God brings all things into existence.[16] Where are we? In a God-wrought world.

Second, not all agency resides with God. While God is the ultimate Creator—artistically fashioning the cosmos from existing material as well as bringing things into being out of nothing—God's means of creating involves the sharing of power. For example, the earth is said to bring forth (*yāṣā'*) vegetation (1:12), and the waters are invited to bring forth (*yāṣā'*) swarms of living creatures (1:20). The sun and moon rule the day and night (1:16), and humans are given the delegated, royal responsibility of ruling (*rādâ*) the earth (1:26). God is not the only holder of power in this story. As Fretheim states: "Both human and nonhuman creatures are called to participate in the creative activity initiated by God."[17] Like a risking parent, God lovingly empowers creation for its own benefit. In other words, creation has the genuine ability to respond. God calls and creatures respond. Where are we? In a responsive world.

Third, creation is cosmos. The chaotic exists, to be sure, but the universe is a place of order and structure, purposefully and lovingly designed by God. Indeed, the universe takes shape as the chaotic waters (*tōhû wābōhû* and *tĕhôm*) are bounded, and despite the ongoing vulnerability of the earth to these chaotic forces, the world remains a cosmos due to God's sustaining breath.[18] Even the orderliness of the very form of the story bespeaks the order of the creative process. Everything has its place. Such a portrayal of cosmic fittingness evokes wonder. As Bernhard Anderson states: "The wonderful order and regularity of the cosmos, in which every creature, animate and inanimate, has its assigned place and function in a marvelous whole, evoke aesthetic feelings of wonder and reverence."[19] Where are we? In a world of wonders, wisely ordered by God.

Fourth, creation is good. As intended by God, creation is good. Indeed, it is very good (*tôb mĕ'ōd*), a judgment that connotes beauty and peace.[20] The universe originates not out of struggle or battle or conflict, as portrayed in so many ancient creation stories, but through a seemingly effortless and struggle-free divine speaking and making. In contrast to other narratives, the biblical narrative testifies to an ontology of peace. Richard Middleton and Brian Walsh put this point especially well:

Rather than begin with conflict amongst the gods, the Scriptures begin with the effortless, joyous calling forth of creation by a sovereign Creator who enters into a relationship of intimacy with his creatures. Therefore creatureliness qua creatureliness is good. . . . This means that a biblical worldview will grant no ontological standing or priority to evil or violence. Indeed, violence is seen, in this worldview, as an illegitimate alien intruder into God's good creation. In contrast to an ontology of violence, then, the Scriptures begin with an ontology of peace.[21]

We have, to use Wendell Berry's phrase, a gift of good land.[22] Where are we? In a world where peace is primordial.

Fifth, the earth is a home for all earthly creatures. The earth is created as a habitat not only for humans (*'ādām*) but for all living things (*nepeš ḥayyâ*). God's intention is to "provide living space for a great variety of living beings."[23] Though unique in being made in God's image and called to rule as God rules,[24] humans are created on the same day as animals and are permitted to eat the same (vegetarian) food. By implication, as Larry Rasmussen fetchingly puts it, "All the createds are relateds."[25] Also, humans are not the only creatures blessed by God, for birds and fish are also blessed. In short, humans and animals share the same house. And so Anderson concludes: "In view of the overall pattern of the account, it is apparent that the emphasis falls not so much on anthropology, that is, on the supremacy of humanity, as on ecology, that is, the earthly habitation that human beings share with other forms of 'living being' (*nepeš ḥayyâh*)."[26] Where are we? In a home we share with many other creatures.

Sixth, the climax of creation is the sabbath. Contrary to many readings of the story, the culmination comes not in the creation of humanity (*'ādām* in the generic sense) on the sixth day; the climax is, rather, the seventh day. This very day is blessed and hallowed by God. As Jürgen Moltmann, among others, persuasively argues, the story reaches its climax with the sabbath rest on the seventh (i.e., perfect) day: "If we look at the biblical traditions that have to do with the belief in creation, we discover that the sabbath is not a day of rest following six working days. On the contrary: the whole work of creation was performed *for the sake of the sabbath*."[27]

The sabbath reminds us, among other things, that the world is in God's loving hands and, therefore, will not fall to pieces if we cease from our work. As Walter Brueggemann contends: "The celebration of a day of rest was, then, the announcement of trust in this God who is confident enough to rest. It was then and is now an assertion that life does not depend upon our feverish activity of self-securing, but that there can be a pause in which life is given to us simply as a gift."[28] Where, then, are we? On an earth not of our own making, blessed by God.

In sum, this founding story affirms that God is a gracious homemaker and the earth is our home. In the first three days, the formless takes form. Because of God's creative word, from an empty void comes a habitable earth. God speaks and separates, and it comes to be. God calls and creation responds. And it is good. No cosmic battles. No primordial violence. No evil woven into the warp and weft of creation. God creates livable places for the plethora of creatures to come. And in the second three days, what is empty is filled. Again because of God's creating-sustaining word, the regions separated out from the chaotic waters are occupied by an increasingly large array of creatures: sun and moon, fish, birds, land animals both domestic and wild, and humans. God is a homemaker showing hospitality to an increasingly diverse range of creaturely inhabitants. Where are we? With a great many other creatures on our home planet, the earth.[29]

With Whom Does God Make a Covenant? (Genesis 6–9)

The story of Noah and the flood is known to many. Indeed, maybe it is too well known, for we assume we know its meaning. But perhaps there is more to the story than meets the eye. Genesis 6–9 is not primarily about Noah or a flood. Like all great stories in the Bible, it is fundamentally about God. It tells a story of a great remembering. Listen to the tale it tells.[30]

> Long ago the earth was filled with wickedness and violence. The creatures made in God's image and entrusted with the care and cultivation of the earth had only evil in their hearts. Then as now things were off-kilter—bent and warped and broken. Like a disease, violence had infected the earth. Like a body out of joint, the earth was dismembered.
>
> And it grieved God's heart that he had brought humans into existence, for it was their wickedness and violence that had wreaked havoc on the earth. Therefore, God resolved to wash away this wickedness—to destroy all flesh and the earth.
>
> But Noah found favor in God's sight, and so God decided to spare Noah and his family and two of every living thing, of all flesh, male and female. Mysteriously God instructed Noah to build a boat—a rather large boat. This craft, the ark, was to hold Noah, his wife, his sons and their wives, and two of every living thing, male and female—birds, animals, creeping things—each according to their kind. And the ark was to carry all the necessary provisions—food and drink not just for the people but also for all the other creatures— because God had made a covenant with Noah and cared for the nonhuman creatures whom Noah was instructed to nudge, cajole, and otherwise load aboard his vessel.
>
> So Noah obediently gathered his menagerie of creatures—wild and domestic, flying and creeping—in numbers sufficient to preserve

their fruitfulness. And with Noah they went into the ark, two and two of all flesh with the breath of life.

Wild animals—hippos and hyenas and hedgehogs.
Domestic animals—dogs and goats and cows.
Birds—quetzels and cockatoos and crows.
Creeping things—scorpions and stink bugs and snakes.

And then the waters came, and came, and came. For a very long time. And everything on the earth in which there was the breath of life died. The waters of chaos once again threatened to engulf the order of creation. Like a pinprick of light in a sea of darkness, only Noah and those with him in the ark were left.

But God remembered.
God remembered Noah.
God remembered all the wild animals in the ark.
God remembered all the domestic animals in the ark.
But God remembered.

With the waters swelling and all else lost save the ark, with the powers of chaos encircling and threatening to overwhelm, with the deep a yawning abyss ready to swallow the lonely ark, God remembered the inhabitants of his floating species preserve. And more. God made a wind blow over the earth, and the waters subsided. Once again, just as in primeval creation, in this act of re-creation God's Spirit brooded and blew over the chaotic waters, and the waters subsided. Chaos was controlled. Shalom—peace, harmony, balance—was restored.

The ark dwellers were thus saved from the waters—waters that, as it turned out, cleansed the earth and provided Noah and his kin with new life. And all the living things in the crazy-making ark were released. Indeed, Noah brought out his restless ark dwellers so that they might multiply and replenish the earth. In language reminiscent of the first creation, where it is said that God blessed the birds and the sea monsters and the swarming aquatic creatures to be fruitful, here too God's purpose is made clear: Noah and his family and all the nonhuman families exited the ark to repopulate the now renewed earth. A new beginning. A clean slate. A fresh start.

After Noah built an altar and made a sacrifice, God resolved never again to curse the ground because of humankind and never again to destroy the earth by water. And God once again blessed the humans, repeating the words given before violence and wickedness entered

the world: "Be fruitful and multiply and fill the earth" (Gen. 9:1).
Only this time, significantly, God does not include the command to
subdue and have dominion over the earth and its creatures, as if God
thought better of giving that command this time, given the mess
humans had made of the earth. Taking the command to rule into
their own hands, mistaking dominion for domination, the human
earth-creatures had perverted their royal responsibility and polluted
the earth. This time, however, God explicitly grants permission to eat
meat, so long as the blood, or life force, is not consumed. Though
humans are now carnivores, respect for life is still the rule. But as
one might expect, fear and dread come upon their prey.

And then God again establishes a covenant. Six times in ten
verses the text speaks of a divine covenant:

1. "I am establishing my covenant with you and your
   descendents after you, and with every living creature that is
   with you, the birds, the domestic animals, and every animal
   of the earth with you, as many as came out of the ark" (Gen.
   9:9–10).
2. "This is the sign of the covenant that I make between me and
   you and every living creature that is with you" (Gen. 9:12).
3. "I have set my bow in the clouds, and it shall be a sign of the
   covenant between me and the earth" (Gen. 9:13).
4. "I will remember my covenant that is between me and you
   and every living creature of all flesh" (Gen. 9:15).
5. "When the bow is in the clouds, I will see it and remember the
   everlasting covenant between [me] and every living creature
   of all flesh that is on the earth" (Gen. 9:16).
6. "This is the sign of the covenant that I have established
   between me and all flesh that is on the earth" (Gen. 9:17).

From the crescendo of God's remembering we come to the majesty
of God's covenanting—God's covenant with the earth and all its
creatures.

Let us now return to our central question. With whom does God establish
a covenant? Clearly, the text speaks of a covenant (běrît) made by God, but it
is not, as is often thought, only a covenant with Noah. This covenant, rather,
is established with "every living creature" (kol-nepeš ḥayyâ), with "every living
creature of all flesh" (kol-nepeš ḥayyâ běkol-bāśār), with "every living creature of
all flesh that is on the earth" (kol-nepeš ḥayyâ běkol-bāśār 'ăšer 'al-hā'āreṣ). The
covenant, put simply in 9:13, is with "the earth" (hā'āreṣ). This text pounds
the point home: this covenant includes all creatures—human and nonhuman.

Bernhard Anderson summarizes the matter very well: "The Noahic covenant, then, is universal in the widest sense imaginable. It is fundamentally an ecological covenant that includes not only human beings everywhere but all animals—every living being (*nepeš ḥayyâ*) of all flesh that is upon the earth (9:16 repeating what was said in 6:19)."[31]

And the bow in the clouds, a careful reading reveals, is not primarily a sign of promise to us of God's faithfulness but a reminder to God of his covenant promise to the earth. The bow (*qešet*) is pointed at God. The traditional reading is that the bow is the rainbow, serving as a colorful reminder to God of his promise. That may be true, but more likely the bow here is the bow and arrow, suggesting that God aims an arrow at his own heart, lest he forget his covenant promise.[32] In other words, God can be counted on to keep this promise. Indeed, though the inclination of the human heart is still evil, unchanged even after the flood (8:21), God nevertheless unilaterally resolves never again to destroy the earth in this way.

Two more features of this covenant merit comment. This covenant is an everlasting covenant (*běrît 'ôlām*). It is not a temporary agreement or provisional pledge but a covenant in perpetuity. It is, furthermore, an unconditional covenant. Unlike the more reciprocal Mosaic covenant, in which conditions are imposed upon the people, God unilaterally and unconditionally establishes this covenant with the earth. This everlasting covenant rests solely on God's steadfast commitment.

With whom does God make a covenant? God covenants with the earth and all its creatures. An everlasting covenant. An unconditional covenant. God covenants with us his faulted people and with this his groaning earth. The God who remembered Noah and all the animals in the ark also re-membered the earth. God, through his chaos-controlling, life-giving Spirit, put the pieces of our dismembered home planet back together again. In this rich and suggestive biblical story we learn of the first endangered species act—initiated by God and obediently carried out by Noah. We learn of God's covenant with the earth.

Who Is at the Center of Things? (Job 38:1–42:6)

Job. The mere mention of the name evokes strong feelings. Remember the story? That blameless and upright and God-fearing man who lost his farm, his family, and his physical well-being. Friends who offered cold comfort. A seemingly cruel and unjust God. Job. A man of suffering in a book about suffering.[33]

Our concern here is with the end of the book. What is all this business about a whirlwind? And what does this have to do with caring for the earth? More precisely, what does the end of this tale tell us about our place in the world? Who exactly is at the center of things? But before we examine the end, let's recall how we get there. Listen again to this fascinating and illuminating story.[34]

Deprived of wealth, posterity, and health, Job refuses to follow his wife's advice that he curse God and die. He is, he insists, a blameless man. He does not curse God, but he does curse the day of his birth. He laments. And then his friends—Eliphaz, Bildad, Zophar—come to offer consolation. They sit with him in silence for a week, and then they offer their own explanations as to why he is suffering. Divine discipline for sin. Retribution for the wrongdoings of his children. Punishment for past iniquity.

Job responds to the third-rate theodicies of his erstwhile friends, attacking their presumption to speak for God and his inscrutable way with the world. Job reaffirms his innocence, and he (again) voices his lament. Finally, he lodges his own complaint directly at God: I'm innocent, he says. I am a just and blameless man.

At long last, God addresses Job. Speaking from a whirlwind, with an onslaught of questions piled one on the other, God responds to Job's lament and his complaint. But God's response is strange, off-putting, elliptical, seemingly not to the point. God's first response is all about cosmology and meteorology and hydrology and animal husbandry and ornithology.

First, earth and sky. "Where were you, Job, when I laid the foundation of the earth? Who was it, Job, who marked the boundaries of the sea? Have you, Job, commanded the morning to come? Were you around, O Job, when the primordial waters were fixed in place? Have you journeyed to the underworld or traveled the expanse of the earth? Did you separate light from darkness? And what about the weather? Do you, Job, know where the snow and hail are stored? Have you knowledge of where lightning comes from or whence the east wind roars? And what, O Job, of the rain? Have you brought it to the desert? Do you provide water to the wasteland? Is it you who begets the ice and frost and snow? Have you, Job, placed the Pleiades in the sky, or fixed Orion and the Great Bear in their celestial circuit?"

Then, animals and birds. "Can you, Job, provide food for the hungry lion? Do you provide for the raven its prey? Do you, Job, know when the wild mountain goats give birth or the wild deer have their young? Is it you, O Job, who let the wild ass go free or made the ox forever wild? And what of the ostrich? Was it your design that it leave its eggs on the earth and deal cruelly with its young? Was it according to your wisdom, Job, that the hawk soar south or the vulture suck the blood of the slain?"

After this cascade of questions, God demands an answer: "Anyone who argues with God must respond" (Job 40:2). Job has publicly reproached God, and now God awaits his answer. Job simply states, "I am small." And so he places his hand over his mouth. Having spoken once, of things he claimed to know but really did not, he will not make the same mistake twice. He has forcibly been shown the limits of his knowledge and power. And so after declaring that he would approach God "like a prince," Job engages in an act of self-humiliation. He now knows his place, and it is not at the center of things.

But this initial exchange, it seems, is not enough, for Job's withdrawal from the disputation may not signal genuine understanding but rather fear and resignation. And so God speaks again from out of the whirlwind. A question remains: Would you discredit my justice? Would you condemn me to justify yourself? And once again a cavalcade of questions issues forth from God's mouth. Job's confrontation with the wild and the inexplicable and the chaotic is not yet complete.

The first questions concern the Behemoth. "What kind of creature is this—this animal of animals that I made just as I made you, O Job? Clearly this animal par excellence is an exceedingly powerful creature. There is strength in its loins and power in its belly. Its sinews and muscles are tight and strong. Its bones are like bronze and its limbs like bars of iron. Indeed, this creature ranks first among my works. Equally clear is the fact that Behemoth lives a life free of fear. The mountains yield food and the marshlands provide shelter. No flooding river or rushing current frightens this creature. The Behemoth, the hippopotamus, fears nothing, least of all capture by humans. Can you, O Job, capture him with hooks, or pierce his nose with a snare? Of course not, for no human is a match for Behemoth. Only I, God, am able to take its life."

Then God speaks of Leviathan, the sea creature par excellence. The voice from the whirlwind begins with a barrage of questions. "Can you, Job, draw out Leviathan with a fishhook? Can you put a rope in its nose, like some captive slave? Can you, Job, make Leviathan your servant? Can you play with it like a pet bird or walk it like a pet dog? Can you, O Job, harpoon it or spear it, to sell in the market? O Job, lay hands or eyes on Leviathan and you will never do it again. Give up hope, my Job, of ever capturing Leviathan.

"For who can face Leviathan and be safe? Mighty is its strength and splendid is its frame. Armored like a warrior, who can pierce its coat of double mail or open the doors of his mouth, ringed with fearsome teeth? Its back has rows of shields so tightly sealed together that no air can pass between them. Its snorting throws out light, and from its mouth come flaming torches. Smoke pours from its nostrils, and its breath sets coals ablaze. Its fleshy neck is firm, its chest hard as rock. Neither sword nor spear nor javelin has any effect on it. Arrows cannot make it flee, clubs are counted as chaff, and it laughs at the rattling of the lance. When Leviathan rises up, even the mighty are afraid. Awesome and terrifying is the power of Leviathan, the crocodilian sea monster. On earth it has no equal."

With this the voice stops, and Job again responds. After the submission and silence of his first response come repentance and acceptance. Job acknowledges that God "can do all things" and that no purpose of God's can be thwarted. And he confesses that he has "uttered what I did not understand, things too wonderful for me, which I did not know" (Job 42:1–2). After expressing his desire to see God, Job now has that desire fulfilled. He has heard God with his own ears and now sees God with his own eyes. He receives not a theodicy but a vision—a vision of God. And with this vision comes a transformation of how he understands himself and the world and his place within it.

What should we make of all this? And more exactly, how does this enigmatic text address the question, who is at the center of things? First, it is clear that we humans are not at the center of things. In this text our anthropocentric pretensions to superiority are laid waste. We, like Job, are put in our rightful place. As Bill McKibben argues, in these speeches "God is describing a world without people—a world that existed long before people, and that seems to have its own independent meaning. Most of the action takes place long before the appearance of humans, and on a scale so powerful and vast that we are small indeed in the picture of things."[35] McKibben further notes that God is "untroubled by the notion of a place where no man lives" and in fact "makes it rain there even though it has no human benefit at all." And so, he concludes, "The first meaning, I think, of God's speech to Job is that we are a part of the whole order of creation—simply a part."[36] In Aldo Leopold's words, we are "plain member and citizen" of the land-community.[37] God, not humanity, is at the center of things.

An implication of this, second, is that "man, who is only one of God's creatures, is *not* the measure of all things and the sole test of the worth of creation."[38] We may be (or try to be) the measurer of all things, but we are not the measure of all things. Behemoth and Leviathan, not to mention the mountain goat and the wild ass, remind us that the scope of God's creative will reaches farther than any human individual or community. Indeed, God nurtures that which is hostile and alien to us. Carol Newsom puts this point especially well:

> The contrast between the horizon [of meaning] within which Job presents himself and the horizon within which God asks Job to locate himself could not be sharper. Job's primary horizon of meaning was the village and the family. God challenges

the parochialism of Job's moral imagination by making the starting point nothing less than the whole of creation. We, too, often tend to think of the moral world as having simply to do with the relation of humans to other humans. Yet human abuse of creation in the wanton destruction of the environment should make modern readers particularly alert to the significance of God's insistence that the questions of human identity and vocation must first be answered in the context of the whole of creation.[39]

It is only in light of the creation-encompassing theocentrism of Scripture that we can answer the questions of who we are and what our specific calling is.

Discerning identity and vocation have to do, third, with shaping and remaking our moral imagination.[40] This text asks of us, as of Job, extended and disciplined attentiveness. Before he is commanded to act, Job is asked to contemplate. Look, behold, appreciate—especially that which is wild, repugnant, dangerous. Newsom's observation is to the point: "There are probably not many ethics courses in colleges or seminaries that spend the first three days in silence—one day in the forest, one day at the shore of the sea, and one night in a field gazing at the stars. Yet something like that is what God requires of Job as the starting point for a new moral understanding."[41] Conduct flows from character, doing from being, actions from basic attitudes. This text prods us to cultivate certain virtues—attentiveness, gratitude, humility—precisely the kind of habitual dispositions required of those called by God to care for the earth.

Fourth, this text adumbrates a moral order. The divine speeches in particular evoke a specific vision of the good. This vision is of a world in which all creatures—even the wild and the untamed, the dangerous and the frightening—have a place. In Newsom's words: "The account of creation in the divine speeches contains metaphors that are strongly suggestive of the formation of a moral order. The imagery of place, limit, and nonencroachment recurs frequently . . . [and is] a language of balance, what we would speak of today as an ecological language."[42] Such imagery and language, as Newsom suggests, generates an ethic of proper place and appropriate limit. In short, the moral order envisioned by this text is an ethic of ecological hospitality and responsibility.

Fifth, in this text not only is the human decentered and properly placed among God's creatures, but something of the character of the created world is revealed. The natural world, not withstanding the chaotic and the unfathomable, displays order and patterned regularity. By analogy, therefore, we can reasonably believe in a moral order, even in the midst of suffering and even if there is much we do not and cannot understand. In the words of Robert Gordis:

> The basic theme—that the universe is a mystery to man—is explicitly set forth in the God speeches. There are, in addition, two other significant ideas implicit in the Lord's words. . . . The first is that the universe was not created exclusively for man's use, and therefore neither it nor its Creator can be judged solely by man's standards and goals. The second is even more significant. The natural world,

though it is beyond man's ken, reveals to him its beauty and order. It is therefore reasonable for man to believe that the universe also exhibits a moral order with pattern and meaning, though it is beyond man's power fully to comprehend.[43]

In other words, it makes sense to believe in a moral order, given that the world is a place of natural order—of beauty and meaning—whose value derives from God its Maker and Sustainer.

Sixth and last, in a subtle but profound way the divine speeches offer comfort to the Jobs of the world, for they connect knowledge of the created order with the isolation and pain of suffering. In his perceptive and eloquent set of meditations, *The Embers and the Stars*, Erazim Kohák ruminates on the gift of night and the power of natural places and, in so doing, provides insightful reflections on this very theme:

> The human alone, surrounded by the gleaming surfaces of his artifacts, cannot bear the pain. He can do that only when the grief can disperse, radiate out and be absorbed. Fellow humans and their works, bearing the same burden, cannot absorb it. . . .
>
> To reconcile, that is what the forest does, silent and accepting, as if God were present therein, taking the grief unto Himself. When humans no longer think themselves alone, masters of all they survey, when they discern the humility of their place in the vastness of God's creation, then that creation and its God can share the pain. For the Christians, the Cross symbolized that reality; confronted with it, the human is not freed from grief, but he is no longer alone to bear it. It is taken up, shared.
>
> That is the age-old wisdom of the book of Job. . . . When God speaks, the framework is different. He speaks not of pain but of the vastness of the creation, of the gazelle in her mountain fastness and the mighty creature of the deep sea. God is not avoiding the issue. He is teaching Job the wisdom of bearing the pain that can neither be avoided nor abolished but can be shared when there is a whole living creation to absorb it.[44]

In other words, God's whirlwind speeches forcibly remind Job not only of God's power but also of the expanse and mystery of the created world—a world not of human making. Such a world, beyond human control or knowledge, is able somehow to absorb the weight of human sorrow. As Belden Lane eloquently observes, in times of grief and pain there is great solace in fierce landscapes.[45] When God is at the center, and the human thereby displaced, there is a world wide and wild enough to absorb the pain of human suffering.

So who is at the center of things? The book of Job is clear: God is at the center of things. Though a blow to our pride, that is the way things are. We must acknowledge our place—an important place to be sure, but also a limited, circumscribed place—and in so doing allow God's wild creatures to have their rightful place. Such is the radical theocentrism of the book of Job.

What Holds the World Together? (Colossians 1:15–20)

Claims to power abound in our age. Best-selling books present their three- or seven- or twelve-step program to success. Sports teams compete for the chance to chant, "We're number one!" Corporations maneuver for market share and consumer dollars. Nations vie for supremacy, often using violence to achieve their ignoble ends. Religious groups promise spiritual enlightenment to those who join their ranks. The claims to power are legion—in our age as in the past. But what is authentic power, and in what or in whom can real power be found? More exactly, what (if anything) holds the world together?

As we seek to explore these questions there is perhaps no better biblical text than Colossians, for in this book Paul addresses, among other things, a cluster of questions concerning power.[46] We will focus on Colossians 1:15–20, but first, a few brief remarks to set the context. After greeting the saints and faithful of Colossae—a small town in the Lycus Valley of Asia Minor, near Laodicea and Hierapolis—Paul speaks of his prayers for the community. He thanks God for the Colossian Christians, for their faith, love, and hope are evidence that the gospel is bearing fruit among them. And Paul asks that the sisters and brothers at Colossae may grow in the knowledge of God, being "made strong with all the strength that comes from his [God's] glorious power" and "prepared to endure everything with patience" (1:11).

They are, furthermore, to give thanks joyfully to God, acknowledging "the Father, who has enabled you to share in the inheritance of the saints in light" (1:12). Why such gratitude? Because God "has rescued us from the power of darkness and transferred us into the kingdom of his beloved Son, in whom we have redemption, the forgiveness of sins" (1:13–14). With echoes of the exodus, Paul declares that God rescues his people and transfers them from one kingdom into another. But what is the nature of this kingdom, and who is this beloved Son? Listen again to Paul and to this familiar text.[47]

Your questions are good ones. To answer them I, Paul, have a poem.

He is the image
of the invisible God,
the firstborn of all creation,
for in him were created all things
in heaven and on earth,
things visible and invisible,
whether thrones or dominions,
whether rulers or powers,
all things have been created
through him and for him.

And he is before all things,
   and all things hold together in him.
And he is the head
   of the body, the church.

He is the beginning,
   the firstborn from the dead,
   so that he might become in all things himself preeminent,
      for in him all the fullness was pleased to dwell
      and through him to reconcile all things to him,
         whether things on earth or things in heaven,
      by making peace through the blood of his cross.

Let me explain. The Son of whom I speak is the very image (*eikōn*) of the invisible God. You Colossians are awash in images, especially of the emperor.[48] Images of Caesar are everywhere. Public festivals and ceremonies that commemorate him are a pervasive feature of your everyday life. But God's beloved Son, not Caesar, is the *true* visible image of the invisible God. Christ is the proper image, for in Christ the nature of God has been perfectly revealed.[49]

Christ is, furthermore, the firstborn of all creation (*prōtotokos pasēs ktiseōs*). Please don't misunderstand me. Christ is not the first being to be created; rather, he is the one by whom the entire creation came into being. As *firstborn*, Christ is both prior to and supreme over creation. And Christ is the firstborn of *all* creation. Christ's reach is cosmic in scope. Nothing is excluded from his sovereign reign.

I know this is an audacious claim, so allow me to say more. Christ is the firstborn because in him were created all things (*hoti en autō ektisthē ta panta*) in heaven and on earth (*en tois ouranois kai epi tēs gēs*), things visible and invisible (*ta horata kai ta aorata*). All things.[50] The universe is not the product of any heavenly principality or power. Neither is it the work of any human ruler or kingdom. In Christ, not Caesar, all things came to be. In Christ, the true image of God, the entire cosmos was created.

Let me be even more specific. The "all things" includes the heavenly and earthly realities of our world that some suppose are ultimate: thrones (*thronoi*), dominions (*kyriotētes*), rulers (*archai*), and powers (*exousiai*).[51] All heavenly principalities and powers are subordinate to Christ.[52] All earthly kings and rulers are subject to Christ. These "powers" are not ultimate; they do not have the last word. *All things* have been created and *continue* to exist (*ta panta ektistai*) through him and for him (*di' autou kai eis auton*). Christ is the agent by whom and the goal for whom creation exists.

But there is more.[53] The mystery deepens. *Christ* is before all things (*pro pantōn*) and all things (*ta panta*) in him are held together (*en autō synestēken*). Before all things. Christ comes first—in both time and status. And, most amazing yet, all things cohere, hang together, in Christ. Christ is the sustainer of the universe and the unifying principle of life. The world hangs together *not* by virtue of any heavenly power. Creation coheres *not* because Caesar reigns. Rather, all things hold together in and through and for *Christ*.[54]

Further, this integrating, coherence-making Lord is the head of the body (*hē kephalē tou sōmatos*), the church (*tēs ekklēsias*). Christ is not only lord and ruler but source and origin of the church. Christ animates and energizes the body, which is us, his people.[55] Therefore, your allegiance is to your assembly of the Lord Christ, not the Roman city. Your identity is found in the church—a community whose founding story is rooted in the history of Israel and the story of Messiah Jesus—rather than in stories of Roman conquest and rule. Your head is not Caesar but Christ.

But there is yet more. Christ is the beginning (*archē*).[56] What does this mean? Not only is Christ the firstborn of all creation, but he is the firstborn *from the dead* (*prōtotokos ek tōn nekrōn*). Christ has been raised from the dead—the first fruits of those who have died, the firstborn among his sisters and brothers.[57] Christ is the founder of a new people.[58] With his death and resurrection the long-expected new age has begun!

Christ has become the firstborn from the dead so that he might become (*hina genētai*) in all things himself preeminent (*en pasin autos prōteuōn*).[59] No thrones or dominions, no rulers or powers can usurp the place of Christ. This preeminence of Christ was the very purpose of the resurrection. And Christ is the beginning, the firstborn from the dead, because in him (*en autō*) all the fullness (*pan to plērōma*) was pleased to dwell (*eudokēsen katoikēsai*). In Christ the completeness of God's self-revelation was focused.[60] Contrary to what you see and hear in Colossae, my sisters and brothers, Caesar is not preeminent, the fullness of deity. That claim properly belongs to Christ.

In Christ all the fullness of God was pleased to dwell, as I said, and pleased through him to reconcile all things to him (*di' autou apokatallaxai ta panta eis auton*).[61]

Through Christ—the agent of redemption as well as creation.
To reconcile—to resolve the deep-seated estrangement of the
    ages.
All things—whether things on earth or things in heaven.
To him—Christ is the goal as well as origin.

And this cosmic reconciliation has been effected, note well, by a
curious kind of peacemaking (*eirēnopoiēsas*). This peace is secured
not through violence or conquest or the merciless bloodletting of
others. This is no *Pax Romana*. This peace is achieved through
the blood of his cross (*dia tou haimatos tou staurou autou*). This is a
different peace—the shalom of the kingdom of God—and a very
different peacemaking—one in which a person voluntarily suffers for
others and in so doing absorbs evil. Making peace through the blood
of his cross. Allelulia and Amen!

Where, then, can power be found? In Christ. How is this power made
manifest? In the creation and preservation of the cosmos and in the cross
and resurrection. What (or better, who) holds the world together? Christ, the
image of the invisible God, the beginning, the firstborn. James Dunn's concluding comments on this text serve as a fitting summary: "The vision is vast.
The claim is mind-blowing. It says much for the faith of these first Christians
that they should see in Christ's death and resurrection quite literally the key
to resolving the disharmonies of nature and the inhumanities of humankind,
that the character of God's creation and God's concern for the universe in its
fullest expression could be so caught and encapsulated for them in the cross
of Christ."[62]

While it may appear at first glance that this text is far removed from matters
ecological, there is in fact much here that bears a closer look. What ecological
wisdom can be gained from this rich and suggestive text? First, our Redeemer
is our Creator. There is no dichotomy between the God who creates and the
God who redeems. F. F. Bruce summarizes this important insight: "So then
the one through whom the divine work of redemption has been accomplished
is the one through whom the divine act of creation took place in the beginning. His mediatorial relation to the created universe provides a setting to
the gospel of salvation which helps his people to appreciate that gospel all
the more."[63] Our Redeemer is our Creator. Not only the substance but the
very style of this poem leads the reader to this conclusion. In the words of
N. T. Wright, "The parallelism between its two halves . . . invites the reader
or listener to draw the conclusion that the creator is also the redeemer, and
vice versa."[64]

This implies, second, that creation and redemption are two acts of one divine
drama. In respect to both creation and redemption, Christ is the firstborn. In
regard to both, Christ is agent and instrument of divine action. Dunn, among
others, notes the striking cohesiveness of the divine economy: "The complemen-
tarity (rather than antithesis) between God's creative activity and redemptive
activity is in a most striking way brought out and maintained by the crucial
middle term, Christ, in, through, and to whom God has accomplished both his
creative and his redemptive purposes."[65] In Christ the divine economy is one.

Third, redemption is the restoration of creation. Redemption does not mean the annihilation of creation but rather its renewal. Salvation is not escape from the earth but the reclamation of the earth. Soteriology (like eschatology) is earth-affirming. Dunn puts this point especially well: "What is being claimed is quite simply and profoundly that the divine purpose in the act of reconciliation and peacemaking was to restore the harmony of the original creation, to bring into renewed oneness and wholeness 'all things,' 'whether things on the earth or things in the heavens.'"[66] This fits, argues Wright, the "creational and covenantal monotheism" of the Jewish tradition, which insists that the covenant God of Israel "will, in fulfilling that covenant, reclaim and redeem his whole creation from that which at present corrupts and threatens it."[67] To paraphrase the medieval adage, grace does not destroy nature but restores it.

Fourth, Christ is Lord, and his reign is cosmic in scope. The ubiquitous "all things" thumps like a constant drumbeat throughout this text, forcibly reminding us that nothing lies outside the creative and redemptive scope of God's grace. As Ralph Martin notes, "Paul goes out of his way to accentuate the teaching on cosmic reconciliation, with no part of the universe unaffected (1:15, 20) and no hostile power unsubdued (2:15)."[68] All things, all things, all things. Christ is Lord over all.

Fifth and finally, this redemption and this rule have begun. The new age has been inaugurated, though not yet consummated. Though caesars of various sorts are still very much with us, everywhere asserting their power and projecting their images, Christ is Lord, here and now, wherever his reign of shalom breaks out. As Wright argues, "The Colossian poem . . . is asserting, astonishingly from the Jewish perspective, that this final redemption, with all that it signified, has already taken place in Jesus Christ."[69] Despite all too many appearances to the contrary, Christ is Lord and he will reign, forever and ever.

While many have commented on this powerful text, none have done so as eloquently as Joseph Sittler. For this pioneering ecological theologian, Colossians 1:15–20 was a biblical touchstone. Therefore, I conclude with words taken from his most famous public address.

These verses sing out their triumphant and alluring music between two huge and steady poles—"Christ" and "all things." Even the Ephesian letter, rich and large as it is in its vision of the church, moves not within so massive an orbit as this astounding statement of the purpose of God. For it is here declared that the sweep of God's restorative action in Christ is no smaller than the six-times repeated *ta panta*. Redemption is the name for this will, this action, this concrete Man who is God with us and God for us—and all things are permeable to his cosmic redemption because all things subsist in him. He comes to all things, not as stranger, for he is the firstborn of all creation, and in him all things were created. He is not only the matrix and *prius* of all things; he is the intention, the fullness, and the integrity of all things: for all things were created through him and for him. Nor are all things a tumbled multitude of facts in an unrelated mess, for in him all things hold together.[70]

God is with us. All things subsist in Christ. In him all things hold together.

What Does God's Good Future Look Like? (Revelation 21:1–22:5)

Disembodied spirits floating in the clouds. Angels playing harps. The earth destroyed and immortal souls clinging to the bosom of Jesus. These are only a few ideas about the future found in the minds of contemporary Christians. But do they adequately capture the biblical vision of the future? According to Scripture, what is the nature of the promised new age? What is the biblical portrayal of life to come, when God's purposes for creation are fulfilled? What does God's good future look like?[71]

To answer such questions I turn to Revelation 21–22. Perhaps no other book is more scrutinized today than Revelation, and yet the early church debated its presence in the canon, Luther relegated it to a subordinate position, and Calvin wrote no commentary on it because, he is reported to have said, "I just don't understand it." To attempt a reading of this highly symbolic apocalyptic text is, therefore, dangerous indeed—foolhardy perhaps. And yet interpret it we must, despite the considerable dangers. As we shall see, this enigmatic last book of the Bible contains much insight and wisdom, especially as we in the twenty-first century, like our brothers and sisters of the first century, wrestle with the principalities and powers of our age. My question is this: What is the nature and character of God's good future? Look again at what this amazing and visually stunning text portrays of our common future.[72]

> And behold, I, John, saw yet another sight.
> Like wizened Isaiah of old, before my eyes there appeared
> a new heaven and a new earth,
> for the first heaven and the first earth
> had passed away—
> the former troubles forgotten,
> the former things remembered no more.
> The chaotic sea,
> out of which the blasphemous beast arose,
> this threatening, abysmal sea was no more.
> And I saw the holy city—the new Jerusalem—
> coming down out of heaven.
> No Babylon this—fallen and frenzied and foul;
> on the contrary, this City of Shalom came from God,
> like a beautiful bride adorned for her husband.

And I heard a loud voice from the throne:
   "Behold, the home of God is among humans.
   Like the Spirit-holding tabernacle in the wilderness,
   like the Word made flesh,
   God will pitch his tent with mortals,
   and they will be God's people,
   and God himself, in person, will be with them.
   And God will wipe every tear from their sorrowing eyes,
   and death will be no more,
   and soulful mourning and crying and pain will be no more,
   for the first things, the former things, have passed away."

And then the One seated on the throne,
in a voice winsome and wild, spoke:
   "Behold, I am making all things new!
   Do you not perceive it?
   A way in the wilderness, rivers in the desert.
   Do you not believe it?
   These words are trustworthy and true. It is done!
   For I am the Alpha and the Omega,
   the Beginning and the End,
   the All-Encompassing One.
   To the thirsty, like the woman at the well,
   I give the water of life.
   To the victor, to those who endure,
   I will be their God and they my children.
   But the cowards, the faithless, the vile, the murderers,
   the sexually immoral, the sorcerers, the idolaters, the liars—
   their place is the burning lake of sulfurous fire.
   Be purged of these practices,
   for the Holy City is a place of righteousness and justice."

Then one of the seven angels showed me the bride of the Lamb—
the Lamb that was slain and now reigns as Lord.
God's messenger, in the power of the Spirit, carried me away,
up to a great, high mountain.
From there the angel showed me the holy city Jerusalem,
coming down out of heaven from God.
It was a sight beyond my wildest imaginings,
my deepest yearnings—
a healing balm for a broken heart.
This heaven-sent, earth-bound city
exuded the weight of God's glory.

Ezekiel's old homecoming vision came alive:
gates on all four sides, each one named for an Israelite tribe,
foundations poured by the great good work of each apostle,
walls of jasper, streets of gold.
A city jeweled with the mineral wealth of the world.
A stupendously enormous city.
A city of perpetually open gates.
An earthly city of safety, and beauty, and shalom.
Our refuge, God's home.

But I saw no temple in this perfect city.
No house for God.
No local place of divine presence.
For the Lord God Almighty and the victorious Lamb—
they were the temple.
God was everywhere immediately present.
So all was holy, nothing common, no place profane.
The very presence of God hallowed everything.
And thus this heaven-on-earth city needed no sun or moon,
for the very glory of God was its light.
The Lamb was the lamp that illumined the way.

And all nations walked by its light,
drawn like birds to the brightness of the dawn.
And the rulers of the earth brought their cultural treasures
through the never-shut gates of this city:
from Midian and Sheba and Tarshish,
from Antioch and Alexandria and Athens,
from Corinth and Laodicea and, yes, even from Rome.
And the nations, people of every tribe and tongue,
carried their goods into this luminous city:
fruits and vegetables grown with tender care,
animals and children raised with familial love,
canoes and cribs crafted with hard-won skill,
dances and songs of exuberant joy,
stories and tales laced with aged wisdom,
words smithed in the forge of respect,
swords burnished into peaceful plowshares.
The true wealth of nations flowed like an ever-rushing stream
into the holy city.

Then the angel showed me the river of the water of life,
bright as crystal, cascading from the throne of God and the Lamb

right smack-dab through the middle of this gardened city.
On the banks, on both sides of this azure-pure river, grew trees.
From seeds sown from the very tree of life,
this flourishing forest, well watered and leaf-full,
produced twelve kinds of fruit,
one for each month—sustenance the year round.
And the leaves of the trees are for the healing of the nations.
No more trees felled for battering rams
to lay siege to medieval cities.
No more trees cut to make sailing masts for colonial warships.
No more trees pulped for paper propaganda
to fuel the fires of ethnic cleansing.
These trees are for life.
These trees are for the healing of the nations.

And in this city, on this heavenly earth, the curse will be no more.
The weight of inherited sorrow will be lifted.
The taint of sin washed clean by the blood of the Lamb.
And the servants of the Lamb will worship God.
And they will see God face to face.
And God's name will be on their foreheads,
marked as God's own forever.
And the Lord God himself will be their light.
And they will reign with God forever and ever!

What sense can we make of this apocalyptic vision? What does this vision tell us about God's good future? First, God's good future is earthly. It includes a renewed heaven and earth. Having brought this world of wonders into existence, covenanted with it, and persistently worked to redeem it, God does not give up on it. This vision is of a new heaven and a new earth (*ouranon kainon kai gēn kainēn*), but the new here connotes new in quality, in contrast to what is old.[73] In keeping with the great vision of Isaiah 65, which (with Ezek. 40–48) informs these chapters of Revelation, God's good future is of a renewed heaven and earth.[74] Eugene Boring captures well this sense of the Seer's vision:

Even though the first earth and the first heaven have passed away, the scene continues very much as a this-worldly scene. This is due, in part, to the fact that the other world can be spoken of only in language and images from this world. More importantly, it is an affirmation of the significance of this world and history, even after the new heaven and new earth arrive. The vision of God in chapter 4 is fulfilled: God is the creator. Yet the one who does not quench a smoking wick or break a bruised reed (Isa. 42:3; Matt. 12:20) does not junk the cosmos and start anew—he renews the old and brings it to fulfillment. The advent of the heavenly city does not abolish all human efforts to build a decent earthly civilization but fulfills them. God does not make "all new things," but "all things new" (21:5).[75]

Not all new things, but all things new. The new, in short, implies continuity with the old. New means renewed, renovated, reclaimed.

Second, in God's good future God himself will dwell with us and with all our creaturely kin. In language reminiscent of John 1:14 and Ezekiel 37:27, the text declares that the home of God (*skēnē tou theou*) is among humans (*anthrōpōn*), that God will tent among us (*skēnōsei met' autōn*).[76] Indeed, Revelation 21:3 emphasizes that God himself (*autos ho theos*) will be with us, and we will be his people. In language rooted deeply in the Old Testament (cf. Exod. 6:7; Lev. 26:12; Jer. 7:23; Ezek. 37:27; Hosea 2:23), the text makes clear that in the holy city God will be known face to face (22:4) and we will belong to God, his name emblazoned on our foreheads (22:4). God will dwell with us, for creation is the home of God.

This implies, third, that in God's good future the separation between heaven and earth is overcome. Life in the new Jerusalem is literally a heaven on earth. The now-distinct realms of heaven and earth are in the future braided together. And they are conjoined because of God's initiative. The holy city comes down (*katabainousan*) from heaven (21:2, 10). Its arrival is no human achievement, its reality no product of human technology or ingenuity. The new Jerusalem is no tower of Babel. In keeping with God's character, God comes to us. As in the parable of the running father (Luke 15:11–32), God initiates redemption. "No longer will there be a great separation between heaven and earth. It is not so much that the redeemed shall be taken to heaven but rather that God will come among us and be part of the new Jerusalem. In the incarnation of Christ, God came among human beings as one of them, but still in a hidden fashion. Now, in this new creation, God will not be hidden, but will come among redeemed humanity in a direct, unmediated way."[77] God comes among us. Heaven on earth. Then we shall know face to face.

Fourth, in God's good future, evil and its consequences are no more. Seven (the perfect number) elements of the old order are abolished, vanquished with the same formula (*ouk estin/estai eti*). The sea, symbolic of primeval chaos and the abode of the beast, is no more. Death itself, not just untimely death, is no more. Mourning and crying and pain are no more (cf. Isa. 65:19–20; Rev. 7:17). So no more death squad murders in the dark of night. No more mothers and fathers mourning their kids killed in battle. No more stillbirths. No more cancer or ebola or AIDS. And all that is under God's curse is no more. The curse of Genesis 3 is repealed, lifted, abrogated. In the words of the old Christmas hymn "Joy to the World," redemption extends "far as the curse is found." And last, the night is no more. The realm of darkness and deception is banished. In sum, this apocalyptic vision vividly portrays a world of shalom.

Fifth, in God's good future we inhabit a most unusual city. The holy city is precisely that—holy—for God is everywhere. There is no temple, no set-apart place, for God himself is the temple. A person has replaced a building. Thus, nothing in this city is profane; nothing is not sacred; all is for the service of God.[78] And this city is a gardened city. In this city flows the river of life, watering (among other things) trees that line its banks. These trees, descendants of the tree of life (Gen. 2), provide fruit year-round, sustenance in every season, and their leaves are a healing balm for the nations. People of all kinds stream into this city, whose gates never close and whose light never ceases. Kings and paupers, friends and enemies, nations both holy and heathen—they all bring their glory and honor to the city (cf. Isa. 60). George Caird captures well this important feature of John's vision:

> Nothing from the old order which has value in the sight of God is debarred from entry into the new. John's heaven is no world-denying Nirvana, into which man may escape from the incurable ills of sublunary existence, but the seal of affirmation on the goodness of God's creation. The treasure that men find laid up in heaven turns out to be **the treasures and wealth of the nations**, the best they have known and loved on earth redeemed of all imperfections and transfigured by the radiance of God. Nothing is excluded but what is **obscene and false**, that is, totally alien to the character of God. Nowhere in the New Testament do we find a more eloquent statement than this of the all-embracing scope of God's redemptive work.[79]

What, then, does God's good future look like? These last chapters of Revelation beckon us with an earthly vision of life made good and right and whole. Heaven and earth are renewed and are one. God dwells with us, at home in creation. Evil and its minions are no more. All is sacred, fit to serve God. All is made new. In short, a world of shalom. Caird's insight into the pastoral nature of this text provides a fitting conclusion:

> The pastoral relevance of the new Jerusalem to the needs of the seven churches becomes still clearer when for the first time since the opening of the visions we hear the voice of God. John is told to **write this**, because this voice from the ultimate future has something urgent to say to the critical present: '**I am making all things new.**' This is not an activity of God within the new creation, after the old has been cast as rubbish to the void; it is the process of re-creation by which the old is transformed into the new. In Smyrna and Thyatira, in Sardis and Laodicea, in all places of his dominion, God is forever making all things new, and on this depends the hope of the world.[80]

Biblical Wisdom and Ecological Vision

Each of these texts holds much wisdom for shaping our ecological imagination. And we have examined only five texts. There is much, much more to explore in Scripture.[81] But these suggestive biblical texts are sufficient to answer some important questions. Where are we? With a plethora of other creatures on our home planet. With whom does God make a covenant? God makes an everlasting and unconditional covenant with the earth and all its creatures. Who is at the center of things? God in all his magnificent and mysterious glory. Who holds the world together? The cosmic Christ, the Lord of creation and redemption. And what does God's good future look like? It is a glorious future—of a renewed heavenly earth, with a cleansing river and healing trees; of a gardened city, gates open to receive the peoples and riches of the world; of God dwelling with us at home in creation. A world of shalom.

Such a powerful ecological vision—a grand sweeping vision of our home and God's economy—should inform how we do our theology and our ethics. No Christian orthodoxy worth its name can ignore this biblical wisdom. Further, this kind of biblically informed theology and ethic should shape how we live— our orthopraxy—for we Christians are a people of the Book, and that Book and its story mold our lives. To the task of shaping a theology and an ethic, and our individual and communal lives, we now turn.

how should we
think of the earth?

a theology and ethic of care for the earth

It is the Holy Spirit who, everywhere diffused, sustains all things, causes them to grow, and quickens them in heaven and in earth.

John Calvin[1]

Given what we have learned about where we are, about the groaning of creation, about why we are in the ecological mess we are in, and about what the Bible has to say, how then are we to think of the earth? More exactly, how are we to think and speak about God and God's relationship to the earth and all its creatures, in light of the fact that everything is connected to everything else, that in the last twenty-four hours three species disappeared forever, that our materialistic patterns of consumption are consuming us and much of the world around us, that Scripture from Genesis to Revelation clearly envisions a world fashioned and loved and renewed by God? And if theology is more (though never less) than thinking clearly and speaking rightly about God—if it involves attaining wisdom (*sapientia*) as well as knowledge (*scientia*)—then it concerns how we act, how we live, how we order our individual and collective lives.

This chapter is a modest attempt to articulate a theology and ethic of care for the earth. It is, in other words, an attempt to state what I (and many other Christians) believe about God and the world and our human responsibilities in that world. I begin by setting forth, in summary fashion, my own theological

111

perspective—my own ecological theology. This is more than merely a restatement of the doctrine of creation or a reformulated theology of nature. Ecological theology involves rethinking all of theology in ecological terms.

In the second half of the chapter I focus on ethics, for if theology seeks wisdom as well as knowledge, then theology is inextricably wedded to ethics, thinking to acting, reflection to life. Thus my question in the latter section is, what kind of ecological ethic emerges from this ecological theology? After a short survey of various perspectives in ecological ethics, I (again all too briefly) put forward my own position, the details of which will be fleshed out in chapter 6. As I will argue, the most promising ecological ethic is one that asks not primarily, what do we need to do? but, who do we need to be?

Evangelical Theology and Care for the Earth

What are the essentials of an evangelical theology of care for the earth?[2] What would such a theology look like? If we claim to bear witness to the gospel, the good news, then what is so good? What exactly is the evangel we evangelicals proclaim? While this is not the place for an extensive answer to these important questions,[3] at least some directions can be given. What follows are the fundamental contours of one such theology.[4]

A Theocentric Vision

As the previous examination of Scripture has made abundantly clear, the biblical vision from Genesis to Revelation places God at the center of things. As Gene McAfee states, "Concerning nature, as concerning everything else, the perspective of both the Hebrew Bible and the New Testament is radically theocentric."[5] Neither anthropocentric (human-centered) nor biocentric (life-centered) nor ecocentric (earth-centered) alternatives can do justice to the testimony of Scripture. God is the measure of all things, not humans. God is the ultimate good, not life. God is the beginning and end, not earth. In such a vision, as portrayed in Dante's mystic rose at the end of his monumental classic *The Divine Comedy*, all things exist to praise God.

One consequence of this starting point is that both human uniqueness and the continuity that humans have with all other creatures are affirmed. Jürgen Moltmann, for example, argues that the "theocentric biblical world picture gives the human being, with his special position in the cosmos, the chance to understand himself as a member in the community of creation."[6] Paul Santmire, likewise, argues that neither cosmocentrism, with its "ethic of adoration," nor anthropocentrism, with its "ethic of exploitation," is adequate since both tacitly assume a dualism between nature and history, differing only in which has priority. Only a theocentric perspective, which refuses to accept such a dualism, is able to cultivate a proper "ethic of responsibility."[7] For these and other reasons Richard Young concludes that "the Christian Scriptures, when interpreted through a theocentric perspective, offer the most satisfying and realistic solution of the environmental problem."[8] If our news is truly good, then we must embrace a theocentric vision of the flourishing of all creatures.

The Doctrine of the Trinity

Such a theocentric vision requires, in my judgment, a recovery of the doctrine of the Trinity.[9] If the good news is truly good, then we must affirm a view of God that properly emphasizes the community of love that God is: three distinct but inseparable persons indwelling each other in a perfect communion of love.[10] And as Denis Edwards persuasively argues, "we need to retrieve a communal model of the Trinity."[11] In other words, we need to retrieve not just any old doctrine of the Trinity, but one in which the community of divine persons is emphasized. God is supreme goodness in whom there is the fullness of love. Such perfect love, to be perfect, must not be centered on itself; it cannot be self-love or private love. Perfect love, rather, flows naturally to another. It involves more than one person. Hence, God, to be the fullness of love, must be a plurality of persons. So argued medieval theologian Richard of St. Victor, using an interpersonal or social metaphor to understand something of the nature of God.[12] Among contemporary theologians, Jürgen Moltmann also emphasizes a social trinitarian understanding of God, for only a "social doctrine of the Trinity" adequately expresses "the history of the Trinity's relations of fellowship" within God's own life, with humans, and with all creation.[13]

God is constituted by three persons with a common divine-nature. While possessing a common divine-nature, each person has a distinctive person-nature determined by the unique relationships with the other persons. The Father is the Father only in virtue of the unique relationships with Son and Spirit. The Son is the Son only in virtue of the unique relationships with Father and Spirit. The Spirit is the Spirit only in virtue of the unique relationships with Father and Son. These perichoretic relations are characterized by mutuality and reciprocity.[14] The classical Christian understanding of God, therefore, makes three affirmations: God is one, God is three, and the three persons are equal.[15] In sum, the one God is a community of mutually engendering and indwelling Love.[16]

This three-personed God, furthermore, creates all things and covenants with the earth and its plethora of creatures.[17] As Genesis affirms and Job reminds us, God creates and sustains all things and enters into covenant relationship with the world. Thus the earth is home for all kinds of creatures, not only humans. All creatures—wild and woolly, dangerous and ugly—have a place, a habitat. As might be expected of a God whose very being is to be in relationship, relationality is a fundamental characteristic of the world. Being-in-relation is the nature of things. Everything is connected to everything else. In the words of

Joseph Sittler, like a fine piece of cloth, "you pull a thread here, and it vibrates throughout the whole fabric."[18] We live in a cosmos designed by a three-in-one God. As Dante (again) reminds us, in this God-wrought world it is Love that moves the spheres and holds the world together. This is, indeed, good news.

The Presence and Power of the Spirit

The natural world, however, not only exhibits an ontology of relations; it also displays its own kind of responsiveness. Scripture attests that creation in various ways responds to God's call to be and become. The earth brings forth living things. Trees clap their hands. Rivers leap in praise of God. There is, as Scott Hoezee reminds us, an "ecology of praise" in which creation's choir "sings a song of high and holy praise" for those with the ears to hear.[19] Without re-enchanting the natural order with quasi-divine status or attributing humanlike agency to birches and bears, we can rightly speak of a kind of response-ability appropriate to nonhuman creatures.[20] As ecologically-minded theologian Joseph Sittler affirms,

> Man is not alone in this world, not even when his aloneness is unalleviated by the companionship of the fellowman. The creation is a community of abounding life—from the invisible microbes to the highly visible elephants, the vastness of mountains, the sweep of the seas, the expanse of land. These companions of our creaturehood are not only *there*: they are there as things without which I cannot be at all! They surround, support, nourish, delight, allure, challenge, and talk back to us.[21]

God calls and his creatures respond—in their own unique ways—and we humans remain ever dependent on these challenging and alluring others.

One way of describing the relationship between God and creation is in terms of the work of the Holy Spirit. John Calvin, quoted in the epigraph at the beginning of this chapter, puts it well: "For it is the Spirit who, everywhere diffused, sustains all things, causes them to grow, and quickens them in heaven and in earth. Because he is circumscribed by no limits, he is excepted from the category of creatures; but in transfusing into all things his energy, and breathing into them essence, life, and movement, he is indeed plainly divine."[22] Calvin, the famous Protestant reformer who died in 1564, sounds very much like the great Cappadocian church father Basil of Caesarea, who died in 379, for Basil likewise speaks of the Holy Spirit as the life-giver present in and with all things.[23] The triune God, three-persons-in-communion, includes the Holy Spirit, who is the sustaining and sanctifying power and presence of God everywhere in the universe.

As both Genesis 1 and Psalm 104 (among other texts) attest, the Holy Spirit is the very breath of life—transfusing and quickening all creatures great and small with shalom-giving energy. God creates through the Spirit. God sustains through the Spirit. God redeems through the Spirit. God sanctifies through the Spirit. We live on a Spirit-enlivened earth. Hence, pneumatology ought not be relegated to the backwaters of theological reflection, nor the Holy Spirit seen as some vague third-rate manifestation of God. As Wesley Granberg-Michaelson affirms, "a fresh understanding of the Holy Spirit is central to the church's faith and witness on behalf of renewing the whole creation."[24] If our good news is truly good, we will have a robust sense of the Holy Spirit as the very power and presence of God.

Image-Bearers

If being-in-relation is the nature of things, then to be human is to exist in relationships. This too is good news. We are not autonomous selves, floating free in a world of atomistic individuals, as many would have us believe. Rather, we are persons related to much more than meets the eye. Created by God, we are dependent on God and made to be in a loving relationship with God. But we are also created to exist among and to live in communion with other humans. We are, as both Scripture and Aristotle remind us, social animals. And we are made from the dust—made out of and absolutely dependent upon the earth ('ādām from the 'ădāmâ, humans from the humus). Thus Sittler concludes, "I am stuck with God, stuck with my neighbor, and stuck with nature (the 'garden'), within which and out of the stuff of which I am made."[25] Humans are thoroughly relational, inextricably related to and bound up not only with God, and not only with other human beings, but also with the animals and plants, the microbes and mountains of this exquisitely complex and beautiful blue-green earth.[26]

However, though we are like all creatures made from the earth, we human earth-creatures are unique. We do not have the sight of an eagle or the strength of a lion. We do not run like a gazelle or swim like a dolphin. We cannot hear like a bat or smell like a bear. But the Bible attests that we are made in God's image, after God's likeness. This means we are God's vice-regents. We are, in other words, called to rule as God rules. Philosopher Tom Regan rightly speaks of our divine imaging in precisely these terms:

> By this I mean that we are expressly chosen by God to be God's vice-regents in our day-to-day affairs of the world; we are chosen by God, that is, to be as loving in our day-to-day dealings with the created order as God was in creating that order in the first place. In this sense, therefore, there is a morally relevant difference between human beings and every other creaturely expression of God. For it is only members of the human species who are given the awesome freedom and responsibility to be God's representatives within creation. And it is, therefore, only we humans who can be held morally blameworthy when we fail to do this, and morally praiseworthy when we succeed.[27]

If our evangel, our good news, is truly good, then we must with joy acknowledge our relatedness to God, neighbor, and natural world, and we must with humility embrace our calling as God's image-bearers. We are unique, but our uniqueness implies not superiority but service.

Sin and Salvation

If the good news is truly good, of course, we must first honestly acknowledge that all is not right with the world. Regan's reference to our moral blameworthiness painfully reminds us that the world is not the way it is supposed to be.[28] Indeed, the world is out of whack because of what we, God's image-bearers, have done and left undone. A contagion called sin haunts our lives and affects all we touch, and so we bear the weight of inherited sorrow and perpetuate in ways known and unknown the brokenness of our lives in the world. Sin, to be sure, violates God's commands. It involves missing the mark and straying from the path of righteousness. But more fundamentally it breaks God's shalom. We violate the intended shalom of God's good future. Ecologically, sin is failure to acknowledge our own finitude. As Larry Rasmussen puts it, "To sin is to overstep and overshoot finitude, deny its potentialities and its limits, and reject creatureliness."[29] Sin, as Augustine taught us long ago, is a species of pride that refuses to accept the fact that we are not God. It is a striving to be like God in ways inappropriate to what it means to be fully human. There is no gospel without an acknowledgment of how our relationships with God, self, others, and earth are broken.

If our news is truly good, furthermore, we must acknowledge that our work as earthkeeping witnesses to God's kingdom is grounded in Christ's own work. Soteriology is, of course, central for any evangelical theology, but in a properly biblical vision the full scope and extent of Christ's work should be explicit. As Colossians, among many biblical texts, makes clear, Christ's work is as wide as creation itself. It is nothing short of the restoration and consummation of all creation.[30] Scott Hoezee says it well: "The redemption that God has in store catches up not just human beings but also trees, shrubs, rivers, lions, lambs, and snakes."[31] Indeed, if Jesus did not die for white-tailed deer, redheaded woodpeckers, blue whales, and green Belizean rain forests, then he did not die for you and me. Jesus comes to save not just us but the whole world. Thus, our work is to be patterned after Christ's reconciling reign as cosmic Lord.[32]

This salvation of all things, accomplished on the cross, is vindicated in the resurrection. The resurrection pertains not only to people; it embraces the earth. As Paul argues, especially in Romans, Christ is the New Adam by whose death and resurrection all things are put right. It is this imagery of "Christ as New Adam," insists Loren Wilkinson, that "does the most justice to the full New Testament teaching of Christ's involvement in the cosmos both as Creator and Redeemer" since neither the satisfaction theory of atonement nor the moral example theory of the atonement "makes the cosmic dimensions of Christ's lordship important."[33] Christ's death on Good Friday and his resurrection on Easter, in other words, must be seen as creation-wide in their redeeming scope. Ray Van Leeuwen puts it well: "If Christ in his death wiped out evil and death, in his resurrection he vindicated the goodness of creation, its renewal and transformation into a new creation."[34] Our witness to God's kingdom is rooted, therefore, in both cross and resurrection—Good Friday and Easter. This is good news indeed.

The Role of Christ

Soteriology is, of course, intimately interconnected with christology. The question of what Christ does cannot be separated from the question of who Christ is. Work and person are interwoven. The above claims about the work of Christ imply a robust doctrine of the person of Christ. The carpenter from Galilee who dies on a Roman cross and is raised from the dead on the third day is the cosmic Christ. The crucified Christ is the cosmic Lord. To use the classical terminology, Christ is both fully human and fully divine—two natures in one person.[35] Christ is, to use the famous words of John 1:14, the very Word of God made flesh. As Joseph Sittler eloquently affirms, "At the heart of the Christian message is the affirmation that God himself enters our dying—that God, the Creator of all things, the life of all life, has himself undergone that which is most common to us humans. The one of whom the church says, 'In him is the fullness of God,' not only dies; he died a crucified convict. The Christian faith says that nothing in human experience is outside the experience of God."[36] Hence, "unless you have a crucified God, you don't have a big enough God."[37] God in person pitches his tent among us. There is no news better than this.

Therefore, because of who Christ is and what Christ does, there is gospel for us and the earth. Because Christ is the one in whom all things hang together, we know that the world is a cosmos and not chaos. Because Christ took on human flesh, we believe matter matters. Because Christ died on a cross, we eschew domination and, by contrast, rule by serving others, including the earth.[38] Because the resurrection is the vindication not only of Christ's work but of creation's goodness, we fearlessly bear witness to the way of the cross and affirm the goodness of earthly life. Because Christ is the firstfruits of the harvest, we are confident that God's good future will come. And because in Christ the restoration and renewal of creation has begun, we yearn as aching visionaries for that day when God's good future of shalom will be fully realized.

A Vision of God's Good Future

If our news is truly good, then we must embrace a properly Christian view of the future. An orthodox Christian eschatology speaks not of the annihilation of the earth but of its renewal and restoration. A Christian view of the future is earth-affirming, not earth-denying. We pray in the Lord's Prayer that God's will be done "on earth as it is in heaven." We confess in the Apostles' Creed that we believe in "the resurrection of the body and life everlasting." We sing in the Doxology that "all creatures here below" praise God. As James Nash rightly puts it, Christian hope "is not for salvation from the body, but rather the redemption of the whole body of creation."[39] The Eastern Orthodox tradition is especially instructive in this regard, with its emphasis on the transfiguration of the earth. Well-known Orthodox theologian Timothy Ware sums up this view: "Not only man's body but the whole of material creation will eventually be transfigured: 'Then I saw a new heaven *and a new earth*; for the first heaven and the first earth has passed away' (Revelation 21:1). Redeemed man is not to be snatched away from the rest of creation, but creation is to be saved and glorified along with him."[40] As many prominent theologians from the mainstream Christian tradition have insisted—from Irenaeus and Augustine through Luther, Calvin, and Wesley—we hope for the redemption of all creation. Cosmic redemption lies at the very heart of the gospel.

Thus Christian eschatology is earth-affirming. Because the earth will not be burned up but rather purified as in a refiner's fire, we can act with confidence that our actions today are not for naught. Because we yearn for a renewed heaven and earth, we can work in expectation that our faithful deeds here and now will be gathered up in the eschaton. Because we rely on God's promises and faithful character rather than human ingenuity or skill, we know that, despite the despoilation of our planetary home, the whole world is, as the song says, in God's hands. In practical terms, if our news is truly good, then recycling and composting and bicycling to work are not whistling in the dark. They are, rather, hope-filled ways of living in harmony with God's own loving, restorative way with the world.

A Community of Faith

Last but not least, if our good news is truly good, then we who call ourselves Christian must be the community God calls us to be. Our indwelling of the Christian story—both Scripture and tradition—must shape our ecclesiology. Much is at stake here, for as Paul Santmire reminds us, "The doing of the church flows from the being of the church. The works of the church flow from the grace given to the church. The life of faithful discipleship grows from the rich soil of faithful communal ritual. The church at work is totally dependent on the church at worship."[41] Santmire's own proposal that the Christian community envision itself as a "martyr church" is most suggestive.

In the life of the church, when it is faithful to its calling, I can see adumbrated the relationship with nature that God originally intended humanity to have in the garden. For, by the cross of Jesus Christ, God has intervened in our sinful history to restore us to our rightful relationship to the divine and therefore to our rightful relationship with other human beings and indeed with the whole world of nature. I can also see fragmentary signs of a communion with nature within the life of the church that is totally new, that is unprecedented, that was not given in our Edenic existence, signs of the New Heavens and the New Earth, when God will be all in all. This is because, by the resurrection of Jesus Christ, God has intervened in our mortal history to give a foretaste of the eternal city and the eternal creation yet to come.

As a community that walks the way of the cross and is driven by the power of the resurrection, the church lives by the grace of God as the embodied, congregated testimony of both the restoration and the foretaste God has brought forth in Christ.[42]

In this way the church is to be a witnessing community—a martyr church in the etymological sense—manifesting the love of the cross and the power of the resurrection.

Santmire fleshes out his proposal by speaking, with regard to the natural world, of four ecclesial callings: to cooperate with nature religiously, to care for nature sensitively, to wonder at nature blessedly, and to anticipate the reign of God joyfully. For example, to be the church today we must never overwork the land or underpay the laborer. We must preserve wild land, care for cultivated land, and view city planning and ecological design as divine sciences. We must pause from our frenetic lives and consider the lilies of the field. We must celebrate the sacraments—eucharist and baptism—as a foretaste of that glorious future banquet of shalom.[43] Santmire concludes:

Life as a Christian has never been easy. Nor should it be any easier today. But, shaped by its ecological and cosmic ritual enactments, and buoyed by its new ecological and cosmic spirituality, this martyr church can rise to this historic occasion today, by the grace of God, to respond to what is perhaps an unprecedented calling, to love God and all God's creatures, as one great and glorious extended family, and in so doing to be a light to the nations and a city set upon a hill, whose exemplary witness cannot be hidden.[44]

By living out these callings, faithfully and joyfully, the body of Christ would be an evangelical church for an ecological age.[45]

Such is my bare-bones ecological theology. From theology proper to ecclesiology, covering most of the traditional doctrinal topics, such are the essentials of an evangelical theology of care for the earth. It is, I believe, gospel—good news—for us and for our endangered earth. What would an ethic informed by this theology look like? In what follows in this chapter, and especially in the next, I attempt to flesh out an ecological ethic of earth-care.

Ecological Ethics and Earth-Care

There is a wide spectrum of views when it comes to ecological ethics. For my purposes I classify views according to two interrelated questions. First, what counts morally? To use the technical terminology, what is morally considerable? What must be taken into account in the process of moral decision-making? What qualifies as a moral beneficiary?[46] Second, of what value are nonhuman creatures? Do they have only instrumental value—worth because of their usefulness to and for humans? Or do they have intrinsic value—worth over and above any usefulness they may have for us?[47] The first question has to do with the scope of moral consideration, while the second has to do with the relative value or worth of that which is under consideration. The first asks what counts, while the second asks how much it counts and why. With these two questions in mind, one can distinguish between at least seven different positions.[48]

Wise Use

Some people argue that the best ethic involves the wise use of natural resources. This ethic, otherwise known as conservationism, is sometimes called (even by its own adherents) "the wise use movement."[49] This position was famously exemplified in the early twentieth century by the resource conservation movement of Gifford Pinchot, the first head of the U.S. National Forest Service.[50] As indicated above, the natural world is envisaged and spoken of as a "natural resource" to be managed as prudently as possible by humans for human good. Nonhuman creatures do not have intrinsic value. Their value is derived exclusively from their usefulness for humans—trees are for lumber, water for human consumption, the prairie for grazing cattle. The natural world is valuable, but only as a means of serving human interests. The scope of what is morally considerable is relatively small—only humans count morally, and usually only humans here and now.

This perspective, often derided by contemporary environmentalists, should not be unfairly criticized, for in times past it represented an advance over the all-too-common view that legitimized the rape, pillage, and plunder of the natural world. Indeed, Pinchot and company were viewed as progressives in their day, acting contrary to then-prevailing trends by working diligently to conserve scarce resources. Today conservationism at its best, as the name implies, opposes any view that sanctions the unchecked or unthinking exploitation of the natural world.

But this position, as many point out, is grossly inadequate, for it is simply too anthropocentric.[51] Yes, the natural world is valuable because it serves human interests, but as Scripture affirms it is also valuable irrespective of any usefulness to humans. The natural world is valuable, Christians insist, simply because God made it and sustains it and loves it. In short, "wise use" still implies that the only value is use, and that simply is not so. The scope of what counts morally must include more than merely presently existing humans. God cares for all the swarms of creatures described in Genesis and calls us to care for (most of) them too. So for all the good it has done, conservationism has serious shortcomings.

Duties to Posterity

The second position is that of those who champion the rights of future generations. We should consider not just the rights and/or interests of humans here and now, proponents of this view argue, but also the rights of humans in the future. We should care not only for our children but for our grandchildren and great-grandchildren, and thus we should care for the world in which they do and will live. Therefore, while we have no direct duties to weasels or warblers or wetlands, we have indirect duties to such things since without them our progeny will not flourish.[52] Or, as some others argue, we are a part of a transgenerational community, and thus we have duties to those not yet born who will come after us. Not love but (intergenerational) justice is the basis for our obligations to future generations.[53] In short, we have duties to posterity.

According to this perspective, nonhuman creatures do not have intrinsic value. They are valuable, but their value is derived from their worth in regard to the flourishing of humans. This position, however, expands the scope of what counts morally to include humans distant in time, and so the circle of moral considerability is significantly enlarged. To borrow from the now famous definition of sustainability put forward in 1987 by the World Commission on Environment and Development, we must strive to meet "the needs of the present without compromising the ability of future generations to meet their own needs."[54] Built into sustainability is an assumption about duties to posterity.

This view is often criticized, and for a variety of reasons. Many argue, as with the previous position, that it is too anthropocentric. It focuses only on human welfare and thus fails to acknowledge the noninstrumental value of the natural world.[55] Others contend that it makes no sense to speak of rights for people not yet born.[56] Yet others simply eschew all rights language as unhelpful and/ or unnecessary.[57] Many of these criticisms are cogent. This position does, however, represent a genuine advance, for at least two reasons. First, it captures a common and legitimate moral intuition, namely, that we should care for those who come after us. Second, it expresses the biblical injunction that we exercise justice through generations—that we take seriously the needs of humans distant from us not only in space but also in time.

Animal Welfare

The third position on the continuum is held by the advocates of animal welfare. With this perspective we move beyond an anthropocentric or human-centered position to a non-anthropocentric point of view, for the animal welfare position claims that we have responsibilities to at least some nonhuman creatures. One of the most common ways of speaking of these responsibilities is in terms of rights: some animals have rights that we humans are duty-bound to respect.[58] For example, you should not mistreat your pet dog, lest you violate the dog's right to decent care and thus be convicted of the inhumane treatment of animals. Beluga whales ought not be captured and put on display in the local aquarium, for they have a right to roam the ocean free. Animal rights is the watchword for this form of the animal welfare tradition.[59]

The other main view within the animal welfare perspective focuses not on respecting rights but on considering consequences. One key plank in this position is the claim that certain animals are sentient, that is, capable of suffering and being conscious of their suffering. The relevant question, as Jeremy Bentham and John Stuart Mill pointed out in the nineteenth century, is not, can the animal think? but rather, can the animal suffer? If certain animals are sentient, and if every sentient being ought to have its interests considered, and if the morally right act is the one that maximizes good consequences for sentient beings, then humans and certain animals are of equal worth when it comes to suffering, and sentient animals, like humans, ought not suffer needlessly. The scope of what counts morally has now been extended to include sentient nonhuman animals, and at least these creatures are viewed as having intrinsic value.

One main criticism lodged against the animal welfare perspective, in either of its two main forms, is that it is too individualistic. It takes into account only isolated animals, irrespective of their larger ecosystemic contexts.[60] In other words, while this position is non-anthropocentric, it is not yet ecocentric. For example, whether it is morally permissible to kill deer in Michigan is a question that can properly be answered only by looking at the entire deer population, as well as the larger ecosystems of which they are a crucial part. Despite this substantial critique, the animal welfare position does enlarge the scope of what counts morally and in so doing expands our ecological imagination. As I will argue in chapter 7, while the animal welfare argument is one of the weakest arguments among those marshaled to support care for the earth, it does, nevertheless, rightly force us to extend moral considerability to include some nonhuman creatures.

Respect for Life

The fourth position on the ecological ethics continuum insists on respect or reverence for life.[61] All living things, not just future human generations or sentient animals, are deserving of our respect and care. This view is called biocentrism (*bios* means "life" in Greek) and usually rests on a basic claim about the inherent worth of all living organisms. All individual animals and plants have value independently of anyone valuing them; thus they deserve our moral concern and we have a prima facie duty to promote their good. The scope of what counts morally is thus extended to include all living organisms, and this extension implies that all living things have intrinsic value. Our duties toward living things do not derive from our duties to other humans. Rather, they are grounded in the value the organisms possess simply by virtue of being alive. Perhaps the most famous representative of this view was Albert Schweitzer— German biblical scholar, musician, missionary—who wrote of the "reverence for life" and tried to live by it.[62] Among contemporary thinkers who follow in Schweitzer's footsteps, Paul Taylor is the most important, with his ethic of "respect for nature" being the most thoroughly and carefully argued biocentric perspective.[63]

There are a number of common criticisms of biocentrism. Many argue that such a view is simply impractical, since one cannot consistently live such a philosophy of life; after all, everyone has to eat. Biocentrism in its more sophisticated versions, however, does not maintain that we ought not consume other organisms, and so the criticism of biocentrism's impracticality attacks a straw man. Others contend that this view is still not sufficiently ecological since only individual organisms are taken into account, while various relationships within the natural world are ignored.[64] This critique surely hits the mark, for biocentrism is life-centered but not yet ecosystem-aware. A perspective that focuses on life, without due attention to the systems and processes within which all living things exist, is not adequately informed about how the world works. Finally, any position that puts life at the center of things must, from a theocentric point of view, be judged inadequate. God lies at the center of things, not life. Despite these problems, biocentrism, like the animal welfare perspective, possesses the not inconsiderable virtue of expanding our moral imagination to include more than merely the human.

Wilderness Preservation

The fifth point on the continuum is wilderness preservation. Long represented by such groups as the Sierra Club and the Wilderness Society, this perspective stresses the need to preserve wild places, to protect unspoiled nature. Preservation, not just conservation, is the watchword. For a variety of reasons, its advocates argue, we need to preserve wild lands: to provide places for human recreation, to maintain nature's services, to protect the habitats of endangered animals and plants. Of special importance are places, to quote the Wilderness Act of 1964, "where the earth and its community of life are untrammeled by man, where man himself is a visitor who does not remain."[65] Intrinsic value is found in places untainted by the human touch. What counts morally are tracts of wild land, as well as the organisms that dwell on and in them. The most well-known representatives of this view are Henry David Thoreau, whose *Walden* remains a classic in American literature, and John Muir—indefatigable mountaineer, founder of the Sierra Club, and tireless advocate for the preservation of wild places.[66]

With the wilderness preservation position we encounter the first bonafide ecocentric perspective. Intrinsic value resides not just in individual creatures but also in entire ecological systems. This claim is evident, for example, in the attention given to larger systems and processes in Thoreau's detailed descriptions of life in and around Walden Pond and in Muir's rapturous reports from his jaunts in the High Sierra. However, with its emphasis on wild land, and usually scenic wilderness such as that found in national parks, this perspective tends, some critics argue, to be not ecological enough. It overlooks the genuine and important ecological value of less aesthetically pleasing places. It tends to value only (or mostly) spectacular scenery and awe-inspiring vistas while ignoring the soil beneath our feet or the park down the street. In addition, modern ideas of wilderness tend to be clouded by "the romantic wilderness myth," which portrays wild places as benign, static, and pristine.[67] In point of fact, few if any places are pristine, none are static, and the natural world is always an admixture of the benign and the harsh. The movement to preserve wilderness is, however, in keeping with the spirit of Job's wild nature poetry. As such it represents a position that removes the human from the center of things, thus engendering humility and fostering hospitality to our nonhuman neighbors.

The Land Ethic

First articulated by Aldo Leopold, in his still widely read and influential *Sand County Almanac*, the land ethic is a full-fledged ecocentric approach.[68] It incorporates knowledge of trophic levels and food webs, of energy flow and cycling systems, of organisms and their niches within habitats and communities and ecosystems. For example, Leopold insists that we must learn to think like a mountain—to see the interdependence of the natural world, to view death as a necessary part of life, to take a long-term view of the earth and its evolution. The emphasis here is on the land organism. To quote Leopold's famous moral maxim, "A thing is right when it tends to preserve the integrity, stability, and beauty of the biotic community. It is wrong when it tends otherwise."[69] The land community itself is given moral standing, along with the animals, plants, and inanimate nature in the ecosystem. And the land and all its creatures have intrinsic value.

There are many strengths to this version of ecocentric holism, to use the technical terminology. It is attuned to how the world works. It captures much of the wisdom of Scripture. The earth and its many creatures are valuable in and for themselves, as well as for their usefulness to humans. All creatures are moral patients and thus must be recipients of moral regard, though it is left open as to how to rank competing moral values. Leopards and loons are not necessarily of the same moral value as Lars and Lucy. Some hierarchy of value is usually acknowledged.

Critics, however, level two main criticisms against the land ethic. First, some accuse Leopold and his followers of engaging in the naturalistic fallacy—of illegitimately moving from is to ought. In other words, the claim is that Leopold derives ethical values from ecological facts, normative prescriptions from scientific descriptions. A judgment of value (e.g., that hunting is morally wrong) cannot be derived from a judgment of fact (e.g., that the deer population is dwindling). The merit of this charge, however, is anything but self-evident. As Holmes Rolston argues, we can and must derive our ethical prescriptions from our ecosystem descriptions.[70] Our moral oughts arise, in part, from our knowledge of how the world works, so values and facts are not always (if ever) independent.

The other major criticism is that the land ethic is a version of "environmental fascism."[71] That is to say, its exclusive focus on the biotic community runs roughshod over the rights of individuals (human or nonhuman) within that community. As a result, there is the grave danger that the good of an individual will be sacrificed for the good of the biotic community. This is, it seems to me, a potent criticism and thus raises a potentially serious problem for certain forms of this ethic. It is not an insuperable problem, however, and various advocates of the land ethic have addressed this perceived shortcoming of Leopold's ethic.[72]

Deep Ecology

The seventh and last perspective on the spectrum is deep ecology. A somewhat diverse movement that encompasses many approaches, this example of "radical ecophilosophy" finds its intellectual moorings primarily in the work of Norwegian philosopher Arne Naess. In a seminal 1973 essay Naess made a distinction between what he called shallow and deep environmental perspectives—between, in essence, anthropocentric and non-anthropocentric positions—and called for a reexamination of the roots of ecological degradation.[73] In collaboration with Bill Devall and George Sessions, Naess developed a platform of basic principles that, among other things, posits the intrinsic value of nonhuman life-forms, affirms the importance of the richness and diversity of nonhuman organisms, and argues that humans have no right to reduce the richness and diversity of nonhuman life except to meet vital needs.[74] Of special importance is the idea of biocentric equality, namely, that all things—humans, animals, plants, bacteria, mountains, rivers, lakes—have an equal right to exist. In other words, deep ecology acknowledges the intrinsic value of the natural world and affirms that nonhuman organisms not only count morally but count equally.

The criticisms of deep ecology are many. Some argue that it is conceptually fuzzy; others, that it is misanthropic; still others, that it smacks of Western imperialism.[75] Each, in my view, has merit. But the most significant charge leveled against deep ecology has to do with its affirmation of biocentric equality.

Insofar as proponents claim that all organisms have equal value or worth, it is unclear how to adjudicate competing interests or goods. As Joseph DesJardins says, "What is to be done when human interests conflict with the interests of the nonhuman world, as so often is the case with environmental issues?"[76] Moreover, how can one consistently put into practice such a position? In the language of philosophy, such a view involves a performative contradiction, for it is impossible to act on what one believes. But we do act, and in so acting we presuppose a scale or hierarchy of values. Better to be honest about what that axiological scale is than to pretend that all organisms are of equal value.

The Land Ethic Revisited

Wise use, duties to posterity, animal welfare, respect for life, wilderness preservation, land ethic, deep ecology—such is (in large part) the landscape of contemporary ecological ethics. As perhaps the preceding comments reveal, I find certain of these seven perspectives more compelling than others. Since I develop in more detail my own ethic of care for the earth in the next chapter, here I will indicate only the broad contours of my own position.

Given what we know of how the world works, summarized in chapter 1; given our understanding of how and why the world is groaning, outlined in chapters 2 and 3; given the witness of Scripture, especially in the texts examined in chapter 4; and given the theological affirmations set forth earlier in this chapter—given all of this, in my view the most adequate ethical perspective (of those surveyed) is the land ethic. Aldo Leopold's vision of the land community, with certain additions and corrections, seems to me to provide the best overarching approach. The additions and corrections include, at a minimum, the following.

First, the land ethic is woefully incomplete for creatures such as us who inhabit the water planet. With approximately 70 percent of the earth's surface covered by water, the land ethic must be extended (and/or renamed) to include the great bodies of water on our blue-green planet. Leopold's claim that "the land ethic simply enlarges the boundaries of the community to include soils, waters, plants, and animals, or collectively: the land"[77] implicitly includes more than land, but this must be made more explicit. The land ethic must be enlarged to include the oceans and great inland lakes, for the ethic we seek is an ethic for the entire earth.

Second, some provision must be made to protect the rights of individual humans.[78] The criticism mentioned above—that the good of a particular person might wrongly be sacrificed for the good of the entire community—must be taken seriously. Therefore, to ensure that the legitimate goods, rights, and interests of persons are protected, certain basic human rights must be acknowledged, and duties that protect those rights must be incorporated into the overarching ethical framework. Baird Callicott argues that the land ethic does just that, namely, acknowledges human rights while also requiring us to respect the nonhuman members of the community.

> The land ethic, therefore, is not draconian or fascist. It does not cancel human morality. . . . While the land ethic, certainly, does not cancel human morality, neither does it leave it unaffected.
>
> Nor is the land ethic inhumane. Nonhuman fellow members of the biotic community have no "human rights," because they are not, by definition, members of the human community. As fellow members of the biotic community, however, they deserve respect.[79]

Despite the impression that Leopold's ethic eschews duties in favor of some sort of calculus of consequences, Callicott maintains that Leopold's land ethic actually gives primacy to duties.[80] Whether or not Callicott's claims regarding the land ethic are true, it is clear that an ethic that combines attention to duties and rights with concern for goods and consequences is more adequate than an ethic that embodies only one or the other.[81]

Third, a hierarchy of value is necessary. For those perspectives that are ecocentric, such as the land ethic, some scale of value is required, for within the biotic community we must make relevant moral discriminations. Holmes Rolston, who follows Leopold in many respects, puts this point especially well. Taking issue with both biocentrism and anthropocentrism, he speaks of the natural world as "bio-systemic and anthropo-apical."

> The system [ecosystem] does not center indiscriminately on life, with one life being equal to another; and the system does not center functionally on humans, who in the ecological sense have little role in the system. Microbes are more important than humans instrumentally. All value does not "center" on humans, though some of it does. Everything of value that happens is not "for" humans; humans defend their own values, and humans need to recognize these values outside themselves. Nevertheless, humans are of the utmost value in the sense that they are the ecosystem's most sophisticated product.[82]

The entire *bios* or living world must be taken into account morally speaking (bio-systemic), even though the human lies at the apex in terms of a certain kind of value (anthropo-apical). Such claims presuppose a scale of value, and Rolston offers for serious consideration his own sophisticated "model of intrinsic, instrumental, and system value."[83]

Fourth, any ecocentric perspective must, from a Christian point of view, be transmuted into a theocentric perspective, for our earthly home, for all its importance, does not lie at the center of things. God is at the center, and all things, whether on earth or in heaven, exist to praise God. While some may doubt the possibility or the advisability of such a transmutation project, it is, in my judgment, a necessary endeavor that is worth the effort. Rolston's own project—in *Environmental Ethics* and other of his writings—is an impressive example of an ethic informed by Leopold but transformed and nuanced in various ways. In the same way, the land ethic could be incorporated into an explicitly theocentric and, more specifically, Christian, theological perspective.

Fifth and finally, while the land ethic fosters certain ecological sensitivities and capacities, little explicit or sustained attention is given to those traits of character known as virtues. As I will argue in the next chapter, while the most adequate ethic gives attention to both rules and consequences, it nevertheless gives pride of place to certain virtues. Leopold's land ethic, while suggestive of virtues such as humility and respect, needs to be developed, supplemented, and corrected by a more thorough examination of the virtues from a Christian perspective.

The Challenge Ahead

The ecological theology and ethic set forth above—informed both by an understanding of the glory and groaning of the earth and by careful attention to Scripture and the teachings of the church—calls us to be caretakers of the earth. It challenges us to live more earth-careful lives.[84] This is not optional. Either we will heed this call in obedience and gratitude or we will, by neglect or malice, fail to act in ways that reflect God's desire for shalom. Hence, as William Dyrness rightly argues, "Our moral responsibility toward the earth cannot be excluded from our Christian calling."[85] It is as false to claim that concern for the earth is not a legitimate feature of authentic Christian discipleship as it is to claim that care for the earth is the sum total of what it means to be a disciple of Christ. As the "Evangelical Declaration on the Care of Creation" puts it, "We resist both ideologies which would presume the Gospel has nothing to do with the care of non-human creation and also ideologies which would reduce the Gospel to nothing more than the care of that creation."[86] The gospel is surely more than caring for the earth, but just as surely it involves nothing less.

The challenge ahead is to persuade Christians that care for the earth is an integral feature of authentic Christian discipleship. It is not the gospel in its entirety, but the gospel is not gospel without it. Jesus saves, to be sure. But from what and for what does he save us? Jesus is Lord, yes. But over whom and over what? Jesus is coming again, most certainly. But for what kind of future should we hope? To answer such fundamental questions, we need to get our theology and our ethic right.

The issue before us is stated clearly by Calvin DeWitt, who speaks of "a perplexing puzzle in the context of geo-crisis." He observes that "Jesus Christ is Creator, Integrator, and Reconciler; yet many who call on his name abuse, neglect, and do not give a care about creation. That irony is there for all to see.

Honoring the Creator in word, they destroy God's works in deed. Praising God from whom all blessings flow, they diminish and destroy God's creatures here below. The pieces of this puzzle do not fit! One piece says, 'We honor the Great Master!' The other piece says, 'We despise his great masterpieces!'"[87] How can this be? How can those who sing the Doxology not care for the creatures here below? How can we honor the Master without caring for his masterpieces? DeWitt concludes his reflections with this challenge to evangelical Christians: "Let us recognize the dismemberment of our Creator and come anew to re-member our Creator. Having re-membered our Creator, reuniting the creative and redemptive work of our Lord, we then can ask our second big question. Is creation a lost cause? And we may respond, Definitely not!"[88]

6

what kind of people ought we be?

earth-care and character

> But lacking the qualities of virtue, can we do the difficult things that will be necessary to live within the boundaries of the earth?
>
> David Orr[1]

Paul tends his forty acres of forest. Thinning and replanting as his arboreal eye sees fit, he takes a long view, for the midlife of the trees of today—some forty years distant—he, now in his own midlife, will most likely not live to see. In so doing, he exhibits the virtues of wisdom and hope. Karen cultivates a creation more domestic than wild. Her garden is regularly gleaned of irises and tulips and daffodils to scent the office at work. Showing an intimate knowledge of soil and flower, with her obvious green thumb she carefully nurtures her backyard garden. In this way she embodies the virtues of benevolence and love. Kent runs a church camp. He puts up solar panels, installs composting toilets, and cultivates an organic garden in unforgiving Adirondack soil. He knows when enough is enough and so resists the pressures to think bigger is better. He manifests the "old-fashioned" virtues of self-restraint and frugality. Wisdom and hope, benevolence and love, self-restraint and frugality—just a few of what I call the "ecological virtues."

More famous earthkeepers could have been mentioned—John Muir, Aldo Leopold, Rachel Carson. But my real though less-than-famous friends well exemplify various virtues needed to care for the earth. And the lives of these real-life earthkeepers prompt the following questions: What kind of people ought we be? What kind of people need we be in order to properly care for the earth? And as the epigraph from David Orr more radically suggests, is it possible to live on our home planet without being people of virtue?

Much has been written in recent years about ecological ethics, including Christian ecological ethics. The vast majority of this scholarship adopts one of two basic ethical perspectives: a focus on rules and obligations (deontology) or attention to goods and consequences (teleology). However, relatively little work in ecological ethics has been done in virtue theory (areteology), especially from a Christian point of view.[2]

This chapter moves the discussion about caring for the earth toward this neglected but important area of study—Christian ecological virtue ethics. Instead of asking, what should we do? it asks, what kind of people should we be? Instead of focusing on conduct it zeros in on character. More exactly, the questions posed here are: What particular virtues arise from a biblically informed Christian ecological ethic? And how important are they? Are they merely nice to have, or are they necessary? Which ones are crucial for the health of household earth? It is my contention that certain virtues are indispensable if Christians are to responsibly fulfill their calling as earthkeepers. Certain traits of character are central to earth-care.

The Nature of Virtue

Virtue is one of those phenomena, like pornography and religion, about which it is sometimes said, "I can't define it, but I know it when I see it." We all have some intuitive sense for what virtue is—or more exactly, what certain virtues are, such as courage and justice and humility—even if we find it difficult to define. But what precisely is virtue? Can it be delimited with any precision? If so, how?

In his famous discussion of virtue in book II of the *Nicomachean Ethics*, Aristotle argues that virtue (*aretē*, better translated "excellence") is neither a passion nor a faculty, but a state of character.[3] And this is so because neither having an emotion nor having a capacity involves choice. For example, passions such as anger and fear, as well as the capacity to have such passions, are part of our natural human endowment and as such are neither praiseworthy nor blameworthy. Virtues and vices, on the other hand, are "modes of choice or involve choice."[4] They are dispositions to act by reference to which we are rightly praised or blamed. In short, a virtue is a settled disposition to act excellently—a state of praiseworthy character developed over time.

This leads to another of Aristotle's conclusions: virtues, especially moral virtues, are formed by habitual behavior. We become people of virtue by developing certain good habits (and people of vice by developing certain bad habits). We become just by doing just acts, and we become brave by doing brave acts. In other words, our doing shapes our being, our conduct forms our character.

Virtue, furthermore for Aristotle, can be described as a mean lying between two extremes. For example, courage is that excellence of character that disposes one to act, when fearful, in neither a rash nor a cowardly way. Moderation is that excellence of character that disposes one to act, when faced with various pleasures, in neither a self-indulgent nor an insensible manner. While I will later argue that it is not always the case that a virtue is a mean between two extremes, most of the time this is true. And since there is no algorithm for determining what the mean is in every situation, in order to know how to act, as Aristotle famously puts it, "to the right extent, at the right time, with the right motive, and in the right way," we need a recognized exemplar of virtue.[5] We need role models, people of virtue, to whom we can look for guidance and insight.

These various strands are tied together in Aristotle's final definition of virtue: "Virtue, then, is a state of character concerned with choice, lying in a mean, i.e., the mean relative to us, this being determined by a rational principle, and by that principle by which the man of practical wisdom would determine it."[6] In other words (bracketing the issue of intellectual virtue), a moral virtue is an excellence of character, developed by conscious choices over time and thus for which one can and should be praised, that disposes one to act in such a way as to avoid extremes—to act, in short, as a wise person would act.

While Aristotle provides insight into the nature of virtue, we can gain further clarity (and correction) from more recent thinkers. Philippa Foot asks how virtue differs from other beneficial qualities such as memory and concentration. She concludes that virtues have as much to do with dispositions, desires, and attitudes as with intentions.[7] While "it is not wrong to think of virtues as belonging to the will," she asserts that the will "must here be understood in its widest sense, to cover what is wished for as well as what is sought."[8] Robert Roberts concurs. There is more to virtue than merely that which belongs to the will, since a number of virtues involve emotions—for example, gratitude, hope, peace, compassion—and other virtues are in large measure skills—for example, courage, moderation, patience.[9] Thus virtues go beyond the will to encompass much more of the human person.

In addition, while virtues can be thought of as traits of character, character in this context refers to that set of attributes or qualities that distinguishes us from others—that complex of traits that marks us as the persons we are. Character is thus more than merely the sum of all we do; character, rather, reflects "the particular direction our agency acquires by choosing to act in some ways rather than others."[10] This way of construing virtue highlights the intimate connection between virtue and vision—a neglected feature of Aristotle's account of virtue. Virtues "influence how we describe the activities in which we engage, what we think we are doing and what we think is important about what we are doing."[11] Thus, as Gilbert Meilaender states, "What duties we perceive—and even what dilemmas—may depend upon what virtues shape our vision of the world."[12] We see the world differently, depending on the virtues that constitute our character. C. S. Lewis captures this brilliantly in *The Chronicles of Narnia*. The creation of Narnia by Aslan looks and feels very different for wicked Uncle Andrew than it does for the children. While the children find it beautiful and understand the words spoken by the animals, Uncle Andrew shrinks back in fear and hears only barking and howling. Because of his evil character he misconstrues the very nature of both Aslan the creator and what is created. As the narrator comments: "For what you see and hear depends a good deal on where you are standing; it also depends on what sort of person you are."[13] Virtue informs vision, and vision shapes action.

Two additional pieces of the puzzle must be added to make the picture (for our purposes here) reasonably complete. As stated above, virtues shape and are shaped by vision, and virtues are formed, in part, by emulating people of recognized wisdom. Each of these statements points to the importance of narrative and community in the shaping of virtue.[14] First, narrative: How we live depends on who we are, and who we are depends on the stories we identify with. Practices are rooted in character, and character is rooted in story. Founding stories shape our desires and attitudes—indeed our basic vision of life. The stories we hear—of the American dream, of material prosperity, of a crazy carpenter from Nazareth—mold and shape our character. Narrative plays a crucial role in the formation of virtue. And, secondly, regarding community: these grand meaning-giving stories, as well as the people in these stories who are held up as role models to follow, are an integral part of the communities in which we live. We are the persons we are in large measure (whether we know it or not and whether we like it or not) because of the various communities of which we have been a part.

In sum, a virtue is a state of praiseworthy character, formed by habits over time, that disposes us to act in certain excellent ways. Knowing which way is the truly excellent way involves avoiding the extremes of vice by looking to people of virtue as role models and by writing our life story as part of a larger narrative in which we find meaning. The settled dispositions to act well, which make us who we are, are nurtured by the stories we imbibe and the communities of which we are a part.

The Ecological Virtues

In each section below I first examine the biblical story. To be precise, I explore certain texts (most of which have not been examined previously in this book) that directly address the issues before us. Such reflections will be brief but of sufficient depth to properly indicate the biblical basis for the ethical claims that follow. I next identify particular theological themes that emerge from the biblical narrative. Not exactly full-fledged doctrines, these theological motifs nevertheless function like doctrines insofar as they, like doctrines, are portable stories.[15] That is, they attempt to summarize in one word or expression what the biblical text narrates. Third, I derive certain ethical principles and moral duties from the theological motifs. And last, I spell out the moral virtues (and vices) corresponding to the motifs and principles.

Respect and Receptivity

We must begin at the beginning—in the book of beginnings, namely, Genesis. As is clear from our discussion in chapter 4, the first chapter of Genesis is a rich and multifaceted narrative. This seminal text communicates much not only about who we are and what God is like but also about the character of that which God creates and sustains. For our purposes here it is important to note a number of things about creation itself.

First, creation has a diversity of creatures. Through God's "let there be" the earth brings forth living creatures of every kind: birds, fish, animals both domestic and wild, flying and creeping things, even sea monsters. Again and again the text speaks of God bringing forth many kinds of creatures. Second, this plethora of creatures is good. God sees what is created and declares it to be good. Indeed, in Genesis 1:31 God sees everything created (not just humans) and declares that it is exceedingly good (tôb mĕ'ōd). Creation is a place of beauty and blessing and delight. Third, creation as a whole evinces integrity or soundness. Because of God's wise and orderly creative activity, the diverse kinds of creatures fit together into a harmonious whole. Creation is a place of flourishing fittedness. In short, biodiversity is an intended result of God's wise and orderly creative activity.

This picture of creational integrity and dependence is reinforced in various psalms. Psalm 104, for example, speaks of all things as having been created by God. Everything in heaven and on earth is a result of God's creative activity. Furthermore, the world God brought into being is a cosmos—a meaningfully ordered whole. This cosmos, moreover, is not autonomous. Rather, it exists solely because of the continuous care and sustenance of God its Creator. All creatures—the wild asses, the cedars of Lebanon, the rock badgers, the young lions—depend on God for their existence and their ability to flourish.

In addition, God's creatures are valuable not because of their usefulness to humans—though some are useful, indeed essential, to us. Instead, they are valuable to each other—for example, the cedars are valuable as places for birds to nest, and the mountains are valuable as places for the wild goats to rest—and, most importantly, rocks and trees, birds and animals are valuable simply because God made them. Their value resides in their being creations of a valuing God, not in their being a means to some human end. Finally, a close reading of this psalm reveals that the human creature is but one creature among God's many creatures. We are to cultivate the earth, but we are to do so in harmony with the needs of other creatures and in such a way that all are enabled to sing praises to God the Creator, since the chief purpose of all creatures is to glorify God.

Psalm 148 is an enthusiastic and eloquent exclamation point to this affirmation concerning the purpose of creation. Here the psalmist calls upon all created things to praise God their Maker: the angels and hosts of heaven, the sun and moon and stars, fire and hail, snow and frost, water and wind, mountains and hills, fruit trees, wild animals, creeping things, kings and princes and rulers, women and men—nothing is left out. God's glory is unsurpassed, and all creatures are invited to sing in a symphony of praise.

In sum, in these texts we find the theological motif of *creational integrity*. Individual creatures and the earth as a whole have an integrity as created by God and as such have more than merely instrumental value. Creatures exist to praise God and are valuable irrespective of human utility. From this theological theme comes the ethical principle of *intrinsic value*. Because species have intrinsic value, they have moral standing. All species, like humanity, count morally. Not all species count the same, of course, but nonhuman creatures do count and thus should be considered when humans make ethical decisions. And because all creatures have moral standing, humans have not only duties *regarding* other species but also duties *to* other species. We have an obligation to protect our watershed not only to preserve safe drinking water for the people who live there but also because we have a direct duty to the trout and herons and muskrats who inhabit that watershed.

Furthermore, given that species are dynamic natural kinds, unique and irreplaceable, I offer the following moral maxim: *Act so as to preserve diverse kinds of life.* More exactly, we have a prima facie duty to protect and preserve nonhuman species. That is, we are obligated to preserve nonhuman species except when other legitimate moral considerations outweigh or overrule this duty.[16] And since such species cannot exist without their homes, we are also obligated to preserve habitats. As Aldo Leopold famously put it, given "the complexity of the land organism . . . to keep every cog and wheel is the first precaution of intelligent tinkering."[17]

Corresponding to the theological motif of creational integrity and the ethical principle of intrinsic value are certain important moral virtues or excellences of character, namely, respect and receptivity. *Respect* is an understanding of and proper regard for the integrity and well-being of other creatures. A respectful person shows both esteem for and deference to another because of the nature or unique character of that other. That which has intrinsic value calls forth a looking back—a re-specting—that acknowledges and regards God-given value. A person who respects neither overlooks nor merely looks over.

Two vices correspond to the virtue of respect. The vice of deficiency is *conceit*, for conceit is ignorance of and disdain for other creatures. It is a failure to recognize the other as other, a lack of proper regard. Conceited people show no genuine interest in another and will if necessary violate the integrity of the other—human or nonhuman—to serve their own self-centered interests.

The vice of excess is *reverence*, or inflated regard for the other. By reverence I mean that a person regards what is not worthy of worship as an object of veneration. Reverence in this sense is misplaced or exaggerated regard. A person worships a creature or creation as a whole rather than the Creator.

Receptivity is shorthand for the acknowledgment of our interdependence with other creatures. It denotes an acceptance of our kinship with our human and nonhuman neighbors—a willing embrace of our mutual dependence. Receptivity also connotes responsiveness to the other. It is a taking in that nevertheless allows the other to remain other—a welcoming of the other. Receptivity, in other words, is a form of hospitality.

The vice of deficiency regarding receptivity is *autonomy*, or the disposition to act as if one does not need others. People who possess this vice think they can survive and even flourish independent of other creatures, as if they are not contingent creatures but rather the makers of their own world and destiny. The autonomous (*autos* + *nomos*) are a law unto themselves. They do their own thing, irrespective of their inescapable emplacement in the natural world. They live as if they exist in self-enclosed isolation from the air, water, and soil that sustain them.

The vice of excess is *addiction*, or unhealthy overdependence on another. This malformed version of receptivity knows no boundaries. It is a form of receiving that knows no limits—a taking in driven by fear and anxiety rather than grace and freedom. In contrast to the isolation of autonomy, addiction implies an inability or unwillingness to let other creatures be.

In short, creation has a God-given integrity and value. Humans have a moral obligation to protect and preserve nonhuman species. Therefore, in the shaping of our character we must cultivate the virtues of respect and receptivity and actively discourage the vices of conceit and reverence, of autonomy and addiction.

Self-Restraint and Frugality

The Genesis creation narrative also emphasizes that the earth is finite. Despite its description of manyness—many individual creatures, many kinds of creatures—the passage does not suggest that the panopoly of God's creatures or the earth itself is unlimited. Creation has definite limits. Moreover, God's word to humans in verse 28 to be fruitful and multiply does not suggest, as some maintain, that the earth has an unlimited supply of "resources" for an ever-growing human population.

First, it is often overlooked that this call by God is also given to all living creatures (v. 22). The sea monsters, the fish, and the birds—indeed, every living creature of every kind is given this invitation. The calling to reproduce is no special privilege unique to humans. Second, this imperative is actually not a command at all but a blessing by God on the swarms of living creatures brought forth by God's creative word. As Susan Bratton states, God's blessing "is not an ethical imperative, nor is it a way to please God by reaching to excess;" rather, God's blessing conveys a reproductive power intended to contribute to the flourishing of all creatures on a finite planet. Bratton concludes, "Human population growth has no mandate to damage or desecrate the cosmos."[18] Creation is finite, and we humans have no biblical warrant to act as if it is infinite.

This theme is present in other biblical texts. For example, after the Israelites escaped from Egypt they wandered in the wilderness on the way to the Promised Land. As narrated in Exodus 16, God provided bread and meat—manna and quail—for them to eat, but only enough for one day at a time. The portions were sufficient for the day. There was to be no excess. The resources were not unlimited, lest the Israelites forget their dependence on the God who not only had delivered them but continued to sustain them.

Jesus calls to mind this experience in the wilderness when he teaches his followers what and how to pray. After three statements emphasizing God's glory, Jesus asks God for human needs. He first prays, "Give us this day our daily bread" (Matt. 6:11). In other words, in the Lord's Prayer we ask the provisioning God of the exodus to give us the nourishment we need for today. As the Israelites received their daily bread, we are to ask for and with gratitude receive food sufficient for the day. This text reiterates the theme of finitude and sufficiency. The biblical witness confirms what photographs from space portray—that the blue-green sphere on which we live is finite.

In sum, these texts provide us with the theological motif of *creational finitude*. The earth is finite. There is only so much to go around. The only seemingly limitless physical resource is the energy from the sun—that divine provision fundamental to all life on earth. All else is limited. As Bill McKibben declares: "There is now a new fact in the world . . . the realization that the natural environment places finite limits on our behavior."[19] From this theological motif comes the ethical principle of *sufficiency*. Enough is enough. Others' (basic) needs take precedence over our (greedy) wants. Our continuing failure to acknowledge this principle portends much future hardship, for there are limits we transgress only at our own (and the earth's) peril.

Given an acknowledgment that the earth is finite, embodied in the ethical principle of sufficiency, I propose a second moral maxim: *Act so as to live within your means*. More precisely, we have a prima facie duty to preserve nonrenewable resources and conserve scarce though renewable resources. This duty applies to a wide range of things—from energy to species. We should, for example, conserve fossil fuels such as coal, oil, and natural gas, for once that solar savings account is depleted it will be a very long time before it is replenished. So too we should preserve species, for that "resource" once gone will never return.

Corresponding to the theological motif of creational finitude and the ethical principle of sufficiency are the moral virtues of self-restraint and frugality. One of the cardinal virtues of the Greeks, *self-restraint* is moderation of inordinate desires. The goal with self-restraint is not the extinction of all desire (as if that were possible), but rather disciplined desire. To use an old-fashioned word, the virtue here is temperance—habitual control of one's appetites. The ecologically temperate (joyfully) say, "I have what I need."

The vice of deficiency that runs contrary to self-restraint is *profligacy*, or un-restrained desire. Profligate people lack sufficient self-control. They are overly self-indulgent. As Aristotle notes, "These people are called belly-gods, this implying that they fill their belly beyond what is right."[20] The ecologically profligate consume the earth beyond what they truly need or what the earth can properly bear.

The vice of excess, in which there is too much self-control, is *austerity*. Overly self-controlled people mistake masochism for moderation. Austerity implies that the passions are inherently evil. Desire per se is dangerous. For the austere all delight in creation's goodness is squeezed out of life and all joy in the fitting use of God's good gifts is squelched.

Frugality is economy of use or efficient use given the limits of the goods available. As its etymology suggests, to be frugal is to enjoy (*frui*) the proper use of the finite goods God has given us. Thus, frugality is characterized not by a parsimonious wish to hold in or keep back, but rather by a desire to use sparingly that which God has provided in order that others may live and flourish. Rightly understood, therefore, frugality represents a form of hospitality.

The vice of deficiency that corresponds to frugality is *greed*—the disposition to excessively acquire, especially beyond one's need. Avarice is perhaps a more accurate term, for it denotes a craving to acquire that is blinded to the limits inherent in creation. Driven by cupidity, the greedy person lacks any sense of the finitude of the world.

The vice of excess is *stinginess*, or thrift as an end in itself. Sparing to the point of being mean, the stingy exhibit no generosity. Fearful of whether there will be enough, the penurious hold in and keep back. Economy for economy's sake is their motto. In the case of each of these vices there is no enjoyment of that which God has provided.

In short, the earth is finite. We have the moral obligation to preserve the resources God has provided and so joyfully to live within our means. Thus, we must cultivate the virtues of self-restraint and frugality, thereby discouraging the currently fashionable vices of profligacy and greed while also avoiding the vices of austerity and stinginess.

If the created world is finite and we are creatures, then it follows that we are finite. It might seem that this rather obvious point needs no special attention. However, we have a penchant for forgetting this central feature of our existence. Indeed, we have a deep desire to avoid looking our finitude, especially our temporal finitude or mortality, straight in the face.[21] To acknowledge the limited nature of our existence produces anxiety and often fear, even as it raises the question of whether death is the end of one's life or whether there is Someone who is sufficiently able and willing to preserve our life beyond biological death, Someone in whom we can rest in spite of our fear and anxiety.[22]

Not surprisingly, the Bible speaks often of human finitude. For example, in Genesis 2 the narrative tells us the human creature is formed out of the ground and made alive by God's life-giving breath (v. 7). We are *'ādām*—earth creature—because we are *'ădāmâ*—clumps of earth, animated by the Spirit of God. We, like all of God's creatures, are finite.

As I indicated in chapter 4, the finitude of humanity is powerfully portrayed in the book of Job. In the deluge of questions asked by God from the whirlwind, Job is, among other things, forcibly reminded of his finitude. Job has not entered the storehouses of the snow or provided prey for the ravens. He does not know when the mountain goats give birth or who let the wild asses go free. That the hawk soars and the eagle mounts up is not Job's doing. Job's power and knowledge are finite. He is a creature.

Even Psalm 8, which speaks of humans as having been created a little lower than God and crowned with glory and honor, reminds us that we are creatures and hence finite. We have a God-given dignity and calling, but we are nevertheless limited. Only God is infinite. Only God is worthy of praise—the one whose name is majestic in all the earth.

But we are not just finite; we are faulted. Though often confused, these two are not the same. Finitude is a good feature of human existence. It is simply how God made us—a feature of our humanity to joyfully accept. Faultedness, however, is not God's intention. The brokenness we know in ourselves and all around us is something we acknowledge with regret and seek with God's grace to overcome.

This feature of human existence is also powerfully depicted in the Genesis narrative. In chapter 3 we learn that Adam and Eve desire to transcend their creaturely finitude and become, like God, omniscient. But in this attempt they fail to trust in God and thus become estranged. Their relationship with God is broken. They become estranged from each other and attempt to pass the blame. They lose touch with their own true and best self and try to hide and conceal their actions. And they become out of joint with the earth such that working the earth becomes burdensome. In these four ways they and we are alienated—from God, from each other, from ourselves, and from the earth. In short, our lives are interwoven with a contagion called sin, which we knowingly and unknowingly perpetuate. The Bible confirms what we know in our hearts: the world is not the way it is supposed to be.[23]

In these and many other biblical texts we find the theological motif of *human finitude and faultedness*. As humans we are creatures—limited in power and knowledge as well as space and time. We are 'ādām from the 'ădāmâ, humans from the humus. We are not God, though we are God's. Furthermore, we are faulted creatures—alienated from God, other humans, ourselves, and the earth. Though we are not God, we all too often think and act as if we were. From this theological motif comes the ethical principle of *responsibility*. Given the limited scope of our human knowledge and power, we must be circumspect and exercise forethought. Given our stubborn unwillingness to admit such limitations, we must be held accountable for our actions.

Therefore, a frank acknowledgment of our limited ability to know the future consequences of our actions and an honest awareness of our penchant for self-aggrandizement and self-deception prompt a third moral maxim: *Act cautiously*. To be more precise, in our care for the earth we have a prima facie duty, before making decisions, to survey as many consequences as possible. This implies neither a God's-eye view of things nor unrealistic expectations of perfection, but it does mean we have a duty to explore alternatives, seek out blind spots, consider worst-case scenarios. Given the manifest evidence of both unforeseen and unintended consequences, we ought not go too fast, cut corners, or ignore opposing points of view. We don't know everything (though we often think we do), and our fat, restless egos often get the best of us. Therefore, we should be careful, exercise caution, go slow.

The theological motif of human finitude and faultedness and the ethical principle of responsibility presuppose the moral virtues of humility and honesty. *Humility* is the proper estimation of one's abilities or capacities. It is the fitting acknowledgment that we humans are earth creatures. Humility thus implies self-knowledge, and especially knowledge of the limits of one's knowledge. Aware of their ignorance, humble folk do not pretend to know more than they really know. Humility also implies genuineness. Aware of their strengths and weaknesses, humble people do not pretend to be other than they are.

The vice of deficiency is *hubris*—exaggerated self-confidence or overweening pride. Hubris is the failure to acknowledge one's own limits, often resulting in tragic consequences for all concerned. Overestimating their abilities, prideful people are vain and boastful. Thinking themselves in control, they make foolish decisions that wreak havoc for themselves and for others. Ecological hubris puts humans at the center, cocky and confident they know best.

The vice of excess is *self-deprecation*. People who display this vice downplay their real abilities and speak disparagingly of their legitimate achievements. They are unable to acknowledge their actual gifts, or they refuse to properly assess their genuine strengths. Aristotle speaks of those who disclaim or belittle their authentic accomplishments as mock modest.[24]

Honesty is the refusal to deceive—others, oneself, or God. Honest people are without guile. They do not have a duplicitous bone in their body. They possess a singleness of intention, a straightforwardness of conduct. Ecological honesty brings with it sincerity and transparency. There is no need to do business at night, no need for cover-ups or slush funds or secrets. Honesty likes the light of day, the open air, telling the truth.

The vice of deficiency with respect to honesty is *deception*, or the culpable failure to be truthful. Deception is willful fraud. Represented in the lowest circles of Dante's Inferno, it is perversion of the truth for personal gain. Deception is cunning misrepresentation, most often fueled by envy or spite. Desperate to get even, the deceptive mislead others (and often themselves) in order to see their enemies harmed and humiliated. The ecologically deceptive skew the data and soft-peddle the downside.

The vice of excess is *uncontrolled candor*. Difficult to name but understood by all, this vice has never known a secret that it did not tell. Persons who exhibit this vice always tell "the truth," even if it means giving over to a rapacious developer the secretly negotiated asking price for a piece of prime greenway land. Those who try to be too honest have no feeling for the relational context of truth telling, famously described by Dietrich Bonhoeffer in his classic essay "What Is Meant by 'Telling the Truth.'"[25] To those who are overly frank, truth is truth and must be told, no matter what the situation.

In short, as humans we are both finite and faulted. Thus we have the moral obligation to act responsibly and with forethought. We must cultivate the virtues of humility and honesty while discouraging the vices of hubris and self-deprecation, deception and uncontrolled candor.

Wisdom and Hope

We have already examined the Genesis texts that speak of God blessing not only humans but all living creatures with the power to reproduce. As we have seen, in 1:22 and 1:28 God wills that fish and birds and humans be fruitful and multiply. The ability to bear fruit—to produce others of one's kind—is an important feature of a flourishing creation. As Calvin DeWitt reminds us, "It is God's will that the *whole of creation* be fruitful, not just people. And thus human fruitfulness may *not* be at the expense of God's blessing of fruitfulness to other creatures."[26]

This concern for reproductivity is also evident in the case law of the Old Testament—the various specific instructions meant to guide the Jews in the living of everyday life. For example, in Deuteronomy 22:6–7 we read, "If you come on a bird's nest, in any tree or on the ground, with fledglings or eggs, with the mother sitting on the fledglings or on the eggs, you shall not take the mother with the young. Let the mother go, taking only the young for yourself, in order that it may go well with you and you may live long." We are permitted to use the fruit of the earth, but we are not allowed to destroy the earth's ability to be fruitful. The kind of wise use that preserves the earth's ability to replenish itself is an important ingredient in living well.

Perhaps the most famous passage that conveys the importance of the fruitfulness of the earth is the story of the flood in Genesis 6–9. Recall from chapter 4 that in this narrative a grieving God decides not only to spare one human family but also to preserve two of every living thing, male and female. Following God's instructions Noah obediently gathers his menagerie of creatures—birds, wild animals, creeping things—to preserve them as well as their ability to reproduce. With Noah and his kin in the ark was "all flesh in which there was the breath of life" (7:15). In the oft overlooked turning point of the story (8:1), God remembers *all* those in the ark—human and nonhuman alike—and sends a redeeming wind, his Holy Spirit, to reorder the chaotic earth.

God, furthermore, makes a covenant with all the creatures in his floating species preserve. Six times in 9:8–17 we are told that God's covenant is with more than just the human. God's everlasting, unconditional covenant, verse 13 affirms, is with "the earth." And the rainbow is a reminder to us of God's promise of faithfulness and a reminder to God of his covenant. God covenants with more than just humans and in so doing acts to preserve the fruitfulness of creatures great and small.

In these texts we find the theological theme of *fruitfulness*. As provisioned by God, the earth is fruitful. Creatures produce sustenance for others and reproduce themselves. In this interdependent world of cycles and systems, even "unimportant" species and "ugly" creatures are valuable. From this theological motif I derive the ethical principle of *sustainability*. We dare not deplete or permanently damage that which supports, maintains, and nourishes our very existence. Nor ought we needlessly or wantonly impair the ability of other creatures to sustain themselves.

From this flows a fourth moral maxim: *Act in such a way that the ability of living creatures to maintain themselves and to reproduce is preserved.* More exactly, we have a prima facie duty to judiciously use those creatures under our care so as to provide for future generations. We need to use plants and animals to survive and to maintain our own existence, and as with all creatures, we affect our surroundings in part by consuming other organisms. However, we have an obligation to provide not only for our own human generations but also for the generations of those nonhuman creatures whose goods and services we use.

The virtues implied by the theological motif of fruitfulness and the ethical principle of sustainability are wisdom and hope. *Wisdom* is sound practical judgment based on uncommon insight honed through long experience and informed by cultivated memory. It is an excellence of intellect that allows one to know what the truly good life is and to live it well. For Christians wisdom originates, as the Wisdom literature in the Old Testament insists, in the fear of God.[27] From a biblical point of view, in other words, wisdom is rooted in the proper worship of God and in knowing the ways of God. Thus, the ecologically wise know that God is at the center of things and that God's good future includes the flourishing of the earth. By their lives, therefore, they bear witness to that future, fostering the fruitfulness of creation over the long haul.

As far as I can tell, wisdom is not a mean; hence, there are not two vices but only one. The vice contrary to wisdom is *foolishness*, or the habitual absence of sound judgment. The fool lacks good sense. He shows no discernment and eschews learning from the past. Ecologically speaking, foolishness is the disposition to act as if the earth is endlessly exploitable and expendable. Ecological services, such as the natural purification of water, are invisible, and ecological costs, such as air pollution, are seen as "externalities." By living only for today the fool acts as if the future does not matter. He eats the last seed corn.

Hope is confident expectation of future good. It is the imagination of some good future, accompanied by the belief that such a future is possible, combined with a desire that this future come to fruition.[28] For Christians this expectation is solidly based on God's promises and God's character as a keeper of promises. Christians hope because they worship a God who keeps covenant with creation and who raised Jesus from the dead as a sign of a coming future restoration of all things. As one of the classic theological virtues, listed with faith and love in 1 Corinthians 13, hope is necessary for life itself.[29] Ecologically, hope is a yearning for shalom rooted in the confidence that a good future lies in God's good hands. Ecological hope remembers, as does God, the rainbow.

The vice of deficiency opposite the virtue of hope is *despair*, for despair is the absence of any expectation of a good future. As its etymology suggests, it is the loss of all hope (de-*sperare*). Despair is cynicism of a profound kind, for it signals a failure or inability to trust. Despair is the hopelessness that leads, as Søren Kierkegaard powerfully describes it, to the sickness unto death.[30] Ecologically speaking, despair is hopelessness in the face of our aching earth. It is an abandonment of belief in the ultimate redemption of all things.

The vice of excess is *presumptuousness*, which can take two forms. Sometimes it has to do with what we call a presumptuous attitude.[31] In contrast to the confident expectation of genuine hope, this kind of false hope exudes an overconfidence that tends to take the good future for granted. It is an unwarranted audacity of belief. Taking the redemption of creation as a given, those with this kind of presumptuousness do nothing about our wounded world.

Another kind of presumptuousness concerns the grounds of belief rather than the level of confidence. Not all objects of hope are worthy of trust. There are many pretenders to hope in our exceedingly anxious world. Prophets (and profits) of easy credulity are lurking virtually everywhere. False hope is abundant. For example, J. Christiaan Beker observes that "just as suffering without hope degenerates into passive resignation, cynicism, or despair, so hope without a relation to suffering degenerates into false hope."[32] This species of presumptuousness presumes that ecological healing will be pain free, that it will not demand anything from us. "We don't have to drive less and recycle more; technology will save us," say its devotees.

In short, the earth is fruitful. We have a moral obligation to use that fruit sustainably. Hence, we must foster the development of people who embody the virtues of wisdom and hope and strive to diminish the vices of foolishness, despair, and presumptuousness.

Patience and Serenity

According to Scripture, work is good. As humans we are called to labor, to till the ground (Gen. 2:15), and in our work we are to find joy and blessing.[33] The curse of the fall is not that we now must work but that our work is toil and drudgery. It is no longer meaningful service to neighbor and a form of worship to God. Even God works. The act of creation itself is a work of God. And God rests. In Genesis 2:1–3 we are told that after the heavens and the earth and their teeming multitude of creatures were made, God rested and "blessed the seventh day and hallowed it." God works and God rests, and so also should we and the creatures under our care. The sabbath rest is, as it were, built into the fabric of the world—a divinely blessed feature of our creaturely existence.

We are reminded of this need for rest in the Ten Commandments. In Exodus 20:8–11 we are called to "remember the sabbath day, and keep it holy," for the seventh day is a sabbath to God on which "you shall not do any work—you, your son or your daughter, your male or female slave, your livestock, or the alien resident in your towns." Notable for our purposes is the injunction to rest animals on the sabbath. Cows and horses and mules need rest too.

The Israelites were instructed in specific ways about how to organize their lives. For example, in Leviticus 25 they were told that the land must be given a sabbath rest every seventh year. In the seventh year "you shall not sow your field or prune your vineyard. You shall not reap the aftergrowth of your harvest or gather the grapes of your unpruned vine" because "it shall be a year of complete rest for the land" (vv. 4–5). Furthermore, after seven seven-year cycles they were to observe a year of jubilee. In the fiftieth year "you shall proclaim liberty throughout the land to all its inhabitants," and "you shall return, every one of you, to your property and every one of you to your family." As in the sabbatical year, so too in the year of jubilee "you shall not sow, or reap the aftergrowth, or harvest the unpruned vines" (vv. 10–11). These stipulations were given, the text makes clear, so that "the land will yield its fruit, and you will eat your fill and live on it securely" (v. 19). Life on the land goes better when one observes God's commandments.

Lest these instructions in shalom-filled living seem quaint or out of date—relics from the (very) Old Testament—we should take note of the inaugural address of Jesus, as recorded in Luke 4. As he begins his public ministry, in his hometown synagogue Jesus quotes from the prophet Isaiah, chapter 61, and boldly declares that this prophetic text has been fulfilled. Empowered by the Holy Spirit, he asserts that he has come "to bring good news to the poor," and "to proclaim release to the captives and recovery of sight to the blind, to let the oppressed go free, and to proclaim the year of the Lord's favor" (Luke 4:18–19). In other words, Jesus announces that in his person the messianic age has come. The year of jubilee—the year of the Lord's favor—is a reality. In short, Jesus the Messiah dramatically reaffirms that the kingdom of God he has come to inaugurate is a reign of redistribution and rest. Those in need will be comforted, those wronged will be set right, and the weary will find rest. Sabbath is gospel.

These texts illustrate the theological motif of *sabbath*. God calls humans to rest from their labors. Indeed, God intends that humans give the people, animals, and land under their care periodic rest and the opportunity for restoration. From this theological motif comes the ethical principle of *rejuvenation*. We all require rest. Such intentional rest and nurture of creatures human and nonhuman not only fit our nature but also resist the relentless use and exploitation that drives much of modern society.

This motif and principle provide the fifth moral maxim: *Act in such a way that the creatures under your care are given their needful rest.* More exactly, we have a prima facie duty to rest the land and its inhabitants in ways appropriate to their needs. Though directed primarily to agricultural land and animals, with a little imagination this duty can be reasonably extended to include other things, such as species and their habitats.

Corresponding to the theological theme of sabbath and the ethical principle of rejuvenation are the moral excellences of patience and serenity. *Patience* is calm forbearance. It is that trait of character that allows us to resist the press of the moment. It steels us against the temptation to take the fast track. Patience presupposes a long view. No aged oak springs from an acorn overnight. No wetland is restored in a week. No endangered species recovers in a year. As Cardinal Newman once said, great acts take time. Patience helps us learn the truth of that aphorism. For Christians patience is grounded in God's merciful forbearance (2 Pet. 3:9). God is patient, not wanting any to perish.

In contrast, the vice of deficiency contrary to patience is *impetuousness*. This is an impulsiveness based on fear of the future that drives us to gratify our desires in the immediate moment, irrespective of the legitimate need of others. Those who exhibit this vice lack the ability to wait. They always eat first at the wilderness supper table. They never put off a purchase in order to pay cash when they can charge it now.

The vice of excess is *timidity*, the disposition to be overly patient—to wait when one must wait no longer. It denotes the failure to act properly when the situation calls for prompt action. Though similar to cowardice, the vice of deficiency of courage, timidity is more a lack of boldness or determination than a disgraceful display of cowardice. The ecologically timid sit on their hands when they should be writing letters or repairing trails.

Serenity is unruffled peacefulness, an inner calm amidst the chaos. It is the relatively rare ability to remain undisturbed by the raging seas that surround. It is tranquility born not of stoic indifference or apathy but rather nurtured by the assurance of God's grace. Mindful that God is continually at work in the world—ordering the chaos, mending the broken, reconciling the alienated—those whose character is marked by this trait go about their earthkeeping business with a calm assurance. Serenity is, in the last analysis, the Augustinian heart finally resting at home in God.

The vice of deficiency is *restlessness*. Characterized by fidgety and directionless activity, it is doing something just to do something, without any clear aim. Lacking any sense of inner peace, the restless person is ruffled by the slightest winds of trouble or discontent. Restlessness is living as if one is never at home. Feeling always on the road or on the run, such a homeless wayfarer never puts down roots, gets to know a place, or builds affection for his surroundings. He can never be an emplaced earthkeeper.

The vice of excess is *passivity*. Unruffled repose can degenerate into a kind of quietude that is indifferent to injustice, sorrow, or joy. There is no virtue in an inner calm that resembles rigor mortis. Tranquility is not lethargy. Being serene is not the same as being passive. The ecologically passive do nothing about restoring the local wetland or promoting the community farmers' market.

In short, all creatures need sabbath rest. We have the moral obligation to rest and rejuvenate the land and its creatures. Thus, we must cultivate the virtues of patience and serenity and actively discourage the vices of impetuousness and timidity, restlessness and passivity.

Benevolence and Love

In the history of the interpretation of Genesis, most of the attention has been given to chapter 1, verses 26 through 28. There we read that humans were given dominion over the fish and the birds and the cattle and the wild animals and the creeping things. For many this means that humans have license to exploit the nonhuman creatures of the earth. That is to say, dominion is understood as domination. As argued in chapters 3 and 4, however, this reading is clearly wrong, not to mention self-serving. Dominion does not mean domination but responsible care. As noted previously, Genesis 1:28 must be placed alongside Genesis 2:15, where we are told that God put the human in the garden "to till it and keep it." To till (*'ābād*) means to serve the earth for its own sake, and to keep (*šāmār*) means to protect the earth as one caringly guards something valuable. In Aaron's benedictory blessing, in which God is called upon to bless and keep his people (Num. 6:22–26), we catch sight of what it means to be a keeper. We are to serve the earth for its own good and to protect creation as God protects us. In summing up the message of this text, Calvin DeWitt puts it well: "Such keeping is not preservation as applied to pickles in a jar; it is the kind of keeping we ask

God to give us. When, in accord with Genesis 2:15, we keep the creation, we make sure that the creatures under our care are maintained with all their proper connections—connections with members of the same species, with the many other species with which they interact, with the soil, air, and water upon which they depend."[34] We are called by God, in short, to be earthkeepers.

That the earth is God's and we are to keep it is reiterated in many of the psalms. Psalm 24:1 declares, "The earth is the LORD's and all that is in it, the world, and those who live in it." Contrary to popular opinion, we do not own the earth or its creatures. God is the owner of the earth, for it was God who created it and continues to sustain it. Psalm 95 invites us to make a joyful noise to God not only because God is our savior but preeminently because "in his hand are the depths of the earth; the heights of the mountains are his also. The sea is his, for he made it, and the dry land, which his hands have formed" (vv. 4–5). And as we have seen with the flood narrative—perhaps the most powerful biblical reminder of our calling to be keepers of the earth—God covenants with more than just humans. All creatures—indeed the earth itself—are in covenant fellowship with God. Through the faithful work of "Noahs" ancient and modern, all living things are kept, protected, preserved.

In sum, these texts reveal the theological motif of *earthkeeping*. God is the rightful and proper owner of the earth, but God gives us the calling to be earthkeepers. We are given the joy and the responsibility to lovingly keep the garden that is the earth—in all its intricate fullness and dynamic relatedness. From this theological motif comes the ethical principle of *beneficence*. Doing good for the sake of the other is the essence of serving and keeping the earth. Conferring benefits on the earth is our God-given human calling.

Put in the form of a sixth moral maxim, this motif and corresponding principle enjoin us to *act so as to care for the earth's creatures, especially those creatures in need*. For example, with respect to nonhuman species, we have a prima facie duty to actively preserve species threatened with extinction. In other words, it is not enough merely to refrain from doing harm; in certain cases we are morally required to do good. We are obligated to act, not just obligated not to act. Thus, failure to promote the good makes one morally blameworthy.

The moral virtues implied by the theological theme of earthkeeping and the ethical principle of beneficence are benevolence and love.[35] *Benevolence* is the willingness to promote the well-being of another. Benevolent people are disposed to act kindly. They have a good (*bene*) will (*voluntas*) and thus usually produce (*facere*) good (*bene*) acts—acts that are beneficial. Further, such good acts are willed even if the bonds of affection are absent. It is in this sense that Jesus commands us to love one another (Matt. 22:34–40; Mark 12:28–34; Luke 10:25–28), for while our affections cannot be commanded, our wills can. We can and should will the good, even to those, such as our enemies (Matt. 5:44; Rom. 12:19–20), for whom we have no good feelings. We can and should will the good to people present and future, animals domestic and wild, ecosystems near and far.

There is only one vice corresponding to this virtue since, as with wisdom, benevolence is not a mean but an intrinsic good that admits of no excess. The vice contrary to benevolence is *malice*. Malice or malevolence is the intention to do evil or cause harm. Malice is ill will. It is the willful and culpable breaking of shalom. While often fueled by envy and resentment toward particular people, it can also be driven by an unexplainable desire to inflict suffering or cause distress—unexplainable in the sense that no feelings of spite or resentment toward the victim(s) necessarily accompany the willing of such actions. The malevolent can and often do act indiscriminately—for example, the terrorist whose evil actions are inflicted on a random group of people. Ecologically considered, malice is the willful destruction of the nonhuman world. Torturing animals. Vandalizing habitats. Disrupting biotic systems. All evidence of the breaking of shalom.

Love, as the term is used here, denotes strong affection for another. It is unselfish concern for the good of that for which one deeply cares. Such bonds of affection and care arise out of personal relationship, such as kinship or friendship, and hence love stands in contrast to benevolence, for which no such feelings are required. Love is, simply put, the disposition to care for the other whom one has come to know. And love is directed not only to people but also to beloved animals and plants—family pets and favorite trees—and to special places—river, forest, desert. These places of the heart evoke loyalty, affection, and care.[36]

As with benevolence and wisdom, love is not a mean, since there is no excess but only deficiency. Given this concept of love, its corresponding vice is *apathy*. Not to love is to lack feeling (*a-pathos*). Not to love is not to care. The opposite of love is not hatred but indifference—that vice singled out by John the Seer in his rebuke of the church at Laodicea (Rev. 3). Ecologically understood, apathy is the absence of any affection for other creatures or places. The ecologically apathetic are oblivious to and unconcerned about the havoc wreaked upon the earth. They live in utopia—no place—since they know no place well enough to really inhabit it. Such people feel no loss, nor do they mourn the absence of anything natural. In contrast, Aldo Leopold laments, "One of the penalties of an ecological education is that one lives alone in a world of wounds."[37]

In short, the earth is the Lord's and the fullness thereof. We humans are not owners but earthkeepers. We have a moral obligation to protect the creatures under our care, especially those whose existence is imperiled. Thus, we must encourage the formation of people who exhibit the virtues of benevolence and love, while discouraging the vices of malice and apathy.

Justice and Courage

Two of the most frequently occurring words in the Bible are "righteousness" and "justice." In the Old Testament God requires, in addition to mercy and compassion, righteousness (*ṣĕdāqâ*) and justice (*mišpāṭ*) of his people. For example, the last half of the Decalogue assumes that justice among humans is a central feature of human flourishing (Exod. 20:12–17). Stealing and bearing false witness, for example, are violations of justice. They are thefts of goods—material possessions and reputation, respectively—that rightly belong to someone else. The covenant stipulations in Leviticus and Deuteronomy often include requirements to execute justice—especially for widows, orphans, and aliens (e.g., Lev. 19:15, 33; Deut. 10:18; 16:20; 24:17)—precisely because such action accords with God's character.

Likewise, the prophets regularly thunder that God's justice be done. Amos proclaims, "Let justice roll down like waters, and righteousness like an ever-flowing stream" (Amos 5:24). Micah summarizes the requirements of right living with these words: "to do justice, and to love kindness, and to walk humbly with your God" (Mic. 6:8). And Jeremiah's bones burn with the message of justice (Jer. 7:1–7). We also find this concern for justice eloquently and passionately articulated in the Wisdom literature. For example, in the first four verses of Psalm 72 the psalmist prays:

> Give the king your justice, O God,
>   and your righteousness to a king's son.
> May he judge your people with righteousness,
>   and your poor with justice.
> May the mountains yield prosperity for the people,
>   and the hills, in righteousness.
> May he defend the cause of the poor of the people,
>   give deliverance to the needy,
>   and crush the oppressor.

The psalm continues in this spirit, interweaving appeals for justice with hope for an abundant and fruitful land. As in many other texts, such as Isaiah 24, here in this psalm justice among people is intimately tied to the health and fruitfulness of the land. Social justice and ecological health are bound together.

In the New Testament the words and deeds of Jesus and the message of the apostle Paul also speak of righteousness and justice. Jesus, for example, redefines for the people of his day what true righteousness is all about. In the Sermon on the Mount, recounted in Matthew 5–7, Jesus emphasizes, often in arresting antitheses, that true piety is a matter of the heart. True righteousness is not a matter of externals but of purity of intention and hunger for justice. In a famous admonition Jesus encourages his followers to seek first the kingdom of God and God's righteousness (*dikaiosynē*; Matt. 6:33), and in so doing they will receive the nourishment and bodily provisions they need. In his inaugural address in Luke 4, as we observed previously, Jesus defines his mission, in part, as bringing justice to the oppressed. The new age dawning, of which Jesus speaks and to which he bears witness, is all about justice. No amount of interpretive gymnastics can drive Jesus' concern for social justice out of the Gospels.

Turning to Paul, some would say that righteousness (*dikaiosynē*) is at the center of his understanding of the gospel.[38] It is, of course, the righteousness or justice of God that is most central for Paul—the righteousness that we cannot attain on our own but that Jesus through his death has achieved for us (Phil. 3:9). But while this idea of righteousness as grace or divine favor is central, for Paul it has an inextricable social dimension. It is justice between people, especially Jews and Gentiles, that also concerns Paul. As James Dunn puts it, "The Christian doctrine of justification by faith begins as Paul's protest not as an individual sinner against a Jewish legalism, but as Paul's protest on behalf of Gentiles against Jewish exclusivism."[39] It was the way Jews separated themselves from non-Jews, creating an us-versus-them mentality, that drew Paul's ire. Hence, justification "cannot be reduced to the experience of individual salvation as though that was all there is to it"; justification by faith, rather, "is Paul's fundamental objection to the idea that God has limited his saving goodness to a particular people."[40]

In sum, these texts and many others like them give rise to the theological motif of *righteousness*. Because the God of the Bible is righteous and just, those who follow this God must be righteous and just. Of particular concern are those most likely to be treated unjustly, namely, the voiceless, the powerless, the homeless. And while this concern is appropriately and most often directed to humans, it also includes those nonhuman creatures whose voices remain silent to human ears. From this theological theme derives the ethical principle of *equity*. Equity is a kind of justice. More precisely, it denotes a type of distributive justice that allocates goods not according to the market, merit, or even equality but according to basic fairness in conjunction with need.[41]

Given this notion of justice as equity, I propose a seventh and final moral maxim: *Act so as to treat others, human or nonhuman, fairly*. More exactly, we have a prima facie duty to treat equals equally and unequals differentially. In other words, equity is not the same as equality. Equality implies sameness: one treats all, regardless of circumstances, the same. Equity implies different treatment when the circumstances warrant it, precisely in order to be fair. As any parent knows, in order to be equitable one must treat similar children in similar circumstances the same but must treat different children in dissimilar situations differently. All the seven-year-olds at your child's birthday party must be given the same amount of ice cream, on pain of loud cries of injustice. But seven-year-olds have privileges (and responsibilities) that four-year-olds do not.

Corresponding to the theological motif of righteousness and the ethical principle of equity are the moral virtues of justice and courage. *Justice* is the disposition to act impartially and fairly. It involves the ability to discern when to treat equals equally and unequals differentially, and thus it implies a kind of practical wisdom. As Lewis Smedes reminds us, justice implies respect— respect for the rights of others.[42] The just person not only respects the rights of the other but also knows how to respect those rights fairly when faced with the competing rights (and needs) of others. Ecological justice names the disposition to act fairly when faced with the competing claims of creatures human and nonhuman, of endangered species and damaged ecosystems.

As with wisdom, benevolence, and love, justice is not a mean and thus has only one corresponding vice, namely, *injustice*. Injustice is the propensity to be partial—to play favorites for no good reason or, more perversely, for personal gain. It is the failure to give people their due. Injustice manifests itself in the continual willingness to violate the rights of others, including the rights of nonhuman creatures. Or if you think that nonhuman creatures have no rights, injustice is the failure of human moral agents to properly exercise our duties to those creatures whose intrinsic value makes them objects of our concern.

Courage is moral strength in the face of danger. It is tenacity in the face of opposition. It is stubborn persistence in the face of adversity. One of the four cardinal virtues for the Greeks, courage implies a firmness of mind and resoluteness of spirit despite the fearful awareness of danger. A virtue particularly sought after by soldiers in the ancient world, in the Christian tradition courage was transmuted into fortitude. In the face of ecological apathy and ignorance and fear, courage is the dogged determination to persevere in caring for the earth.

The vice of deficiency is *cowardice*, or the inability to overcome fear without being reckless. Paralyzed with fear, the coward lacks the ability to act when the situation calls for decisive or swift action. Danger becomes debilitating. The ecological crisis is too much—too overwhelming, too scary, too fearful—and so the coward does nothing.

The vice of excess associated with courage is *rashness*. While courageous people honestly face their fear and persevere in spite of its sometimes paralyzing effects, rash people refuse to acknowledge their fear and thus act hastily or without proper caution. In so doing they often put themselves and/or others in danger. Often masquerading as bravado, this vice is really a recklessness that foolishly ignores signs of danger. The ecologically rash stuff their fear and rush off "to save the earth," but in so doing they often do more damage than good.

In short, righteousness and justice are integral features of God's world of shalom. We have the moral obligation to treat others fairly, giving special care to those creatures who by virtue of circumstance require it. Therefore, we must cultivate the moral excellences of justice and courage—while discouraging the vices of injustice, cowardice, and rashness—in the formation of our individual and collective character.

On Being Caretakers of the Earth

What kind of people ought we be, and why should we strive to become such people? First, the various kinds of animals and plants that populate the earth are created by God and are, therefore, valuable, irrespective of their usefulness to us. Such value implies that we must not needlessly harm those species under our care. We must respect our nonhuman neighbors and with receptivity acknowledge our common dependence on God. Second, the earth and its creatures are finite. Thus, we must live within our means, conserving and preserving our resources by exercising self-restraint and living frugally. In so doing we show hospitality.

Third, we are limited and often self-deceived in how we view the world. Though we sometimes think we have infallible insight into the future, we do not and never will. Thus, we must be cautious, acting with humility and honesty when making decisions about the future of the earth and its inhabitants. Fourth, the God-designed world is fruitful and able to sustain itself. We must wisely use the creatures under our care so as to provide for future generations. We dare not eat the last seed corn. We must preserve the earth's fruitfulness. In so doing we witness to the divinely inspired hope that is within us.

Fifth, work is good, but so is rest. We all—people, animals, land—need a sabbath from our labors. We must allow for times of rejuvenation. With patience and serenity we must resist the relentless drive to exploit. Sixth, the earth is God's, not ours. We are not owners but earthkeepers—called to serve and protect the earth. We must be willing to promote the well-being of all those who live within the garden. Fighting malice and apathy with benevolence and love, we follow the pattern of Christ.

Seventh and last, the cries for righteousness and justice must not go unheeded. God, who is just, calls us to do justice, not only in regard to suffering humans but also with respect to an aching earth. We must have the courage of our convictions and treat others justly. That which needs special treatment—homeless people, fragile land, rare species—we are obligated to treat with special care. In all that we do and say, we must gratefully acknowledge our Creator-Redeemer, the Maker of heaven and earth, who richly provisions us for the journey.

There is much work to be done. With regard to caring for the earth there is much good work to be done. There are biological field studies to perform. There are groundwater remediation experiments to run. There are creation awareness centers to set up. There are school-yard ecology programs to implement. There are old milk cartons to recycle. There are lights to turn off. There is compost to turn.

But very little of that good work of keeping the earth will be accomplished without the concrete embodiment of the virtues just discussed. Therefore, while this subject is in one sense theoretical, it is in fact intensely practical, for virtues, after all, should not only be studied but should also be put into practice. As Aristotle reminds us in his own book of ethics, "Surely, as the saying goes, where there are things to be done the end is not to survey and recognize the various things, but rather to do them; with regard to virtue, then, it is not enough to know, but we must try to have and use it."[43] Or as James reminds us in his contribution to the New Testament, "So faith by itself, if it has no works, is dead" (James 2:17). The good work of earthkeeping is impossible without respect, receptivity, self-restraint, frugality, humility, honesty, wisdom, hope, patience, serenity, benevolence, love, justice, and courage. To do the work God calls us to do, these fundamental traits of character are necessary. *Character is central to the care of the earth.*

But lest we succumb to the alluring though false belief that human character is not only necessary but also sufficient—that the virtues listed above will be enough to silence the groaning of the earth—Wendell Berry reminds us that caring for the earth is not our task alone, and we dare not think that on our slim shoulders the world and its fate rest.

> Whatever is foreseen in joy
> Must be lived out from day to day.
> Vision held open in the dark
> By our ten thousand days of work.
> Harvest will fill the barn; for that
> The hand must ache, the face must sweat.
>
> And yet no leaf or grain is filled
> By work of ours; the field is tilled
> And left to grace. That we may reap,
> Great work is done while we're asleep.
>
> When we work well, a Sabbath mood
> Rests on our day, and finds it good.[44]

The Ecological Virtues

Theological Motif	Ethical Principle	Virtue	Vice (deficiency)	Vice (excess)
Creational Integrity	Intrinsic Value	Respect Receptivity	Conceit Autonomy	Reverence Addiction
Creational Finitude	Sufficiency	Self-restraint Frugality	Profligacy Greed	Austerity Stinginess
Human Finitude and Faultedness	Responsibility	Humility Honesty	Hubris Deception	Self-deprecation Uncontrolled Candor
Fruitfulness	Sustainability	Wisdom Hope	Foolishness Despair	Presumptuousness
Sabbath	Rejuvenation	Patience Serenity	Impetuousness Restlessness	Timidity Passivity
Earthkeeping	Beneficence	Benevolence Love	Malice Apathy	—— ——
Righteousness	Equity	Justice Courage	Injustice Cowardice	—— Rashness

why worry about galapagos penguins and the jack pine?

arguments for earth-care

> I have never been able to entertain a God-idea which was not integrally related to the fact of chipmunks, squirrels, hippopotamuses, galaxies, and light years.
>
> Joseph Sittler[1]

One of the lesser known stories by Dr. Seuss is *The Lorax*. I discovered this treasure, first published in 1971, in an anthology while searching for a story for my three daughters as part of our nightly bedtime ritual. The Lorax, it seems, was shortish, oldish, brownish, mossy, and spoke with a voice that was sharpish and bossy. But he did so because his vocation was to speak for the trees. Since the Truffula Trees had no tongues, the Lorax gave voice to their concerns as well as those of the Brown Bar-ba-loots, the Swomee-Swans, the Humming-Fish, and all the other creatures who flourished down where the Grickle-grass grows.

Alas, his voice was no match for the biggering and biggering that turned Truffula Trees into thneeds—those all-purpose items that everyone needs. And so when the ax fell on the very last Truffula Tree—and after the Swomee-Swans could no longer sing a note because of the smogulous smoke deep down in their throat—the Lorax heisted himself and took leave of that place through

155

a hole in the smog without leaving a trace. But that, we discover, is not quite right, for the Lorax did leave something behind. The narrator tells us that the Lorax left here in this mess a small pile of rocks with the word "Unless." And in retelling the story our worrisome narrator-friend, the Once-ler, unlocks the meaning of the Lorax's puzzling legacy: "Now that you are here the word of the Lorax seems perfectly clear. UNLESS someone like you cares a whole awful lot, nothing is going to get better. It's not."[2]

With that insight the Once-ler entrusts the reader with the last remaining Truffula seed, and in hope-filled words that conclude the story he declares that if we "plant a new Truffula and treat it with care, give it clean water and feed it fresh air, grow a forest and protect it from axes that hack, then the Lorax and all of his friends may come back."[3]

Who speaks for the trees? And why worry about them in the first place? Why in particular should Christians consider, like the Lorax, speaking—and caring— for our equivalents of Truffula Trees and Brown Bar-ba-loots and Humming-Fish? After all, isn't all this concern for ecology just another passing fad? And won't new technologies be invented to address our ecological problems? And, ultimately, why care for a world that will be completely destroyed when Jesus comes again? Besides, who wants to be a Lorax, fighting for lost and impossible causes? Why care for the earth?

In chapter 3 I attempted to rebut various arguments against caring for the earth, demonstrating how the main claims that constitute the so-called ecological complaint against Christianity are problematic. My strategy there was to give reasons for not accepting certain arguments, for why supposedly sound arguments are in fact not persuasive. The ecological complaint, I argued, is eminently rejectable. I did not, however, offer reasons as to why we should care for the earth. That more positive or constructive task is the focus of this penultimate chapter.

In the press, in popular literature, and in scholarly books and articles, many arguments are made for why we should take better care of the earth. What follows here are ten of the most important arguments. My purpose, however, is not merely to explain and analyze these arguments. I intend, rather, to present a cumulative case for earth-care. By cumulative I mean that the arguments all support the same conclusion. Despite their considerable differences and various problems, these arguments provide a compelling rationale—moving from prudence to piety—for taking better care of our home planet.[4] To use the language of logic, these ten arguments together constitute a conductive argument or convergent support pattern in favor of the claim that we ought to care for the earth. In a manner similar to a braided climbing rope, in which various strands are woven together to provide the strength necessary to support the weight of a falling climber, these arguments taken together are stronger than any argument by itself.

Some of these arguments, I readily acknowledge, are more persuasive than others.[5] They are not all of equal rhetorical value. For example, the animal rights argument is, in my view, quite problematic. It is, however, an important part of the contemporary debate and despite its problems raises a number of significant questions that must be addressed. The fact that you or I find certain of these arguments more persuasive than others does not necessarily imply that the others are not useful or of value. In short, all the arguments here presented are valuable, though some may be more compelling than others.[6] So what exactly are the arguments? Why should we Christians speak for the trees?

If You Breathe, Thank a Tree

"Your Air Is Being Polluted" shouted the headline of a fundraising letter from a well-known environmental organization. Send a financial contribution to support our efforts to enact more earth-friendly legislation, the letter continued. Why? It is in your self-interest. Perhaps the most common argument, prominent especially in the popular media and in public policy debates, is the self-interest argument, or what I call the "if you breathe, thank a tree" argument. It says that it is in our self-interest to care for the earth. It is in our interest as individuals (and as cities, countries, and ultimately a species) to take better care of the earth and its various creatures. For example, it is in our self-interest to protect the rain forests since the very air we breathe—more exactly, the oxygen we need to survive—comes from, among other things, the trees of the earth. Or it is in our self-interest to preserve the quantity and protect the quality of our drinking water since either scarce or contaminated water spells hardship (if not doom) for the human community. This argument is used with respect to a variety of necessary but threatened "resources" of human existence, but the basic form is the same. We should care for the earth because if we destroy or even severely diminish certain organisms, communities, or ecosystems, then we imperil our own existence.

This argument is simple and, for many people, quite compelling. All of us do, after all, have to breathe. We all desire and depend on that most basic elixir of life—water. Thus, a recognition of the inescapable dependence of human life—and of our own life in particular—on features of our planetary home, such as air and water, can be a persuasive motivation for changed thinking and acting. Experience living in places where basic necessities such as air and water are significantly compromised has prompted me to reconsider how I live—simply, truth be told, in order to make my *own* life better. No concern here for future human generations or the health of endangered species. And given the human propensity to self-interest, prudential arguments such as these will always find a receptive public this side of the eschaton.

As with most arguments that rely only on self-interest, however, the "if you breathe, thank a tree" argument leaves much to be desired. While realistic in its assessment of human nature, it is inadequate in its understanding of human ethics. While not all appeals to personal welfare or prudence are illegitimate—indeed, some say we have certain duties to self—most of us want and expect *more* in an ethics argument than simply an appeal to enlightened self-interest. We may think that not many people will live up to them, but in the offering of moral arguments we expect an appeal to moral standards. We may think that not many people will seriously consider them, but in the giving of moral reasons we expect some attention to moral goods. We may think that not many people will be found embodying them, but in the analysis of moral behavior we expect to find displayed some moral virtues. Indeed, for many people an argument that depends entirely on an appeal to self-interest, however enlightened, is a defective argument. Psychologically persuasive, perhaps, but morally defective. Therefore, despite its simplicity and charm, this argument will not suffice. We must move beyond mere prudence.

On Loan from Our Children

Another argument, quite common in both popular and professional literature, seeks to overcome some of the deficiencies of the self-interest argument and to give voice to a common moral intuition. I call this the "on loan from our children" argument. It is, in slightly more technical language, the "obligations for future generations" argument. The basic claim is captured well in the statement, we not only inherit the earth from our ancestors but borrow it from our children. Or to paraphrase the Great Law of the Haudenosaunee, in our every deliberation, we must consider the impact of our decisions on the next seven generations. The earth is on loan to us from our children and our children's children. We do not own the earth—its minerals, soils, plants, animals. We are to use them, to be sure; indeed, we cannot but do so, for all organisms must use other organisms to survive and flourish. But, properly understood, the earth and its plethora of inhabitants are entrusted to us to use in such a way that our human progeny will also be enabled to flourish. At the heart of this argument is the claim that our descendents, some of whom do not yet exist, are entitled to an inhabitable earth. This right of future generations to a livable planet entails that we today have certain duties or obligations. In short, we should care for the earth because we owe it to our children.

This argument is quite compelling. Who among us does not think about the legacy left to upcoming generations? What caring mother does not wish for her son or daughter a future bright with possibility and hope? What loving father does not order his life so that his daughters and sons will be enabled to realize their dreams? We naturally feel obligated—by bonds of family and tribe and nation—to pass on a goodly inheritance to those who come after us. The moral intuition lying behind this argument is not just common but time-honored. It rightly articulates what at its best is not an onerous "duty" but a thing of joy: passing on one's inheritance, whether it be cherished beliefs, identity-sustaining stories, or grandma's piano. So too, this argument rightly asserts, we ought to live in such a sustainable way that we pass on to our children an earth replenished and replenishable. If we truly care for our children, then we will strive to preserve their most all-encompassing habitat—the earth.

But, someone will assert, it is one thing to affirm a grand moral principle, high in the stratosphere of ethical theory; it is quite another to apply such a principle in the muddiness of life. For example, our interlocutor continues, what precisely do we owe to our children, ecologically speaking? To use a simple but apt example, some backpackers hike with the moral maxim that they owe it to those who come after them on the trail to leave it in as good a shape as they found it. In other words, pick up your own trash, but don't feel obligated to pick up anyone else's. Others follow a maxim that stipulates they should leave the woods in even better condition than it was before they stumbled up Rattlesnake Hill or camped on Lake Ucantipovertu. So they pack out all garbage—regardless of the source—and often at considerable cost in toil and sweat. To the latter group, those in the former group are moral slackards, happy to get by with the moral minimum. To the former group, those in the latter group are masochistic do-gooders whose works of supererogation may earn them entry into ecological heaven but whose sense of duty is unnecessarily high. In short, which obligations are the *correct* obligations?

This query carries some force. In an entitlement age, when everyone seems to think they have a right to almost anything, we should be cautious about extending too far the umbrella of rights.[7] In a culture in which bumper stickers declare, "Prosperity is my divine right," we should most certainly ask questions about whether claims are legitimate and obligations appropriate. But while there may be little consensus as to whether we are obligated to give people what they merely want, it is fairly uncontroversial that we are morally obligated to give people what they truly need.[8] Basic needs such as air, water, food, and shelter are inalienable; hence, the term "sustenance rights."[9] Proper skepticism about your neighbors' claim that they have a right to a BMW or tiresome debates about competing moral duties should not obscure the fact that we do have certain duties to others by virtue of their legitimate claims on us. Further, in a world in which over a billion people have inadequate daily nutrition—enough people to stretch shoulder-to-shoulder around the world at the equator over thirteen times—many justifiably question the consumption patterns of those of us in the overdeveloped West.[10] Christians especially ought to be concerned about patterns of consumption that deprive many people of having their most basic needs met. Thus, despite criticism, the "on loan from our children" argument has considerable merit and is for many a persuasive reason to better care for the earth.

'Tis a Gift to Be Simple

Discussion of our current patterns of living in the affluent West leads to the third argument—what I call, borrowing from the famous Shaker hymn, the "'tis a gift to be simple" argument. Otherwise known as the joyful simplicity argument, those who champion this approach reason, appropriately, quite simply. In the words of Bill McKibben, "The secret weapon of environmental change and of social justice must be this—living with simple elegance is more *pleasurable* than living caught in the middle of our consumer culture."[11] Cultural norms to the contrary, more is not necessarily better, for us or for the earth. As social psychologist David Myers concludes after an exhaustive review of the literature, there is no correlation whatsoever between wealth and well-being.[12] He goes on to affirm, "Realizing that well-being is something other than being well-off is liberating."[13] A simpler way of life liberates us from emulating "the lifestyles of the rich and famous" and thereby enables us to find authentic happiness. As the Shaker hymn refrain states: "'tis the gift to be simple, 'tis the gift to be free, 'tis the gift to come down where you ought to be; and when we find ourselves in the place just right, 'twill be in the valley of love and delight." In sum, we should care for the earth because an earth-friendly way of life is simply more joyful.

This argument rings true for an increasing number of people today. Henry David Thoreau said it many years ago: "Most of the luxuries, and many of the so-called comforts of life, are not only not indispensable, but positive hindrances to the elevation of mankind."[14] Centuries before that a wandering Jewish rabbi insisted that a person could not serve both the God of Abraham, Isaac, and Jacob and the god of wealth (Matt. 6:24). Contemporary culture-watchers verify this ancient wisdom. The thesis of Paul Wachtel's insightful book, with the telling title *The Poverty of Affluence*, is that "our society's preoccupation with goods and with material productivity is in large measure irrational and serves needs similar to those which motivate neurotic defense mechanisms in individuals." In other words, our society is sick. Our consumer culture of getting and spending all too often masks an inner spiritual emptiness we lack the courage to face. Thus, Wachtel concludes, "So long as we persist in defining well-being predominately in economic terms and in relying on economic considerations to provide us our primary frame of reference for personal and social policy decisions, we will remain unsatisfied."[15] The bumper sticker's proclamation that "whoever dies with the most toys wins" is a bald-faced lie. The emphasis on simplicity, with its challenge to uncomplicate our lives by recognizing what is truly worthwhile, is a much-needed antidote to the fearful and anxious acquisitiveness that so characterizes our age.

The joyful simplicity argument has further merit in lifting to consciousness the central place of the virtues in the moral life, since simplicity is, as one contemporary writer puts it, one of the ecological virtues.[16] A virtue, recall from the last chapter, is a habitual disposition to act in an excellent way—a praiseworthy character trait. As alluded to above, the virtue of simplicity refers to the disposition to discern the truly valuable and thus live a life of uncluttered contentment. People who embody this virtue live against the grain of the avariciousness of our culture, for example, by using fewer nonrenewable natural resources. In short, this argument reminds us of the importance of character and virtue, including ecological virtues such as simplicity, respect, self-restraint, frugality, serenity, justice, and humility.

But, some object, the "'tis a gift to be simple" argument is merely a smoke screen for a self-serving individualism. It legitimates a concern for the self, which isolates people from their neighbors. Furthermore, the very foundation of our social order depends on the increasing consumption of goods. Our way of life would collapse if too many people adopted a simpler lifestyle. And even if it were the morally excellent thing to do, it is unrealistic to believe that people in any great number will really change the way they live. Advocates of simpler living are, like Don Quixote, tilting at windmills. A grand idea, perhaps, but an impossible ideal.

The last objection might have some punch if one assumed that probable results or consequences are the ultimate moral litmus test. But why make that assumption? Why assume that to be morally good your action must produce noteworthy consequences? Should we not, especially we Christians, simply do the right thing, regardless of the results? Since when are Christians consequentialists? The objection about consumption voices a common complaint, namely, that any attempt to scale back our desires and spending habits will push the economy into a tailspin and destroy "the American way of life." Truth be told, however, our current way of life is in many respects unsustainable,[17] and it is already showing signs of collapse.[18] Maybe our way of life ought not revolve around the constant quest for more stuff. Christians most of all ought to question whether consumeristic materialism is worthy of allegiance. Given the God we serve, can we justify a way of life predicated on the inordinate desire for that which moth and rust consume?

As for the first objection, the true aim of simplicity is not isolation but community, not individual enrichment but shalom for one's neighbors in need. As the old motto puts it: "Live simply so that others may simply live." Simplicity is not driven by a desire to be parsimonious for parsimony's sake; rather, we live simply in order to unclutter our lives so as to focus on what is truly important. The "'tis a gift to be simple" argument, therefore, should not be dismissed. Indeed, maybe simplicity will function as McKibben predicts—as a secret weapon to liberate those souls caught in the all-consuming whirlwind of our consumer culture.

Poor and Oppressed Unite

One might call the fourth argument "poor and oppressed unite," since it posits a link between various forms of oppression. It is more commonly called the ecojustice argument, since it is grounded in an appeal to justice. This argument has a variety of specific forms. For example, contemporary Christian feminist theologian Rosemary Radford Ruether argues that "we cannot criticize the hierarchy of male over female without ultimately criticizing and overcoming the hierarchy of human over nature."[19] Sexism, in other words, is integrally connected to anthropocentrism, and anthropocentrism contributes to ecological degradation.[20] Thus, those who work to overcome the domination of women must realize that the success of their struggle is dependent on the struggle to stop the exploitation of the earth. Conversely, ecology activists must realize that their work goes hand in hand with those fighting for greater equity for women. Like many ecofeminists, Ruether claims: "Women must see that there can be no liberation for them and no solution to the ecological crisis within a society whose fundamental model of relationships continues to be one of domination. They must unite the demands of the women's movement with those of the ecological movement to envision a radical reshaping of the basic socioeconomic relations and the underlying values of this society."[21]

Another form of this argument concerns not sexism but racism. Commenting on the revealing 1987 study "Toxic Wastes and Race in the United States," Charles Lee states, "The racial composition of a community is the single variable best able to explain the existence or non-existence of commercial hazardous waste facilities in that area. Racial minorities, primarily African-Americans and Hispanics, are strikingly overrepresented in communities with such facilities."[22] Lee and others thus speak of "environmental racism" and insist that we must link the issues of environmental pollution and racial equity.[23] Ecological sustainability and social justice must be seen as interdependent goals.[24] If we care for humans who are treated unjustly, then we should also care for an exploited earth. In short, we should care for the earth because the various forms of oppression are interlinked.

This argument, as many have increasingly recognized, is persuasive and important. For example, there is a growing body of empirical evidence for the existence of environmental racism.[25] There are positive correlations and, many argue, causal links between the location of toxic waste sites and the residences of people of color. Given that sexism and racism and the exploitation of the earth are connected, concern for one should entail concern for the others. The ecology movement and the various movements for human liberation, which have for too long been separate and at times antagonistic projects, must see themselves as allies in a common quest. There is, happily, growing recognition of this fact.[26] No one has made this point more forcibly than Paul Hawken, who writes, "A Native American taught me that the division between ecology and human rights was an artificial one, and that the environmental and social justice movements addressed two sides of a single larger dilemma. The way we harm the earth affects all people, and how we treat one another is reflected in how we treat the earth."[27] The environmental movement and the social justice movement are two of the "three basic roots" (along with the movement of indigenous peoples against globalization) of the larger worldwide movement Hawken exhaustively catalogues and describes.

However, while this argument at its foundation is sound, some of its specific forms are not. For example, it is a non sequitur to claim that a necessary condition for equality between women and men is that all hierarchy between humans and nonhumans, or humans and God, be abolished.[28] It simply does not follow that gender equity is possible only if marmots and junipers and people are put on equal moral footing. It does not follow that responsible care for the earth is possible only if God is reconceived as wholly immanent. But one does not need to accept such axiological egalitarianism in order to agree with the main claim about the connection between various forms of oppression.

Others object that while these movements must be seen as interrelated, it is often impossible to devote time and energy to all such causes. In other words, how does one committed to both social justice and ecological harmony—sheltering the homeless and protecting the water quality of the local river—devote adequate time to each? Our time and energy are finite; would it not be better to concentrate on one or the other? This query deserves respect, for it usually arises out of a genuine concern. It also perceptively points out a curious logic in the ecojustice argument, namely, the assumption that unless our actions somehow connect the issues of ecological degradation and social injustice, they are suspect, as if doing nothing, in order to preserve consistency, was the more moral tack. Lest we fall victim to what I call the fallacy of erroneous consistency, we should heed Edmund Burke's wise words: No one made a greater mistake than the person who did nothing because he or she could not do everything. We can rightly acknowledge the many links between ecological despoilation and social injustice even if we devote ourselves more to addressing one set of problems than the other.

In sum, the "poor and oppressed unite" argument, despite criticisms, is an important strand in the cumulative case here being woven. Our passion for justice should embrace all creatures—for their sake and for the sake of our human neighbors whose voices cry out for justice to roll down like waters and righteousness like an ever-flowing stream.

Spotted Owls Have Rights Too

Some years ago there was considerable media attention devoted to the forests of the Pacific Northwest, since there was controversy over the plight of the northern spotted owl (*Strix occidentalis caurina*). The spotted owl's status as a threatened species had limited logging in some of the forests, and the media pitched the conflict as "loggers versus owls." Hence I have dubbed the fifth argument, which focuses on the rights of animals, the "spotted owls have rights too" argument.

The most well-known scholarly proponent of the animal rights argument is Tom Regan. Regan's argument, in essence, is this: If an organism is the subject of a life—that is, a conscious being with interests—then that organism has inherent value; certain animals are in fact subjects of a life; thus, those animals have inherent value; if an organism has inherent value, then it has moral rights; therefore, certain animals have moral rights. Thus, the concept of natural rights should be extended to include certain nonhuman creatures.[29] As indicated in chapter 5, the basic claim is that if certain animals have the same relevant characteristics as humans, then they too have the same rights—rights that entail certain duties for us as humans. In other words, we should care for the earth, or at least certain kinds of nonhuman creatures, because they are entitled to such care.

One need not accept every point in the reasoning to appreciate the intuitive force of this argument. We usually extend the domain of moral considerability to include those creatures most akin to us. That is, we rightly include certain nonhuman creatures within the realm of what counts morally. For example, we acknowledge certain duties to our pet dog Elvis or farm cow Bessie that do not pertain to the flea in Elvis's hair or the fly buzzing around Bessie's head. We have no compunction about killing the flea but would rightly have moral scruples about killing the dog, at least without good reason. Indeed, such moral scruples are codified in laws proscribing the inhumane treatment of animals. In other words, we de facto operate with a scale of value that some would say implicitly grants rights to certain creatures, such as pets and farm animals, which are not given to other creatures, such as insects or microorganisms.

However, as a number of critics maintain, animal rights arguments too often fail to recognize the larger ecosystemic context within which individual animals exist. Environmental philosopher Holmes Rolston persuasively argues that individual animals must be viewed in the context of their ecosystem, since only then can the legitimate and competing needs of other creatures be taken into account.[30] For example, is it morally permissible to kill wild deer? For Rolston, it all depends on the ecosystem within which the deer live. How large is the total deer population? What are the effects of the existing deer population on the ability of other animals and plants within that ecosystem to flourish? An animal rights perspective that prohibits all deer hunting fails to take into consideration those instances in which hunting deer is not just morally permissible but obligatory due to deer overpopulation and stress on the ecosystem. The fact that a deer may qualify as a subject of a life, to use Regan's terms, and hence have a right to live, is largely irrelevant, since the locus of value lies beyond the life of any individual deer. Only if the larger ecosystemic context is considered may decisions be properly made about the care of individual animals. Thus, the animal rights approach, in sum, is too individualistic.

Furthermore, some critics perceptively ask whether rights language is the most appropriate way to think and speak about this intuition concerning the care humans should properly give to certain nonhuman creatures. While it is clear that rights entail duties, it is not the case that duties necessarily imply rights. In other words, I may have a duty to someone or something regardless of whether that person or thing has the appropriate right. We may have duties to Elvis or Bessie even if they do not have any moral rights, and it may make more sense to think about those duties without using rights language. The "spotted owls have rights too" argument is nevertheless valuable insofar as it gives voice to an important moral intuition and leads us to think through the moral backing of a legal code most of us strongly support.

Value Generates Duty

A central question—perhaps *the* central question—in the discussion of ecological responsibility is this: Do nonhuman creatures have value irrespective of their usefulness to humans? The "value generates duty" argument, or the intrinsic value argument, answers this question with a resounding yes. Since intrinsic or noninstrumental value is objectively present in the natural world, and since the presence of such value generates certain duties for human agents, humans have obligations to care for the natural world. As Holmes Rolston puts it, "We follow what we love, and the love of an intrinsic good is always a moral relationship. Value generates duty."[31] Unlike the animal rights argument, this argument hinges not on the fact that certain nonhuman creatures have rights but rather on the fact that human moral agents have duties to, as Rolston argues, sentient life, organic life, endangered species, and even entire ecosystems. Thus, if marmots, sequoias, spotted owls, and old growth forests have value over and above any usefulness to humans, then we have duties to protect them, regardless of whether they have rights. We should care for the earth because certain animals, plants, and entire ecosystems are valuable for their own sake.

There has been much discussion concerning this argument, in particular the concept of intrinsic value.[32] As indicated previously (chapter 5, note 47), there are two sets of important distinctions—instrumental and intrinsic value, and subjective and objective value—that we must have clear in our minds. Instrumental value refers to the value something has because of its usefulness to humans. Intrinsic value refers to the value something has irrespective of its usefulness for human ends. So the worth of a maple tree as X board feet of lumber or as a location for a tree house is an example of instrumental value, while the worth of that maple tree as habitat for cardinals or as a creature that praises God is an example of intrinsic value. Subjective value indicates that something becomes valuable only if some human values it, while objective value refers to the value something has whether anyone values it or not. In other words, according to those who believe in subjective value, the maple tree is valuable only because some humans value it; for those who espouse objective value, the maple tree is valuable regardless of whether any human values it. Our valuing of the tree does not make it valuable; our valuing is a recognition of the value already there.

Given this understanding of the terms, Christians certainly have good grounds for accepting the initial premise of the argument above, namely, that there is intrinsic value objectively present in the natural world. For example, Psalm 104 insists that nonhuman creatures have value irrespective of their value to us. The mountains are valuable for the wild goats, the cedars are valuable for the storks, and the seas are valuable for Leviathan. And as Psalms 96 and 148 declare, all creatures are designed to sing praises to God. They have, one could say, doxological value as part of the grand symphony of creation—value regardless of whether any human values them. If this is the case, and given the truth of the premise concerning the relationship between value and duty, the conclusion follows: humans have duties to nonhuman creatures. We have a duty to ensure that the rocks and trees and rivers are able to praise God. To see a tree as only so many board feet of wood and a river as only a place to dump your waste are forms of myopic anthropocentrism (and utilitarianism) that reduce all value to human terms. A focus *only* on human use—even if wise use—is a stunted viewpoint that fails to acknowledge the value present in a world not of our making.

Some object, however, claiming that this argument implies that duties to nonhuman creatures are on par with duties to humans. Thus, it flies in the face of clear differences in value between humans and nonhumans. This approach necessarily entails, our objector continues, a biocentrism that levels important differences in value among the diverse creatures of the earth: it assumes that we have the same duties to marmots as to cousins Mary and Mark. But it does *not* necessarily follow from the intrinsic value argument that we have the *same* kind of duties to dogs or sequoias or rain forests that we have to humans. All that follows is that we have moral obligations to a wider range of creatures. The complicated business of sorting out the relative weight of competing duties is one of the thorny issues of this approach.[33] Such complications, however, should not detract from the cogency of this argument any more than they would an argument involving the conflicting duties we owe humans.

Another critic objects that nonhuman creatures do not value. Isn't valuing a distinctly human enterprise? And if so, how can one properly claim that value is objectively present in the natural world? This criticism, however, conflates value with valuing. Even if you assume that valuing is a uniquely human project—something only we humans do—why does it follow that no value is present in the nonhuman world? As Rolston nicely puts it in arguing against moral subjectivism, "We humans cannot know the value of something in the natural world without some feeling about it, but it does not follow that the value is just how we feel about it. The value comes mediated, communicated by our experience, but it does not follow that the value just is the experience."[34]

But in point of fact, valuing is not something only humans do, for God values creation. In God's eyes creation is, as Genesis 1:31 relates, very good. In sum, the "value generates duty" argument is an important argument. It reminds us that we have duties to care for nonhuman creatures for their own good, as well as for the goods we acquire from them.

We're All in This Together

We have all seen the photos—the earth from space, a single seamless web of a planet, devoid of political boundaries, dramatically evoking a sense of our finitude, our connectedness, our fragility. Such photos and feelings illustrate what I call the "we're all in this together" argument, sometimes referred to as the earth community argument. The main claim is that all of us on the earth are bound together in such a way that our ability to flourish is interdependent. One of the most influential arguments for this view is Aldo Leopold's land ethic. As outlined in chapter 5, for Leopold, "All ethics rest upon a single premise: that the individual is a member of a community of interdependent parts."[35] From this premise Leopold formulates his famous ethical maxim: "A thing is right when it tends to preserve the integrity, stability, and beauty of the biotic community. It is wrong when it tends otherwise."[36] Eight decades prior to Leopold, John Muir invoked a similar argument by asserting that "when we try to pick out anything by itself, we find it hitched to everything else in the universe."[37] The entire interconnected community that is the earth forms the proper context for human action and should guide our ethical decision-making.

While on the surface similar to the self-interest argument, this argument is actually quite different, since it is grounded not in an appeal to individual self-interest but in an acknowledgment of the common good. In other words, there is a recognition of the intricate web of life and multiple ways in which organisms are valuable within the community. For example, the preservation of trees is important not just because they are necessary for humans but also because the trees themselves—and the squirrels, birds, cicadas, and a host of other creatures who live in them—will be enhanced by such action. Planting and preserving trees is good for the health of the entire community. In sum, we should care for the earth because such care is in the best interest of the entire biotic community.

There are specifically Christian forms of this argument. For example, sounding very much like Muir, pioneering ecological theologian Joseph Sittler states that "nature is like a fine piece of cloth; you pull a thread here and it vibrates through the whole fabric."[38] Therefore, as evident in the epigraph to this chapter, Sittler concludes, "I have never been able to entertain a God-idea which was not integrally related to the fact of chipmunks, squirrels, hippopotamuses, galaxies, and light years."[39] Echoing Sittler, contemporary Lutheran theologian

Larry Rasmussen states, "The basic premise for future actions and outlook is the simple sentence above: all that exists, coexists. Community rests at the heart of things."[40] We should care for the earth because all creatures are created in community for the glory of God.

The merits of this argument are many. It not only recognizes one of the givens of ecology—that everything is connected to everything else—but it also, in its Christian articulations, takes seriously often overlooked aspects of Scripture. For example, as we have seen, the covenant spoken of in Genesis 6–9 is not just with humans, as is usually thought, but is with the earth and all its creatures. In addition, as demonstrated earlier, Psalms 104 and 148 speak of the value of and praise given by nonhuman members of the community of being. It is in fact the case, though we are sadly slow to realize it, that we are all in this together—men and women, whites and nonwhites, rich and poor, north and south and east and west, humans and nonhumans.

In addition, like the intrinsic value argument, this argument rightly calls into question the anthropocentrism of our age. Though we are the measurers of all things, we are not the measure of all things.[41] Such was the conceit of the Enlightenment, and such is the hubris of our own age. But such overweening pretensions to autonomy are destructive—of the earth, of our attempts at human community, of our own self-identity, of our relationship with God. The earth community argument displaces us from the center of the universe. It forcibly reminds us that *God* is the center of the cosmos, and our task and privilege is to worship the Maker of heaven and earth, in concert with all other creatures. As argued in various ways already, theocentrism rather than either anthropocentrism or biocentrism is the more appropriate stance for Christians to take.

One of the criticisms of this argument is that the mere acknowledgment of an overarching common good provides little specific guidance in making actual decisions. While this may be true, such an acknowledgment is no small achievement and should not be discounted. For example, while the land ethic may not in fact easily resolve every particular decision (and which ethic does?), it does instill a sensibility that renders such decision-making more ecologically informed. It enlarges our moral imagination and informs it as to how the world works. Reflection on our Christian responsibilities as earthkeepers is simply more ecologically and theologically informed when Sittler's chipmunks, squirrels, hippopotamuses, galaxies, and light years are taken into account, lest the notion of earthkeeper devolve into a managerial notion of steward, devoid of the care befitting the biblical term.

As indicated in chapter 5, other critics assert that common good arguments such as this one can too easily legitimate injustice. Without the presence of some rule or principle to safeguard certain basic rights, those rights run the risk of being violated for the sake of the end (the common good) in view. For example, some property owners claim they are treated unjustly—their property rights are violated—when certain restrictions are placed on the use of their property because of the presence of endangered species and/or their habitats. True enough, there is the danger of good ends sanctioning unjust means. But the earth community argument can be modified to preclude this possibility and thus defuse this criticism. In the above case, the current U.S. Endangered Species Act includes provisions for taking the concerns of property owners seriously, for example, incidental take permits and habitat conservation plans. Hence, despite these criticisms, the "we're all in this together" argument is a significant addition to the cumulative case for caring for the earth.

God Says So

The eighth argument, and perhaps the most straightforward, is the "God says so" argument. Otherwise known as the divine command argument, this position takes various forms, but the basic structure is simple: God commands that we care for the earth; authentic faith demands that we obey God; therefore, we should care for the earth. For example, the often neglected Genesis 2:15 states that God created humankind to serve and protect the earth. We are called by God to be earthkeepers; therefore, we should strive to keep the earth just as God promises in the Aaronic blessing of Numbers 6 to keep us. Further, in Leviticus 25 we are commanded to give the land a sabbath. Regardless of whether such legislation was ever followed in ancient Israel, God's command is clear. We should regularly rest the land, its animals, and its workers. Excessive exploitation is prohibited in order to preserve the land's fruitfulness. Genuine Christian discipleship requires that we obey God's commands, one of which is that we care for the earth and its creatures. We should care because God says so.

It is difficult to find fault with this argument. God's command to care for our home planet is clear, and obedience to God lies at the very center of the Christian life. Not surprisingly, therefore, the divine command argument is, for most Christians, a powerful argument.[42] If God prescribes certain actions and proscribes others, then faithful Christians, desirous of following God's commands, will enact that which God enjoins and abstain from that which God prohibits.

But, the critic will interject, why pick Genesis 2:15 and Leviticus 25 as the passages to live by? On what basis does one choose which commands—which texts—to take seriously? Doesn't the divine command argument run aground on the tricky business of knowing which of the many biblical commands are important for us here and now? This is a fair question, for very few if any Christians believe that all the commands in the Bible should be taken seriously today. Many of the injunctions in Leviticus—for example, the length of hair and type of dress—are rightly viewed as culturally specific and thus no longer required of us. However, not all the commands in Scripture can or should be dismissed. The Ten Commandments (Exod. 20:1–17; Deut. 5:1–21) have for Christians through the ages properly given guidance for living well. The various commands of Jesus—for example, to love God and neighbor (Matt. 22:34–40; Mark 12:28–34; Luke 10:25–28) and to love others as Jesus loved (John 13:34–35)—are naturally taken as divine commands by which to order one's life. In the case of ecological concerns, one must proceed on a text-by-text basis, and I can only state (and not here argue) that the texts cited above constitute commands that are still binding.

But even if we agree on which commands are binding, the critic continues, how do we figure out what God's will is in specific situations? How do God's commands apply in particular circumstances, and what do we do when there are apparently conflicting commands? Knowing God's will is easy in the abstract, but what about in the nitty-gritty of life? This is a legitimate concern because the business of discerning the will of God is not easy. Often we are puzzled, in the thick of a particular situation, about what to do. So we pray for divine guidance. We learn how the world works by being informed by the best science. We read the Bible. We talk to trusted friends. We do our homework on public policy issues. And we hope for a flash of insight or dose of wisdom. But despite our many questions about God's will and our genuine perplexity in certain situations, we usually know what God commands. The real problem most of the time, if we are honest, is doing it. The problem resides not in our knowing what we need to do but in willing what we know we should do. The spirit is willing, as Jesus says, but the flesh is weak (Matt. 26:41; Mark 14:38). It is clear from Scripture that one of God's commands is that we should care for the earth.

God's Concerns Are Our Concerns

The ninth argument is the "God's concerns are our concerns" argument, or the image of God argument. It states that since humans are meant to be God's image-bearers, and since being an image-bearer of God involves, among other things, caring for the needs of others, humans are called to show the kind of care that God exhibits. The classic scriptural warrant is Genesis 1:26–27. We are created in the image of God. We are God's vice-regents, meant to represent God and rule as God rules. And how does God rule? With care and compassion, remembering his covenant love and listening for and hearing the cries of the suffering and oppressed. Such a conclusion, drawn from throughout the Old Testament, is reinforced by New Testament texts such as Matthew 5–7 and John 13. Being an image-bearer of God means imitating Christ—the Christ who shares in our suffering, washes our feet, and voluntarily takes up a cross for our sake. Given that God is concerned for all creatures, the scope of our concern must include the nonhuman as well as human. In short, we should care for the earth because we are God's image-bearers, and since God cares about all creatures, so should we.

This, too, is a compelling argument. Given an acknowledgment that God is concerned about more than just humans, and given that we are called to image or represent God, it follows that we should care for more than just our own kind or our own place. Our care should include humid wetlands and arid deserts, the beautiful Western prairie orchid and the not-so-pretty Houston toad, soaring bald eagles and the American burying beetle. God cares about marmots and meadows and mountains, and so should we, since we are to reflect the all-encompassing and profoundly transforming love of God.

But, our friendly critic rejoins, the image of God argument actually undercuts care for the earth. For example, by indicating that only humans are created *imago Dei*, the Genesis 1 text emphasizes that we are of much greater value than nonhuman creatures. Since God obviously values people more than lizards or conifers, he argues, so should we. While it is true that only humans are created in the image of God, and that this makes us unique in important ways vis-à-vis other creatures, it does not follow that human uniqueness undermines our calling as earthkeepers. We are supremely valuable, but other creatures are valuable too. Our uniqueness does not exempt us from extending care but rather summons us to faithfully exercise our God-given responsibility to till and keep the garden that is the earth. Human uniqueness is not a license for exploitation but a call to service. If God cares for nonhuman creatures, then as God's image-bearers, so should we.

But on the broad canvas of history, our critic continues, God is concerned about more important things than snail darters and California condors. We should take care of first things first—saving souls, feeding people, preaching the gospel—and worry about grey wolves and northern falcons only after we have attended to God's primary concerns. Let's focus on the unadulterated gospel, he contends, and leave saving the earth to the secular tree huggers.

This objection voices an important concern. Care for the earth should never be construed as somehow anti-people. Christian earthkeepers are not misanthropes. This objection, however, wrongly assumes that the gospel is somehow unconnected to the earth, as if the message of the Bible concerns only disembodied souls in heaven, as if in the eschaton the canvas of creation will be annihilated, as if our Redeemer is not our Creator. In a properly expansive Christian vision, as set forth in the previous three chapters, worrying about wolves and warblers is part and parcel of the gospel—the good news that nothing is beyond God's wide redemptive embrace.[43] Thus, this criticism badly misses the mark by truncating the gospel. The "God's concerns are our concerns" argument is a persuasive reason to take seriously our calling to care for the earth, for it tells us who we are and what we are to do as members of God's kingdom.

For the Beauty of the Earth

The tenth and final argument is, to borrow from a famous hymn, the "for the beauty of the earth" argument. Perhaps better named the grateful heart argument, it claims that care for the earth and its inhabitants is a fitting response of gratitude for creatures who experience God's bountiful and gracious provisions. In the words of the hymn—responding to the gifts of earth and sky, hill and vale, tree and flower, sun and moon and stars of light—we sing, "Lord of all to thee we raise, this our hymn of grateful praise." Gratitude is the grammar of a grace that fosters respectful care for God's creatures and humble contentment with one's provisions.[44] We care for the earth because it is the appropriate and proper response to God's providential care for us.

This is a very persuasive argument. Indeed, in my view it is the most compelling reason, from a Christian point of view, to care for the earth. The phenomenology of grace and gratitude, whether between humans or between humans and God, suggests that the experience of gracious provision readily and rightly evokes a response of gratitude and care. In other words, when given a gift, especially a valuable gift or a gift that meets basic needs, the appropriate response is gratitude to the giver and care for the gift. Grace begets gratitude, and gratitude begets care.

Christians within the Reformed tradition should especially find this argument congenial given that gratitude is one of the theological themes emphasized within that tradition. For example, John Calvin repeatedly refers to creation as "this most beautiful theatre" and "this magnificent theatre of heaven and earth, crammed with innumerable miracles," for which we should thank and praise God.[45] Indeed, Calvin writes that "if the testimonies of Scripture were lacking, and they are very many and very clear, nature itself also exhorts us to give thanks to the Lord, because he has brought us into its light, granted us the use of it, and provided all the necessary means to preserve it."[46] As Calvin scholar Susan Schreiner comments, "The universe struck him [Calvin] as a constant course of revelation," and therefore, "illustrations and arguments from nature fill Calvin's writings."[47] For Calvin, the created order is divine gift, and gratitude the fitting response.

This spirit of gratitude pervades the most loved of the Dutch Reformed confessions, namely, the Heidelberg Catechism. Commenting on its three-part structure of guilt, grace, and gratitude, Henry Stob affirms: "What drives the Christian to love and obedience is thankfulness. This gives to the moral life a characteristic note of joy. Appreciative of God's mercy, thankful for his unspeakable gift, happy in his gracious conferments, the Christian seeks with might and main to show forth [God's] praises and to do [God's] will."[48] God's provisions—evident preeminently in the person of Jesus Christ but also manifest in the natural world—evoke gratitude and prompt joyful care. We live as we do, not because we should but because we may. Not obligation but thanksgiving drives the Christian moral life.

One necessary condition for this argument to be persuasive, however, is an acknowledgment of creation as a manifestation of divine grace—a recognition that earth and sky, hill and vale, tree and flower are in fact gifts. This itself presupposes both belief in God as Creator and some degree of knowledge of creation as the intricate, interdependent, and truly amazing system that it is. In other words, this argument is compelling only insofar as one acknowledges the Giver and the giftedness of creation. For those who believe in God but have little concrete knowledge about creation, and hence not much appreciation for the giftedness of the earth, or for those who know much about ecology but do not believe there is any Creator, this argument will not have much persuasive force. Despite this limitation, however, the "for the beauty of the earth" argument remains a compelling argument, for if we can begin to experience in the wondrous world around us God's extravagant and steadfast love, we will care for this provisioned earth not out of obligation or duty but out of gratitude and love.

So why care for the earth? For many reasons—many good reasons. Because our own existence is imperiled. Because we owe it to our children. Because an earth-friendly way of life is more joyful. Because various forms of oppression are of a piece. Because certain nonhuman creatures are entitled to our care. Because the earth is valuable for its own sake. Because it is in the best interest of the entire earth community. Because God says so. Because we are God's image-bearers. Because grace begets gratitude, and gratitude begets care. Because, in sum, care for the earth is integral to what it means to be a Christian—it is an important part of our piety, our spirituality, our collective way of being authentically Christian. Care for the earth is an expression of our devotion to the God whom we love and serve. Joseph Sittler once again articulately and accurately captures the theological heart of this matter: "We must expand our doctrine of God to acknowledge that he is not only the Lord to whom I flee in times of trouble, but he is also the maker of heaven and earth—God of all that is. When we say, 'I believe in the Holy Spirit, the Lord and giver of life,' the reference is not just to religious life, devotional life, prayer-book life. It means all of life."[49] If we embraced such an expansive theology, we would take better care of the earth. And if so, then maybe the Lorax and all his friends would come back. The last Truffula seed is in our hands.

where is there hope?

christian faith at home on earth

O God, we thank you for this universe, our great home; for its vastness and its riches, and for the manifoldness of the life which teems upon it and of which we are a part. We praise you for the arching sky and the blessed winds, for the driving clouds and the constellations on high. We praise you for the salt sea and the running water, for the everlasting hills, for the trees, and for the grass under our feet. We thank you for our senses by which we can see the splendor of the morning and hear the jubilant songs of love, and smell the breath of the spring-time. Grant us, we pray you, a heart wide open to all this joy and beauty, and save our souls from being so steeped in care or so darkened by passion that we pass heedless and unseeing when even the thornbush by the wayside is aflame with the glory of God.

Walter Rauschenbusch[1]

It has been a long journey, this book. We have gone from explorations of specific places and learning from our home planet to analyses of the many degradations of the natural world. From explanations as to why creation is groaning to exegeses of biblical texts. From an examination of Christian theology and ethics to a discussion of virtue and vice and various arguments for why we ought to care for the earth. In this dialogue between ecology and theology we have covered much ground. But what, at the end of the day, does it all amount to? More precisely, given the ecological challenges ahead, as well as the mandate to care for the earth, the burning question is: in what may we hope?[2] In an age of increasing cynicism and despair, where is hope? In a world of wounds, how do we find hope? There are no more existentially important questions to ask.

A response to such questions could be sought in any number of ways. One could, for example, find confidence in contemporary stories of ecological success. For example, in *Hope, Human and Wild* Bill McKibben speaks of three places on the earth—the Indian state of Kerala, the Brazilian city of Curitiba, and the Adirondacks of upstate New York—that offer gritty, realistic hope in the face of seemingly overwhelming obstacles and challenges.[3] Inroads are being made in regard to illiteracy and poverty. Pollution is being checked. Forests are growing back. Do not despair, he argues, and he is right. In telling such stories, McKibben kindles the (sometimes) dwindling flame of hope.

Or one could give an account of the various social movements aiming to produce a better planet. In *Blessed Unrest* Paul Hawken writes about literally thousands of groups around the globe that are working to change the world for the better. In the words of his subtitle he describes "how the largest social movement in history is restoring grace, justice, and beauty to the world."[4] The book's appendix alone is over one hundred pages long—filled with categories (and the number of organizations that fit those categories) and terms that describe different facets of this movement—ample evidence, Hawken argues, of social and environmental progress, and thus a firm foundation for hope.

Or one could recite recent breakthroughs in technology that hold out the promise of taming the twin dragons of consumption and pollution. The list is long and still growing: fuel-cell engines for motor vehicles that quadruple fuel efficiency, inexpensive and efficient photovoltaic technology, recycling of heretofore unusable materials, large-scale composting technology.[5] While the danger of placing one's faith in technological prowess is ever present, especially in our technology-infatuated age,[6] we should not overlook these and other innovations, for they do foster hope that we can adequately address at least some of our ecological problems.

Or one could refer to informed and sophisticated proposals to rethink our economy in ways more conducive to the health of the planet, especially in light of "the end of oil."[7] For example, in *The Bridge at the Edge of the World* James Speth outlines in considerable detail the opportunities we have for a "new consciousness" and "a new politics" as we engage in a large-scale transformation from a form of capitalism blind to the natural world to one that takes ecological sustainability as a given.[8] And in *Deep Economy* Bill McKibben offers a compelling case for moving beyond an economy in which growth is the paramount ideal to an economy characterized by genuine wealth and, as the subtitle indicates, a durable future.[9]

Or one could point to a growing awareness of ecological issues in the public consciousness. Or to polls showing an increasing number of people who rank the environment as one of the most important challenges facing us today. Or to continuing support for environmental legislation. Or to ecologically informed science curricula in schools. Or to citywide recycling programs. Or to wetlands restoration. All of the above are promising signs of hope.[10] All of these are important. None should be overlooked or dismissed.

But are these human seeds of hope enough? Do they provide a sufficient basis for genuine hope? In seeking to answer these questions Christians—evangelicals perhaps most of all—instinctively seek wisdom in Scripture, for if "the hopes and fears of all the years are met in Thee tonight," as the old Christmas carol claims, then the Bible and its witness to a God who tents among us offer just the hope we earth-dwellers need and so desperately seek. While many biblical texts address the question of hope, a lesser-known Old Testament text offers, I believe, precisely the vision of hope, and of a God of hope, that speaks to our burning questions and our aching need.

Learning from Isaiah 54

The woman took her place in line with the others. Her dark yet graying hair, penetrating and luminous eyes, and richly colored skin caused me to do a double take as she made her way among the guests at the homeless shelter that night. With her late-thirty-something son in tow, she sauntered up to the counter for the evening supper. That night we served a meager meal of spuds and rice, with whole milk thick as cow's cream for dessert. To them it was a feast. Them: "street people" to some, "homeless" to many, "guests" to us who worked at the shelter. After supper, to the mixed rhythm of chirps and snores, those with their homes on their backs or in their bags—Isodore, her son, and eighteen others—bedded down for the night.

Homelessness. Hopelessness. Living in exile. It comes in many forms.[11] One philosopher describes life today as "coping with the flux"—learning to get along in the concrete details of life without the guardrails of metaphysics or stable systems of thought.[12] Our time is a time of ever-accelerating change, motion, movement: faster computers, smaller cell phones, cell phones that are computers, next-day delivery, minute rice. And finding your way is for many a dizzying and confusing endeavor. Living in a whirlwind is disorienting. All the familiar landmarks seem to be gone or are, at best, only vaguely perceived.

This sense of coping with the flux is related to a pervasive sense of rootlessness. Many people perceive themselves as homeless wayfarers. As Frances FitzGerald puts it, commenting on communities as vastly different as Liberty Baptist Church, the Sun City Center retirement village in Florida, and the Rajneeshpuram commune in Oregon, "Rootlessness and the search for self-definition" are "characteristic features of American life."[13] Or as psychologist Paul Wachtel observes, "We are not only restless but rootless. In the pursuit of more, in the effort to better ourselves, we must leave behind what we previously had."[14] Or in the poignant words of one twenty-something nomad, "I have no beliefs. I belong to no community, tradition, or anything like that. I'm lost in this vast, vast world. I belong nowhere. I have absolutely no identity."[15] People feel homeless.

Such is the context of Isaiah 54. The people of Israel are in exile, homeless, hopeless. All is in flux. Their identity is at stake. Indeed, their theology is in crisis. Have the gods of Babylon triumphed? How do we sing the Lord's song in a strange land? Where is God in the midst of our suffering, our exile? In a foreign land, away from the temple, feeling deserted and abandoned by God, their hope had disappeared as fast as a drop of water on a sun-scorched weed. As you read the words below, can you feel the desperate craving for the security and serenity of home? The longing to belong? The desire to see and smell and taste the familiarity of home? Can you sense the God-forsakenness of exile? The temple destroyed? My box for God dismantled?

> Sing, O barren one who did not bear;
>   burst into song and shout,
>   you who have not been in labor!
> For the children of the desolate woman will be more
>   than the children of her that is married, says the Lord.
> Enlarge the site of your tent,
>   and let the curtains of your habitations be stretched out;
> do not hold back; lengthen your cords
>   and strengthen your stakes.
> For you will spread out to the right and to the left,
>   and your descendents will possess the nations
>   and will settle the desolate towns.
>
> Do not fear, for you will not be ashamed;
>   do not be discouraged, for you will not suffer disgrace;
> for you will forget the shame of your youth,
>   and the disgrace of your widowhood you will remember no more.
> For your Maker is your husband,
>   the Lord of hosts is his name;
> the Holy One of Israel is your Redeemer,
>   the God of the whole earth he is called.
> For the Lord has called you
>   like a wife forsaken and grieved in spirit,
> like the wife of a man's youth when she is cast off,
>   says your God.
> For a brief moment I abandoned you,
>   but with great compassion I will gather you.
> In overflowing wrath for a moment
>   I hid my face from you,
> but with everlasting love I will have compassion on you,
>   says the Lord, your Redeemer.

This is like the days of Noah to me:
Just as I swore that the waters of Noah
would never again go over the earth,
so I have sworn that I will not be angry with you
and will not rebuke you.
For the mountains may depart
and the hills be removed,
but my steadfast love shall not depart from you,
and my covenant of peace shall not be removed,
says the LORD, who has compassion on you.

Isaiah 54:1–10

In the midst of their homelessness and hopelessness comes the voice of the prophet: "Sing, . . . burst into song and shout, . . . enlarge the site of your tent, . . . lengthen your cords" (vv. 1–2). And more: "Do not fear, . . . do not be discouraged, . . . forget the shame of your youth" (v. 4). The excruciating pain of exile—like the pain felt by a widow grieving for her dead husband—remember no more. What could possibly warrant such outrageous hope? What could motivate such impossible actions? What could render believable such dangerous promises?

Only one thing, the text tells us. Only one thing: The remembrance that our Redeemer is our Creator, and that this God is a God of steadfast love. And peace. And compassion. The poem is candid. It frankly acknowledges hopelessness, abandonment, and despair—indeed, that God "for a brief moment" abandoned Israel (v. 7). Yet it affirms, against the oppressive reality of exile, God's longsuffering fidelity and great compassion. Verse 10 exclaims, "The mountains may depart and the hills be removed, but my steadfast love shall not depart"—God's covenant of shalom shall not be removed.

As the prophet has already reminded us in chapter 49, verses 14–16, God is like a nursing mother who shows compassion for the child of her womb. Or as he makes clear in chapter 52, verse 7, against all human expectation the messenger brings gospel, good news, that God is triumphant over the chaos-making powers of Babylon. The peace of God—when the king rules with justice and righteousness, delivering the needy and the poor and the oppressed so that all creatures flourish and sing praises to God, and God's glory fills the entire earth (Ps. 72)—is here in Isaiah affirmed in the very midst of violence, oppression, and exile. For the homeless, there is a mind-boggling promise of homecoming. For the hopeless, there arises a bright morning star of hope. Because of who God is. Our Redeemer is our Creator, a God of unfathomable love.

Few of us are in Isodore's straits, homeless in that sense, moving from shelter to shelter to keep out of the cold. But all of us are (or have been) in exile—shorn of faith, forlorn of hope, seeking shelter in a loveless place. For some it means being in a new place, with new people (and perhaps a new language), facing questions such as, Is this where God wants me to be? For others homelessness is the death of a loved one—spouse, child, parent—the exile of loss, of a long loneliness, of a grief that seemingly knows no end. There's a hole in the world now, and it no longer feels quite like home. For yet others exile is the death of a dream, a cherished relationship, a vision of some good future, or perhaps the loss of a job, a friendship, some long-awaited hope now unfulfilled.

In addition, increasingly we feel like exiles on the earth—ecological exiles. As our sense that things are ecologically out of kilter increases, we feel homeless on our home planet. For example, Australians are feeling homesick because their landscape is dramatically changing due to global warming. Writes Clive Thompson, "They no longer feel like they know the place they've lived in for decades." Thompson reports that Australian philosopher Glenn Albrecht has coined a new term, solastalgia, to denote this "pining for a lost environment."[16] We grieve the loss of what once was. We worry about what may be. We yearn for an earth filled with God's shalom. In whom and for what may we hope?

Isaiah's words hit home. Wherein lies hope? This text powerfully reminds us of this: in a world of wounds, there is hope amid hopelessness, for our Redeemer is the Creator—a God of unsearchable compassion and unquenchable love. The One who woos us with his costly love is the same One who wrought us and this world in the beginning and who will renew and restore all things in the end.

Radical Faith in a Troubled World

This biblical vision that animates hope amidst hopelessness is not to be confused with optimism.[17] When asked to explain how he kept going during the decades of despair prior to the liberation of the Czech Republic from a repressive communism, Václav Havel replied: "I am not an optimist . . . I am a person of hope. . . . I cannot imagine that I would strive for anything if I did not carry hope in me."[18] Elsewhere Havel puts it this way: "Hope is not prognostication. It is an orientation of the spirit, an orientation of the heart; it transcends the world that is immediately experienced, and is anchored somewhere beyond its horizons. . . . Hope is definitely not the same thing as optimism."[19] As Scott Russell Sanders perceptively comments, "Havel's actions make clear that he is not saying that our hope should be *invested* elsewhere, in heaven or a utopian future, but that it *comes from* elsewhere, to encourage and strengthen us for good works here."[20] Like optimism, hope is for this world. In that sense hope is *this*-worldly. But unlike optimism, the source of hope does not derive from this world. Its source lies *beyond*.

More exactly, optimism is generally based on a modernist faith in progress, while hope is rooted in faith in God. As N. T. Wright argues, optimism is based on "a belief in Progress," born of the Enlightenment, that claims "the world is getting better and better" because of our "industrial progress" and "technological innovation." Such progress, it is believed, will produce "a world in which old evils will be left behind," to which Wright remarks, "Try telling that to a Holocaust survivor, a Tutsi refugee, a Honduran peasant." Such belief in a perfectible world flies in the face of the facts of history. In contrast to optimism, affirms Wright, hope has to do "not with steady progress, but with a belief that the world is God's world and that God has continuing plans for it."[21]

But how can we live in such hope? Sanders provides an articulate and compelling answer. We can live in hope, he believes, because the "leaping up in expectation" that is hope is anchored in many things: wildness, bodiliness, family, fidelity, skill, simplicity, beauty, and ultimately God.[22] In short, there are certain features of our common human experience that ground our hope. Built into the created order are signs of God's good and loving presence. As Wright affirms, the signs of hope "are not the evidences of an evolution from lower to higher forms of life, or from one ethical or political system to another, but the signs built into the created order itself: music, the birth of a baby, the appearance of spring flowers, grass growing through concrete, the irrepressibility of human love." So, he concludes, "some parts of our world simply point beyond themselves, and say, 'Look! Despite all, there is hope.'"[23] This sacramental universe is one basis of hope.

Wendell Berry gets at the same thing when he writes that "authentic underpinnings of hope" can still be found in the very dynamics of nature. "Though we have caused the earth to be seriously diseased," he continues, "it is not yet without health. The earth we have before us now is still abounding and beautiful." And so Berry concludes, "The health of nature is the primary ground of hope—if we can find the humility and wisdom to accept nature as our teacher."[24]

But this brings us back to imagination. One can perceive the health of nature as a ground of hope only if one has eyes to see. One can see how this world of wonders points beyond itself only if one views the world sacramentally. Indeed, one can live in hope only if that hope is anchored somewhere beyond the horizons of present reality. Hope can be sustained only by an imagination that is rooted in memories that go deeper than the present age and in a vision that can see beyond the seemingly ubiquitous forces of death.

Faith rooted in a Christian imagination is a bold witness in our troubled world. Such a faith stands in striking contrast to the pervasive fear and indifference and hopelessness that characterize our age. But such faith is also more than a bit dangerous. In ways we often do not acknowledge, we attempt to tame God and make God (and our faith) safe and easy. Annie Dillard offers a much-needed reminder:

On the whole, I do not find Christians, outside of the catacombs, sufficiently sensible of conditions. Does anyone have the foggiest idea what sort of power we so blithely invoke? Or, as I suspect, does no one believe a word of it? The churches are children playing on the floor with their chemistry sets, mixing up a batch of TNT to kill a Sunday morning. It is madness to wear ladies' straw hats and velvet hats to church; we should all be wearing crash helmets. Ushers should issue life preservers and signal flares; they should lash us to our pews. For the sleeping god may wake and take offense, or the waking god may draw us out to where we can never return.[25]

"Draw us out to where we can never return." Perhaps that is what we all need: to be drawn out by God—the undomesticatable God, the wildest being there is[26]—to where we can no longer depend on our technology, our intelligence, our wealth, our own strength, our good works. This is the realm of dangerous faith—that anxious country where our yearning is most precarious and hence our trust most real.

The practical consequences of such a radical faith are themselves radical. For example, discussions of what is "realistic" take on a different tone. The answer, of course, all depends on what is really real. If God is really at the center of things and God's good future is the most certain reality, then the truly realistic course of action is to buck the dominant consequentialist ethic of our age—which says that we should act only if our action will most likely bring about good consequences—and simply, because we are people who embody the virtue of hope, do the right thing. Therefore, if we believe it is part of our task as earthkeepers to recycle, then we ought to recycle, whether or not it will change the world. Do the right thing. If we think it part and parcel of our ecological obedience to drive less and walk more, then that is what we ought to do. Do the right thing. If we feel called to run for public office, then run we must. Do the right thing. We should fulfill our calling to be caretakers of the earth regardless of whether global warming is real or there are holes in the ozone layer or three nonhuman species become extinct each day. Our vocation is not contingent on results or the state of the planet. Our calling simply depends on our identity as God's response-able human image-bearers.

If we have this kind of faith (and hope and love), then the words of a famous Gerard Manley Hopkins poem become, Christianly speaking, the most profoundly realistic.[27]

> The world is charged with the grandeur of God.
>> It will flame out, like shining from shook foil;
>> It gathers to a greatness, like the ooze of oil
> Crushed. Why do men then now not reck his rod?
> Generations have trod, have trod, have trod;
>> And all is seared with trade; bleared, smeared with toil.
>> And wears man's smudge and shares man's smell: the soil
> Is bare now, nor can foot feel, being shod.

And for all this, nature is never spent;
    There lives the dearest freshness deep down things;
And though the last lights off the black West went
    Oh, morning, at the brown brink eastward, springs—
Because the Holy Ghost over the bent
    World broods with warm breast and with ah! bright wings.

Perhaps at the end of the day we should heed that most passionate medieval evangelical, St. Francis of Assisi, who is said to have admonished all who follow Christ to preach the gospel always, and if necessary, use words. We Christians tend to be too wordy, too preachy, not incarnational enough. Perhaps we should speak only when necessary and spend more time preaching with our actions. That is, after all, the most genuine evangelism. The world is watching, and what we do and fail to do with respect to the earth speaks volumes. This is what was on Joseph Sittler's mind when he penned these last lines of his prophetic 1973 essay, "Evangelism and the Care of the Earth": "If *in piety* the church says, 'The earth is the Lord's and the fulness thereof' (Psalm 24:1), and *in fact* is no different in thought and action from the general community, who will be drawn to her word and worship to 'come and see' that her work or salvation has any meaning? Witness in saying is irony and bitterness if there be no witness in doing."[28]

For the beauty of the earth. May we each be so moved by love and gratitude that we bear witness to the good news of the gospel. In so doing we will with our lives proclaim the hope that lies within us—the hope of God's good future of shalom.

notes

Introduction Ecology and Theology in Dialogue

1. Thomas Aquinas, *Summa contra Gentiles*, II.3, trans. James F. Anderson (Notre Dame: University of Notre Dame Press, 1992).

2. Wendell Berry, *Sex, Economy, Freedom, and Community* (New York: Pantheon, 1992), 98.

3. David Orr, *Ecological Literacy: Education and the Transition to a Postmodern World* (Albany: State University of New York Press, 1992).

4. James Nash, *Loving Nature: Ecological Integrity and Christian Responsibility* (Nashville: Abingdon, 1991), chap. 3.

5. For more on this theme, see Steven Bouma-Prediger and Brian Walsh, *Beyond Homelessness: Christian Faith in a Culture of Displacement* (Grand Rapids: Eerdmans, 2008).

6. Aldo Leopold, *A Sand County Almanac* (New York: Ballantine, 1970), 197.

7. See, e.g., Augustine, *On Christian Doctrine*, trans. D. W. Robertson Jr. (New York: Macmillan, 1958), chaps. 27–29.

8. Joseph Sittler, "Evangelism and the Care of the Earth," in *Evocations of Grace: The Writings of Joseph Sittler on Ecology, Theology, and Ethics*, ed. Steven Bouma-Prediger and Peter Bakken (Grand Rapids: Eerdmans, 2000), 202. Please note regarding gender-exclusive language that when I cite another author, I will not change the text (or add "*sic*") but will allow the language to stand as is.

9. Steven Bouma-Prediger, *The Greening of Theology: The Ecological Models of Rosemary Radford Ruether, Joseph Sittler, and Jürgen Moltmann* (Atlanta: Scholars, 1995), esp. chap. 8.

10. Christopher Kaiser, "The Integrity of Creation: In Search of a Meaning," *Perspectives* 11 (April 1996): 8–11. On the basis of his reading of Gen. 1–2, Michael Welker, likewise, criticizes the abstractness of the term "creation"; see *Creation and Reality* (Minneapolis: Fortress, 1999), chap. 1.

11. Joseph Sittler, *Gravity and Grace* (Minneapolis: Augsburg, 1986), 15.

Chapter 1 Where Are We? An Ecological Perception of Place

1. Gabriel Marcel, quoted in Edward Relph, *Place and Placelessness* (London: Pion, 1976), 43.

2. Jose Ortega y Gasset, quoted in Belden C. Lane, *Landscapes of the Sacred: Geography and Narrative in American Spirituality* (New York: Paulist Press, 1988), vii. For insight into the relation between environmental perception and human attitudes and values, see Yi-Fu Tuan, *Topophilia: A Study of Environmental Perception, Attitudes, and Values* (New York: Columbia University Press, 1974); Steven Feld and Keith Basso, eds., *Senses of Place* (Santa Fe, NM: School of American Research Press, 1996); and Winifred Gallagher, *The Power of Place* (New York: HarperCollins, 1993).

3. Aldo Leopold, *A Sand County Almanac* (New York: Ballantine, 1970), 262.

4. David Orr, *Ecological Literacy: Education and the Transition to a Postmodern World* (Albany: State University of New York Press, 1992), 83. See also David Orr, *Earth in Mind: On Education, Environment, and the Human Prospect* (Washington, DC: Island, 1994); and *The Nature of Design: Ecology, Culture, and Human Intention* (New York: Oxford University Press, 2002).

5. Garrett Hardin, *Filters against Folly: How to Survive Despite Economists, Ecologists, and the Merely Eloquent* (New York: Penguin, 1985), 24, and chap. 7.

6. Orr, *Ecological Literacy*, 92.

7. Ibid.

8. Ibid.

9. A number of fine books provide such knowledge, e.g., Ernest Callenbach, *Ecology: A Pocket Guide* (Berkeley: University of California Press, 1998); and more in-depth, Frank Golley, *A Primer for Environmental Literacy* (New Haven: Yale University Press, 1998). See also Henry Art, ed., *The Dictionary of Ecology and Environmental Science* (New York: Henry Holt, 1993), for excellent information on all manner of things environmental.

10. Orr, *Ecological Literacy*, 93.

11. Chapter 2 will provide a detailed argument in support of the use of this term, but a sampling of recent titles also suggests that "crisis" is not an overstatement: James Gustave Speth, *The Bridge at the Edge of the World: Capitalism, the Environment, and Crossing from Crisis to Sustainability* (New Haven: Yale University Press, 2008); Elizabeth Kolbert, *Field Notes from a Catastrophe: Man, Nature, and Climate Change* (New York: Bloomsbury, 2006); Peter Annin, *The Great Lakes Water Wars* (Washington, DC: Island, 2006).

12. In addition to its well-known publication *State of the World*, the Worldwatch Institute also publishes a very useful compendium of environmental trends called *Vital Signs*. Many other sources for taking the pulse of the planet can be found in the notes to chapter 2.

13. Orr, *Ecological Literacy*, 93.

14. See Alfred Crosby's pivotal work in environmental history, *The Columbian Exchange: Biological and Cultural Consequences of 1492* (Westport, CT: Praeger, 2003). For an overview of the history of the world from an environmental perspective, see Clive Ponting, *A Green History of the World: The Environment and the Collapse of Great Civilizations* (New York: Penguin, 1991).

15. See Ted Steinberg's illuminating study, *Down to Earth: Nature's Role in American History* (New York: Oxford University Press, 2002). Also fascinating is J. R. McNeill's *Something New under the Sun: An Environmental History of the Twentieth-Century World* (New York: Norton, 2000).

16. See Jared Diamond's enlightening volume *Collapse: How Societies Choose to Fail or Succeed* (New York: Viking, 2005). See also his award-winning *Guns, Germs, and Steel: The Fate of Human Societies* (New York: Norton, 1999).

17. Orr, *Ecological Literacy*, 94.

18. Leopold, *Sand County Almanac*, 240.

19. Holmes Rolston III, *Environmental Ethics: Duties to and Values in the Natural World* (Philadelphia: Temple University Press, 1988), 32–44.

20. Orr, *Ecological Literacy*, 94.

21. James Speth delineates some of the major problems with GDP, e.g., that GDP does not count costs and benefits that occur outside the market, in *Bridge at the Edge of the World*, 138–40.

22. The ISEW is set forth by Herman Daly and John Cobb in *For the Common Good: Redirecting the Economy toward Community, the Environment, and a Sustainable Future* (Boston: Beacon, 1989), 401–55. The GPI is from the work of Jason Venetoulis and Cliff Cobb and the Redefining Progress Sustainability Indicators Program, available at www.rprogress.org. For more on the WISP, developed by Richard Estes, go to www.sp2.upenn.edu/~restes/world.html. See Speth, *Bridge at the Edge of the World*, 138–44, for more examples of alternative measures of well-being.

23. E. F. Schumacher, *Small Is Beautiful* (New York: Harper and Row, 1973).

24. A tip of the iceberg: Sim Van Der Ryn and Stuart Cowan, *Ecological Design* (Washington, DC: Island, 1996); Nancy Jack Todd and John Todd, *From Eco-Cities to Living Machines: Principles of Ecological*

Design (Berkeley: North Atlantic Books, 1993); William McDonough and Michael Braungart, *Cradle to Cradle: Remaking the Way We Make Things* (New York: North Point, 2002).

25. Orr, *Ecological Literacy*, 95.

26. To learn more about the "how to's" of ecological literacy, in addition to books already mentioned, see these oldies but goodies: Michael Schut, ed., *Simpler Living, Compassionate Life* (Denver: Morehouse, 1999); Art Meyer and Jocele Meyer, *Earthkeepers* (Scottdale, PA: Herald, 1991); and Loren Wilkinson and Mary Ruth Wilkinson, *Caring for Creation in Your Own Backyard* (Vancouver: Regent, 1992). In addition, local nature centers and museums, county parks and their programs, school projects and family vacations—all these can be ways to boost one's knowledge of how the world works.

27. The places need not be wild. But for the purposes of illustrating how the natural world works—of learning from the discipline of ecology—I have chosen three places where humans live relatively lightly on the land, and thus places where the intricate workings of the natural world are perhaps more obvious.

28. Tuan, *Topophilia*; see also David Barnhill, ed., *At Home on the Earth: Becoming Native to Our Place* (Berkeley: University of California Press, 1999); and Peter Sauer, ed., *Finding Home: Writing on Nature and Culture from Orion Magazine* (Boston: Beacon, 1992).

29. "On a per unit area basis, rain forests are more than twice as productive as northern coniferous forests, half again as productive as temperate forests, and between four and five times as productive as savanna and grasslands" (John Kricher, *A Neotropical Companion: An Introduction to the Animals, Plants, and Ecosystems of the New World Tropics* [Princeton: Princeton University Press, 1989], 66–67). While consisting of only one-third of the world's total forest area, tropical forests contain four-fifths of the earth's vegetation.

30. See, e.g., John Terborgh, *Diversity and the Tropical Rain Forest* (New York: Scientific American Library, 1992), 32–35.

31. Kricher, *Neotropical Companion*, 90.

32. Ibid., 44.

33. Billy Goodman, *The Rain Forest* (New York: Tern Enterprise, 1991), 28.

34. Kricher, *Neotropical Companion*, 166–67.

35. "The web of symbiosis is yet more intricately woven. Networks of plant and tree roots pervade the leaf-cutters' labyrinth and lend structural support to their extensive catacombs. Recent research on the fungus grown by the ants shows that it exhibits biological activity against certain plant pathogens, thus protecting the supporting trees" (Arnold Newman, *Tropical Rainforest* [New York: Facts On File Books, 1990], 86).

36. Adult botflies often lay their eggs on mosquitoes. When the mosquito bites, the botfly egg comes in contact with the skin, hatches, and burrows under. With a breathing tube sticking up to the surface to gain needed air, the larval fly grows ever bigger. Its body covered with sharp little black spines, like miniature fishhooks, when the larvae moves it can cause considerable pain. Removal is recommended, though not always easy to accomplish.

37. Kricher, *Neotropical Companion*, chaps. 2, 4.

38. Goodman, *Rain Forest*, 33.

39. Kricher, *Neotropical Companion*, 124.

40. John Muir, *The Mountains of California* (San Francisco: Sierra Club, 1988), 2.

41. Verna Johnston, *The Sierra Nevada* (Boston: Houghton Mifflin, 1970), 172.

42. Charles Little, *The Dying of the Trees: The Pandemic in America's Forests* (New York: Penguin, 1995), 74.

43. Johnston, *Sierra Nevada*, 78.

44. The ring count of one old logged sequoia reveals the monarch was 3,200 years old when it died—a sapling when David slew Goliath.

45. William Tweed, *Sequoia–Kings Canyon* (Las Vegas: KC Publications, 1980), 30.

46. Johnston, *Sierra Nevada*, 81.

47. John Muir, *My First Summer in the Sierra* (San Francisco: Sierra Club, 1988), 109–10. Elsewhere Muir comments that "one is constantly reminded of the infinite lavishness and fertility of Nature—

inexhaustible abundance amid what seems enormous waste. And yet when we look into any of her operations that lie within the reach of our minds, we learn that no particle of her material is wasted or worn out. It is eternally flowing from use to use, beauty to yet higher beauty" (168).

48. Percy Knauth, *The North Woods* (New York: Time-Life, 1972), 26.

49. Famous Boundary Waters naturalist Sigurd Olson reported seeing a beaver dam that was a half-mile long and strong enough to hold a horse and wagon (Knauth, *North Woods*, 86).

50. Glenda Daniel and Jerry Sullivan, *A Sierra Club Naturalist's Guide: The North Woods of Michigan, Wisconsin, and Minnesota* (San Francisco: Sierra Club, 1981), 374.

51. Mark Stensaas, *Canoe Country Wildlife: A Field Guide to the Boundary Waters and Quetico* (Duluth, MN: Pfeifer-Hamilton, 1993), 28.

52. Daniel and Sullivan, *Sierra Club Naturalist's Guide*, 375.

53. Knauth, *North Woods*, 94.

54. Often confused with habitat, "niche" refers not to where an organism lives but to its function or role within an ecosystem.

55. Stensaas, *Canoe Country Wildlife*, 187.

56. The word "boreal" comes from Boreas, the Greek god of the north wind.

57. Stensaas, *Canoe Country Wildlife*, 206.

58. Daniel and Sullivan, *Sierra Club Naturalist's Guide*, 243.

59. Ibid., 130.

60. Stensaas, *Canoe Country Wildlife*, 2.

61. Ibid., 44.

62. Daniel and Sullivan, *Sierra Club Naturalist's Guide*, 371.

63. Stensaas, *Canoe Country Wildlife*, 45.

64. Sigurd Olson, *Sigurd Olson's Wilderness Days* (New York: Alfred Knopf, 1972), 192.

65. This is one of Miller's "principles for understanding and sustaining the earth" (G. Tyler Miller Jr., *Living in the Environment*, 7th ed. [Belmont, CA: Wadsworth, 1992], inside front cover). The Paddler's Golden Rule adaptation of this principle goes something like this: "Do unto those downstream as you would have those upstream do unto you." In what follows in this section I sometimes borrow Miller's helpful terminology.

66. Callenbach, *Ecology*, dedication page.

67. Hardin, *Filters against Folly*, 57.

68. Ibid., 58.

69. Callenbach, *Ecology*, dedication page.

70. Ibid.

71. Daniel Botkin, *Discordant Harmonies: A New Ecology for the Twenty-First Century* (New York: Oxford University Press, 1990), 6.

72. E. O. Wilson, *The Diversity of Life* (New York: Norton, 1999), 144. See also Yvonne Baskin, *The Work of Nature: How the Diversity of Life Sustains Us* (Washington, DC: Island, 1998).

73. Miller, *Living in the Environment*, 7th ed., inside front cover.

74. See, e.g., Roger Lewin, *Complexity: Life at the Edge of Chaos*, 2nd ed. (Chicago: University of Chicago Press, 1999).

Chapter 2 What's Wrong with the World? The Groaning of Creation

1. Calvin DeWitt, "Biogeographic and Trophic Restructuring of the Biosphere: The State of the Earth under Human Domination," *Christian Scholar's Review* 32 (Summer 2003): 347–48. Elsewhere DeWitt speaks of "seven degradations of creation": (1) alteration of planetary energy exchange, (2) land degradation, (3) deforestation, (4) species extinction, (5) water degradation, (6) global toxification, and (7) human and cultural degradation. See Calvin DeWitt, *Caring for Creation: Responsible Stewardship of God's Handiwork* (Grand Rapids: Baker, 1998), chap. 1.

2. Stuart Pimm, *The World according to Pimm: A Scientist Audits the Earth* (New York: McGraw Hill, 2001), 233. The work of many other notable scientists could also be cited, e.g., E. O. Wilson, Norman Myers, and Peter Raven.

3. Aldo Leopold, *A Sand County Almanac* (New York: Ballantine, 1970), 197.

4. Danielle Nierenberg, "Population Rise Slows but Continues," in *Vital Signs 2007–2008*, 51.

5. Population pyramids are available at the U.S. Census Bureau Web site: www.census.gov/ipc/www/idb/worldpopinfo.html.

6. Nierenberg, "Population Rise Slows," 50.

7. Lester Brown, "Challenges of the New Century," in *State of the World 2000* (New York: Norton, 2000), 5.

8. James Gustave Speth, *Red Sky at Morning: America and the Crisis of the Global Environment* (New Haven: Yale University Press, 2004), 120.

9. Christopher Flavin, "The Legacy of Rio," in *State of the World 1997* (New York: Norton, 1997), 7, 16.

10. Lester Brown, Gary Gardner, and Brian Halweil, *Beyond Malthus: Nineteen Dimensions of the Population Challenge* (New York: Norton, 1999), 19.

11. Flavin, "Legacy of Rio," 18.

12. Ibid., 18–19.

13. Brown, Gardner, and Halweil, *Beyond Malthus*, 36.

14. Wendell Berry, *Home Economics* (New York: North Point, 1987), 149–50 (italics in the original).

15. Assuming two feet per person and a circumference of 24,906 miles.

16. *The State of the Food Insecurity in the World 2006*, Food and Agriculture Organization of the United Nations, 1; see also "The Millennium Development Goals Report 2005" (New York: United Nations, 2005), www.unfpa.org/icpd/docs/mdgrept2005.pdf.

17. Most of the chronically undernourished are not literally starving to death, but in receiving less than 90 percent of the minimum daily calorie intake they do not have enough energy for an active working life. By contrast, the malnourished suffer from severe deficiencies of protein and/or vitamins and minerals.

18. Lester Brown, "Why Ethanol Production Will Drive World Food Prices Even Higher in 2008," Earth Policy Institute, January 24, 2008, http://earthpolicy.org/Updates/2008/Update69.htm. See also *Vital Signs 2007–2008*, 21.

19. Gary Gardner, "Grain Area Shrinks Again," in *Vital Signs 2000*, 45.

20. Brown, "Why Ethanol Production." Brown, among many others, decries the massive increase in grain used for the production of ethanol. The biofuel effect on world food prices is projected to dramatically increase the number of hungry people in the world. Indeed, with the escalation of food prices in 2008, such an increase in global hunger is, sadly, already under way. How can we morally justify feeding grain to our motor vehicles instead of to hungry people?

21. John Tuxill, *Losing Strands in the Web of Life: Vertebrate Declines and the Conservation of Biological Diversity* (Washington, DC: Worldwatch Institute, 1998), 9. See also E. O. Wilson, *The Diversity of Life* (New York: Norton, 1999); and Norman Myers, *The Sinking Ark* (New York: Pergamon, 1979).

22. *Ecosystems and Human Well-being: Biodiversity Synthesis*, Millennium Ecosystem Assessment (Washington, DC: World Resources Institute, 2005), 3. www.millenniumassessment.org/documents/document.354.aspx.pdf.

23. Norman Myers, "Biotic Holocaust," *National Wildlife Federation*, March/April 1999, 31.

24. Elroy Bos, "Threats to Species Accelerate," in *Vital Signs 2007–2008*, 97. For more extensive (and up-to-date) data, see the IUCN Red List at www.iucnredlist.org. The picture painted by the U.S. Fish and Wildlife Service concerning endangered and threatened species is similarly distressing. For an explanation of the Endangered Species Act and a discussion of why it ought to be strengthened, see Steven Bouma-Prediger and Virginia Vroblesky, *Assessing the Ark: A Christian Perspective on Non-Human Creatures and the Endangered Species Act* (Wynnewood, PA: Crossroad, 1997).

25. Bos, "Threats to Species Accelerate," 96.

26. See, e.g., the 2007 Red List (www.iucnredlist.org), tables 3a and 3b.

27. Tuxill, *Losing Strands*, 11–12.

28. See, e.g., Kevin Eckerle, "Climate Change Affects Terrestrial Biodiversity," in *Vital Signs 2007–2008*, 94–95.

29. See, e.g., Gretchen Daily, ed., *Nature's Services: Societal Dependence on Natural Ecosystems* (Washington, DC: Island, 1997), esp. chaps. 6 and 14.

30. V. Heywood, ed., *Global Biodiversity Assessment* (Cambridge: Cambridge University Press, 1995).

31. Rebecca Lindsey, "Tropical Deforestation," NASA Earth Observatory, March 30, 2007, 16. Lindsey's claim is based on 2005 data from the Food and Agriculture Organization of the United Nations. This is a low estimate. Norman Myers puts the total at 37 million acres per year (see Daily, *Nature's Services*, 224).

32. For a perceptive discussion of the role of trees and forests in Western thought, see Robert Pogue Harrison, *Forests: The Shadow of Civilizations* (Chicago: University of Chicago Press, 1992). For an interesting treatment of the psychological and mythological power of trees, see Michael Perlman, *The Power of Trees* (Woodstock, CT: Spring, 1994).

33. Gary Gardner, "Forest Loss Continues," in *Vital Signs 2005*, 92.

34. Lindsey, "Tropical Deforestation," 16. See also Gardner, "Forest Loss Continues," 92.

35. Thomas Rudel et al., "Tropical Deforestation Literature: Geographical and Historical Patterns in the Availability of Information and Analysis of Causes," Forestry Department, Food and Agriculture Organization of the United Nations, 8.

36. Despite the common belief that the computer age would decrease paper usage, recent studies confirm my own anecdotal observations that paper usage has actually increased. Molly O'Meara summarizes the findings: "Between 1988 and 1998, average per capita consumption of printing and writing paper in industrial countries shot up by 24 percent. Computers have not sated the appetite of paper-hungry industrial countries—they have merely altered their tastes" ("Harnessing Information Technologies for the Environment," in *State of the World 2000*, 129).

37. Janet Abramovitz, *Taking a Stand: Cultivating a New Relationship with the World's Forests* (Washington, DC: Worldwatch Institute, 1998), 8.

38. Charles Little, *The Dying of the Trees: The Pandemic in America's Forests* (New York: Penguin, 1995), ix.

39. Ibid., 188.

40. See, e.g., Abramovitz, *Taking a Stand*, 9–16; and Daily, *Nature's Services*, chap. 12.

41. "Coping with Water Scarcity, World Water Day 2007," United Nations World Health Organization, 1. www.euro.who.int/watsan/issues/20080818_5.

42. "August 2006 Monthly Update: Water Scarcity," World Resources Institute, 2. http://earthtrends.wri.org/images/sectoral_water_withdrawals.jgp.

43. Janet Abramovitz, *Imperiled Waters, Impoverished Future: The Decline of Freshwater Ecosystems* (Washington, DC: Worldwatch Institute, 1996), 31.

44. Brown, Gardner, and Halweil, *Beyond Malthus*, 37.

45. Sandra Postel, *Dividing the Waters: Food Security, Ecosystem Health, and the New Politics of Scarcity* (Washington, DC: Worldwatch Institute, 1996). 32. See also Sandra Postel, *Liquid Assets: The Critical Need to Safeguard Freshwater Ecosystems* (Washington, DC: Worldwatch Institute, 2005), 19, 25.

46. *The Water Atlas* (New York: New Press, 2004), 64–65. See also Lester Brown, "Water Deficits Growing in Many Countries," *Great Lakes Directory*, August 9, 2002, www.greatlakesdirectory.org/zarticles/080902_water_shortages.htm; and Postel, *Dividing the Waters*, 20–21.

47. Eleanor Sterling, "Blue Planet Blues: Demand for Freshwater Threatens to Outstrip Supply," *Natural History*, November 2007, 29–31; reprinted in *Water Supply*, ed. Richard Joseph Stein (New York: H. W. Wilson, 2008), 6.

48. Brown, Gardner, and Halweil, *Beyond Malthus*, 39.

49. Postel, "Redesigning Irrigated Agriculture," in *State of the World 2000* (New York: Norton, 2000), 43–44.

50. Abramovitz, *Imperiled Waters*, 34–35.

51. "Water, Sanitation, and Hygiene Links to Health," World Health Organization, November 2004. www.who.int/water_sanitation_health/publications/facts2004/en/print.html.

52. Postel, *Liquid Assets*, 16–17.

53. David Pimentel, "Soil Erosion: A Food and Environmental Threat," *Environment, Development and Sustainability* 8 (2006): 123.

54. Pimentel, "Soil Erosion," 124.

55. Ibid.

56. Norman Myers, *Gaia: An Atlas of Planet Management*, cited in Pimentel, "Soil Erosion," 123. As Pimentel states, this is very likely a conservative estimate.

57. Pimentel, "Soil Erosion," 123.

58. G. Tyler Miller Jr., *Living in the Environment*, 11th ed. (Pacific Grove, CA: Brooks/Cole, 2000), 356–57.

59. 1999 Sierra Club Sprawl Report, at www.sierraclub.org/sprawl/report99/.

60. "Population Growth and Suburban Sprawl," Sierra Club, 2003. www.sierraclub.org/spawl/sprawlpop_2003.pdf.

61. *The State of the Cities 2000: Megaforces Shaping the Future of the Nation's Cities*, U.S. Department of Housing and Urban Development, 2000. In addition to various environmental problems there are many serious health issues associated with sprawl; see, e.g., Howard Frumpkin, "Urban Sprawl and Public Health," *Public Health Reports* 117 (May–June 2002).

62. "Municipal Solid Waste Generation, Recycling, and Disposal in the United States: Facts and Figures for 2006," United States Environmental Protection Agency, 2007, www.epa.gov/waste/nonhaz/municipal/pubs/msw06.pdf. For a very helpful analysis of waste of all kinds, see Kim Martens Evans, *The Environment: A Revolution in Attitudes* (Farmington Hills, MI: Gale, Cengage Learning, 2008).

63. "Municipal Solid Waste Generation," 2.

64. Ibid., 3–4.

65. Miller, *Living in the Environment*, 11th ed., 580. Data from the late 1990s.

66. G. Tyler Miller Jr., *Living in the Environment*, 15th ed. (Pacific Grove, CA: Brooks/Cole, 2006), 533. For more specific data on these other kinds of waste, see Evans, *Environment*, 89–92.

67. Alan Durning, *How Much Is Enough?* (New York: Norton, 1992), 48. See also Durning's more recent *This Place on Earth: Home and the Practice of Permanence* (Seattle: Sasquatch Books, 1996). In each book Durning asks perceptive questions about our profligate living in the United States (and other so-called developed countries) and offers practical advice on making a home in a world of consumption and impermanence.

68. David Myers, *The Pursuit of Happiness: Who Is Happy—and Why* (New York: William Morrow, 1992), 44 (italics in the original). See also David Myers, *The American Paradox: Spiritual Hunger in an Age of Plenty* (New Haven: Yale University Press, 2000), whose subtitle gives away the book's thesis.

69. James Gustave Speth, *The Bridge at the Edge of the World: Capitalism, the Environment, and Crossing from Crisis to Sustainability* (New Haven: Yale University Press, 2008), 126.

70. See, e.g., the videos "Affluenza" and "Escape from Affluenza," produced by KCTV, Seattle Public Television, and the subsequent book by John DeGraaf, David Wann, and Thomas Naylor, *Affluenza: The All-Consuming Epidemic* (San Francisco: Berrett-Koehler, 2001).

71. "GEO-2000, Global Environment Outlook," United Nations Environment Programme, www.unep.org/geo2000/index.htm.

72. Janet Sawin and Ishani Mukherjee, "Fossil Fuel Use Up Again," in *Vital Signs 2007–2008*, 32.

73. See the graph of energy consumption versus GDP, created by Frank van Mierlo, based on data from "2006 Key World Energy Statistics," from the International Energy Agency, at http://en.wikipedia.org/wiki/File:World_Energy_consumption.png.

74. Brown, Gardner, and Halweil, *Beyond Malthus*, 46.

75. For an extensive discussion of peak oil, see Richard Heinberg, *The Party's Over: Oil, War and the Fate of Industrial Societies*, rev. ed. (Gabriola Island, BC: New Society, 2005), chap. 3. See also Paul Roberts, *The End of Oil: On the Edge of a Perilous New World* (Boston: Houghton Mifflin, 2004).

76. Brown, Gardner, and Halweil, *Beyond Malthus*, 48.

77. Janet Sawin, "Wind Power Still Soaring," in *Vital Signs 2007–2008*, 36–37.

78. Janet Sawin, "Solar Power Shining Bright," in *Vital Signs 2007–2008*, 38–39.

79. Sawin and Mukherjee, "Fossil Fuel Use Up Again," 32.

80. "Acidification," The Swedish NGO Secretariat on Acid Rain, 1. www.atmosphere.mpg.de/enid/3-Acid_Rain/-_Impact_1_zx.html.

81. *Global Ecology Handbook* (Boston: Beacon, 1990), 225. See also Miller, *Living in the Environment*, 11th ed., 480.

82. "Acid Rain: Downpour in Asia?" World Resources Institute, www.wri.org/publication/content/8434.

83. "Is Rain Getting More or Less Acidic?" Environment Canada, www.ec.gc.ca/acidrain/acidwater.html.

84. "Some Questions and Answers on Acid Rain," New York State Department of Environmental Conservation, 1. http://www.dec.ny.gov/chemical/8418.html.

85. Jeff Jones, "Rain Check," *Adirondack Life*, March/April 1997, 51.

86. The scientific primer on acid rain in the Adirondacks is Jerry Jenkins et al., *Acid Rain and the Adirondacks: A Research Summary* (Ray Brook, NY: Adirondack Lakes Survey Corporation, 2005). See also Jerry Jenkins et al., *Acid Rain in the Adirondacks: An Environmental History* (Ithaca, NY: Cornell University Press, 2008).

87. For more on the effects of acid rain, see Evans, *Environment*, chap. 5.

88. Chris Bright, "Anticipating Environmental 'Surprise,'" in *State of the World 2000*, 34.

89. In 2007 just seven states (Illinois, Indiana, Kentucky, Michigan, Ohio, Pennsylvania, West Virginia) produced 21 percent of the sulfur dioxide and 36 percent of the nitrogen oxides (analysis based on data from the EPA Web site, http://camddataandmaps.epa.gov/gdm/index.cfm?fuseaction=iss.progressresults).

90. E. G. Nisbet, *Leaving Eden: To Protect and Manage the Earth* (Cambridge: Cambridge University Press, 1991), 83–84.

91. See the latest graphs from the EPA ("Air Trends," www.epa.gov/air/airtrends/).

92. The fourteen warmest years, in descending order: 2005, 1998 and 2007 tied, 2002, 2003, 2006, 2004, 2001, 1997, 1995, 1990, 1999, 1991, 2000 (Goddard Institute for Space Studies, available at http://data.giss.nasa.gov/gistemp/).

93. The first report came out in 1990, the second in 1995, the third in 2001, and the fourth in 2007.

94. "IPCC, 2007: Summary for Policymakers," in *Climate Change 2007: The Physical Science Basis* (contribution of Working Group I to the Fourth Assessment Report of the Intergovernmental Panel on Climate Change; Cambridge: Cambridge University Press, 2007), 5. Also available online at www.ipcc.ch/pdf/assessment-report/ar4/wg1/ar4-wg1-spm.pdf.

95. Ibid., 2.

96. Jonathan Amos, "Deep Ice Tells Long Climate Story," *BBC News*, September 4, 2006, http://news.bbc.co.uk/2/hi/science/nature/5314592.stm. The natural level of CO_2 over most of the past 800,000 years has been 180–300 ppm. According to Eric Wolff of the British Antarctic Survey: "The scary thing was the rate of change now occurring in CO_2 concentrations. In the ice core, the fastest increase seen was of the order of 30 ppmv over a period of roughly 1000 years. The last 30 ppmv of increase has occurred in just 17 years. We really are in the situation where we don't have an analogue in our records" (Amos, "Deep Ice").

97. Miller, *Living in the Environment*, 11th ed., 500.

98. "IPCC, 2007," 4.

99. Ibid., 10 (italics in the original). The term "very likely," one of eight terms of assessed likelihood, is precisely defined as greater than a 90 percent chance of occurrence.

100. Bill McKibben, *The End of Nature* (New York: Doubleday, 1989), 45.

101. "IPCC, 2007," 5–8. See also the contribution of Working Group II to the Fourth Assessment Report of the IPCC, 2007. With better quality data and greater confidence in conclusions than in previous reports, this report describes in detail how global climate change is currently affecting many

natural systems and human communities. For more on this issue, see Lisa Mastay, "Global Ice Melting Accelerating," in *Vital Signs 2005*; Mark Lynas, *High Tide: The Truth about Our Climate Crisis* (New York: Picador, 2004); and Elizabeth Kolbert, *Field Notes from a Catastrophe: Man, Nature, and Climate Change* (New York: Bloomsbury, 2006).

102. "IPCC, 2007," 15–18.

103. Ibid., 8–9.

104. Molly Aeck, "Weather-Related Disasters Near a Record," in *Vital Signs 2005*, 50–51.

105. For other examples see Bill McKibben, *Hope, Human and Wild: True Stories of Living Lightly on the Earth* (St. Paul: Hungry Mind, 1995).

106. Despite the substantial evidence given above (as well as firsthand experience of ecological degradation) some today apparently think that our home planet is doing quite well, environmentally speaking. There are some, in other words, who say: "It's not so bad." One example is the "Cornwall Declaration on Environmental Stewardship," which states that "some unfounded or undue concerns include fears of destructive manmade global warming, overpopulation, and rampant species loss." These are "merely alleged problems" of "very low and largely hypothetical risk." One wonders how to respond to such claims. Given the manifold evidence of degradation and the crucial goods and services provided by a biologically diverse earth, how can concern for the loss of biodiversity be seen as "unfounded"? Given even a modicum of knowledge of how the world works, how can the risk be called "very low"?

107. Nisbet, *Leaving Eden*, 140.

108. Ibid., 140–42.

Chapter 3 Is Christianity to Blame? The Ecological Complaint against Christianity

1. Ludwig Feuerbach, *The Essence of Christianity* (New York: Harper and Row, 1957), 287.

2. *Sierra*, May–June 1993, 112.

3. This is the title of chapter 3 in James Nash, *Loving Nature: Ecological Integrity and Christian Responsibility* (Nashville: Abingdon, 1991).

4. Ibid., 72.

5. Ibid. (italics in the original). Or as the subtitle of H. Paul Santmire's enlightening historical survey indicates, Christian theology has in the past represented "an ambiguous ecological promise." See *The Travail of Nature: The Ambiguous Ecological Promise of Christian Theology* (Philadelphia: Fortress, 1985).

6. Nash, *Loving Nature*, 72, 74.

7. Wendell Berry, *Sex, Economy, Freedom, and Community* (New York: Pantheon, 1992), 94.

8. Ibid., 94–95.

9. Nash, *Loving Nature*, 68. In addition to chapter 3 of Nash, an insightful discussion of "the argument over Christianity" can be found in chapter 4 of Robert Booth Fowler's *The Greening of Protestant Thought* (Chapel Hill: University of North Carolina Press, 1995).

10. Arnold Toynbee, "The Religious Background of the Present Environmental Crisis," in *Ecology and Religion in History*, ed. David Spring and Eileen Spring (New York: Harper and Row, 1974), 146.

11. Ibid., 147.

12. Ibid., 148.

13. Roderick Nash, *The Rights of Nature: A History of Environmental Ethics* (Madison: University of Wisconsin Press, 1989), 90.

14. Wallace Stegner, *Marking the Sparrow's Fall: The Making of the American West* (New York: Henry Holt, 1998), 121. Many others make this same charge, e.g., Ian McHarg, "The Place of Nature in the City of Man," in *Western Man and Environmental Ethics*, ed. Ian Barbour (Reading, PA: Addison-Wesley, 1973), 174–75.

15. Stegner, *Marking the Sparrow's Fall*, 122.

16. Berry, *Sex, Economy, Freedom, and Community*, 105.

17. John Passmore, *Man's Responsibility for Nature* (New York: Scribner's, 1974), 12–13.

18. Rosemary Radford Ruether, *New Woman/New Earth: Sexist Ideologies and Human Liberation* (New York: Seabury, 1975), 195.

19. Lynn White Jr., "The Historical Roots of Our Ecologic Crisis," in Barbour, *Western Man and Environmental Ethics*, 25. Originally published in *Science* 155 (March 10, 1967): 1203–7.

20. Ibid., 26.

21. Ibid., 27.

22. Ibid. (italics in the original).

23. Max Oelschlaeger, *Caring for Creation: An Ecumenical Approach to the Environmental Crisis* (New Haven: Yale University Press, 1994), 2.

24. Another (in)famous proponent of this eschatology is James Watt, the first Reagan-era Secretary of the Interior. In response to a question during a discussion (on Feb. 5, 1981) with a committee of the House of Representatives regarding why his agency was acting contrary to its expressed mandate, Watt, a devout Christian, said, "I do not know how many future generations we can count on before the Lord returns." In other words, since Jesus is coming back soon, and since everything will be destroyed when Jesus returns, why care about the earth? See Ron Wolf, "God, James Watt, and the Public Lands," *Audubon* 83, no. 3 (May 1981): 58–65. But others argue that Watt was not really an otherworldly apocalypticist but was someone who minimized or downplayed the effects of ecological degradation. See, e.g., David Larson, "God's Gardeners: American Protestant Evangelicals Confront Environmentalism, 1967–2000" (PhD dissertation, University of Chicago Divinity School, 2001).

25. Lindsey's famous book, *The Late Great Planet Earth* (Grand Rapids: Zondervan, 1970), was a blockbuster best seller; LaHaye's current coauthored series of fictional works—the Left Behind series—has sold tens of millions of copies.

26. Jerry Jenkins as quoted by Lon Carlozo, "Apocalypse soon: For series' authors, the ending justifies their means," *Chicago Tribune*, sec. 5, March 13, 2002.

27. Nash, *Rights of Nature*, 91–92. For more on the "end times" literature and attitudes toward creation, see Fowler, *Greening of Protestant Thought*, chap. 3.

28. Bill Moyers, "On Receiving Harvard Medical School's Global Environment Citizen Award" (public address, December 1, 2004, www.commondreams.org/views04/1206-10.htm).

29. The use of the term "person" invites a larger discussion that we have no room for here. Suffice to say, by that term I mean to denote a unique set of attributes or qualities, usually limited to humans, that make possible responsible action and thus moral culpability.

30. See, e.g., Joseph Sittler, "Ecological Commitment as Theological Responsibility," *Zygon* 5 (June 1970): 175.

31. Wendell Berry, *What Are People For?* (New York: North Point, 1990), 98.

32. Nash, *Loving Nature*, 74–75.

33. See Carolyn Merchant, *The Death of Nature* (San Francisco: Harper and Row, 1980); and Clarence Glacken, *Traces on the Rhodian Shore: Nature and Culture in Western Thought from Ancient Times to the End of the Eighteenth Century* (Berkeley: University of California Press, 1967).

34. Nash, *Loving Nature*, 77.

35. Backing for this claim can be found in Hans Walter Wolff, *Anthropology of the Old Testament* (Philadelphia: Fortress, 1981); G. E. Ladd, *Theology of the New Testament* (Grand Rapids: Eerdmans, 1974), chaps. 29, 34; Herman Ridderbos, *Paul: An Outline of His Theology* (Grand Rapids: Eerdmans, 1975), chaps. 3, 6.

36. On the former, see G. C. Berkouwer, *Man: The Image of God* (Grand Rapids: Eerdmans, 1962), chap. 6. On the latter, see John Cooper, *Body, Soul, and Life Everlasting* (Grand Rapids: Eerdmans, 1989). For one example (among many) of a Christian non-dualist anthropology, see Kevin Corcoran, *Rethinking Human Nature: A Christian Materialist Alternative to the Soul* (Grand Rapids: Baker Academic, 2006). For more on this larger discussion, see the essays in Warren Brown, Nancey Murphy, and H. Newton Malony, eds., *Whatever Happened to the Soul? Scientific and Theological Portraits of Human Nature* (Minneapolis: Fortress, 1998); and the essays in Joel Green, ed., *What about the Soul? Neuroscience and Christian Anthropology* (Nashville: Abingdon, 2004).

37. See, e.g., Plato's *Phaedo* and *Phaedrus*.

38. Berry, *Sex, Economy, Freedom, and Community,* 106 (italics in the original).

39. Nash, *Loving Nature*, 79.

40. Ibid.

41. Santmire, *Travail of Nature,* chap. 2. See also Susan Power Bratton, *Christianity, Wilderness, and Wildlife: The Original Desert Solitaire* (Scranton, PA: University of Scranton Press, 1993).

42. Wesley Granberg-Michaelson, *Ecology and Life: Accepting Our Environmental Responsibility* (Waco: Word, 1988), 33. For other critical responses to the Lynn White thesis, see, e.g., the essays by Louis Moncrief and Rene Dubos in Barbour, *Western Man and Environmental Ethics*; Rene Dubos, "Franciscan Conservation versus Benedictine Stewardship," in Spring and Spring, *Ecology and Religion in History*; and Jeremy Cohen, "The Bible, Man, and Nature in the History of Western Thought: A Call for Reassessment," *Journal of Religion* 65, no. 2 (April 1985): 155–72.

43. See, e.g., Eugene Klaaren, *Religious Origins of Modern Science* (Grand Rapids: Eerdmans, 1977); and Roger Hooykaas, *Religion and the Rise of Modern Science* (Edinburgh: Scottish Academic, 1972).

44. See, e.g., David Lindberg and Ronald Numbers, *God and Nature: Historical Essays on the Encounter between Christianity and Science* (Berkeley: University of California Press, 1986).

45. Nash, *Loving Nature,* 88.

46. On the Maya, see, e.g., Clive Ponting, *A Green History of the World: The Environment and the Collapse of Great Civilizations* (New York: Penguin, 1991), chap. 5. See also Jared Diamond, *Collapse: How Societies Choose to Fail or Succeed* (New York: Viking, 2005). Augustine's lament can be found in his *City of God.* Plato's observations are in his *Critias,* chap. 3.

47. For example, in *Capitalism and Progress: A Diagnosis of Western Society* (Grand Rapids: Eerdmans, 1979), Bob Goudzwaard argues that modern capitalism (and socialism), with its ultimate belief in economic progress, has been a significant contributor to ecological degradation. Brian Walsh and Richard Middleton, in *The Transforming Vision* (Downers Grove, IL: InterVarsity, 1984), also point to a misplaced faith in economic prosperity or economism as one of the leading factors in ecological despoilation. And Alan Miller makes a similar argument in chap. 5 of *Gaia Connections* (Savage, MD: Rowman and Littlefield, 1991).

48. White, "Historical Roots," 30.

49. A discussion of textual criticism is beyond the scope of this project. Suffice it to say that the earliest and best attested manuscripts, reflected in both the United Bible Society and the Nestle-Aland Greek New Testaments, have *heurethēsetai* here in 2 Pet. 3:10. For discussion of this text, see Bruce Metzger, *A Textual Commentary on the Greek New Testament,* 2nd ed. (London: United Bible Society, 1994); and Richard Bauckham, *Jude and 2 Peter,* Word Biblical Commentary 50 (Waco: Word, 1983), 303–22. For excellent background on this entire issue, see Al Wolters, "Worldview and Textual Criticism in 2 Peter 3:10," *Westminster Theological Journal* 49, no. 2 (Fall 1987): 405–13.

50. For corroboration of this reading, see Bauckham, *Jude and 2 Peter.*

51. Susan Schreiner, *The Theatre of His Glory: Nature and the Natural Order in the Thought of John Calvin* (Grand Rapids: Baker, 1991), 99.

52. Thomas Finger, "Evangelicals, Eschatology, and the Environment," Scholars Circle monograph 2 (Evangelical Environmental Network, 1998), 5.

53. Cicero, *Letters to Atticus* 8.16.2 and 16.11.6.

54. N. T. Wright, *Surprised By Hope: Rethinking Heaven, the Resurrection, and the Mission of the Church* (New York: HarperCollins, 2008), 133.

55. Barbara Rossing, *The Rapture Exposed: The Message of Hope in the Book of Revelation* (Boulder, CO: Westview, 2004), 2. This book offers a thorough and trenchant critique of the rapture and Left Behind eschatology. See also "Not Left Behind," the appendix in Craig Hill's fine book, *In God's Time: The Bible and the Future* (Grand Rapids: Eerdmans, 2002), in which he offers a compelling critique of Left Behind biblical interpretation, concluding that "contemporary America's most popular Christian eschatology is unscriptural" (207).

56. Finger, "Evangelicals, Eschatology, and the Environment," 27 (italics in the original).

57. Ibid.

58. Nash, *Loving Nature,* 74.

59. Donald Worster, *The Wealth of Nature: Environmental History and the Ecological Imagination* (New York: Oxford University Press, 1993), 208–10 (italics in the original).

60. Ibid., 210.

61. Ibid., 211.

62. Ibid., 214.

63. Ibid., 214–16.

64. Ibid., 217. Wendell Berry makes the same claim: our local human economies derive from and depend on the larger economy of nature, and ultimately on God's economy; see his essay "Two Economies" in *Home Economics* (New York: North Point, 1987).

65. Worster, *Wealth of Nature*, 217.

66. Ibid., 218 (italics in the original). This judgment is shared by a number of other astute observers of Western culture. For example, in *The Poverty of Affluence: A Psychological Portrait of the American Way of Life* (Philadelphia: New Society, 1989), Paul Wachtel speaks of "pollution and the problem of environmental limits" as "the weightiest of all the denied realities of the consumer life" (48).

67. Worster, *Wealth of Nature*, 18.

68. Norman Wirzba, *The Paradise of God: Renewing Religion in an Ecological Age* (New York: Oxford University Press, 2003), 61–62 (italics in the original).

69. Ibid., 62.

70. Ibid., 65.

71. Ibid., 67.

72. Ibid., 68.

73. Ibid., 69.

74. Ibid., 69–70.

75. Ibid., 72.

76. Ibid., 73.

77. For more on this, see Steven Bouma-Prediger and Brian Walsh, *Beyond Homelessness: Christian Faith in a Culture of Displacement* (Grand Rapids: Eerdmans, 2008), chaps. 7–8.

78. Wirzba, *Paradise of God*, 77.

79. Ibid., 78 (bold in the original).

80. Ibid., 78–79 (bold in the original). See also Neil Postman, *Technopoly: The Surrender of Culture to Technology* (New York: Vintage, 1993); Albert Borgmann, *Power Failure: Christianity in the Culture of Technology* (Grand Rapids: Brazos, 2003); and Bill McKibben, *Enough: Staying Human in an Engineered Age* (New York: Henry Holt, 2003).

81. Wirzba, *Paradise of God*, 81.

82. Ibid., 85.

83. Ibid., 89.

84. Ibid., 90.

85. Ibid., 91.

86. Granberg-Michaelson, *Ecology and Life*, 34.

87. See, e.g., Merchant, *Death of Nature*. The list of Enlightenment thinkers—Bacon, Descartes, Hobbes, Locke, Newton, Smith, Kant—who contributed in sundry ways to the shaping of what we call modernity well illustrates the power of this intellectual movement.

88. Of the many studies on the rise of modernity, see, e.g., Charles Taylor, *Sources of the Self: The Making of the Modern Identity* (Cambridge: Harvard University Press, 1989); Stephen Toulmin, *Cosmopolis: The Hidden Agenda of Modernity* (Chicago: University of Chicago Press, 1990); Alasdair MacIntyre, *After Virtue*, 2nd ed. (Notre Dame: University of Notre Dame Press, 1984). On the cultural captivity of the church, see, e.g., William Placher, *Unapologetic Theology: A Christian Voice in a Pluralistic Conversation* (Louisville: Westminster/John Knox, 1989); John Milbank, *Theology and Social Theory: Beyond Secular Reason* (Oxford: Blackwell, 1993).

89. Wendell Berry, *Sex, Economy, Freedom, and Community*, 114–15.

90. Granberg-Michaelson, *Ecology and Life*, 35.

91. James Gustafson, *Ethics from a Theocentric Perspective: Theology and Ethics* (Chicago: University of Chicago Press, 1981), 91.

92. Holmes Rolston III, *Environmental Ethics: Duties to and Values in the Natural World* (Philadelphia: Temple University Press, 1988), 32 (italics in the original).

93. See, e.g., Jurgen Moltmann, *God in Creation: A New Theology of Creation and the Spirit of God* (San Francisco: Harper and Row, 1985); Joseph Sittler, *Essays on Nature and Grace* (Philadelphia: Fortress, 1972); and Richard Young, *Healing the Earth: A Theocentric Perspective on Environmental Problems and Their Solutions* (Nashville: Broadman and Holman, 1994).

94. Granberg-Michaelson, *Ecology and Life*, 37. Such a claim finds strong support from a host of other astute culture watchers, e.g., Jacques Ellul, E. F. Schumacher, and Neil Postman.

95. Walsh and Middleton, *Transforming Vision*, 135.

96. Postman, *Technopoly*, xii.

97. Langdon Gilkey, *Society and the Sacred* (New York: Crossroad, 1981).

98. Granberg-Michaelson, *Ecology and Life*, 40.

99. See, e.g., the Belgic Confession, article 2, where these two books are mentioned in response to the question of how God is made known to us.

100. Granberg-Michaelson, *Ecology and Life*, 41.

101. Sittler, "Ecological Commitment as Theological Responsibility," 179 (italics in the original). Others who note this *Schöpfungsvergessenheit* include Per Lonning, *Creation—An Ecumenical Challenge?* (Macon, GA: Mercer, 1989), 5; Ian Barbour, *Religion in an Age of Science* (San Francisco: Harper and Row, 1990), 217; and Gustav Wingren, "The Doctrine of Creation: Not an Appendix but the First Article," *Word and World* 4 (Fall 1984): 353–71.

102. Glacken, *Traces on the Rhodian Shore*, 181.

103. Walsh and Middleton, *Transforming Vision*, 44.

104. Granberg-Michaelson, *Ecology and Life*, 42.

105. See, e.g., Gennadios Limouris, ed., *Justice, Peace, and the Integrity of Creation: Insights from Orthodoxy* (Geneva: World Council of Churches, 1990).

106. See, e.g., David Hallman, *Ecotheology: Voices from South and North* (Geneva: World Council of Churches, 1994); and Leonardo Boff, *Ecology and Liberation: A New Paradigm* (Maryknoll, NY: Orbis, 1995).

107. See, e.g., the Religions of the World and Ecology series, published by Harvard University Press. Ten volumes are now out—on Buddhism, Christianity, Confucianism, Judaism, Hinduism, Indigenous Traditions, Islam, Jainism, Shinto, and Taoism.

Chapter 4 What Is the Connection between Scripture and Ecology? Biblical Wisdom and Ecological Vision

1. Thomas Berry (lecture, Christianity and Ecology conference, Harvard Divinity School, Cambridge, MA, April 1998).

2. For a helpful discussion of different ways of viewing Scripture, see Donald McKim, *What Christians Believe about the Bible* (Nashville: Thomas Nelson, 1985).

3. The literature on hermeneutics is vast. For a solid introduction, with special attention to biblical interpretation, see Donald McKim, *A Guide to Contemporary Hermeneutics: Major Trends in Biblical Interpretation* (Grand Rapids: Eerdmans, 1986). For a comprehensive and responsible in-depth treatment, see Anthony Thiselton, *New Horizons in Hermeneutics* (Grand Rapids: Zondervan, 1992). For a superb overview of the history of interpretation of the Bible, see Robert Grant and David Tracy, *A Short History of the Interpretation of the Bible* (Philadelphia: Fortress, 1984). For an excellent discussion of the larger issues in epistemology, see Richard Bernstein, *Beyond Objectivism and Relativism: Science, Hermeneutics, and Praxis* (Philadelphia: University of Pennsylvania Press, 1983).

4. The expression comes from Thomas Nagel, *The View from Nowhere* (New York: Oxford University Press, 1986), but the classic contemporary presentation of our ineliminable human finitude in understanding remains Hans-Georg Gadamer, *Truth and Method* (New York: Continuum, 1975).

5. Richard Rorty, *Philosophy and the Mirror of Nature* (Princeton: Princeton University Press, 1979), 176.

6. Paul Ricoeur, *The Conflict of Interpretations: Essays in Hermeneutics*, ed. Don Ihde (Evanston, IL: Northwestern University Press, 1974), 148. For an illuminating example of learning from these masters, see Merold Westphal, *Suspicion and Truth: The Religious Uses of Modern Atheism* (Grand Rapids: Eerdmans, 1993).

7. For examples of such creative appropriation by Christians, see Merold Westphal, ed., *Postmodern Philosophy and Christian Thought* (Bloomington: Indiana University Press, 1999); and James K. A. Smith, *Who's Afraid of Postmodernism? Taking Derrida, Lyotard, and Foucault to Church* (Grand Rapids: Baker Academic, 2006).

8. Bernstein, *Beyond Objectivism and Relativism*, esp. part 4.

9. Willard Swartley, *Slavery, Sabbath, War, and Women* (Scottdale, PA: Herald, 1983).

10. Bernhard Anderson, *From Creation to New Creation* (Minneapolis: Augsburg Fortress, 1994), 134.

11. My approach is very similar to that of Paul Santmire, in both of the ways just mentioned. First, Santmire, too, is explicit about the role of interpretive frameworks. Like a pair of glasses, they are necessary if one is to see clearly and accurately the world of the text. In his words, "We need an interpretive framework that, together with the most rigorous forms of historical study, will help us hear the witness of the Scriptures." And, second, Santmire outlines his own interpretative position and strategy, especially as he attempts to recover the biblical story beyond the distorting glasses of typical Western anthropocentrism. According to Santmire, we must hear the witness of Scripture "as Augustine heard that witness," namely, as testimony to the universal vision of the city of God, and so Santmire proposes to read Scripture from "'first things' (protology) to 'last things' (eschatology)" (H. Paul Santmire, *Nature Reborn: The Ecological and Cosmic Promise of Christian Theology* [Minneapolis: Augsburg Fortress, 2000], 31).

Santmire's own approach is also inspired by the evocative and influential writings of Joseph Sittler. Conscious of the many different voices in the Bible, and aware of how what we bring to the biblical text influences how we read it, Sittler nevertheless speaks of a "rhetoric of cosmic extension" in the Bible, especially in the New Testament, which testifies to the universal scope of God's grace. See, e.g., Joseph Sittler, *Essays on Nature and Grace* (Philadelphia: Fortress, 1972), 36–50.

12. Santmire, *Nature Reborn*, 31.

13. E.g., Anderson, *From Creation to New Creation*, chaps. 4, 8; Walter Brueggemann, *Genesis*, Interpretation (Atlanta: John Knox, 1982), 3–4; and Terence Fretheim, "The Book of Genesis," in *The New Intrepreter's Bible*, vol. 1 (Nashville: Abingdon, 1994), 322–23. See also Terence Fretheim's magisterial *God and the World in the Old Testament* (Nashville: Abingdon, 2005), esp. chap. 2.

14. Fretheim, "Book of Genesis," 321.

15. Many works inform my rendering, e.g., Brueggemann, *Genesis*; Fretheim, "Book of Genesis" and *God and the World in the Old Testament*; Gerhard von Rad, *Genesis*, rev. ed., Old Testament Library (Philadelphia: Westminster, 1972); Gordon Wenham, *Genesis 1–15*, Word Biblical Commentary 1 (Waco: Word, 1987); and Claus Westermann, *Genesis 1–11* (Minneapolis: Augsburg, 1984). Also informative is Anderson, *From Creation to New Creation*. The work of J. Richard Middleton is especially insightful on what it means to be made in God's image; see "The Liberating Image? Interpreting the *Imago Dei* in Context," *Christian Scholar's Review* 24, no. 1 (September 1994): 8–25; and especially his *The Liberating Image: The Imago Dei in Genesis 1* (Grand Rapids: Brazos, 2005), which is the definitive work on this important topic.

16. For more on the creation myths of the day, and on Genesis 1–11 as a critique of the ideology of those myths, see Middleton, *Liberating Image*, chaps. 3–4.

17. Fretheim, *God and the World in the Old Testament*, 38. Fretheim emphasizes this power sharing:

Moreover, and especially important, the divine creating often entails a speaking *with* that which is *already* created: let the earth bring forth (1:11, 24); let the waters bring forth (1:20). Genesis 1:12 differs from 1:20, 24 in that it specifically states that "the earth brought forth." That such a statement is not present in 1:20, 24, however, should not be interpreted to mean that the earth and waters were not actual participants in these cases; rather, God's creative act is mediated in and through these creatures, and God as sole stated subject is a variation of 1:11–13, where the earth is stated as the only subject. Grammatically the use of the jussive "let" means that God's speaking does not function as an imperative; it leaves room for creaturely response, not unlike the cohortative "let us make" (1:26) leaves room for consultation and the "[let them] have dominion" (1:28) entails a sharing of power (38, italics in the original).

18. For a discussion of chaos and the formless void, see Fretheim, *God and the World in the Old Testament*, 43–46.

19. Anderson, *From Creation to New Creation*, 154.

20. "Good" does not necessarily mean, as many readers assume, perfect. Creation is good, but not perfect, at least not (as is commonly understood) in the Platonic sense of perfect as unchanging or static. Though good, the earth still needs to be developed, worked, cared for—the responsibility and the privilege of the human earth-creature.

21. Richard Middleton and Brian Walsh, *Truth Is Stranger Than It Used To Be* (Downers Grove, IL: InterVarsity, 1995), 153. See also John Milbank, *Theology and Social Theory: Beyond Secular Reason* (Oxford: Blackwell, 1993), 262.

22. Wendell Berry, *The Gift of Good Land* (San Francisco: North Point, 1981).

23. Anderson, *From Creation to New Creation*, 154.

24. On the meaning of the *imago Dei*, see Brueggemann, *Genesis*, 32; Westermann, *Genesis 1–11*, 143–45; and Middleton, "The Liberating Image?"

25. Larry Rasmussen, *Earth Community Earth Ethics* (Maryknoll, NY: Orbis, 1996), 262.

26. Anderson, *From Creation to New Creation*, 139.

27. Jürgen Moltmann, *God in Creation: A New Theology of Creation and the Spirit of God* (San Francisco: Harper and Row, 1985), 277 (italics in the original).

28. Brueggemann, *Genesis*, 35.

29. For more on reading the Bible in terms of home/homelessness/homecoming, see Steven Bouma-Prediger and Brian Walsh, *Beyond Homelessness: Christian Faith in a Culture of Displacement* (Grand Rapids: Eerdmans, 2008).

30. Once again many works inform my rendering, including commentaries (Brueggemann, *Genesis*; Fretheim, "Book of Genesis" and *God and the World in the Old Testament*; von Rad, *Genesis*; Wenham, *Genesis 1–15*; Westermann, *Genesis 1–11*) and monographs (Anderson, *From Creation to New Creation*; Robert Murray, *The Cosmic Covenant: Biblical Themes of Justice, Peace, and the Integrity of Creation* [London: Sheed and Ward, 1992]; Ronald Simkins, *Creator and Creation: Nature in the Worldview of Ancient Israel* [Peabody, MA: Hendrickson, 1994]).

31. Anderson, *From Creation to New Creation*, 157.

32. My thanks to Hope College colleague Barry Bandstra for this insight.

33. Indeed it is about suffering, but it is also about much more. The overall question of the book, I believe, is revealed in chapter 1, verse 9. In that text Satan, the adversary, queries the Lord: "Does Job fear God for nothing?" In other words, Does Job serve God only because of the goods, material and spiritual, that he receives? Or does he worship God simply because it is right and fitting to do so, come what may? Satan obviously thinks Job's faith is an example, to use Merold Westphal's fetching phrase, of "piety for profit" (*God, Guilt, and Death: An Existential Phenomenology of Religion* [Bloomington: Indiana University Press, 1984], 125). God thinks otherwise; Job's faith, God bets, is the real thing. The drama of the plot is in discovering who is right—God or Satan. In short, while suffering and one's response to it do constitute an important theme in the story, the book is fundamentally a polemic against fraudulent faith. The story of Job alerts us to the danger of a false consciousness that, believing its faith to be genuine, actually engages in idolatry.

34. My rendering is informed by the following works: Robert Gordis, *The Book of Job: Commentary, New Translation, and Special Studies* (New York: Jewish Theological Seminary of America, 1978); idem, *The Book of God and Man: A Study of Job* (Chicago: University of Chicago Press, 1965); Norman Habel, *The Book of Job* (Philadelphia: Westminster, 1985); Marvin Pope, *Job*, 3rd ed., Anchor Bible 15 (New York: Doubleday, 1973); and especially Carol Newsom's insightful commentary, "The Book of Job," in *The New Interpreter's Bible*, vol. 4 (Nashville: Abingdon, 1996).

35. Bill McKibben, *The Comforting Whirlwind: God, Job, and the Scale of Creation* (Grand Rapids: Eerdmans, 1994), 36.

36. Ibid., 37.

37. Aldo Leopold, *A Sand County Almanac* (New York: Ballantine, 1970), 240.

38. Gordis, *Book of Job*, 467.

39. Newsom, "Book of Job," 625–26.

40. For more on the role of moral imagination see Bruce Birch and Larry Rasmussen, *Bible and Ethics in the Christian Life*, rev. ed. (Minneapolis: Augsburg Fortress, 1989); Samuel Wells, *Improvisation: The Drama of Christian Ethics* (Grand Rapids: Brazos, 2004); and David Cunningham, *Christian Ethics: The End of the Law* (New York: Routledge, 2008).

41. Newsom, "Book of Job," 626.

42. Ibid.

43. Gordis, *Book of Job*, 435.

44. Erazim Kohák, *The Embers and the Stars: A Philosophical Inquiry into the Moral Sense of Nature* (Chicago: University of Chicago Press, 1984), 45. Reflecting on the gifts of nature, Kohák affirms the decentering power of the natural world: "In the solitude at dusk, the world which presents itself to the dweller is not a world of his making, nor does it derive its meaning from him. He is not its center, but a dweller within it" (43).

45. Belden C. Lane, *The Solace of Fierce Landscapes: Exploring Desert and Mountain Spirituality* (New York: Oxford University Press, 1998).

46. The question of the authorship of Colossians is contested. Many commentators argue that it was not written by St. Paul, while others (e.g., Martin and Wright, see next note) believe that Paul is, in fact, the author. For a variety of reasons, I side with this latter group and so shall refer to the author as Paul.

47. My rendering of this text is informed by the following: F. F. Bruce, *The Epistles to the Colossians, to Philemon, and to the Ephesians*, New International Commentary on the New Testament (Grand Rapids: Eerdmans, 1984); James D. G. Dunn, *The Epistles to the Colossians and to Philemon*, New International Greek Testament Commentary (Grand Rapids: Eerdmans, 1996); Andrew Lincoln, "The Letter to the Colossians," in *The New Interpreter's Bible*, vol. 11 (Nashville: Abingdon, 2000); Ralph Martin, *Ephesians, Colossians, and Philemon*, Interpretation (Atlanta: John Knox, 1991); Peter O'Brien, *Colossians and Philemon*, Word Biblical Commentary 44 (Waco: Word, 1982). I am especially indebted to the work of N. T. Wright; see especially *The Climax of the Covenant* (Minneapolis: Fortress, 1992); *The Epistles of Paul to the Colossians and to Philemon*, The Tyndale New Testament Commentaries (Grand Rapids: Eerdmans, 1986); and *The Resurrection of the Son of God* (Minneapolis: Fortress, 2003). I am also persuaded by Brian Walsh and Sylvia Keesmaat, *Colossians Remixed: Subverting the Empire* (Downers Grove, IL: InterVarsity, 2003), that the letter cannot be understood rightly without proper attention to its imperial Roman context. For an introduction to these issues, see, e.g., Richard Horsley, ed., *Paul and Empire: Religion and Power in Roman Imperial Society* (Harrisburg, PA: Trinity Press International, 1997).

48. As in North America at Christmas, when the sights and sounds and smells of the holiday are virtually everywhere, in Colossae and other cities in Asia Minor the emperor cult "permeated public life and the culture generally as well as public space." In particular, "the imperial image, which emanated from and represented the center [of the empire], became omnipresent and was widely venerated in the Greek cities" (Horsley, *Paul and Empire*, 21–22).

49. See Prov. 8:22 and Wis. 7:25 for the Hellenistic Jewish background of the notion of divine Wisdom personified and described as the image of God's goodness.

50. Both the merism (heaven and earth) and the inclusio (heaven / earth // visible / invisible) emphasize that nothing is excluded from the "all things."

51. While these terms, given their uses in Hellenistic Jewish texts, are usually thought to refer to astral or heavenly powers, the ubiquity and power of the emperor cult makes it difficult to believe that Paul did not have Roman imperial rule in mind. As Neil Elliot makes clear, in other Pauline writings these terms refer to historical powers and form the context for Paul's "anti-imperial message of the

cross" ("The Anti-Imperial Message of the Cross," in Horsley, *Paul and Empire*, 167). See also Horsley, *Paul and Empire*, 172–76 and 179–81.

52. Virtually all commentators assume these terms refer only to heavenly realities. For example, Dunn claims that "all four terms thus refer only to the invisible, heavenly realm" (*Epistles to the Colossians and to Philemon*, 92). Thus is the text depoliticized, and any possibility that one or more of these terms might refer to actual historical thrones or dominions, rulers or powers, is dismissed. In other words, that the throne might be Caesar's or the dominion that of Rome or the power that of the empire is not seriously considered.

53. In the two parallel lines of the middle section of the poem, which thematically connect the two main strophes, the supremacy of Christ is reinforced. See, e.g., Wright's suggestive and insightful literary analysis in *Climax of the Covenant*, 104.

54. The cosmos holds together because, in the words of Brian Walsh, Christ is "nothing less than the ontological linchpin of creation" ("Subversive Poetry and Life in the Empire," *Third Way* 23, no. 3 [April 2000]: 4).

55. While *ekklēsia* is usually translated "church," the term means "assembly," and has both political and religious meanings. As Horsley comments: "By general consensus, while *ekklēsia* comes to Paul from the Septuagint (the Jewish Bible in Greek) with strong connotations of the 'assembly' of (all) Israel, its primary meaning in the Greek-speaking eastern Roman empire was the citizen 'assembly' of the Greek *polis*. *Ekklēsia* is thus a political term with certain religious overtones" (*Paul and Empire*, 208). Thus Paul's assemblies or churches are alternative local communities that stand over against the Roman imperial order.

56. In language reminiscent of Gen. 1:1 and Prov. 8:22, Christ is here proclaimed to be the beginning. As with the term "firstborn," beginning has to do with primacy, whether in time or with reference to sovereignty.

57. See, respectively, 1 Cor. 15:20, 23 and Rom. 8:29.

58. See, e.g., Gen. 49:3, where both terms, "firstborn" and "beginning," together designate the founder of a new people.

59. The use of the rare word *prōteuōn* combined with the seemingly omnipresent "all things" emphasizes (again) the full scope of Christ's superiority.

60. Dunn comments: "The wholeness of God's interaction with the universe is summed up in Christ." In this way Paul's thought "reaches well beyond that of Wisdom or even God 'dwelling in' a good and compassionate person . . . to grasp at the idea of the wholeness of divine immanence dwelling in Christ" (*Epistles to the Colossians and to Philemon*, 101).

61. See also Eph. 2:16 and Col. 1:22.

62. Dunn, *Epistles to the Colossians and to Philemon*, 104.

63. Bruce, *Colossians, Philemon, Ephesians*, 62–63.

64. Wright, *Climax of the Covenant*, 107.

65. Dunn, *Epistles to the Colossians and to Philemon*, 86.

66. Ibid., 104.

67. Wright, *Climax of the Covenant*, 108.

68. Martin, *Ephesians, Colossians, and Philemon*, 95.

69. Wright, *Climax of the Covenant*, 109.

70. Sittler, "Called to Unity," in *Evocations of Grace: The Writings of Joseph Sittler on Ecology, Theology, and Ethics*, ed. Steven Bouma-Prediger and Peter Bakken (Grand Rapids: Eerdmans, 2000), 39. Of all those in the twentieth century to champion the "cosmic Christ," none did so as well as Sittler, whose famous plenary speech at the 1961 meeting of the World Council of Churches in New Delhi, India, was in fact an extended meditation on Col. 1:15–20.

71. Such questions, contrary to the views of many, are not idle or speculative or worthless. These questions are anything but pie in the sky, by-and-by, for what we believe about the future is integrally connected to how we act in the present. Our eschatology shapes our ethics.

72. My interpretive rendering is informed by the following: David Aune, *Revelation 17–22*, Word Biblical Commentary 52c (Nashville: Thomas Nelson, 1998); G. K. Beale, *The Book of Revelation*, New

International Greek Testament Commentary (Grand Rapids: Eerdmans, 1999); G. R. Beasley-Murray, *The Book of Revelation*, New Cambridge Bible Commentary (Grand Rapids: Eerdmans, 1981); M. Eugene Boring, *Revelation*, Interpretation (Louisville: Westminster/John Knox, 1989); G. B. Caird, *The Revelation of St. John the Divine* (New York: Harper and Row, 1966); Catherine Gunsalus González and Justo L. González, *Revelation*, Westminster Bible Companion (Louisville: Westminster/John Knox, 1997); George Eldon Ladd, *A Commentary on the Revelation of John* (Grand Rapids: Eerdmans, 1972); Paul Minear, *I Saw a New Earth* (Washington, DC: Corpus, 1968); and Christopher Rowland, "The Book of Revelation," in *The New Interpreter's Bible*, vol. 12 (Nashville: Abingdon, 1998).

For a superb presentation of what the Bible (and the church on its better days) says about the future, see N. T. Wright, *Surprised by Hope: Rethinking Heaven, the Resurrection, and the Mission of the Church* (New York: HarperCollins, 2008). For a short repudiation of "rapture theology," see the appendix, "Not Left Behind," in Craig Hill, *In God's Time: The Bible and the Future* (Grand Rapids: Eerdmans, 2002). For a more extensive and thoroughly devastating critique, see Barbara Rossing, *The Rapture Exposed: The Message of Hope in the Book of Revelation* (Boulder, CO: Westview, 2004).

73. The Greek *neos* is a temporal term denoting that which is young, new in time, or previously non-existent. The term *kainos* is an eschatological term, having to do with the promise and realization of the messianic age to come, denoting something previously unknown or unprecedented, something with a new character. With its background usage in the Hebrew prophets, *kainos* suggests that which is better, of a superior nature. See Colin Brown, ed., *The New International Dictionary of New Testament Theology*, vol. 2 (Grand Rapids: Zondervan, 1976), 669–76; and Gerhard Kittel and Gerhard Friedrich, eds., *Theological Dictionary of the New Testament* (Grand Rapids: Eerdmans, 1974), 388–89, 628. See also Paul Minear's perceptive analysis of these terms in *I Saw a New Earth*, 272–73. Beale says it well: "Indeed, *kainos* ('new'), as we have seen, refers predominantly to a change in quality or essence rather than something new that has never previously been in existence" (*Book of Revelation*, 1040).

74. Claus Westermann summarizes the gist of Isaiah 65: "Instead, the world, designated as 'heaven and earth,' is to be miraculously renewed" (*Isaiah 40–66* [Philadelphia: Westminster, 1969], 408). In a similar manner Paul Hanson affirms: "No goal short of the restoration of all of God's creation to its intended wholeness will satisfy the yearning of the Servant of the Lord" (*Isaiah 40–66*, Old Testament Library [Louisville: John Knox, 1995], 246).

75. Boring, *Revelation*, 220. See also George Ladd, who affirms: "Throughout the entire Bible, the ultimate destiny of God's people is an earthly destiny. . . . Biblical thought always places man on a redeemed earth, not in a heavenly realm removed from earthly existence" (*Revelation*, 275).

76. As Caird reminds us: "The word *skēnē* (dwelling) has a long and important theological history. It is the word regularly used in the Septuagint for the Hebrew *mishkan* (tent), which was the symbol of God's abiding presence in the midst of Israel in the wilderness" (*Revelation of St. John the Divine*, 263).

77. González and González, *Revelation*, 138.

78. Caird comments: "The sphere of the holy has expanded to include all that is capable of being offered to God, and all that is unfit for God has been forever excluded. The presence of God, no longer confined to a sanctuary apart, pervades the whole life and being of the city, which accordingly needs no created light" (*Revelation of St. John the Divine*, 279).

79. Ibid., 279–80. For an enlightening commentary on Isa. 60, see Richard Mouw, *When the Kings Come Marching In* (Grand Rapids: Eerdmans, 1983).

80. Caird, *Revelation of St. John the Divine*, 265–66.

81. In addition to the books already cited, see Theodore Hiebert, *The Yahwist's Landscape: Nature and Religion in Early Israel* (New York: Oxford University Press, 1996); William P. Brown, *The Ethos of the Cosmos: The Genesis of Moral Imagination in the Bible* (Grand Rapids: Eerdmans, 1999); William P. Brown and S. Dean McBride Jr., eds., *God Who Creates: Essays in Honor of W. Sibley Towner* (Grand Rapids: Eerdmans, 2000); and the Earth Bible series, 5 vols., edited by Norman Habel (Sheffield: Sheffield Academic, 2000–2002). See also *The Green Bible*, published in 2008 by HarperCollins—the NRSV translation, with all verses that pertain to the earth or earthkeeping highlighted in green. This Bible also includes a number of interpretive essays, a series of Bible studies on creation care, a resource guide of Web sites, and a "green" subject index.

Chapter 5 How Should We Think of the Earth? A Theology and Ethic of Care for the Earth

1. John Calvin, *Institutes of the Christian Religion*, ed. John McNeill (Philadelphia: Westminster, 1960), 1.13.14.

2. Historian Robert Booth Fowler concludes his enlightening study of contemporary Protestantism with these words: "My argument has been that at all levels of Protestantism there is now a considerable consensus on the necessity of action by Christian people to address the environment" (*The Greening of Protestant Thought* [Chapel Hill: University of North Carolina Press, 1995], 175). His study includes a discerning look at evangelicals, about whom he comments that "the most significant current trend within organized Protestant environmentalism" is "the emergence of vigorous evangelical support for the ecological movement" (ibid., 17). If this was true in the early to mid 1990s, it is even truer now, with a growing wave of interest by evangelicals in creation care in the early twenty-first century.

3. For a more thorough and rigorous discussion of the shape of an ecological theology of care for the earth, see Steven Bouma-Prediger, *The Greening of Theology: The Ecological Models of Rosemary Radford Ruether, Joseph Sittler, and Jürgen Moltmann* (Atlanta: Scholars, 1995), esp. chap. 8.

4. A number of evangelicals have authored books on care of the earth, going back at least to Francis Schaeffer's *Pollution and the Death of Man: The Christian View of Ecology* (Wheaton, IL: Tyndale, 1970). More recent volumes authored or edited by evangelicals include: Loren Wilkinson et al., *Earthkeeping: Christian Stewardship of Natural Resources* (Grand Rapids: Eerdmans, 1980), and its subsequent second revised edition, *Earthkeeping in the '90s: Stewardship of Creation* (Grand Rapids: Eerdmans, 1991); Wesley Granberg-Michaelson, *A Worldly Spirituality: The Call to Take Care of the Earth* (San Francisco: Harper and Row, 1984); Calvin DeWitt, *Earth-Wise: A Biblical Response to Environmental Issues* (Grand Rapids: CRC Publications, 1994); Fred Van Dyke et al., *Redeeming Creation: The Biblical Basis for Environmental Stewardship* (Downers Grove, IL: InterVarsity, 1996); Calvin DeWitt, *Caring for Creation: Responsible Stewardship of God's Handiwork* (Grand Rapids: Baker, 1998); R. J. Berry, ed., *The Care of Creation* (Leicester, UK: Inter-Varsity, 2000); Sarah Tillett, ed., *Caring for Creation: Biblical and Theological Perspectives* (Oxford: A Rocha, 2005); Tri Robinson, *Saving God's Green Earth: Rediscovering the Church's Responsibility to Environmental Stewardship* (Norcross, GA: Ampelon, 2006); Matthew Sleeth, *Serve God, Save the Planet: A Christian Call to Action* (White River Junction, VT: Chelsea Green, 2006); Ed Brown, *Our Father's World: Mobilizing the Church to Care for Creation* (Downers Grove, IL: InterVarsity, 2008); Ben Lowe, *Green Revolution: Coming Together to Care for Creation* (Downers Grove, IL: InterVarsity, 2009).

5. Gene McAfee, "Ecology and Biblical Studies," in *Theology for Earth Community*, ed. Dieter Hessel (Maryknoll, NY: Orbis, 1996), 36.

6. Jürgen Moltmann, *God in Creation: A New Theology of Creation and the Spirit of God* (San Francisco: Harper and Row, 1985), 31.

7. H. Paul Santmire, *Brother Earth* (New York: Thomas Nelson, 1970), chaps. 1–2.

8. Richard Young, *Healing the Earth: A Theocentric Perspective on Environmental Problems and Their Solutions* (Nashville: Broadman and Holman, 1994), 260.

9. Given the raft of books on the Trinity written in recent years, there is ample evidence that such a recovery is underway. Not much of this, however, has (yet) found a connection with ecological concerns. See, e.g., David Cunningham, *These Three Are One: The Practice of Trinitarian Theology* (Oxford: Blackwell, 1998); Colin Gunton, *The Promise of Trinitarian Theology* (Edinburgh: T&T Clark, 1991); Catherine Mowry LaCugna, *God for Us: The Trinity and Christian Life* (San Francisco: HarperCollins, 1991); Ted Peters, *God as Trinity: Relationality and Temporality in Divine Life* (Louisville: Westminster/John Knox, 1993); William Placher, *The Triune God: An Essay in Postliberal Theology* (Louisville: Westminster/John Knox, 2007); Miroslav Volf, *After Our Likeness: The Church as the Image of the Trinity* (Grand Rapids: Eerdmans, 1998); John Zizioulas, *Being as Communion: Studies in Personhood and the Church* (Crestwood, NY: St. Vladimir's Seminary Press, 1985). Three notable examples of authors in whose writings Trinitarian theology and ecological theology do engage are: Denis Edwards (*Jesus the Wisdom of God: An Ecological Theology* [Maryknoll, NY: Orbis, 1995]; idem, *Breath of Life: A Theology of the Creator Spirit* [Maryknoll, NY: Orbis, 2004]); Jürgen Moltmann (*The Trinity and the Kingdom* [San Francisco: Harper and Row,

1981]; idem, *God in Creation: A New Theology of Creation and the Spirit of God* [San Francisco: Harper and Row, 1985]), and H. Paul Santmire (*Nature Reborn: The Ecological and Cosmic Promise of Christian Theology* [Minneapolis: Augsburg Fortress, 2000]; idem, *Ritualizing Nature: Renewing Christian Liturgy in a Time of Crisis* [Minneapolis: Fortress, 2008]).

10. Person is not the same as individual. Understood in the classical Christian tradition from the time of Boethius until the last few centuries, person necessarily implies relationship. In other words, being a person means being-in-relationship. The premodern notion of person is thus very different than the modern idea of the autonomous individual or solitary self.

11. Edwards, *Jesus the Wisdom of God*, 92.

12. See Richard of St. Victor, *De Trinitate* books I–III; for commentary see Edwards, *Jesus the Wisdom of God*, 93–101.

13. Moltmann, *Trinity and the Kingdom*, 19.

14. In the early Christian tradition, the intratrinitarian relations were described in terms of *perichorēsis* (in Greek) and *circumincession* (in Latin)—each signifying mutual indwelling.

15. Thus tritheism, modalism, and subordinationism are all heterodox formulations of the doctrine of God.

16. For Moltmann, to capture the reality of God we must speak of "the love story of the God whose very life is the eternal process of engendering, responding and blissful love" (*Trinity and the Kingdom*, 157).

17. For more on the motif of covenant and creation, see Wesley Granberg-Michaelson, "Covenant and Creation," in *Liberating Life: Contemporary Approaches to Ecological Theology*, ed. Charles Birch, William Eakin, and Jay McDaniel (Maryknoll, NY: Orbis, 1990), 27–36.

18. Joseph Sittler, *Gravity and Grace* (Minneapolis: Augsburg, 1986), 22.

19. Scott Hoezee, *Remember Creation: God's World of Wonder and Delight* (Grand Rapids: Eerdmans, 1998), 45.

20. The responsiveness of creation and the possibility of creature-specific forms of agency has been explored by Brian Walsh, Marianne Karsh, and Nik Ansell in "Trees, Forestry, and the Responsiveness of Creation," *Cross Currents* 44, no. 2 (1994): 149–62. They argue that both a careful reading of the Bible and a creational listening to the earth lead to the conclusion that trees have their own peculiar kind of responsiveness.

21. Joseph Sittler, "Evangelism and the Care of the Earth," in *Evocations of Grace: The Writings of Joseph Sittler on Ecology, Theology, and Ethics*, ed. Steven Bouma-Prediger and Peter Bakken (Grand Rapids: Eerdmans, 2000), 102. Elsewhere Sittler speaks of the earth as our sister, who "unquenchably sings out her violated wholeness, and in groaning and travail awaits with man the restoration of all things" ("A Theology for Earth," in *Evocations of Grace*, 25). Paul Santmire employs the same sibling imagery when he speaks of the world as "brother earth."

22. Calvin, *Institutes*, 1.13.14. See Susan Schreiner, *The Theatre of His Glory: Nature and Natural Order in the Thought of John Calvin* (Grand Rapids: Baker, 1991) for an excellent exposition of Calvin's views of the natural world.

23. Basil's classic work on this topic is *On the Holy Spirit*. For an enlightening discussion of Basil's views, see Denis Edwards, *Breath of Life*, chap. 2; and Jaroslav Pelikan, *The Emergence of the Catholic Tradition*, vol. 1 in *The Christian Tradition: A History of the Development of Doctrine* (Chicago: University of Chicago Press, 1971), 211–25.

24. Wesley Granberg-Michaelson, "Renewing the Whole Creation," *Sojourners* (February–March 1990): 13.

25. Sittler, "Evangelism and the Care of the Earth," 204.

26. Two (among the many) insightful books that describe this embeddedness of humans in various ways in the world are: Anna Peterson, *Being Human: Ethics, Environment, and Our Place in the World* (Berkeley: University of California Press, 2001); and Robert Wennberg, *God, Humans, and Animals: An Invitation to Enlarge Our Moral Universe* (Grand Rapids: Eerdmans, 2003).

27. Tom Regan, "Christianity and Animal Rights," in Birch, Eakin, and McDaniel, *Liberating Life*, 80.

28. For an excellent discussion of sin and its many dimensions, see Neal Plantinga, *Not the Way It's Supposed To Be: A Breviary of Sin* (Grand Rapids: Eerdmans, 1995).

29. Larry Rasmussen, *Earth Community Earth Ethics* (Maryknoll, NY: Orbis, 1996), 275.

30. There are two major understandings in the Christian tradition of why the Word became flesh: to consummate the creation, regardless of sin; to restore creation, because of sin. Most theologians emphasize one view or the other. Paul Santmire consciously embraces both traditions when he concludes: "The Incarnation of the Word is thus a response to the human condition of alienation from God and rebellion against God, as well as a divine cosmic unfolding intended to move the whole of cosmic history into its final stage" (*Nature Reborn*, 59). For an insightful examination of these two streams within the tradition, see Chul Won Suh, *The Creation-Mediatorship of Jesus Christ: A Study in the Relationship between the Incarnation and the Creation* (Amsterdam: Rodopi, 1979).

31. Hoezee, *Remember Creation*, 79.

32. A theme emphasized by Loren Wilkinson, "Cosmic Christology and the Christian's Role in Creation," *Christian Scholar's Review* 11, no. 1 (1981): 18–40.

33. Loren Wilkinson, "Christ as Creator and Redeemer," in *The Environment and the Christian*, ed. Calvin DeWitt (Grand Rapids: Baker, 1991), 39–40.

34. Ray Van Leeuwen, "Christ's Resurrection and the Creation's Vindication," in DeWitt, *The Environment and the Christian*, 61. Van Leeuwen cites approvingly the work of Oliver O'Donovan, who also emphasizes the Pauline image of Christ as the New Adam (see, e.g., *Resurrection and Moral Order: An Outline for Evangelical Ethics* [Grand Rapids: Eerdmans, 1986]).

35. This language was, of course, worked out in the fourth and fifth centuries AD. Its usage did not imply—nor does it now imply—a full grasp of the incarnation, for like the Trinity and the origin of evil, the incarnation is a genuine mystery. The function of doctrine is to provide proper language and thus foster understanding as far as possible for finite and fallen minds.

36. Joseph Sittler, *Grace Notes and Other Fragments*, ed. Robert Herhold and Linda Marie Delloff (Philadelphia: Fortress, 1981), 119. In another context Sittler observes: "The doctrine of the Trinity arose precisely because of the magnitude of the Christian community's claim about Christ. The community knew that if God is subtracted from Jesus the remainder is not Jesus" ("The Scope of Christological Reflection," *Interpretation* 26 [July 1972]: 331).

37. Sittler, *Grace Notes*, 119. See also Jürgen Moltmann's classic work, *The Crucified God* (New York: Harper and Row, 1974).

38. As Brian Walsh points out, to have dominion (Gen. 1:26–28) is to follow the one we Christians call *Domine*, Lord, which means "to lay down one's life for that which we have dominion over" (*Subversive Christianity: Imaging God in a Dangerous Time* [Bristol: Regius, 1992], 23).

39. James Nash, *Loving Nature: Ecological Integrity and Christian Responsibility* (Nashville: Abingdon, 1991), 124.

40. Timothy Ware, *The Orthodox Church* (London: Penguin, 1991), 239 (italics in the original). See also his very fine introduction to Orthodox theology, *The Orthodox Way* (Crestwood, NY: St. Vladimir's Seminary Press, 1979).

41. Santmire, *Nature Reborn*, 76.

42. Ibid., 118–19.

43. Ibid., 120–28.

44. Ibid., 128.

45. Santmire's more recent book, *Ritualizing Nature: Renewing Christian Liturgy in a Time of Crisis*, is a richly suggestive discussion of how we Christians can and should shape our lives, most especially our worship lives, in order to become better caretakers of creation.

46. Moral considerability is thus to be distinguished from moral agency. Being a recipient of moral regard need not imply being able to give moral regard. Moral patients need not be moral agents. For example, that we humans in our moral deliberations take into account a white pine does not imply that the tree has a conscience or is able to make moral choices or has moral duties.

47. Most ethicists distinguish between *instrumental value* (value because of utility for some human purpose) and *intrinsic value* (value in and for itself and not because of a thing's utility for human ends).

There is another important distinction between *subjective value* (something becomes valuable only if someone values it) and objective value (something has value whether or not anyone values it). The latter is sometimes called *inherent worth* (value independent of any human valuing). In other words, there are two related but logically distinct questions: (1) Is X valuable in and for itself, irrespective of any usefulness it provides to us? If the answer is yes, then X has intrinsic value. If the answer is no, then X has only instrumental value, if it has any value at all; and (2) Does our valuing of X make X valuable? If the answer is yes, then X has subjective value. X has value, whether intrinsic or instrumental or both, only because someone values it. The valuer gives value to X. If the answer is no, then X has objective value. X has value independently of any valuer valuing it. See, e.g., Louis Pojman, *Global Environmental Ethics* (Mountain View, CA: Mayfield, 2000), 140, 187.

48. For a similar, though more detailed, continuum of ethical perspectives, see Max Oelschlaeger, *The Idea of Wilderness: From Prehistory to the Age of Ecology* (New Haven: Yale University Press, 1991).

49. Unfortunately the term "wise use" has been, as Louis Pojman points out, co-opted by an umbrella organization—the Wise Use Movement—"dedicated to fighting the environmentalist agenda" (see Pojman, *Global Environmental Ethics*, 360–61).

50. One standard history of the environmental movement in the United States is Roderick Nash, *Wilderness and the American Mind*, rev. ed. (New Haven: Yale University Press, 1973). See also Nash's more recent *The Rights of Nature: A History of Environmental Ethics* (Madison: University of Wisconsin Press, 1989).

51. Many environmental ethics textbooks, and a whole raft of monographs, take issue with this perspective. See, e.g., Lawrence Johnson, *A Morally Deep World: An Essay on Moral Significance and Environmental Ethics* (Cambridge: Cambridge University Press, 1991); Nash, *Rights of Nature*; Pojman, *Global Environmental Ethics*; Laura Westra, *An Environmental Proposal for Ethics: The Principle of Integrity* (Lanham, MD: Rowman and Littlefield, 1994).

52. A direct duty is an obligation that some person has *to* someone or something else, while an indirect duty is an obligation *regarding* someone or something else. So some argue that while humans have no direct duties to trees, humans may have indirect duties regarding trees, because of direct duties to other humans.

53. For a sustained argument for the coherence of future generations language, and for intergenerational justice, see Avner de-Shalit, *Why Posterity Matters: Environmental Policies and Future Generations* (London: Routledge, 1995). See also R. I. Sikora and Brian Barry, eds., *Obligations to Future Generations* (Philadelphia: Temple University Press, 1978).

54. World Commission on Environment and Development, *Our Common Future* (New York: Oxford University Press, 1987).

55. See, e.g., Holmes Rolston III, *Conserving Natural Value* (New York: Columbia University Press, 1994), esp. chap. 6.

56. For an informed discussion of the question of the rights of future generations—both whether it is coherent to speak of such rights and whether it is plausible to believe possible or future people have such rights, with arguments on both sides—see Joseph DesJardins, *Environmental Ethics: An Introduction to Environmental Philosophy*, 2nd ed. (Belmont, CA: Wadsworth, 1997), chap. 4.

57. For example, Holmes Rolston III, *Environmental Ethics: Duties to and Values in the Natural World* (Philadelphia: Temple University Press, 1988), chap. 2.

58. Rights entail duties, but duties do not necessarily entail rights. So if you have a right to your pocketbook, I have a duty to keep my hands off it. But I may have a duty to protect Kirtland warblers, even if they do not have any rights.

59. The leading advocate of animal rights is Tom Regan. See, e.g., *The Case for Animal Rights* (Berkeley: University of California Press, 1983).

60. Rolston, *Environmental Ethics*, chap. 2. Other major criticisms lodged against utilitarian arguments are, for example, that the end does not always justify the means, that privileging the greatest good for the greatest number often violates certain rights or results in injustice, that following a calculus of satisfying one's personal preferences is often counterintuitive.

61. As will become evident in the next chapter, I clearly distinguish between respect and reverence. However, advocates of biocentrism often use the terms interchangeably.

62. See, e.g., Albert Schweitzer, *Reverence for Life*, ed. Thomas Kiernan (New York: Philosophical Library, 1965); and *Civilization and Ethics* (London: A&C Black, 1946).

63. Paul Taylor, *Respect for Nature: A Theory of Environmental Ethics* (Princeton: Princeton University Press, 1986).

64. Rolston, *Environmental Ethics*, chap. 2.

65. For a history of the idea of wilderness, see Oelschlaeger, *Idea of Wilderness*.

66. Probably the best introduction to the writings of Muir is his own *My First Summer in the Sierra* (San Francisco: Sierra Club, 1988). Among the biographies, the best are Frederick Turner, *Rediscovering America: John Muir in His Time and Ours* (San Francisco: Sierra Club, 1985); and Michael Cohen, *The Pathless Way: John Muir and the American Wilderness* (Madison: University of Wisconsin Press, 1984).

67. See, e.g., DesJardins, *Environmental Ethics*, chap. 8.

68. The best biography of Leopold is by Curt Meine, *Aldo Leopold: His Life and Work* (Madison: University of Wisconsin Press, 1988). See also Susan Flader, *Thinking Like a Mountain: Aldo Leopold and the Evolution of an Ecological Attitude toward Deer, Wolves, and Forests* (Columbia: University of Missouri Press, 1974). The standard commentary on Leopold's magnum opus is J. Baird Callicott, ed., *Companion to "A Sand County Almanac": Interpretive and Critical Essays* (Madison: University of Wisconsin Press, 1987).

69. Aldo Leopold, *A Sand County Almanac* (New York: Ballantine, 1970), 262.

70. Rolston, *Environmental Ethics,* chap. 6, especially 230–32.

71. The charge leveled by Tom Regan in *The Case for Animal Rights*, 361–62.

72. One of the most vigorous defenders of the land ethic is Baird Callicott. For a short presentation and defense of the land ethic, see his essay, "The Conceptual Foundations of the Land Ethic," in *Companion to "A Sand County Almanac,"* 186–217. For a more thorough and detailed discussion, see his *In Defense of the Land Ethic* (Albany: State University of New York, 1989). See also Rolston, *Environmental Ethics*, for a very sophisticated theory of moral value and duty—inspired by, if not based on, Leopold's land ethic—that addresses these major criticisms.

73. See Arne Naess, "The Shallow and the Deep, Long-Range Ecology Movement," *Inquiry* 16 (1973): 95–100.

74. Bill Devall and George Sessions, *Deep Ecology* (Salt Lake City: Peregrine Smith Books, 1985), chap. 5.

75. These and other criticisms are summarized in DesJardins, *Environmental Ethics*, 227–29. See Oelschlaeger, *Idea of Wilderness*, 301–9, for another list of criticisms and an informed discussion of them.

76. DesJardins, *Environmental Ethics*, 216.

77. Leopold, *Sand County Almanac*, 239.

78. This discussion brackets the question of whether it is appropriate to speak of the rights of non-human creatures—an issue taken up in chapter 8—and here focuses on human rights.

79. Callicott, "The Conceptual Foundations of the Land Ethic," 208.

80. Ibid., 212–14.

81. For an illuminating example of such a mixed approach, see Lewis Smedes, *Choices: Making Right Decisions in a Complex World* (San Francisco: Harper and Row, 1986).

82. Rolston, *Environmental Ethics*, 73. Elsewhere he remarks: "Each natural kind has its place, integrity, even perfections, but none of the others reaches the eminence of personality. Without faulting the animals for their lack of civility, an animal capable of culture (represented by Einstein) realizes a greater range of values in its life than does an animal incapable of culture (a kangaroo rat). Emphatically, this does not deny that kangaroo rats have intrinsic worth or that humans have duties toward them; rather, it discriminates differentials in value richness that are ethically relevant" (68).

83. Ibid., 216–29. For example, rivers, rocks, and mountains have less intrinsic value than amoebas, which have less than baboons, which have less than humans. The instrumental value, however, is roughly inversely proportional to intrinsic value, with rivers and grasses of more instrumental value than squirrels or humans.

84. The phrase is from Lionel Basney's wonderful book, *An Earth-Careful Way of Life* (Downers Grove, IL: InterVarsity, 1994).

85. William Dyrness, "The Ecology of Hope" (paper delivered at the National Association of Evangelicals conference, "Compassion and the Care for Creation," Malone College, Canton, OH, March 3, 1999), 10.

86. Available at http://www.creationcare.org/resources/declaration.php.

87. DeWitt, *Caring for Creation*, 16.

88. Ibid., 58.

Chapter 6 What Kind of People Ought We Be? Earth-Care and Character

1. David Orr, *Earth in Mind: On Education, the Environment, and the Human Prospect* (Washington, DC: Island, 1994), 62.

2. Scholars who have explored ecological virtue theory include: Philip Cafaro and Ronald Sandler, eds., *Environmental Virtue Ethics* (Lanham, MD: Rowman and Littlefield, 2005); Geoffrey Frasz, "Environmental Virtue Ethics: A New Direction for Environmental Ethics," *Environmental Ethics* 15 (1993): 259–74; Jay McDaniel, *Of God and Pelicans: A Theology of Reverence for Life* (Louisville: Westminster/ John Knox, 1989), 73–74; James Nash, *Loving Nature: Ecological Integrity and Christian Responsibility* (Nashville: Abingdon, 1991), 63–67; idem, "Toward the Revival and Reform of the Subversive Virtue: Frugality," *The Annual of the Society of Christian Ethics* 15 (1995): 137–60; Michael Northcott, *The Environment and Christian Ethics* (Cambridge: Cambridge University Press, 1996); John Patterson, "Maori Environmental Virtues," *Environmental Ethics* 16 (1994): 397–409; Ronald Sandler, *Character and Environment: A Virtue-Oriented Approach to Environmental Ethics* (New York: Columbia University Press, 2007); Paul Taylor, *Respect for Nature: A Theory of Environmental Ethics* (Princeton: Princeton University Press, 1986), 198–218; Louke van Wensveen, "Christian Ecological Virtue Ethics: Transforming a Tradition," in *Christianity and Ecology: Seeking the Well-Being of Earth and Humans*, ed. Dieter Hessel and Rosemary Radford Ruether (Cambridge: Harvard University Press, 2000), 155–71; idem, *Dirty Virtues: The Emergence of Ecological Virtue Ethics* (Amherst, NY: Humanity Books, 2000); Laura Westra, *An Environmental Proposal for Ethics: The Principle of Integrity* (Lanham, MD: Rowman and Littlefield, 1994). In addition to this book, my own contributions in this area can be found in "Creation Care and Character: The Nature and Necessity of the Ecological Virtues," *Perspectives on Science and Christian Faith* 50, no. 1 (March 1998): 6–21; and "Response to Louke van Wensveen: A Constructive Proposal," in Hessel and Ruether, *Christianity and Ecology*, 173–82.

3. There are at least two objections to using Aristotle as a guide on this issue. First, a feminist critique would question the individualism inherent in Aristotle's account of the virtues. See, for example, Nel Noddings, *Caring: A Feminine Approach to Ethics and Moral Education* (Berkeley: University of California Press, 1984). While this critique is on target, it does not, as far as I can see, nullify my appropriation of Aristotle for the purposes of this project. I readily acknowledge the interpersonal nature of virtue, and attempt to incorporate this into my understanding of virtue.

The second objection is theological. John Milbank, for example, also notes and critiques the individualism of antique ethics, but lodges an additional complaint against the ethics of Aristotle. According to Milbank (who is following the lead of Augustine), the Greeks and Romans "think there can only *be* virtue where there is something to be defeated, and virtue therefore consists for them, not only in the attainment and pursuit of a goal desirable in itself, but also in a 'conquest' of less desirable forces" (*Theology and Social Theory: Beyond Secular Reason* [Oxford: Blackwell, 1993], 390–91). In short, virtue assumes conflict, *aretē* assumes *agōn*. The Christian story, by contrast, celebrates "the ontological priority of peace over conflict" (390) and therefore repudiates the heroic construal of the virtues. Virtue is, from a Christian perspective, not an achievement that presumes conflict, but a gift offered through reconciliation and the forgiveness of sins.

Milbank's point is well taken, but it does not necessarily preclude a Christian appropriation of Aristotle. Aquinas is a case in point (see, e.g., *Summa Theologiae* I–II, questions 49–67, *Treatise on the Virtues*, trans. John A. Oesterle (Notre Dame: University of Notre Dame Press, 1984). For Aquinas a virtue is "a good quality of the mind, by which we live rightly, of which no one can make bad use, which God works in us without us" (question 55, article 4). With his claim that "God works in us without us" Aquinas argues that the efficient cause of infused virtue is God and that there is not necessarily any conflict or conquest. In short, while Aquinas leans heavily on Aristotle in his understanding of virtue, he recontextualizes and thereby transforms Aristotle's concept of virtue.

4. Aristotle, *Nicomachean Ethics*, in *The Basic Works of Aristotle*, ed. Richard McKeon (New York: Random House, 1941), 1106a 4.

5. Ibid., 1109a 27.

6. Ibid., 1107a 1.

7. Philippa Foot, *Virtues and Vices and Other Essays in Moral Philosophy* (Berkeley: University of California Press, 1978), 4–5.

8. Ibid., 5.

9. Robert Roberts, *Spirituality and Human Emotion* (Grand Rapids: Eerdmans, 1982), 12–15.

10. Stanley Hauerwas, *Character and the Christian Life: A Study in Theological Ethics* (San Antonio: Trinity University, 1985), 115–17.

11. Ibid., 11; cf. 5, 17. See also Stanley Hauerwas, *Vision and Virtue: Essays in Christian Ethical Reflection* (Notre Dame: Fides, 1974), chap. 2.

12. Gilbert Meilaender, "Virtue in Contemporary Religious Thought," in *Virtue—Public and Private*, ed. Richard John Neuhaus (Grand Rapids: Eerdmans, 1986), 9.

13. C. S. Lewis, *The Magician's Nephew* (New York: Macmillan, 1978), 125.

14. On the fundamental role of narrative, and especially the biblical metanarrative, see J. Richard Middleton and Brian Walsh, *Truth Is Stranger Than It Used To Be* (Downers Grove, IL: InterVarsity, 1995), chaps. 4–5. On the centrality of community in the formation of moral vision, see Stanley Hauerwas, *A Community of Character: Toward a Constructive Christian Social Ethic* (Notre Dame: University of Notre Dame Press, 1981). On both, see also Steven Bouma-Prediger and Brian Walsh, *Beyond Homelessness: Christian Faith in a Culture of Displacement* (Grand Rapids: Eerdmans, 2008), 208–12.

15. This understanding of doctrine is developed in N. T. Wright, *The New Testament and the People of God* (Philadelphia: Fortress, 1992), chap. 5.

16. Holmes Rolston proposes the following yet more precise specification of this duty: While we have "no duty of benevolence to preserve rare species from natural extinction," except to save certain endangered species as resources or museum pieces, we do have "a duty of nonmaleficence to avoid artificial" or anthropogenic extinction. That is to say, we have an obligation to avoid human-caused extinction of species, and in some cases we are obligated to preserve species whose extinction is, as far as we can tell, a product of nonhuman factors. This duty of nonmaleficence is a prima facie duty and thus can be overridden in certain cases, e.g., smallpox or malaria. But the duty to avoid harming non-human species still holds and so the burden of proof always resides with those who wish to do harm. See Holmes Rolston III, *Environmental Ethics: Duties to and Values in the Natural World* (Philadelphia: Temple University Press, 1988), 155.

17. Aldo Leopold, *A Sand County Almanac* (New York: Ballantine, 1970), 190.

18. Susan Power Bratton, *Six Billion and More: Human Population Regulation and Christian Ethics* (Louisville: Westminster/John Knox, 1992), 43. On the theme of blessing in Scripture, see Claus Westermann, *Blessing in the Bible and the Life of the Church* (Philadelphia: Fortress, 1978).

19. Bill McKibben, *The Comforting Whirlwind: God, Job, and the Scale of Creation* (Grand Rapids: Eerdmans, 1994), 10.

20. Aristotle, *Nicomachean Ethics*, 1118b 19.

21. For a powerful and insightful analysis of the human tendency to deny mortality and in so doing create and perpetuate evil, see Ernest Becker, *Denial of Death* (New York: Macmillan, 1973) and *Escape from Evil* (New York: Macmillan, 1975).

22. Perhaps the classic presentation of this question is Leo Tolstoy's short story, "The Death of Ivan Ilych."

23. Two books that illuminate the phenomenon of sin very clearly are Ted Peters, *Sin: Radical Evil in Soul and Society* (Grand Rapids: Eerdmans, 1995); and Neal Plantinga, *Not the Way It's Supposed To Be: A Breviary of Sin* (Grand Rapids: Eerdmans, 1995).

24. Aristotle, *Nicomachean Ethics*, 1127a 22.

25. Dietrich Bonhoeffer, *Ethics* (New York: Macmillan, 1955), 363–72.

26. Calvin DeWitt, "Take Good Care: It's God's Earth," *Prism* 1 (December 1993–January 1994): 10 (italics in the original).

27. See, e.g., Job 28:28; Ps. 111:10; Prov. 1:7. For more on ecological wisdom, see Bouma-Prediger and Walsh, *Beyond Homelessness*, 221–24.

28. For a perceptive and lucid exposition of hope, see Lewis Smedes, *Standing on the Promises: Keeping Hope Alive for a Tomorrow We Cannot Control* (Nashville: Thomas Nelson, 1998).

29. On the indispensability of hope for living a human life, see Victor Frankl, *Man's Search for Meaning* (New York: Simon and Schuster, 1963), and the writings of Elie Wiesel, e.g., *Night* (New York: Bantam, 1958). The centrality of hope in Christian theology is evident in the many works of Jürgen Moltmann, e.g., *Theology of Hope: On the Ground and the Implications of a Christian Eschatology* (New York: Harper and Row, 1967).

30. Søren Kierkegaard, *The Sickness Unto Death* (Princeton: Princeton University Press, 1980).

31. See, e.g., Thomas Aquinas, *Summa Theologiae* I–II.64.4.

32. J. Christiaan Beker, *Suffering and Hope: The Biblical Vision and the Human Predicament* (Grand Rapids: Eerdmans, 1994), 89.

33. See, e.g., Lee Hardy, *The Fabric of This World: Inquiries into Calling, Career Choice, and the Design of Human Work* (Grand Rapids: Eerdmans, 1990).

34. DeWitt, "Take Good Care," 10.

35. For an explication of the difference between beneficence and benevolence, see William Frankena, *Ethics* (Englewood Cliffs, NJ: Prentice-Hall, 1973), 45.

36. See William Vitek and Wes Jackson, eds., *Rooted in the Land: Essays on Community and Place* (New Haven: Yale University Press, 1996); and Terry Tempest Williams, *Refuge: An Unnatural History of Family and Place* (New York: Vintage, 1992).

37. Leopold, *Sand County Almanac*, 197.

38. For example, the Lutheran tradition in general and, among recent NT scholars, Ernst Käsemann in particular.

39. James Dunn and Alan Suggate, *The Justice of God* (Grand Rapids: Eerdmans, 1993), 25. See also N. T. Wright, *Surprised by Hope: Rethinking Heaven, the Resurrection, and the Mission of the Church* (New York: HarperCollins, 2008), 213–22.

40. Ibid., 28.

41. For more on justice and equity, see Bouma-Prediger and Walsh, *Beyond Homelessness*, 214–17.

42. Lewis Smedes, *Mere Morality: What God Expects from Ordinary People* (Grand Rapids: Eerdmans, 1983), chap. 2.

43. Aristotle, *Nicomachean Ethics*, 1179a 35–1179b 4.

44. Wendell Berry, *Sabbaths* (San Francisco: North Point, 1987), 19.

Chapter 7 Why Worry about Galapagos Penguins and the Jack Pine? Arguments for Earth-Care

1. Joseph Sittler, "Ecological Commitment as Theological Responsibility," *Zygon* 5 (June 1970): 173.

2. Dr. Seuss, *The Lorax* in *Six by Seuss* (New York: Random House, 1991), 342.

3. Ibid., 345.

4. By "prudence" I mean what most people today mean by that term, namely, shrewdness in the management of one's own affairs, a kind of self-interest. I do not mean what Aristotle means by *phronēsis*, that is, sound judgment in securing the means necessary to attain the good life. By "piety" I mean earnest

devotion to a religious way of life, fidelity to one's religious tradition; specifically here I mean those forms of religious devotion known as Christian spirituality.

5. Indeed, some people need only a single argument to be persuaded that caring for the earth is important—for example, the self-interest argument. Many Christians find the divine command argument sufficient unto itself to foster greater concern for God's nonhuman creatures and the earth on which we live. For others a particular combination of arguments convinces them to take their ecological responsibilities more seriously. This is not surprising, since the force of arguments is person-relative; that is, their cogency or persuasive appeal is relative to a person's beliefs, dispositions, desires, virtues, and the like.

6. I am aware that much more needs to be said about each of these arguments, and that greater attention must be given to the implications for specific public policies. But my aim here is quite modest, namely, simply to present and discuss each of these answers to the question "Why care for the earth?" For examples of the application of a Christian ethical framework to a particular public policy issue, see Steven Bouma-Prediger and Virginia Vroblesky, *Assessing the Ark: A Christian Perspective on Non-Human Creatures and the Endangered Species Act* (Wynnewood, PA: Crossroad, 1997); or Robert Grant, *A Case Study in Thomistic Enviromental Ethics: The Ecological Crisis in the Loess Hills of Iowa* (Lewiston: Edwin Mellon, 2007).

7. Indeed, some question whether this perspective is adequately captured by the use of rights language itself. Is the language of rights and duties appropriate in this context? For example, are the "obligations" one feels for one's children really obligations at all? But as the backpacker examples illustrate, it does make sense to speak of duties in cases where familial affection is lacking. We at times do rightly feel bound by obligations to future generations whom we do not necessarily know.

8. On the sorting of rules and duties, see Lewis Smedes, *Choices: Making Right Decisions in a Complex World* (San Francisco: Harper and Row, 1986), chaps. 3–4.

9. On sustenance rights, see Nicholas Wolterstorff, *Until Justice and Peace Embrace* (Grand Rapids: Eerdmans, 1983). These rights, in most discussions, are for presently existing people. I do not here engage the controversial and important topic of whether it makes sense to speak of rights for humans not yet existing. Obviously for this argument to function as intended, that is, to apply to more than just currently existing humans, it must be coherent to speak of rights for possible people. See Avner de-Shalit, *Why Posterity Matters: Environmental Policies and Future Generations* (London: Routledge, 1995) for one defense of the rights of future human generations. See also R. I. Sikora and Brian Barry, eds., *Obligations to Future Generations* (Philadelphia: Temple University Press, 1978).

10. See, e.g., Bob Goudzwaard, *Aid for the Overdeveloped West* (Toronto: Wedge, 1975); *Capitalism and Progress: A Diagnosis of Western Society* (Grand Rapids: Eerdmans, 1979); and his co-authored volume, with Harry de Lange, *Beyond Wealth and Poverty* (Grand Rapids: Eerdmans, 1995).

11. Bill McKibben, *The Comforting Whirlwind: God, Job, and the Scale of Creation* (Grand Rapids: Eerdmans, 1994), 89.

12. David Myers, *The Pursuit of Happiness: Who Is Happy—and Why* (New York: William Morrow, 1992), chap. 2. For further confirmation of this claim, see also his *The American Paradox: Spiritual Hunger in an Age of Plenty* (New Haven: Yale University Press, 2000).

13. Myers, *Pursuit of Happiness*, 46.

14. Henry David Thoreau, *Walden and Other Writings*, ed. Joseph Wood Krutch (New York: Bantam, 1981), 115.

15. Paul Wachtel, *The Poverty of Affluence: A Psychological Portrait of the American Way of Life* (Philadelphia: New Society, 1989), 1–2.

16. James Nash, *Loving Nature: Ecological Integrity and Christian Responsibility* (Nashville: Abingdon, 1991), 63–67.

17. See, e.g., Herman Daly and John Cobb, *For the Common Good: Redirecting the Economy toward Community, the Environment, and a Sustainable Future* (Boston: Beacon, 1989); Robert Gottfried, *Economics, Ecology, and the Roots of Western Faith* (Lanham, MD: Rowman and Littlefield, 1995); Goudzwaard and de Lange, *Beyond Wealth and Poverty*; and Bill McKibben, *The End of Nature* (New York: Doubleday, 1989).

18. The swift and dramatic collapse of the global economic system in 2008–2009 is only one telling indication of the pervasive problems in the world. Another key indicator is the various stressed ecological systems noted in chapter 2. For a perceptive analysis of the key factors that cause societal collapse, see Jared Diamond, *Collapse: How Societies Choose to Fail or Succeed* (New York: Viking, 2005).

19. Rosemary Radford Ruether, *Sexism and God-Talk: Toward a Feminist Theology* (Boston: Beacon, 1983), 73.

20. For backing for these claims see Steven Bouma-Prediger, *The Greening of Theology: The Ecological Models of Rosemary Radford Ruether, Joseph Sittler, and Jürgen Moltmann* (Atlanta: Scholars, 1995), chaps. 2, 5.

21. Rosemary Radford Ruether, *New Woman/New Earth: Sexist Ideologies and Human Liberation* (New York: Seabury, 1975), 204.

22. Charles Lee, "Evidence of Environmental Racism," *Sojourners* (February–March 1990), 25.

23. For more on environmental racism, see Steven Bouma-Prediger, "Environmental Racism," in *Handbook of U.S. Theologies of Liberation*, ed. Miguel de la Torre (St. Louis: Chalice, 2004).

24. Indeed, the language of the "triple bottom line"—social justice, environmental sustainability, and economic prosperity—is being adopted increasingly by business groups, non-profits, and governmental units.

25. See, e.g., the work of Bunyon Bryant and Paul Mohai, *Environmental Racism: Issues and Dilemmas* (Ann Arbor: University of Michigan Office of Minority Affairs, 1991); Robert Bullard, *Dumping in Dixie: Race, Class, and Environmental Quality* (Boulder, CO: Westview, 1990); and Richard Hofrichter, ed., *Toxic Struggles: The Theory and Practice of Environmental Justice* (Philadelphia: New Society, 1993).

26. For example, in recent years environmental organizations such as the Sierra Club have acknowledged that they must adopt ecojustice as one of their goals and work for a more just and equitable human society if their environmental aims are to be achieved.

27. Paul Hawken, *Blessed Unrest: How the Largest Social Movement in History Is Restoring Grace, Justice, and Beauty to the World* (New York: Penguin, 2007), 2, 13.

28. For an example of this claim, see Rosemary Radford Ruether, *To Change the World: Christology and Cultural Criticism* (New York: Crossroad, 1981), 67. For a critique, see Richard Mouw, *The God Who Commands: A Study in Divine Command Ethics* (Notre Dame: University of Notre Dame Press, 1991), 161–63.

29. See, e.g., Tom Regan, *The Case for Animal Rights* (Berkeley: University of California Press, 1983). Another influential spokesperson for this general perspective is Peter Singer, though he adopts a utilitarian stance. Singer's argument goes like this: some animals have the capacity to suffer, that is, are sentient organisms; sentient organisms have an interest in not suffering; if any organism has an interest, then it has moral standing; therefore some animals have moral standing. See, e.g., Peter Singer, *Animal Liberation: A New Ethic for Our Treatment of Animals* (New York: Avon Books, 1975).

30. Holmes Rolston III, *Environmental Ethics: Duties to and Values in the Natural World* (Philadelphia: Temple University Press, 1985), chap. 2.

31. Ibid., 41.

32. See, e.g., Joseph DesJardins, *Environmental Ethics: An Introduction to Environmental Philosophy*, 2nd ed. (Belmont, CA: Wadsworth, 1997), 144–45.

33. See Rolston, *Environmental Ethics*, chap. 6, for a sophisticated method of sorting comparative value.

34. Ibid., 28.

35. Aldo Leopold, *A Sand County Almanac* (New York: Ballantine, 1970), 239.

36. Ibid., 262.

37. John Muir, *My First Summer in the Sierra* (San Francisco: Sierra Club, 1988), 10.

38. Joseph Sittler, *Gravity and Grace* (Minneapolis: Augsburg, 1986), 22.

39. Sittler, "Ecological Commitment as Theological Responsibility," 173.

40. Larry Rasmussen, *Earth Community Earth Ethics* (Maryknoll, NY: Orbis, 1996), 324. See also Jürgen Moltmann, *God in Creation: A New Theology of Creation and the Spirit of God* (San Francisco: Harper and Row, 1985), 139.

41. For a perceptive and well-argued defense of this claim, see Norman Wirzba, *The Paradise of God: Renewing Religion in an Ecological Age* (New York: Oxford University Press, 2003), chap. 4. See also James Gustafson, *A Sense of the Divine: The Natural Environment from a Theocentric Perspective* (Cleveland: Pilgrim, 1994).

42. For one contemporary affirmation of divine command ethics, see, e.g., Richard Mouw, *God Who Commands*.

43. This biblical understanding of God's kingdom as inclusive of all things is winsomely put forward in N. T. Wright's *Surprised by Hope: Rethinking Heaven, the Resurrection, and the Mission of the Church* (New York: HarperCollins, 2008).

44. Calvin DeWitt points to the connection between gratitude and contentment: "As all creatures pour forth praise for God's everflowing blessings, so should we. Satisfied with God's provision, we should find contentment to be our greatest profit" (*The Environment and the Christian* [Grand Rapids: Baker, 1991], 108).

45. John Calvin, *Institutes of the Christian Religion*, ed. John McNeill (Philadelphia: Westminster, 1960), 1.14.20, 2.6.1; see also 1.6.2 and 3.10.2.

46. Ibid., 3.9.3. See also 1.14.22, where, writing on the goodness of creation, Calvin states: "We are, therefore, also to petition [God] for whatever we desire: and we are to recognize as a blessing from [God], and thankfully to acknowledge, every benefit that falls to our share."

47. Susan Schreiner, *The Theatre of His Glory: Nature and Natural Order in the Thought of John Calvin* (Grand Rapids: Baker, 1991), 106. And as Schreiner makes abundantly clear, "Calvin's belief in God's faithfulness to his original purpose in creation governed his understanding of the role of creation in redemption. In Calvin's theology, God is reclaiming all of his creation: the cosmos, human nature, and society" (111).

48. Henry Stob, *Ethical Reflections: Essays on Moral Themes* (Grand Rapids: Eerdmans, 1978), 78; see also Allen Verhey, *Living the Heidelberg: The Heidelberg Catechism and the Moral Life* (Grand Rapids: Christian Reformed Church, 1986), chaps. 8–9.

49. Sittler, *Gravity and Grace*, 35.

Chapter 8 Where Is There Hope? Christian Faith at Home on Earth

1. Walter Rauschenbusch, *Prayers of the Social Awakening* (Boston: Pilgrim, 1910), 47.

2. This is the last of Immanuel Kant's three fundamental questions. The first two questions are, What can I know? and, What must I do? See Immanuel Kant, *Critique of Pure Reason*, trans. Norman Kemp Smith (New York: St. Martin's Press, 1965), 635; in other editions, see the canon of pure reason, section 2 (A805/B833).

3. Bill McKibben, *Hope, Human and Wild: True Stories of Living Lightly on the Earth* (St. Paul: Hungry Mind, 1995), chaps. 2–4.

4. Paul Hawken, *Blessed Unrest: How the Largest Social Movement in History Is Restoring Grace, Justice, and Beauty to the World* (New York: Penguin, 2007).

5. The books and articles are too numerous to mention, but a good place to start is the Worldwatch Institute, www.worldwatch.org.

6. See, e.g., Bill McKibben, *Enough: Staying Human in an Engineered Age* (New York: Henry Holt, 2004); and Albert Borgmann, *Power Shift: Christianity in the Culture of Technology* (Grand Rapids: Brazos, 2003).

7. On oil consumption, see Paul Roberts, *The End of Oil: On the Edge of a Perilous New World* (New York: Houghton Mifflin, 2004); and Richard Heinberg, *The Party's Over: Oil, War and the Fate of Industrial Societies*, rev. ed. (Gabriola Island, BC: New Society, 2005).

8. James Gustave Speth, *The Bridge at the Edge of the World: Capitalism, the Environment, and Crossing from Crisis to Sustainability* (New Haven: Yale University Press, 2008). See also James Gustave Speth, *Red Sky at Morning: America and the Crisis of the Global Environment* (New Haven: Yale University Press, 2004).

9. Bill McKibben, *Deep Economy: The Wealth of Communities and the Durable Future* (New York: Holt, 2007).

10. Evidence of growing awareness in the public consciousness is virtually everywhere—from headlines in local newspapers to major stories in national and international journals and magazines. For more on public opinion polls, go to the Pew Research Center Web site: www.pewresearch.org/pubs/. As I write this, major legislation on global warming is being presented in the U.S. Senate, with additional legislation soon to follow on a host of other issues. Ecologically informed science curricula are being developed and implemented all over the world; in southwestern Michigan, the Outdoor Discovery Center is just one of many organizations that help educate children in kindergarten through high school on how the world works ecologically speaking. Finally, recycling programs are expanding, as are wetlands restoration initiatives in many parts of the United States.

11. See Steven Bouma-Prediger and Brian Walsh, *Beyond Homelessness: Christian Faith in a Culture of Displacement* (Grand Rapids: Eerdmans, 2008), chaps. 1–2.

12. John Caputo, *Radical Hermeneutics: Repetition, Deconstruction, and the Hermeneutic Project* (Bloomington: Indiana University Press, 1987), 239.

13. Frances FitzGerald, *Cities on a Hill: A Journey through Contemporary American Cultures* (New York: Simon and Schuster, 1986), 390.

14. Paul Wachtel, *The Poverty of Affluence: A Psychological Portrait of the American Way of Life* (Philadelphia: New Society, 1989), 95.

15. Walter Truett Anderson, *Reality Isn't What It Used to Be* (San Francisco: HarperCollins, 1990), 51.

16. Clive Thompson, "Global Mourning" *Wired* (January 2008): 70. See also chaps. 5–6 in Bouma-Prediger and Walsh, *Beyond Homelessness*.

17. A number of the following paragraphs are taken from Bouma-Prediger and Walsh, *Beyond Homelessness*, chap. 9.

18. Václav Havel, quoted in Lewis Smedes, *Standing on the Promises: Keeping Hope Alive for a Tomorrow We Cannot Control* (Nashville: Abingdon, 1998), 30.

19. Václav Havel, *Disturbing the Peace* (New York: Alfred Knopf, 1990), 181.

20. Scott Russell Sanders, *Hunting for Hope* (Boston: Beacon, 1998), 27 (italics in the original).

21. N. T. Wright, *The Millennium Myth* (Louisville: Westminster/John Knox, 1999), 39.

22. Sanders, *Hunting for Hope*, 20. See also chaps. 4, 5, 7, 8, 9, 11, 12, 13.

23. Wright, *Millennium Myth*, 39–40.

24. Wendell Berry, *Sex, Economy, Freedom, and Community* (New York: Pantheon, 1992), 11.

25. Annie Dillard, *Teaching a Stone to Talk* (New York: Harper and Row, 1982), 58–59.

26. God is "the wildest being in existence," who is "not to be fenced in, under human control, like some domestic creature" (Berry, *Sex, Economy, Freedom, and Community*, 101).

27. Gerard Manley Hopkins, "God's Grandeur," in *Poems and Prose* (London: Penguin, 1985), 27.

28. Joseph Sittler, "Evangelism and Care of the Earth," in *Preaching and the Witnessing Community*, ed. Herman Stuempfle (Philadelphia: Fortress, 1973), 104.

bibliography

Abramovitz, Janet. *Imperiled Waters, Impoverished Future: The Decline of Freshwater Ecosystems*. Washington, DC: Worldwatch Institute, 1996.

———. *Taking a Stand: Cultivating a New Relationship with the World's Forests*. Washington, DC: Worldwatch Institute, 1998.

Aeck, Molly. "Weather-Related Disasters Near a Record." In *Vital Signs 2005*, 50–51.

Amos, Jonathan. "Deep Ice Tells Long Climate Story." *BBC News*, September 4, 2006. http://news.bbc.co.uk/2/hi/science/nature/5314592.stm.

Anderson, Bernhard, ed. *Creation in the Old Testament*. Philadelphia: Fortress, 1984.

———. *Creation versus Chaos*. Philadelphia: Fortress, 1987.

———. *From Creation to New Creation*. Minneapolis: Augsburg Fortress, 1994.

Anderson, Walter Truett. *Reality Isn't What It Used to Be*. San Francisco: HarperCollins, 1990.

Annin, Peter. *The Great Lakes Water Wars*. Washington, DC: Island, 2006.

Aristotle. *Nicomachean Ethics*. In *The Basic Works of Aristotle*, edited by Richard McKeon, 927–1112. New York: Random House, 1941.

Art, Henry, ed. *The Dictionary of Ecology and Environmental Science*. New York: Henry Holt, 1993.

Augustine. *On Christian Doctrine*. Translated by D. W. Robertson Jr. New York: Macmillan, 1958.

Aune, David. *Revelation 17–22*. Word Biblical Commentary 52c. Nashville: Thomas Nelson, 1998.

Barbour, Ian. *Religion in an Age of Science*. San Francisco: Harper and Row, 1990.

———, ed. *Western Man and Environmental Ethics*. Reading, PA: Addison-Wesley, 1973.

Barnhill, David, ed. *At Home on the Earth: Becoming Native to Our Place*. Berkeley: University of California Press, 1999.

Baskin, Yvonne. *The Work of Nature: How the Diversity of Life Sustains Us*. Washington, DC: Island, 1998.

Basney, Lionel. *An Earth-Careful Way of Life*. Downers Grove, IL: InterVarsity, 1994.

Bauckham, Richard. *Jude and 2 Peter*. Word Biblical Commentary 50. Waco: Word, 1983.

Beale, G. K. *The Book of Revelation*. New International Greek Testament Commentary. Grand Rapids: Eerdmans, 1999.

Beasley-Murray, G. R. *The Book of Revelation*. New Cambridge Bible Commentary. Grand Rapids: Eerdmans, 1981.

Becker, Ernest. *Denial of Death*. New York: Macmillan, 1973.

———. *Escape from Evil*. New York: Macmillan, 1975.

Beker, J. Christiaan. *Suffering and Hope: The Biblical Vision and the Human Predicament*. Grand Rapids: Eerdmans, 1994.

Berkouwer, G. C. *Man: The Image of God*. Grand Rapids: Eerdmans, 1962.

Bernstein, Richard. *Beyond Objectivism and Relativism: Science, Hermeneutics, and Praxis*. Philadelphia: University of Pennsylvania Press, 1983.

Berry, R. J., ed. *The Care of Creation*. Leicester, UK: Inter-Varsity, 2000.

Berry, Wendell. *The Gift of Good Land*. San Francisco: North Point, 1981.

———. *Home Economics*. New York: North Point, 1987.

———. *Sabbaths*. San Francisco: North Point, 1987.

———. *Sex, Economy, Freedom, and Community*. New York: Pantheon, 1992.

———. *What Are People For?* New York: North Point, 1990.

Birch, Bruce, and Larry Rasmussen. *Bible and Ethics in the Christian Life*. Rev. ed. Minneapolis: Augsburg Fortress, 1989.

Birch, Charles, William Eakin, and Jay McDaniel, eds. *Liberating Life: Contemporary Approaches to Ecological Theology*. Maryknoll, NY: Orbis, 1990.

Boff, Leonardo. *Ecology and Liberation: A New Paradigm*. Maryknoll, NY: Orbis, 1995.

———. *Trinity and Society*. Maryknoll, NY: Orbis, 1988.

Bonhoeffer, Dietrich. *Ethics*. New York: Macmillan, 1955.

Borgmann, Albert. *Power Failure: Christianity in the Culture of Technology*. Grand Rapids: Brazos, 2003.

Boring, M. Eugene. *Revelation*. Interpretation. Louisville: Westminster/John Knox, 1989.

Bos, Elroy. "Threats to Species Accelerate." In *Vital Signs 2007–2008*, 96–97.

Botkin, Daniel. *Discordant Harmonies: A New Ecology for the Twenty-First Century*. New York: Oxford University Press, 1990.

Bouma-Prediger, Steven. "Creation Care and Character: The Nature and Necessity of the Ecological Virtues." *Perspectives on Science and Christian Faith* 50, no. 1 (March 1998): 6–21.

———. "Environmental Racism." In *Handbook of U.S. Theologies of Liberation*, edited by Miguel de la Torre, 281–87. St. Louis: Chalice, 2004.

———. *The Greening of Theology: The Ecological Models of Rosemary Radford Ruether, Joseph Sittler, and Jürgen Moltmann*. Atlanta: Scholars, 1995.

———. "Response to Louke van Wensveen: A Constructive Proposal." In Hessel and Ruether, *Christianity and Ecology*, 173–82.

Bouma-Prediger, Steven, and Peter Bakken, eds. *Evocations of Grace: The Writings of Joseph Sittler on Ecology, Theology, and Ethics*. Grand Rapids: Eerdmans, 2000.

Bouma-Prediger, Steven, and Virginia Vroblesky. *Assessing the Ark: A Christian Perspective on Non-Human Creatures and the Endangered Species Act*. Wynnewood, PA: Crossroad, 1997.

Bouma-Prediger, Steven, and Brian Walsh. *Beyond Homelessness: Christian Faith in a Culture of Displacement*. Grand Rapids: Eerdmans, 2008.

Bratton, Susan Power. *Christianity, Wilderness, and Wildlife: The Original Desert Solitaire*. Scranton, PA: University of Scranton Press, 1993.

———. *Six Billion and More: Human Population Regulation and Christian Ethics*. Louisville: Westminster/John Knox, 1992.

Bright, Chris. "Anticipating Environmental 'Surprise.'" In *State of the World 2000*, 22–38. New York: Norton, 2000.

Brown, Colin, ed. *The New International Dictionary of New Testament Theology*, vol. 2. Grand Rapids: Zondervan, 1976.

Brown, Ed. *Our Father's World: Mobilizing the Church to Care for Creation*. Downers Grove, IL: InterVarsity, 2008.

Brown, Lester. "Challenges of the New Century." In *State of the World 2000*, 3–21. New York: Norton, 2000.

———. "Why Ethanol Production Will Drive World Food Prices Even Higher in 2008." Earth Policy Institute. January 24, 2008. http://earthpolicy.org/Updates/2008/Update69.htm.

Brown, Lester, Gary Gardner, and Brian Halweil. *Beyond Malthus: Nineteen Dimensions of the Population Challenge*. New York: Norton, 1999.

Brown, Warren, Nancey Murphy, and H. Newton Malony, eds. *Whatever Happened to the Soul? Scientific and Theological Portraits of Human Nature*. Minneapolis: Fortress, 1998.

Brown, William. *The Ethos of the Cosmos: The Genesis of Moral Imagination*. Grand Rapids: Eerdmans, 1999.

Brown, William P., and S. Dean McBride Jr., eds. *God Who Creates: Essays in Honor of W. Sibley Towner*. Grand Rapids: Eerdmans, 2000.

Bruce, F. F. *The Epistles to the Colossians, to Philemon, and to the Ephesians*. New International Commentary on the New Testament. Grand Rapids: Eerdmans, 1984.

Brueggemann, Walter. *Genesis*. Interpretation. Atlanta: John Knox, 1982.

———. *The Land*. Philadelphia: Fortress, 1977.

———. *Theology of the Old Testament*. Minneapolis: Augsburg Fortress, 1997.

Bryant, Bunyon, and Paul Mohai. *Environmental Racism: Issues and Dilemmas*. Ann Arbor: University of Michigan Office of Minority Affairs, 1991.

Bullard, Robert. *Dumping in Dixie: Race, Class, and Environmental Quality*. Boulder, CO: Westview, 1990.

Cafaro, Philip, and Ronald Sandler, eds. *Environmental Virtue Ethics*. Lanham, MD: Rowman and Littlefield, 2005.

Caird, G. B. *The Revelation of St. John the Divine*. New York: Harper and Row, 1966.

Callenbach, Ernest. *Ecology: A Pocket Guide*. Berkeley: University of California Press, 1998.

Callicott, J. Baird, ed. *Companion to "A Sand County Almanac": Interpretive and Critical Essays*. Madison: University of Wisconsin Press, 1987.

———. *In Defense of the Land Ethic*. Albany: State University of New York Press, 1989.

Calvin, John. *Institutes of the Christian Religion*. Edited by John McNeill. Philadelphia: Westminster, 1960.

Caputo, John. *Radical Hermeneutics: Repetition, Deconstruction, and the Hermeneutic Project*. Bloomington: Indiana University Press, 1987.

Cohen, Jeremy. "The Bible, Man, and Nature in the History of Western Thought: A Call for Reassessment." *Journal of Religion* 65, no. 2 (April 1985): 155–72.

Cohen, Michael. *The Pathless Way: John Muir and the American Wilderness*. Madison: University of Wisconsin Press, 1984.

Cooper, John. *Body, Soul, and Life Everlasting*. Grand Rapids: Eerdmans, 1989.

"Coping with Water Scarcity, World Water Day 2007." UN World Health Organization. www.euro.who.int/watsan/issues/20080818_5.

Corcoran, Kevin. *Rethinking Human Nature: A Christian Materialist Alternative to the Soul*. Grand Rapids: Baker Academic, 2006.

Crosby, Alfred. *The Columbian Exchange: Biological and Cultural Consequences of 1492*. Westport, CT: Praeger, 2003.

Cunningham, David. *Christian Ethics: The End of the Law*. New York: Routledge, 2008.

————. *These Three Are One: The Practice of Trinitarian Theology*. Oxford: Blackwell, 1998.

Daily, Gretchen, ed. *Nature's Services: Societal Dependence on Natural Ecosystems*. Washington, DC: Island, 1997.

Daly, Herman, and John Cobb. *For the Common Good: Redirecting the Economy toward Community, the Environment, and a Sustainable Future*. Boston: Beacon, 1989.

Daniel, Glenda, and Jerry Sullivan. *A Sierra Club Naturalist's Guide: The North Woods of Michigan, Wisconsin, and Minnesota*. San Francisco: Sierra Club, 1981.

DeGraaf, John, David Wann, and Thomas Naylor. *Affluenza: The All-Consuming Epidemic*. San Francisco: Berrett-Koehler, 2001.

De-Shalit, Avner. *Why Posterity Matters: Environmental Policies and Future Generations*. London: Routledge, 1995.

DesJardins, Joseph. *Environmental Ethics: An Introduction to Environmental Philosophy*. 2nd ed. Belmont, CA: Wadsworth, 1997.

Devall, Bill, and George Sessions. *Deep Ecology*. Salt Lake City: Peregrine Smith, 1985.

DeWitt, Calvin. "Biogeographic and Trophic Restructuring of the Biosphere: The State of the Earth under Human Domination." *Christian Scholar's Review* 32 (Summer 2003): 347–64.

————. *Caring for Creation: Responsible Stewardship of God's Handiwork*. Grand Rapids: Baker, 1998.

————. *Earth-Wise: A Biblical Response to Environmental Issues*. Grand Rapids: CRC Publications, 1994.

————, ed. *The Environment and the Christian: What Does the New Testament Say about the Environment?* Grand Rapids: Baker, 1991.

————. "Take Good Care: It's God's Earth." *Prism* 1 (December 1993–January 1994): 8–11.

Diamond, Jared. *Collapse: How Societies Choose to Fail or Succeed*. New York: Viking, 2005.

————. *Guns, Germs, and Steel: The Fate of Human Societies*. New York: Norton, 1999.

Dillard, Annie. *Teaching a Stone to Talk*. New York: Harper and Row, 1982.

Dunn, James D. G. *The Epistles to the Colossians and to Philemon*. New International Greek Testament Commentary. Grand Rapids: Eerdmans, 1996.

Dunn, James D. G., and Alan Suggate. *The Justice of God*. Grand Rapids: Eerdmans, 1993.

Durning, Alan. *How Much Is Enough?* New York: Norton, 1992.

————. *This Place on Earth: Home and the Practice of Permanence*. Seattle: Sasquatch Books, 1996.

Dyrness, William. "The Ecology of Hope." Paper delivered at the National Association of Evangelicals conference, "Compassion and the Care for Creation," Malone College, Canton, OH, March 3, 1999.

Eckerle, Kevin. "Climate Change Affects Terrestrial Biodiversity." In *Vital Signs 2007–2008*, 94–95.

Ecosystems and Human Well-being: Biodiversity Synthesis. Millennium Ecosystem Assessment. Washington, DC: World Resources Institute, 2005. www.millenniumassessment.org/documents/document.354.aspx.pdf.

Edwards, Denis. *Breath of Life: A Theology of the Creator Spirit.* Maryknoll, NY: Orbis, 2004.

———. *Jesus the Wisdom of God: An Ecological Theology.* Maryknoll, NY: Orbis, 1995.

Evans, Kim Martens. *The Environment: A Revolution in Attitudes.* Farmington Hills, MI: Gale, Cengage Learning, 2008.

Farley, Benjamin. *In Praise of Virtue: An Exploration of the Biblical Virtues in a Christian Context.* Grand Rapids: Eerdmans, 1995.

Feld, Steven, and Keith Basso, eds. *Senses of Place.* Santa Fe, NM: School of American Research, 1996.

Feuerbach, Ludwig. *The Essence of Christianity.* New York: Harper and Row, 1957.

Finger, Thomas. "Evangelicals, Eschatology, and the Environment." Scholars Circle monograph 2. Evangelical Environmental Network, 1998.

———. *Self, Earth, and Society: Alienation and Trinitarian Transformation.* Downers Grove, IL: InterVarsity, 1997.

FitzGerald, Frances. *Cities on a Hill: A Journey through Contemporary American Cultures.* New York: Simon and Schuster, 1986.

Flader, Susan. *Thinking Like a Mountain: Aldo Leopold and the Evolution of an Ecological Attitude toward Deer, Wolves, and Forests.* Columbia: University of Missouri Press, 1974.

Flavin, Christopher. "The Legacy of Rio." In *State of the World 1997*, 3–22. New York: Norton, 1997.

Foot, Philippa. *Virtues and Vices and Other Essays in Moral Philosophy.* Berkeley: University of California Press, 1978.

Fowler, Robert Booth. *The Greening of Protestant Thought.* Chapel Hill: University of North Carolina Press, 1995.

Frankena, William. *Ethics.* Englewood Cliffs, NJ: Prentice-Hall, 1973.

Frankl, Victor. *Man's Search for Meaning.* New York: Simon and Schuster, 1963.

Frasz, Geoffrey. "Environmental Virtue Ethics: A New Direction for Environmental Ethics." *Environmental Ethics* 15 (1993): 259–74.

Fretheim, Terence. "The Book of Genesis." In *The New Interpreter's Bible*, vol. 1. Nashville: Abingdon, 1994.

———. *God and the World in the Old Testament.* Nashville: Abingdon, 2005.

Frumpkin, Howard. "Urban Sprawl and Public Health." *Public Health Reports* 117 (May–June 2002): 201–17.

Gadamer, Hans-Georg. *Truth and Method.* New York: Continuum, 1975.

Gallagher, Winifred. *The Power of Place.* New York: HarperCollins, 1993.

Gardner, Gary. "Forest Loss Continues." In *Vital Signs 2005*, 92–93.

———. "Grain Area Shrinks Again." In *Vital Signs 2000*, 44–45.

"GEO-2000: Global Environment Outlook." United Nations Environment Programme. www
.unep.org/geo2000/index.htm.

Gilkey, Langdon. *Society and the Sacred*. New York: Crossroad, 1981.

Glacken, Clarence. *Traces on the Rhodian Shore: Nature and Culture in Western Thought from Ancient Times to the End of the Eighteenth Century*. Berkeley: University of California Press, 1967.

Global Ecology Handbook. Boston: Beacon, 1990.

Golley, Frank. *A Primer for Environmental Literacy*. New Haven: Yale University Press, 1998.

González, Catherine Gunsalus, and Justo L. González. *Revelation*. Westminster Bible Companion. Louisville: Westminster/John Knox, 1997.

Goodman, Billy. *The Rain Forest*. New York: Tern Enterprise, 1991.

Gordis, Robert. *The Book of God and Man: A Study of Job*. Chicago: University of Chicago Press, 1965.

———. *The Book of Job: Commentary, New Translation, and Special Studies*. New York: Jewish Theological Seminary of America, 1978.

Gottfried, Robert. *Economics, Ecology, and the Roots of Western Faith*. Lanham, MD: Rowman and Littlefield, 1995.

Goudzwaard, Bob. *Aid for the Overdeveloped West*. Toronto: Wedge, 1975.

———. *Capitalism and Progress: A Diagnosis of Western Society*. Grand Rapids: Eerdmans, 1979.

Goudzwaard, Bob, and Harry de Lange. *Beyond Wealth and Poverty*. Grand Rapids: Eerdmans, 1995.

Granberg-Michaelson, Wesley. "Covenant and Creation." In Birch, Eakin, and McDaniel, *Liberating Life*, 27–36.

———. *Ecology and Life: Accepting Our Environmental Responsibility*. Waco: Word, 1988.

———. "Renewing the Whole Creation." *Sojourners* (February–March 1990): 10–14.

———, ed. *Tending the Garden: Essays on the Gospel and the Earth*. Grand Rapids: Eerdmans, 1987.

———. *A Worldly Spirituality: The Call to Take Care of the Earth*. San Francisco: Harper and Row, 1984.

Grant, Robert. *A Case Study in Thomistic Environmental Ethics: The Ecological Crisis in the Loess Hills of Iowa*. Lewiston: Edwin Mellon, 2007.

Grant, Robert, and David Tracy. *A Short History of the Interpretation of the Bible*. Philadelphia: Fortress, 1984.

Green, Joel, ed. *What about the Soul? Neuroscience and Christian Anthropology*. Nashville: Abingdon, 2004.

Gunton, Colin. *Christ and Creation*. Grand Rapids: Eerdmans, 1992.

———. *The One, the Three, and the Many: God, Creation, and the Culture of Modernity*. Cambridge: Cambridge University Press, 1993.

———. *The Promise of Trinitarian Theology*. Edinburgh: T&T Clark, 1991.

Gustafson, James. *Ethics from a Theocentric Perspective: Theology and Ethics*. Chicago: University of Chicago Press, 1981.

———. *A Sense of the Divine: The Natural Environment from a Theocentric Perspective*. Cleveland: Pilgrim, 1994.

Habel, Norman. *The Book of Job*. Philadelphia: Westminster, 1985.

————, ed. *Earth Bible*. 5 vols. Sheffield: Sheffield Academic, 2000–2002.

Hallman, David, ed. *Ecotheology: Voices from South and North*. Geneva: World Council of Churches, 1994.

Hanson, Paul. *Isaiah 40–66*. Louisville: John Knox, 1995.

Hardin, Garrett. *Filters against Folly: How to Survive Despite Economists, Ecologists, and the Merely Eloquent*. New York: Penguin, 1985.

Hardy, Lee. *The Fabric of This World: Inquiries into Calling, Career Choice, and the Design of Human Work*. Grand Rapids: Eerdmans, 1990.

Harrison, Robert Pogue. *Forests: The Shadow of Civilization*. Chicago: University of Chicago Press, 1992.

Hauerwas, Stanley. *Character and the Christian Life: A Study in Theological Ethics*. San Antonio: Trinity University, 1985.

————. *A Community of Character: Toward a Constructive Christian Social Ethic*. Notre Dame: University of Notre Dame Press, 1981.

————. *Vision and Virtue: Essays in Christian Ethical Reflection*. Notre Dame: Fides, 1974.

Havel, Václav. *Disturbing the Peace*. New York: Alfred Knopf, 1990.

Hawken, Paul. *Blessed Unrest: How the Largest Social Movement in History Is Restoring Grace, Justice, and Beauty to the World*. New York: Penguin, 2007.

Heinberg, Richard. *The Party's Over: Oil, War and the Fate of Industrial Societies*. Rev. ed. Gabriola Island, BC: New Society, 2005.

Hendry, George. *Theology of Nature*. Philadelphia: Westminster, 1980.

Hessel, Dieter, ed. *Theology for Earth Community*. Maryknoll, NY: Orbis, 1996.

Hessel, Dieter, and Rosemary Radford Ruether, eds. *Christianity and Ecology: Seeking the Well-Being of Earth and Humans*. Cambridge: Harvard University Press, 2000.

Heywood, V., ed. *Global Biodiversity Assessment*. Cambridge: Cambridge University Press, 1995.

Hiebert, Theodore. *The Yahwist's Landscape: Nature and Religion in Early Israel*. New York: Oxford University Press, 1996.

Hill, Craig. *In God's Time: The Bible and the Future*. Grand Rapids: Eerdmans, 2002.

Hoezee, Scott. *Remember Creation: God's World of Wonder and Delight*. Grand Rapids: Eerdmans, 1998.

Hofrichter, Richard, ed. *Toxic Struggles: The Theory and Practice of Environmental Justice*. Philadelphia: New Society, 1993.

Hooykaas, Roger. *Religion and the Rise of Modern Science*. Edinburgh: Scottish Academic, 1972.

Hopkins, Gerard Manley. *Poems and Prose*. London: Penguin, 1985.

Horsley, Richard, ed. *Paul and Empire: Religion and Power in Roman Imperial Society*. Harrisburg, PA: Trinity Press International, 1997.

"IPCC, 2007: Summary for Policymakers." In *Climate Change 2007: The Physical Science Basis*, 1–18. Contribution of Working Group I to the Fourth Assessment Report of the Intergovernmental Panel on Climate Change. Cambridge: Cambridge University Press, 2007. Also available online at www.ipcc.ch/pdf/assessment-report/ar4/wg1/ar4-wg1-spm.pdf.

Jenkins, Jerry, Karen Roy, Charles Driscoll, and Christopher Buerkett. *Acid Rain and the Adirondacks: A Research Summary*. Ray Brook, NY: Adirondack Lakes Survey Corporation, 2005.

————. *Acid Rain in the Adirondacks: An Environmental History*. Ithaca, NY: Cornell University Press, 2008.

Johnson, Lawrence. *A Morally Deep World: An Essay on Moral Significance and Environmental Ethics*. Cambridge: Cambridge University Press, 1991.

Johnston, Verna. *The Sierra Nevada*. Boston: Houghton Mifflin, 1970.

Jones, Jeff. "Rain Check." *Adirondack Life*, March/April 1997, 48–68.

Kaiser, Christopher. "The Integrity of Creation: In Search of a Meaning." *Perspectives* 11 (April 1996): 8–11.

Kant, Immanuel. *Critique of Pure Reason*. Translated by Norman Kemp Smith. New York: St. Martin's Press, 1965.

Kierkegaard, Søren. *The Sickness Unto Death*. Princeton: Princeton University Press, 1980.

Kittel, Gerhard, and Gerhard Friedrich, eds. *Theological Dictionary of the New Testament*. Grand Rapids: Eerdmans, 1974.

Klaaren, Eugene. *Religious Origins of Modern Science*. Grand Rapids: Eerdmans, 1977.

Knauth, Percy. *The North Woods*. New York: Time-Life, 1972.

Kohák, Erazim. *The Embers and the Stars: A Philosophical Inquiry into the Moral Sense of Nature*. Chicago: University of Chicago Press, 1984.

Kolbert, Elizabeth. *Field Notes from a Catastrophe: Man, Nature, and Climate Change*. New York: Bloomsbury, 2006.

Kricher, John. *A Neotropical Companion: An Introduction to the Animals, Plants, and Ecosystems of the New World Tropics*. Princeton: Princeton University Press, 1989.

LaCugna, Catherine Mowry. *God for Us: The Trinity and Christian Life*. San Francisco: HarperCollins, 1991.

Ladd, George Eldon. *A Commentary on the Revelation of John*. Grand Rapids: Eerdmans, 1972.

————. *Theology of the New Testament*. Grand Rapids: Eerdmans, 1974.

Lane, Belden C. *Landscapes of the Sacred: Geography and Narrative in American Spirituality*. New York: Paulist Press, 1988.

————. *The Solace of Fierce Landscapes: Exploring Desert and Mountain Spirituality*. New York: Oxford University Press, 1998.

Larson, David. "God's Gardeners: American Protestant Evangelicals Confront Environmentalism, 1967–2000." PhD dissertation, University of Chicago Divinity School, 2001.

Lee, Charles. "Evidence of Environmental Racism." *Sojourners* (February–March 1990): 21–25.

Leopold, Aldo. *A Sand County Almanac*. New York: Ballantine, 1970.

Lewin, Roger. *Complexity: Life at the Edge of Chaos*. 2nd ed. Chicago: University of Chicago Press, 1999.

Lewis, C. S. *The Magician's Nephew*. New York: Macmillan, 1978.

Limouris, Gennadios, ed. *Justice, Peace, and the Integrity of Creation: Insights from Orthodoxy*. Geneva: World Council of Churches, 1990.

Lincoln, Andrew. "The Letter to the Colossians." In *The New Interpreter's Bible*, vol. 11. Nashville: Abingdon, 2000.

Lindberg, David, and Ronald Numbers, eds. *God and Nature: Historical Essays on the Encounter between Christianity and Science*. Berkeley: University of California Press, 1986.

Lindsey, Hal. *The Late Great Planet Earth*. Grand Rapids: Zondervan, 1970.

Lindsey, Rebecca. "Tropical Deforestation." NASA Earth Observatory. March 30, 2007. http://earthobservatory.nasa.gov/Features/Deforestation/.

Little, Charles. *The Dying of the Trees: The Pandemic in America's Forests.* New York: Penguin, 1995.

Lonning, Per. *Creation—An Ecumenical Challenge?* Macon, GA: Mercer, 1989.

Lovins, Amory. *The Negawatt Revolution.* Snowmass, CO: Rocky Mountain Institute, 1990.

Lowe, Ben. *Green Revolution: Coming Together to Care for Creation.* Downers Grove, IL: InterVarsity, 2009.

Lynas, Mark. *High Tide: The Truth about Our Climate Crisis.* New York: Picador, 2004.

MacIntyre, Alasdair. *After Virtue.* 2nd ed. Notre Dame: University of Notre Dame Press, 1984.

Martin, Ralph. *Ephesians, Colossians, and Philemon.* Interpretation. Atlanta: John Knox, 1991.

McAfee, Gene. "Ecology and Biblical Studies." In Hessel, *Theology for Earth Community,* 31–44.

McDaniel, Jay. *Of God and Pelicans: A Theology of Reverence for Life.* Louisville: Westminster/John Knox, 1989.

McDonough, William, and Michael Braungart. *Cradle to Cradle: Remaking the Way We Make Things.* New York: North Point, 2002.

McHarg, Ian. "The Place of Nature in the City of Man." In Barbour, *Western Man and Environmental Ethics,* 171–86.

McKibben, Bill. *The Comforting Whirlwind: God, Job, and the Scale of Creation.* Grand Rapids: Eerdmans, 1994.

———. *Deep Economy: The Wealth of Communities and the Durable Future.* New York: Holt, 2007.

———. *The End of Nature.* New York: Doubleday, 1989.

———. *Enough: Staying Human in an Engineered Age.* New York: Henry Holt, 2003.

———. *Hope, Human and Wild: True Stories of Living Lightly on the Earth.* St. Paul: Hungry Mind, 1995.

McKim, Donald. *A Guide to Contemporary Hermeneutics: Major Trends in Biblical Interpretation.* Grand Rapids: Eerdmans, 1986.

———. *What Christians Believe about the Bible.* Nashville: Thomas Nelson, 1985.

McNeill, J. R. *Something New under the Sun: An Environmental History of the Twentieth-Century World.* New York: Norton, 2000.

Meilaender, Gilbert. *The Theory and Practice of Virtue.* Notre Dame: University of Notre Dame Press, 1984.

———. "Virtue in Contemporary Religious Thought." In *Virtue—Public and Private,* edited by Richard John Neuhaus, 7–29. Grand Rapids: Eerdmans, 1986.

Meine, Curt. *Aldo Leopold: His Life and Work.* Madison: University of Wisconsin Press, 1988.

Merchant, Carolyn. *The Death of Nature.* San Francisco: Harper and Row, 1980.

Metzger, Bruce. *A Textual Commentary on the Greek New Testament.* 2nd ed. London: United Bible Society, 1994.

Meyer, Art, and Jocele Meyer. *Earthkeepers.* Scottdale, PA: Herald, 1991.

Middleton, J. Richard. "The Liberating Image? Interpreting the *Imago Dei* in Context." *Christian Scholar's Review* 24, no. 1 (September 1994): 8–25.

———. *The Liberating Image: The Imago Dei in Genesis 1*. Grand Rapids: Brazos, 2005.

Middleton, J. Richard, and Brian Walsh. *Truth Is Stranger Than It Used To Be*. Downers Grove, IL: InterVarsity, 1995.

Milbank, John. *Theology and Social Theory: Beyond Secular Reason*. Oxford: Blackwell, 1993.

"Millennium Development Goals Report 2005." New York: United Nations, 2005. www.unfpa.org/icpd/docs/mdgrept2005.pdf.

Miller, Alan. *Gaia Connections*. Savage, MD: Rowman and Littlefield, 1991.

Miller, G. Tyler, Jr. *Living in the Environment*. 7th ed. Belmont, CA: Wadsworth, 1992.

———. *Living in the Environment*. 11th ed. Pacific Grove, CA: Brooks/Cole, 2000.

———. *Living in the Environment*. 15th ed. Pacific Grove, CA: Brooks/Cole, 2006.

Minear, Paul. *Christians and the New Creation: Genesis Motifs in the New Testament*. Louisville: Westminster/John Knox, 1994.

———. *I Saw a New Earth*. Washington, DC: Corpus, 1968.

Moltmann, Jürgen. *The Coming of God: Christian Eschatology*. Minneapolis: Fortress, 1996.

———. *The Crucified God*. New York: Harper and Row, 1974.

———. *God in Creation: A New Theology of Creation and the Spirit of God*. San Francisco: Harper and Row, 1985.

———. *The Spirit of Life: A Universal Affirmation*. Minneapolis: Fortress, 1992.

———. *Theology of Hope: On the Ground and the Implications of a Christian Eschatology*. New York: Harper and Row, 1967.

———. *The Trinity and the Kingdom*. San Francisco: Harper and Row, 1981.

Mouw, Richard. *The God Who Commands: A Study in Divine Command Ethics*. Notre Dame: University of Notre Dame Press, 1991.

———. *When the Kings Come Marching In*. Grand Rapids: Eerdmans, 1983.

Muir, John. *The Mountains of California*. San Francisco: Sierra Club, 1988.

———. *My First Summer in the Sierra*. San Francisco: Sierra Club, 1988.

"Municipal Solid Waste Generation, Recycling, and Disposal in the United States: Facts and Figures for 2006." United States Environmental Protection Agency, 2007. www.epa.gov/waste/nonhaz/municipal/pubs/msw06.pdf.

Murray, Robert. *The Cosmic Covenant: Biblical Themes of Justice, Peace, and the Integrity of Creation*. London: Sheed and Ward, 1992.

Myers, David. *The American Paradox: Spiritual Hunger in an Age of Plenty*. New Haven: Yale University Press, 2000.

———. *The Pursuit of Happiness: Who Is Happy—and Why*. New York: William Morrow, 1992.

Myers, Norman. "Biotic Holocaust." *National Wildlife Federation*, March/April 1999, 31–39.

———. *The Sinking Ark*. New York: Pergamon, 1979.

Naess, Arne. "The Shallow and the Deep, Long-Range Ecology Movement." *Inquiry* 16 (1973): 95–100.

Nagel, Thomas. *The View from Nowhere*. New York: Oxford University Press, 1986.

Nash, James. *Loving Nature: Ecological Integrity and Christian Responsibility*. Nashville: Abingdon, 1991.

————. "Toward the Revival and Reform of the Subversive Virtue: Frugality." *The Annual of the Society of Christian Ethics* 15 (1995): 137–60.

Nash, Roderick. *The Rights of Nature: A History of Environmental Ethics*. Madison: University of Wisconsin Press, 1989.

————. *Wilderness and the American Mind*. Rev. ed. New Haven: Yale University Press, 1973.

Newman, Arnold. *Tropical Rainforest*. New York: Facts On File Books, 1990.

Newsom, Carol. "The Book of Job." In *The New Interpreter's Bible*, vol. 4. Nashville: Abingdon, 1996.

Nierenberg, Danielle. "Population Rise Slows but Continues." In *Vital Signs 2007–2008*, 50–51.

Nisbet, E. G. *Leaving Eden: To Protect and Manage the Earth*. Cambridge: Cambridge University Press, 1991.

Noddings, Nel. *Caring: A Feminine Approach to Ethics and Moral Education*. Berkeley: University of California Press, 1984.

Northcott, Michael. *The Environment and Christian Ethics*. Cambridge: Cambridge University Press, 1996.

O'Brien, Peter. *Colossians and Philemon*. Word Biblical Commentary 44. Waco: Word, 1982.

O'Donovan, Oliver. *Resurrection and Moral Order: An Outline for Evangelical Ethics*. Grand Rapids: Eerdmans, 1986.

Oelschlaeger, Max. *Caring for Creation: An Ecumenical Approach to the Environmental Crisis*. New Haven: Yale University Press, 1994.

————. *The Idea of Wilderness: From Prehistory to the Age of Ecology*. New Haven: Yale University Press, 1991.

Olson, Sigurd. *Sigurd Olson's Wilderness Days*. New York: Alfred Knopf, 1972.

O'Meara, Molly. "Harnessing Information Technologies for the Environment." In *State of the World 2000*. Washington, DC: Worldwatch Institute, 2005.

Orr, David. *Earth in Mind: On Education, Environment, and the Human Prospect*. Washington, DC: Island, 1994.

————. *Ecological Literacy: Education and the Transition to a Postmodern World*. Albany: State University of New York Press, 1992.

————. *The Nature of Design: Ecology, Culture, and Human Intention*. New York: Oxford University Press, 2002.

Passmore, John. *Man's Responsibility for Nature*. New York: Scribner's, 1974.

Patterson, John. "Maori Environmental Virtues." *Environmental Ethics* 16 (1994): 397–409.

Pelikan, Jaroslav. *The Emergence of the Catholic Tradition*. Vol. 1 of *The Christian Tradition: A History of the Development of Doctrine*. Chicago: University of Chicago Press, 1971.

Perlman, Michael. *The Power of Trees*. Woodstock, CT: Spring, 1994.

Peters, Ted. *God as Trinity: Relationality and Temporality in Divine Life*. Louisville: Westminster/John Knox, 1993.

————. *Sin: Radical Evil in Soul and Society*. Grand Rapids: Eerdmans, 1995.

Peterson, Anna. *Being Human: Ethics, Environment, and Our Place in the World*. Berkeley: University of California Press, 2001.

Pimentel, David. "Soil Erosion: A Food and Environmental Threat." *Environment, Development, and Sustainability* 8 (2006): 119–37.

Pimm, Stuart. *The World according to Pimm: A Scientist Audits the Earth*. New York: McGraw Hill, 2001.

Placher, William. *The Triune God: An Essay in Postliberal Theology*. Louisville: Westminster/ John Knox, 2007.

———. *Unapologetic Theology: A Christian Voice in a Pluralistic Conversation*. Louisville: Westminster/John Knox, 1989.

Plantinga, Neal. *Not the Way It's Supposed To Be: A Breviary of Sin*. Grand Rapids: Eerdmans, 1995.

Pojman, Louis. *Global Environmental Ethics*. Mountain View, CA: Mayfield, 2000.

Ponting, Clive. *A Green History of the World: The Environment and the Collapse of Great Civilizations*. New York: Penguin, 1991.

Pope, Marvin. *Job*. 3rd ed. Anchor Bible 15. New York: Doubleday, 1973.

"Population Growth and Suburban Sprawl." Sierra Club, 2003. www.sierraclub.org/sprawl/ sprawlpop_2003.pdf.

Postel, Sandra. *Dividing the Waters: Food Security, Ecosystem Health, and the New Politics of Scarcity*. Washington, DC: Worldwatch Institute, 1996.

———. *Liquid Assets: The Critical Need to Safeguard Freshwater Ecosystems*. Washington, DC: Worldwatch Institute, 2005.

———. "Redesigning Irrigated Agriculture." In *State of the World 2000*, 39–58. Washington, DC: Worldwatch Institute, 2000.

Postman, Neil. *Technopoly: The Surrender of Culture to Technology*. New York: Vintage, 1993.

Rasmussen, Larry. *Earth Community Earth Ethics*. Maryknoll, NY: Orbis, 1996.

Rauschenbusch, Walter. *Prayers of the Social Awakening*. Boston: Pilgrim, 1910.

Regan, Tom. *The Case for Animal Rights*. Berkeley: University of California Press, 1983.

———. "Christianity and Animal Rights." In Birch, Eakin, and McDaniel, *Liberating Life*, 73–87.

Relph, Edward. *Place and Placelessness*. London: Pion, 1976.

Ricoeur, Paul. *The Conflict of Interpretations: Essays in Hermeneutics*. Edited by Don Ihde. Evanston, IL: Northwestern University Press, 1974.

Ridderbos, Herman. *Paul: An Outline of His Theology*. Grand Rapids: Eerdmans, 1975.

Roberts, Paul. *The End of Oil: On the Edge of a Perilous New World*. New York: Houghton Mifflin, 2004.

Roberts, Robert. *Spirituality and Human Emotion*. Grand Rapids: Eerdmans, 1982.

Robinson, Tri. *Saving God's Green Earth: Rediscovering the Church's Responsibility to Environmental Stewardship*. Norcross, GA: Ampelon, 2006.

Rolston, Holmes, III. *Conserving Natural Value*. New York: Columbia University Press, 1994.

———. *Environmental Ethics: Duties to and Values in the Natural World*. Philadelphia: Temple University Press, 1988.

Rorty, Richard. *Philosophy and the Mirror of Nature*. Princeton: Princeton University Press, 1979.

Rossing, Barbara. *The Rapture Exposed: The Message of Hope in the Book of Revelation*. Boulder, CO: Westview, 2004.

Rowland, Christopher. "The Book of Revelation." In *The New Interpreter's Bible*, vol. 12. Nashville: Abingdon, 1998.

Rudel, Thomas, Kevin Flesher, Diane Bates, Sandra Baptista, and Peter Holmgren. "Tropical Deforestation Literature: Geographical and Historical Patterns in the Availability of Information and Analysis of Causes." Forest Resources Assessment Programme Working Paper No 27. Forestry Department, Food and Agriculture Organization of the United Nations, 2007.

Ruether, Rosemary Radford. *New Woman/New Earth: Sexist Ideologies and Human Liberation*. New York: Seabury, 1975.

———. *Sexism and God-Talk: Toward a Feminist Theology*. Boston: Beacon, 1983.

———. *To Change the World: Christology and Cultural Criticism*. New York: Crossroad, 1981.

Sanders, Scott Russell. *Hunting for Hope*. Boston: Beacon, 1998.

Sandler, Ronald. *Character and Environment: A Virtue-Oriented Approach to Environmental Ethics*. New York: Columbia University Press, 2007.

Santmire, H. Paul. *Brother Earth*. New York: Thomas Nelson, 1970.

———. "I-Thou, I-It, and I-Ens." *Journal of Religion* 48 (July 1968): 260–73.

———. *Nature Reborn: The Ecological and Cosmic Promise of Christian Theology*. Minneapolis: Augsburg Fortress, 2000.

———. *Ritualizing Nature: Renewing Christian Liturgy in a Time of Crisis*. Minneapolis: Fortress, 2008.

———. *The Travail of Nature: The Ambiguous Ecological Promise of Christian Theology*. Philadelphia: Fortress, 1985.

Sauer, Peter, ed. *Finding Home: Writing on Nature and Culture from Orion Magazine*. Boston: Beacon, 1992.

Sawin, Janet, and Ishani Mukherjee. "Fossil Fuel Use Up Again." In *Vital Signs 2007–2008*, 32–33.

Schaeffer, Francis. *Pollution and the Death of Man: The Christian View of Ecology*. Wheaton, IL: Tyndale, 1970.

Schreiner, Susan. *The Theatre of His Glory: Nature and Natural Order in the Thought of John Calvin*. Grand Rapids: Baker, 1991.

Schumacher, E. F. *Small Is Beautiful*. New York: Harper and Row, 1973.

Schut, Michael, ed. *Simpler Living, Compassionate Life*. Denver: Morehouse, 1999.

Schweitzer, Albert. *Civilization and Ethics*. London: A&C Black, 1946.

———. *Reverence for Life*. Edited by Thomas Kiernan. New York: Philosophical Library, 1965.

Schweizer, Eduard. *The Letter to the Colossians*. Minneapolis: Augsburg, 1982.

Sikora, R. I., and Brian Barry, eds. *Obligations to Future Generations*. Philadelphia: Temple University Press, 1978.

Simkins, Ronald. *Creator and Creation: Nature in the Worldview of Ancient Israel*. Peabody, MA: Hendrickson, 1994.

Singer, Peter. *Animal Liberation: A New Ethic for Our Treatment of Animals*. New York: Avon Books, 1975.

Sittler, Joseph. "Ecological Commitment as Theological Responsibility." *Zygon* 5 (June 1970): 172–81.

———. *Essays on Nature and Grace*. Philadelphia: Fortress, 1972.

———. "Evangelism and the Care of the Earth." In *Preaching and the Witnessing Community*, edited by Herman Stuempfle, 100–104. Philadelphia: Fortress, 1973.

———. *Grace Notes and Other Fragments*. Edited by Robert Herhold and Linda Marie Delloff. Philadelphia: Fortress, 1981.

———. *Gravity and Grace*. Minneapolis: Augsburg, 1986.

———. "The Scope of Christological Reflection." *Interpretation* 26 (July 1972): 328–37.

Sleeth, Matthew. *Serve God, Save the Planet: A Christian Call to Action*. White River Junction, VT: Chelsea Green, 2006.

Smedes, Lewis. *Choices: Making Right Decisions in a Complex World*. San Francisco: Harper and Row, 1986.

———. *Mere Morality: What God Expects from Ordinary People*. Grand Rapids: Eerdmans, 1983.

———. *Standing on the Promises: Keeping Hope Alive for a Tomorrow We Cannot Control*. Nashville: Thomas Nelson, 1998.

Smith, James K. A. *Who's Afraid of Postmodernism? Taking Derrida, Lyotard, and Foucault to Church*. Grand Rapids: Baker Academic, 2006.

"Some Questions and Answers on Acid Rain." New York State Department of Environmental Conservation. http://www.dec.ny.gov/chemical/8418.html.

Speth, James Gustave. *The Bridge at the Edge of the World: Capitalism, the Environment, and Crossing from Crisis to Sustainability*. New Haven: Yale University Press, 2008.

———. *Red Sky at Morning: America and the Crisis of the Global Environment*. New Haven: Yale University Press, 2004.

Spring, David, and Eileen Spring, eds. *Ecology and Religion in History*. New York: Harper and Row, 1974.

The State of Food Insecurity in the World 2006. Food and Agriculture Organization of the United Nations, 2006. http://www.fao.org/docrep/009/a0750e/a0750e00.htm.

The State of the Cities 2000: Megaforces Shaping the Future of the Nation's Cities. U.S. Department of Housing and Urban Development, 2000.

Stegner, Wallace. *Marking the Sparrow's Fall: The Making of the American West*. New York: Henry Holt, 1998.

Steinberg, Ted. *Down to Earth: Nature's Role in American History*. New York: Oxford University Press, 2002.

Stensaas, Mark. *Canoe Country Wildlife: A Field Guide to the Boundary Waters and Quetico*. Duluth, MN: Pfeifer-Hamilton, 1993.

Sterling, Eleanor. "Blue Planet Blues: Demand for Freshwater Threatens to Outstrip Supply." *Natural History*, November 2007, 29–31. Reprinted in *Water Supply*, edited by Richard Joseph Stein, 5–9. New York: H. W. Wilson, 2008.

Stob, Henry. *Ethical Reflections: Essays on Moral Themes*. Grand Rapids: Eerdmans, 1978.

Stone, Christopher. *Earth and Other Ethics: The Case for Moral Pluralism*. New York: Harper and Row, 1987.

Suh, Chul Won. *The Creation-Mediatorship of Jesus Christ: A Study in the Relationship between the Incarnation and the Creation*. Amsterdam: Rodopi, 1979.

Swartley, Willard. *Slavery, Sabbath, War, and Women*. Scottdale, PA: Herald, 1983.

Taylor, Charles. *Sources of the Self: The Making of the Modern Identity*. Cambridge: Harvard University Press, 1989.

Taylor, Paul. *Respect for Nature: A Theory of Environmental Ethics*. Princeton: Princeton University Press, 1986.

Terborgh, John. *Diversity and the Tropical Rain Forest*. New York: Scientific American Library, 1992.

Thiselton, Anthony. *New Horizons in Hermeneutics*. Grand Rapids: Zondervan, 1992.

Thomas Aquinas. *Summa contra Gentiles*. Translated by James F. Anderson. Notre Dame: University of Notre Dame Press, 1992.

————. *Treatise on the Virtues*. Translated by John Oesterle. Notre Dame: University of Notre Dame Press, 1984.

Thompson, Clive. "Global Mourning." *Wired* (January 2008): 70.

Thoreau, Henry David. *Walden and Other Writings*. Edited by Joseph Wood Krutch. New York: Bantam, 1981.

Tillett, Sarah, ed. *Caring for Creation: Biblical and Theological Perspectives*. Oxford: A Rocha, 2005.

Todd, Nancy Jack, and John Todd. *From Eco-Cities to Living Machines: Principles of Ecological Design*. Berkeley: North Atlantic Books, 1993.

Toulmin, Stephen. *Cosmopolis: The Hidden Agenda of Modernity*. Chicago: University of Chicago Press, 1992.

Toynbee, Arnold. "The Religious Background of the Present Environmental Crisis." In Spring and Spring, *Ecology and Religion in History*, 137–49.

Tuan, Yi-Fu. *Topophilia: A Study of Environmental Perception, Attitudes, and Values*. New York: Columbia University Press, 1990.

Tucker, Mary Evelyn, and John Grim, eds. *Worldviews and Ecology*. Maryknoll, NY: Orbis, 1994.

Turner, Frederick. *Rediscovering America: John Muir in His Time and Ours*. San Francisco: Sierra Club, 1985.

Tuxill, John. *Losing Strands in the Web of Life: Vertebrate Declines and the Conservation of Biological Diversity*. Washington, DC: Worldwatch Institute, 1998.

Tweed, William. *Sequoia–Kings Canyon*. Las Vegas: KC Publications, 1980.

Van Der Ryn, Sim, and Stuart Cowan. *Ecological Design*. Washington, DC: Island, 1996.

Van Dyke, Fred, David Mahan, Joseph Sheldon, and Raymond Brand. *Redeeming Creation: The Biblical Basis for Environmental Stewardship*. Downers Grove, IL: InterVarsity, 1996.

Van Leeuwen, Ray. "Christ's Resurrection and the Creation's Vindication." In DeWitt, *The Environment and the Christian*, 57–71.

Van Wensveen, Louke. "Christian Ecological Virtue Ethics: Transforming a Tradition." In Hessel and Ruether, *Christianity and Ecology*, 155–71.

————. *Dirty Virtues: The Emergence of Ecological Virtue Ethics*. Amherst, NY: Humanity Books, 2000.

Verhey, Allen. *Living the Heidelberg: The Heidelberg Catechism and the Moral Life*. Grand Rapids: Christian Reformed Church, 1986.

Vital Signs 2000. Washington, DC: Worldwatch Institute, 2000.

Vital Signs 2005. Washington, DC: Worldwatch Institute, 2005.

Vital Signs 2007–2008. Washington, DC: Worldwatch Institute, 2008.

Vitek, William, and Wes Jackson, eds. *Rooted in the Land: Essays on Community and Place*. New Haven: Yale University Press, 1996.

Volf, Miroslav. *After Our Likeness: The Church as the Image of the Trinity*. Grand Rapids: Eerdmans, 1998.

Von Rad, Gerhard. *Genesis*. Rev. ed. Old Testament Library. Philadelphia: Westminster, 1972.

Wachtel, Paul. *The Poverty of Affluence: A Psychological Portrait of the American Way of Life*. Philadelphia: New Society, 1989.

Walsh, Brian. *Subversive Christianity: Imaging God in a Dangerous Time*. Bristol: Regius, 1992.

————. "Subversive Poetry and Life in the Empire." *Third Way* 23, no. 3 (April 2000): 4.

Walsh, Brian, Marianne Karsh, and Nik Ansell. "Trees, Forestry, and the Responsiveness of Creation." *Cross Currents* 44, no. 2 (1994): 149–62.

Walsh, Brian, and Sylvia Keesmaat. *Colossians Remixed: Subverting the Empire*. Downers Grove, IL: InterVarsity, 2003.

Walsh, Brian, and J. Richard Middleton. *The Transforming Vision*. Downers Grove, IL: InterVarsity, 1984.

Ware, Timothy. *The Orthodox Church*. London: Penguin, 1991.

————. *The Orthodox Way*. Crestwood, NY: St. Vladimir's Seminary Press, 1979.

The Water Atlas. New York: New Press, 2004.

Wells, Samuel. *Improvisation: The Drama of Christian Ethics*. Grand Rapids: Brazos, 2004.

Welker, Michael. *Creation and Reality*. Minneapolis: Fortress, 1999.

Wenham, Gordon. *Genesis 1–15*. Word Biblical Commentary 1. Waco: Word, 1987.

Wennberg, Robert. *God, Humans, and Animals: An Invitation to Enlarge Our Moral Universe*. Grand Rapids: Eerdmans, 2003.

Westermann, Claus. *Blessing in the Bible and the Life of the Church*. Philadelphia: Fortress, 1978.

————. *Genesis 1–11*. Minneapolis: Augsburg, 1984.

————. *Isaiah 40–66*. Old Testament Library. Philadelphia: Westminster, 1969.

Westphal, Merold. *God, Guilt, and Death: An Existential Phenomenology of Religion*. Bloomington: Indiana University Press, 1984.

————, ed. *Postmodern Philosophy and Christian Thought*. Bloomington: Indiana University Press, 1999.

————. *Suspicion and Truth: The Religious Uses of Modern Atheism*. Grand Rapids: Eerdmans, 1993.

Westra, Laura. *An Environmental Proposal for Ethics: The Principle of Integrity*. Lanham, MD: Rowman and Littlefield, 1994.

White, Lynn, Jr. "The Historical Roots of Our Ecologic Crisis." *Science* 155 (March 10, 1967): 1203–7. Reprinted in Barbour, *Western Man and Environmental Ethics*, 18–30.

Wiesel, Elie. *Night*. New York: Bantam, 1958.

Wilkinson, Loren. "Christ as Creator and Redeemer." In DeWitt, *The Environment and the Christian*, 25–44.

————. "Cosmic Christology and the Christian's Role in Creation." *Christian Scholar's Review* 11, no. 1 (1981): 18–40.

Wilkinson, Loren, and Mary Ruth Wilkinson. *Caring for Creation in Your Own Backyard.* Vancouver: Regent, 1992.

Wilkinson, Loren, Peter De Vos, Calvin DeWitt, Eugene Dykema, Vernon Ehlers. *Earthkeeping in the '90s: Stewardship of Creation.* 2nd ed. Grand Rapids: Eerdmans, 1991. Originally published as *Earthkeeping: Christian Stewardship of Natural Resources.* Grand Rapids: Eerdmans, 1980.

Williams, Terry Tempest. *Refuge: An Unnatural History of Family and Place.* New York: Norton, 1999.

Wilson, E. O. *The Creation: An Appeal to Save Life on Earth.* New York: Norton, 2006.

———. *The Diversity of Life.* Cambridge: Harvard University Press, 1992.

Wingren, Gustav. "The Doctrine of Creation: Not an Appendix but the First Article." *Word and World* 4 (Fall 1984): 353–71.

Wirzba, Norman. *The Paradise of God: Renewing Religion in an Ecological Age.* New York: Oxford University Press, 2003.

Wolf, Ron. "God, James Watt, and the Public Lands." *Audubon* 83, no. 3 (May 1981): 58–65.

Wolff, Hans Walter. *Anthropology of the Old Testament.* Philadelphia: Fortress, 1981.

Wolters, Al. "Worldview and Textual Criticism in 2 Peter 3:10." *Westminster Theological Journal* 49, no. 2 (Fall 1987): 405–13.

Wolterstorff, Nicholas. *Until Justice and Peace Embrace.* Grand Rapids: Eerdmans, 1983.

World Commission on Environment and Development. *Our Common Future.* New York: Oxford University Press, 1987.

Worster, Donald. *The Wealth of Nature: Environmental History and the Ecological Imagination.* New York: Oxford University Press, 1993.

Wright, N. T. *The Climax of the Covenant.* Minneapolis: Fortress, 1992.

———. *The Epistles of Paul to the Colossians and to Philemon.* The Tyndale New Testament Commentaries. Grand Rapids: Eerdmans, 1986.

———. *The Millennium Myth.* Louisville: Westminster/John Knox, 1999.

———. *The New Testament and the People of God.* Philadelphia: Fortress, 1992.

———. *The Resurrection of the Son of God.* Minneapolis: Fortress, 2003.

———. *Surprised by Hope: Rethinking Heaven, the Resurrection, and the Mission of the Church.* New York: HarperCollins, 2008.

Young, Richard. *Healing the Earth: A Theocentric Perspective on Environmental Problems and Their Solutions.* Nashville: Broadman and Holman, 1994.

Zizioulas, John. *Being as Communion: Studies in Personhood and the Church.* Crestwood, NY: St. Vladimir's Seminary Press, 1985.

subject index

Gross Domestic Product (GDP), 5, 186n21
Gustafson, James, 78

habitats, 24
habits, 132–33, 134
Hansen, James, 48
Hanson, Paul, 202n74
Hardin, Garrett, 4, 19
Havel, Václav, 180
Hawken, Paul, 162–63, 176
heaven, 107–8
heaven and earth, 88, 200n50
Heidelberg Catechism, 172
hermeneutics, 82–84, 197n3
hierarchy, 126, 127, 162–63
historic premillennialism, 70
Hobbes, Thomas, 196n87
Hoezee, Scott, 114, 116
Holy Spirit, as breath of life, 114–15
homelessness, 177–80, 199n29
homeostasis, 20
honesty, 141, 142, 153, 154
hope, 144–45, 153, 154, 175–83, 210n29
hopelessness, 144, 177–80, 181
Hopkins, Gerard Manley, 182–83
Horsley, Richard, 201n55
hospitality, 97, 137, 153
hubris, 80, 141
humanity
    embedded in creation, 63–64, 204n26
    finitude of, 116, 140–42
    and habitat, 4–6
    uniqueness of, 171
humility, 80, 84, 141, 153, 154, 161
hunger, 27–28, 54

image of God, 57, 63, 89, 115–16, 170–71, 182
imagination, 181. *See also* moral imagination
imitation of Christ, 170
impetuousness, 146
incarnation, 205n30, 205n35
Index of Sustainable Economic Welfare, 5, 186n22
individualism, 115, 122, 161, 208n3
individual rights, 125, 126–27
industrialism, 73, 74, 181
infant mortality, 37
injustice, 152, 168
instrumental value, 165, 205n47, 207n83
interdependence, 10, 76, 137
intergenerational justice, 206n53
Intergovernmental Panel on Climate Change, 49, 52

International Energy Agency, 46
International Union for the Conservation of Nature, 30
interpretive frameworks, 198n11
interrelatedness, of world, 14, 19
intrinsic value, 136, 165–67, 168, 205n47, 207n83
Irenaeus, 118
irrelevance of God, 76–77

Jenkins, Jerry, 62, 70
Jesus Christ
    death and resurrection of, 102, 117
    Lordship of, 103, 117, 128–29
    as New Adam, 116
    teaching of, 150
justice, 121, 149–51, 153, 154, 161, 162
justification by faith, 151

Kaiser, Christopher, xv
Kant, Immanuel, 196n87, 213n2
Kasemann, Ernst, 210n38
Keeling, David, 49
Kierkegaard, Søren, 144
kingdom of God, 79, 146
knowledge, 111
Kohák, Erazim, 98, 200n44

Ladd, George, 202n75
LaHaye, Tim, 62, 70, 194n25
lakes, 14–18
land degradation, 24, 38–39, 54
land ethic, 124–25, 126–28, 167
Lane, Belden, 98
Lee, Charles, 162
Left Behind series, 62, 194n25, 195n55
legislation, 176
Leopold, Aldo, xiv, 3, 24, 96, 124–25, 126–28, 131, 135, 149, 167, 207n68
Leviathan, 96
Levinas, Emmanuel, 83
Lewis, C. S., 134
life, respect for, 122–23, 125
limits, 20
Lindsey, Hal, 62, 194n25
Little, Charles, 35
Locke, John, 72, 196n87
Lorax, The (Dr. Seuss), 155–56, 173
Lord's Prayer, 118, 138
love, 113–14, 149, 154, 170, 154
Luther, Martin, 82, 104, 118

Macatawa River, 21–22
malice, 149

scripture index

Micah

6:8 150

Wisdom of Solomon

7:25 200n49

Matthew

5–7 150, 170
5:44 148
6:11 138
6:24 160
6:33 150
12:20 107
22:34–40 148, 170
25:6 69
26:41 170

Mark

12:28–34 148, 170
14:38 170

Luke

4 150
4:18–19 146
10:25–28 148, 170
15:11–32 108

John

1:14 108, 117
13 170
13:34–35 170

Acts

28:15 70

Romans

8 xii, 24
8:19–23 23
8:29 201n57
12:19–20 148

1 Corinthians

13 144
15:20 201n57
15:23 201n57

Ephesians

2:16 201n61

Philippians

3:9 151

Colossians

1:11 99

1:12 99
1:13–14 99
1:15 103
1:15–20 99–104, 201n70
1:16–17 79
1:20 103
1:22 201n61
2:15 103

1 Thessalonians

4 69, 70
4:15 69
4:16 69
4:17 69

James

2:17 154

2 Peter

3 68, 69
3:7 69
3:9 68, 146
3:10 68, 81, 195n49

Revelation

3 149
7:17 108

21–22 xiii, 104
21:1 118
21:1–22:5 103–9
21:2 108
21:3 108
21:5 108
21:10 108
22:1–2 81
22:4 108